1041 SERMON ILLUSTRATIONS, IDEAS, AND EXPOSITIONS

1041
Sermon Illustrations, Ideas, and Expositions
TREASURY OF THE CHRISTIAN WORLD

Compiled and edited by A. GORDON NASBY

Foreword by George M. Docherty

BAKER BOOK HOUSE
Grand Rapids, Michigan

Special acknowledgment is made to the *Christian World,* and to the following publishers in the United States of America who have granted permission for the reprinting of copyrighted material from their publications:

Abingdon-Cokesbury Press for item 594, from *What Are We Living For?* by John Sutherland Bonnell, copyright, 1950, by Abingdon-Cokesbury Press; for item 615, from *Why Do Men Suffer?* by Leslie D. Weatherhead, copyright, 1936, by Abingdon-Cokesbury Press.

Oxford University Press for items 34, 155 and 674 from *No Coward Soul* by David A. MacLennan, copyright, 1949, by Oxford University Press.

Charles Scribner's Sons for items 104 and 347 from *The Heading Cross* by H. H. Farmer, copyright, 1939, by Charles Scribner's Sons.

PHOTOLITHOPRINTED BY CUSHING - MALLOY, INC.
ANN ARBOR, MICHIGAN, UNITED STATES OF AMERICA
1976

FOREWORD

Richard Hope Hillary in his moving war book *The Last Enemy* makes this illuminating comment on the craft of the writer: "A writer is constantly digging into himself, penetrating the life and nature of man, and thus realizing himself." What is true of the creative writer is no less applicable to the preacher. Week by week he digs deeply into his own experience. The sermon is the declaration of some facet of his life to his people. No preacher really ever says anything new in the sense that what he says has never before been expressed. The originality of his preaching consists in the fact that it is true for him. This process of constantly digging into oneself constitutes both the agony and the glory of preaching—he shares something of the glory of Michelangelo when he beheld in the block of marble the image of King David; the agony is the discovery that there is nothing to declare when one introspects.

The preacher differs from the writer, however, in that this "digging into himself" is also a meditation on God. He withdraws himself from the world and broods upon God. It was said of Alexander Whyte of Free St. George's, Edinburgh, when he came into the pulpit, that it seemed as if he had come straight from the presence of God. He did no less. For two hours prior to the service, he was alone in his study in prayer and meditation. The creative companion in this communion with God is, of course, Holy Scripture. As with the scribes he "is like unto a man who is an householder which bringeth forth out of his treasure things new and old."

What is new for him is the impact of the Eternal Holy Spirit with his frail humanity as he sits at his desk with his Bible. True exegesis is a gift from God. And he can be assured of this: that what is true for him will have been shared and recognized by others.

Essential, however, to the preacher is the reading of literature in general and the writings of other preachers. In this he will confirm what he has found "in his own solitariness" as Whitehead defines religion. And more—that others have plumbed deeper into the eternal mystery of God and have comprehended a wider grasp of the human situation. The necessity of building up literary capital week by week is the only safeguard against those bleak and arid deserts when the fount of creative work all but dries up. In the modern ministry this experience is far too common. The multitudinous duties of parish and congregation drive a wedge between the preacher's desk and his pulpit. At best, he feeds his mind on the secondhand pleasure of "thumbing through" literary reviews.

On top of this is an added burden. The nature of the work of the ministry is becoming more and more soullessly executive, demanding qualifications for dealing with technical details of organization and planning that once were used exclusively in the commercial world. This ecclesiastical machinery stalls the creative urge. Inner intellectual and spiritual resources dwindle to the merest trickle. Sunday races toward him like a traffic signal—and showing red—seen through the windshield of a speeding car. He steps on the brakes and finds himself once more thrown back upon his own resources. The spider may spin its web out of the mystery of its own body, but the preacher who has fallen behind in his reading has no such alchemy. Week by week he sings the same tune; his people know it too well and tire of the melody. He frantically searches for stories; then piously hopes for a text to make them a sermon.

Into this far too common situation in the life of the present-day ministry comes a book like *Treasury of the Christian World*. It is not an attempt to write a man's sermons, nor provide a homiletical first-aid post. It does not even make claim simply to provide him with illustrations, though this it does abundantly. It rather seeks to rekindle the old creative urge that now seems cold and black, like last night's fire. In this book one experiences the new-found joy of meeting in the company of good and great thinkers and preachers of the present and the past. Their fresh, clear insights into the wide range of subjects that are classified cannot but bring real renewal of mind and blessing to the heart of every preacher who reads this book.

I have never been able to keep a commonplace book for any length of time. It always seemed that the ideas I noted down, I never used in my sermons; and the thoughts and quotations that came singing to my mind in the white heat of preparation, I vaguely remembered having read somewhere but would never have dreamed of noting them down at the time. As I turn the pages of *Treasury of the Christian World*, I also, like the householder, bring forth things new and old. It is like renewing acquaintance with old friends again. Here is Gilbert Keith Chesterton, for instance, with his pungent paradoxes, telling us that when we first look at the Sermon on the Mount, it turns everything upside down, but later you discover that it turns everything right side up. Instinctively, my hand reaches out to my bookshelf to read again his *Orthodoxy* or *Heretics*. Chesterton lives again for me, and my mind is refreshed in our meeting. Sometimes it is a new word from an old source. One thinks of Lincoln's comment when he said he did not like a certain Cabinet member's face. "But the poor man is not responsible for his face," replied his advocate. "Every man over forty is responsible for his face," countered Abraham Lincoln; and the shadow of this giant looms the larger. The man whose choice was a dictionary if he were to be cast on a desert island with one book is to be commended. Words have their own history and story to tell. They are living symbols of experience. They have a life of their own. *Treasury of the Christian World* gives us insights into a living heritage. In such company the preacher is really sure and greatly blessed. With this book near at hand he will never again feel the half-terror, half-desolation as he sits down to prepare his work.

GEORGE M. DOCHERTY

PREFACE

W<small>HILE</small> browsing through second-hand books in Blessings Book Store, Chicago, some twelve years ago, I came upon two hand-sewn, coverless volumes of the *Christian World Pulpit*. Some minister had obviously once greatly treasured his weekly issues of the *Christian World Pulpit*, judging from the care he had taken in their preservation. Looking back on my ministry, I consider the discovery of the *Christian World Pulpit* and its companion publication, the *Christian World*, early in my ministry, enriching to it.

Many Americans, of course, have long been familiar with these two publications, which have for so many decades enjoyed such great success. Published weekly at 110–1 Fleet Street, London, E.C. 4, the *Christian World Pulpit* has printed many of the outstanding sermons preached in the pulpits of the English-speaking world. In its columns have appeared the sermons of the greatest preachers of the last century. Great pulpit masters such as Henry Ward Beecher, W. L. Watkinson, D. L. Moody, F. W. Farrar, Lyman Abbott, Theodore Cuyler, C. H. Spurgeon, J. H. Jowett, and others were frequent contributors in their time. The most able of modern preachers and theological writers are also well represented.

For more than eleven years I have collected these volumes, studied, selected, and arranged what in my estimation are the illustrative and thought high lights of this grand series of sermons. More than eighteen thousand sermons have been read in this search. In addition, the editor of the *Christian World*, E. H. Jeffs, has granted permission to use material from the columns of this religious weekly. Over two thousand articles of the *Christian World* were also read in preparation for this volume.

The *Christian World Pulpit* and the *Christian World* have long been used in Britain as devotional reading for the home. Readers will no doubt find these selections suitable for that purpose. Ministers should find much inspiration and help in sermon preparation. Teachers and speakers will likewise profit from the convenient arrangement of the material according to subjects.

I hope the book will be read from cover to cover at various times. There is no contents page since the topics are included in the Subject Index at the end of the book.

The more than one thousand selections are chosen from nearly five hundred authors. Readers will no doubt discover new favorites by being introduced to authors included here. Contributors come from all major denominations. Varying theological positions are stated.

From a study of the sermons and articles made during the preparation of the book, one becomes aware of the capacity for illustration the great preachers have possessed. Nearly all selections rely heavily on illustration as a means of teaching. In this modern day little defense need be made for the illustrative method. Strangely, Jesus seemed wholly in agreement that the illustrative method was most effective. In this connection, John Hutton once wrote, "Truth cannot be taught by formulas and propositions and arguments; but only by an illustration and a tale, as our Lord acknowledged who educated the human race on God by telling half a dozen great stories."

The choice of selections has been made on the basis of human interest appeal, and I have sought to select such material as would engage the attention of not simply the clergy but also the rank and file of those with a loyalty to Christianity.

The book is presented in the hope that it may deepen and excite the consecration of all who turn its pages.

I wish to express sincere appreciation to the *Christian World* and its editor for permission to reprint the material included in this book, all of which appeared originally in their columns. In cases where there was a possibility that the material included in the book had also appeared in America in book form, an effort was made to determine the fact and credits given on the copyright page. Gratitude is expressed to the many authors, including Robert McCracken, Harry Emerson Fosdick, Paul Scherer, McEwan Lawson, D. W. Langridge, Ralph Sockman, Harold W. Ruopp, John W. McKelvey, John Sutherland Bonnell, James MacKay, David A. MacLennan, H. H. Farmer, E. L. Allen, George Buttrick, Leslie D. Weatherhead, John Bishop and Andrew Blackwood. In the event that credits have been omitted, proper acknowledgement will be made in future editions.

Thanks are also extended my wife, Constance, who typed the manuscript and prepared the author index, and to Mrs. Deo Coomer for checking the final copy.

A. GORDON NASBY

Chicago, Illinois

Absolute

1   A friend of the late Professor Foster, of the University of Chicago, says that he asked the brilliant apostle of relativity a few months before his death what he was doing. "I am hunting for the Absolute in history," Foster replied. "Have you found it?" inquired his friend. "No," said the great teacher, "but I am convinced that if it cannot be found that means the death of religion."

James A. Beebe

Adversity

2   F. W. Boreham in one of his essays refers to the occasion when the great naturalist, Alfred Russell Wallace, tried to help an emperor moth, and only harmed it by his well-intentioned efforts. He discovered the moth struggling wildly to break its way through the cocoon which covered it. It was a handsome creature of fine proportions, and Wallace was moved by the sight of its severe ordeal. So he split the cocoon, and released the moth from further struggle. But that moth never developed; its wings never expanded; the colors and tints that should have adorned them never appeared. In the end it died undeveloped, stunted, ruined. That hard and severe struggle with the cocoon was Nature's method of developing its splendid wings, of bringing forth the glory and beauty of the creature. The moth had been saved from struggle, but the naturalist's ill-considered ministry had ruined and slain it.

J. D. Jones

✳✳

3   Once, years ago, a man sent me a letter from somewhere in Wales, telling of a sermon which he heard Joseph Parker preach in the City Temple in the mid-seventies. The question of the sermon was, "Does God Forsake the Righteous?" and in the course of it the preacher described the abode of the poor widow. He spoke of it as a "place out of which even a sheriff's officer could not take more than a shadow, and would not take that because he could not sell it." There was a figure to stick in the memory. Later the preacher said: "I have been as nearly forsaken as any man in the world. I looked around on all sides, but could see no way out—no lateral way, only a vertical one!"

Joseph Fort Newton

✳✳

4   The late F. A. Atkins, a brilliant journalist, was lunching one Sunday in a London club with a well-known minister who was in deep trouble, very ill and very tired. Yet that morning, says Mr. Atkins, "he had preached one of the most searching and inspiring sermons I had ever heard. I laughingly remarked that he always preached best when things were at their worst. He looked at me and said, very quietly, 'We get help.'"

                                                                    J. T. Hodgson

✳✳

5   There is a story of a German baron who made a great Aeolian harp by stretching the wires from tower to tower of his castle. When the harp was ready he listened for the music. But it was in the still air; the wires hung silent. Autumn came with its gentle breezes and there were faint whispers of song. At length the winter winds swept over the castle, and now the harp answered in majestic music.

Such a harp is the human heart. It does not yield its noblest music in the summer days of joy, but in the winter of trial. The sweetest songs on earth have been sung in sorrow. The richest things in character have been reached in pain. Even of Jesus we read that He was made perfect through suffering.

                                                                    Dean Stanley

✳✳

6   Luther used to say there were many of the Psalms he could never understand until he was afflicted. Rutherford declared he got a new Bible through the furnace. Even the heathen Bion said, "It's a great misfortune not to endure misfortunes"; and Anaxagoras, when his house was in ruins and his estate wasted, afterwards remarked, "If they had not perished, I should have perished." So said one, brought to himself by blindness, "I could never see till I was blind." Trials bring many to God. Joab would not come to Absalom till Absalom set his cornfield on fire.

Adversity, Overcoming

7   Over in India there is a monument in memory of six children of the Lees of Calcutta, buried in a landslide of the slopes of the Himalayas at Darjeeling. What do you suppose those terribly bereaved parents put on it? "Thanks be unto God, which giveth us the victory through our Lord Jesus Christ." He does give us the victory in and through and over life's disasters. God does not send the disasters which afflict His children. But in them He sends the chance to fight and overcome. Shall we not praise Him?

                                                                    David A. MacLennan

Affliction

8   Dr. Fosdick tells of a friend of his who was stricken with infantile paralysis in her youth. Someone sympathizing with her said, "Affliction does so color life." "Yes," she said quietly, "and I propose to choose the color."

Agnosticism

9   Agnosticism is dangerous. You can see its danger in the last sentence of Somerset Maugham's summing up: "The practical outcome of agnosticism is that you act as though God did not exist." If all mankind adopted this position the result would be chaos; there could be no common brotherhood, no co-operation in the world. Each man would seek his own pleasure only. Duty would lose all sanctions, and life would be as Thomas Hobbes described it: "No arts, no letters, no society, and which is worst of all, continual fear and danger of violent death, and the life of man solitary, poor, nasty, brutish and short." That is the danger of agnosticism; lack of belief leads inevitably to lack of morality: but belief in God is the corrective to chaos. So we are back to that position which has been emphasized over and over again: the issue before the world is not merely belief or lack of it, but God or chaos.

Adam Jack

✳✳

10   "I am an agnostic," said a young soldier to me the other day. He said it with a smirk, as though all the secrets of religion had been revealed to him. "Of course you are an agnostic," I replied. "You can't expect to know much about religion at your age. You want to study the New Testament for ten years and then come and talk to me." I should never dream of saying to a scientist, with some kind of satisfaction to myself, that I was an agnostic in scientific matters. Jesus demanded a thoroughly honest approach to life and religion, when a man would seek the way of life eternal.

R. Morton Stanley

✳✳

11   Dr. L. P. Jacks tells of an agnostic who said to another agnostic, on his death-bed, "Stick to it, Tom." "Yes," gasped Tom, "but there's nothing to stick to."

W. Francis Gibbons

Alcohol

12   Why do people turn to alcohol?

1. They may have inherited an unbalanced nervous equipment from alcoholism in their family. Then someone starts them off and away they go plunging down hill like a loosely balanced stone kicked by a careless foot.

2. Folk are frightened by life. They don't look as though they are because we all wear masks. But we are frightened, and we are weak, and things look threatening and things go wrong. Then alcohol for a little time makes us feel twice our size.

3. We are shy and we are lonely. We may be sexually tormented. We are very conscious of being inferior, life catches us some very hard smacks, and alcohol helps us to forget for a little.

4. We have no plan for life. We are lost on the road, quite forlorn, and very bored. We have done something wrong, or failed in something and the memory haunts us like a ghost.   McEwan Lawson

✻✻

13   We read the considered judgment of Upton Sinclair, the American novelist. "All my life I have lived in the presence of fine and beautiful men going to their death through alcohol. I call it the greatest trap that life has set for the feet of genius; and I record my opinion that the Prohibition amendment was the greatest step in progress taken by America since the freeing of the slaves."

James Colville

Ambition

14   Lord Tennyson was once conversing with a friend who made the remark that his greatest ambition in life was to leave the world better than he found it. Lord Tennyson replied that his greatest ambition was to obtain a clearer vision of God. Much of the poet's noble work can leave no doubt as to the perfect sincerity of that remark.   •   Walter Wynn

Ancestry

15   Let me tell you a fine story that comes from the third Christian century. Away in North Africa, in Tunisia, lay the city of Carthage, famed down all the centuries. It was not only a great centre of North African civilization, but also a great centre of North African Christianity, and its bishops had wide influence

over many churches. Not least among these bishops was Cyprian. In the middle of the third century there fell upon the Christian Church in Carthage, as upon many other Churches in the Roman Empire, the devastating persecution organized by Decius, the Emperor. Christians were sought out, imprisoned and massacred in a way reminiscent of Hitler's treatment of the Jews. Bishops were tortured and put to death, even the most aged and the most learned. But another trial befell Carthage at the same time—an awful plague which took off hundreds of people. At this time, in spite of all the dangers, Cyprian called on the persecuted Christians of Carthage to minister to the heathen folk who lay sick and dying within her walls, and gave them this noble reason for their bravery: "We must be worthy of our birth." Now are we children of God . . . a grand deed with a grand motive! There is to be a courtly dignity about Christian people, for "we have a noble ancestor." Maxwell O. Janes

Anniversary

16   I suggest that an Anniversary should be planned to have at least three main effects.

The congregation, including, of course, the church members, should have a justifiable pride in their church's history and its personalities stimulated. Frankly I take a poor view of the present-day tendency in churches to let the past fade into oblivion, to ignore our indebtedness to it; slothfully to refrain from entering into the impulses and devotedness of those who saw the vision of what a church could do in this place or that. A gross lack of imaginativeness and sympathetic love! Knowing what our own efforts to maintain the churches cost us, we might be expected to understand and to admire the cost of founding them. And why do we ministers so readily assent to the removal of photographs and other references to those who went before us in the ministry? Do we not ourselves hope to be just a little remembered after we are gone? If we are doing our level best, we need not fear to stress the precious things of days and men now gone. I believe this note is indispensable to a good Anniversary, to be sounded deeply, sincerely, generously. What heart-warming possibilities lie in a well-organized reunion of past and present members!

Another essential at the Anniversary celebrations is that as many people as possible shall be involved in enjoyable participation. All the joys of the living Church at work should be experienced in a special way at this moment. The old-time Anniversary tea may be out of the question, but other forms of fellowship and enterprise are possible. My present church has a fine scheme for the Anniversary Saturday evening. Every organization was asked to contribute an item to a variety program not exceeding ten minutes in time. What surprises!

What fun! What general interest! The more people working, the greater the enjoyment! Very few visiting preachers and speakers can of themselves make the Anniversary outstanding. The effect is certainly less valuable and less permanent.

Finally, a real Anniversary should be a time for new or at least renewed objectives—definite ones. The Deacons' and Church Meetings should face the things which ought to be done, and other things it would be good to do in the next twelve months, and these should boldly be proclaimed. Pious comments are weak in spiritual vitamins. It is so easy to go back into a doze when the Anniversary is past.   William H. S. Webb

Appearance

17   It is said that Abraham Lincoln, when he was President of the United States, was advised to include a certain man in his Cabinet. When he refused he was asked why he would not accept him. "I don't like his face," the President replied. "But the poor man isn't responsible for his face," responded his advocate. "Every man over forty is responsible for his face," countered Abraham Lincoln.   E. G. Manby

Appreciation

18   Thomas Carlyle married probably the cleverest woman in England; she adored him; he loved her as far as Thomas Carlyle could love anyone, next to his mother. She ached and longed for words that were never said; and she wrote in her diary once: "Carlyle never praises me. If he says nothing I have to be content that things are all right." And after her death Carlyle discovered from her diary that he had had fellowship with a woman whose heart had been aching for years for the things he never said.   Robert Bond

Atheism

19   Atheism has never been able to steady the heart, still the conscience, satisfy the intellect, explain the universe or account for the undying and inextinguishable aspirations of the soul. It cannot provide a refuge in the storms of life or rob death of its sting. Atheism always fails in the presence of death. No wonder Robert Hall exclaimed: "I buried my materialism in the grave of my father."
                                                                                    James L. Gordon

✵✵

20 The pious man and the atheist always talk of religion; the one speaks of what he loves, and the other of what he fears.

Author unknown

Atheists, Making of

21 The history of intolerance reveals the patent way for making atheists. It is written in five rules: (1) Meet the young, sturdy, and independent thinker, to whom the Bible is not quite as easy as ABC, and the mysteries of the Gospel are not revealed as clearly as the facts of everyday life—meet his inquiries with rebuke. If he asks for explanation, tell him he is proud and has a bad heart, and bid him believe. (2) Next, seeing he persists in trying to understand the grounds of his faith, call him a "blasphemer" against good men. It will sting him to call him names. (3) Injure him if you can in his temporal life. (4) On no account show him any sympathy, or he may come to think that Christianity is love, like its Creator. (5) When he appears on a "secularist" platform, stand up and pray for him.

That is the short and easy way to make atheists. In that way they have been made by the hundred; and if Bradlaugh's life only brings home to us the folly and the iniquity of this procedure, and makes clear to the churches that their chief need is more of Christ's Spirit, more of His love for men, of His sympathy with those who feel the actual difficulties of life and of faith, and who are facing them with agonizing earnestness; if it only does this, then, in very deed, his story will have conferred on the churches a real and lasting benefit.

John Clifford

Atom

22 It is said that Sir Oliver Lodge prayed that we might never discover the secret of the atom until we were good enough and great enough to control its use for the well-being of mankind.

W. H. Campbell

Atonement

23 Lord Balfour in his *Foundations of Belief* says, "If the Atonement were not too wide for our intellectual comprehension, it would be too narrow for our spiritual necessities." That is a magnificent phrase. Some people seem to think that they want something deeper to preach about, and something more intellectual to listen to. I contend that the subject of a Christ crucified is a theme for

a lifetime, for an eternity. You may think it is not up-to-date preaching; but, in reality, it is the only kind of preaching that is up-to-date.

Dinsdale T. Young

⁂

24   When Lionel Fletcher, the Australian evangelist, was in Britain he related an incident of his boyhood days on the farm. Hearing a great commotion in the farmyard he ran there and found a hen being savagely attacked by a hawk. He was too late to save her, for she soon succumbed to her wounds. Why had she not fled to the safety of the barn with the other hens? This was apparent when from under her wings there emerged a number of little chicks—and lo! On each was blood, the blood of the mother-love that sacrificed itself for their salvation.

"O Jerusalem, Jerusalem, that killest the prophets, and stonest them which are sent unto thee, how often would I have gathered thy children together, even as a hen gathereth her chickens under her wings, and ye would not! Behold, your house is left unto you desolate."

T. J. Lewis

Atrophy

25   "Up to the age of thirty," says Charles Darwin, "or beyond it, poetry of many kinds gave me great pleasure; and even as a schoolboy I took intense delight in Shakespeare, especially in the historical plays. Pictures gave me considerable, and music very great, delight. I cannot read Shakespeare now. I have also lost my taste for music and pictures. My mind seems to have become a kind of machine for grinding laws out of a large collection of facts; but why this should have caused the atrophy of that part of the brain alone on which the higher tastes depend I cannot conceive. The loss of those tastes is a loss of happiness, and may possibly be injurious to the intellect and more probably to the moral character by enfeebling the emotional part of our nature." He then proceeds to say that if he had his life to live over again he would read poetry and listen to music at least once a week.

John Macmillan

Authority in Preaching

26   Dr. R. F. Horton contended that "every living preacher must receive his message in a communication direct from God, and the constant purpose of his life must be to receive it uncorrupted, and to deliver it without addition or subtraction." Having a due sense of the seriousness and responsibility of the com-

mission laid upon him, the minister will strive to interpret accurately the message God has laid upon his heart and mind. A little boy was watching his father write a sermon. "Daddy," he asked, "does God tell you what to say?" "Er—er—yes, my son," came the slightly hesitating reply. "Well," challenged the boy, "why do you cross out so much?"

Stanley Herbert

Baptism

27 The Sacrament of Baptism should be in public, whether it be the baptism of an adult or an infant. It must be a public confession of faith, and the child is received only because of his parents' faith and that confession is always to be openly repeated. If the Sacrament cannot be administered at the hour of worship, the Church ought to be represented at the ordinance. The person administering the Sacrament should be an officer of the Church. That is not based on any express command in the New Testament. It is not bound up with any doctrine of ordination. There is no hint of any priest or priestly consecration in the records of baptism. Yet because it is a Sacrament of the Church, and the ceremony by which the Church receives the converted into its membership, it is fitting that the person baptizing should be a duly appointed officer of the Church.

John Bishop

Beauty, Effect of

28 Years ago, the rector of a parish in one of the lowest districts of Central London used occasionally to visit a poor widow who occupied a garret in a foul and noisy slum. Among her scanty possessions was a flower-pot containing a stunted geranium, which she tended with anxious care. One day the clergyman inquired why she spent her pains on keeping the puny little plant alive. "It reminds me," she replied, "that God is here."

Robert L. Ottley

Belief

29 In a brilliant essay, one of our great historians, G. M. Trevelyan, sums up Cromwell's religious belief and practice as consisting of a sense of sin, and of his own human worthlessness save when redeemed by God's grace, and a continual communion with God through Christ in the sanctuary of his own mind and heart. He goes on to say that this personal intercourse with God is the essence of religion—that it is a mighty power, and that in Cromwell's day it wrought

mightily. The significance of these words is that they were written by a historian summing up one of the most momentous eras in the story of our nation. Prayer wrought mightily; it produced great men who wrought great deeds.

J. Pickthall

** **

30 There was one of our good men, a plain, good minister, in one of our churches in a country town, whom I well remember. There was an infidel in the town, a man of business; and on one Sunday evening this plain, simple brother of mine saw that infidel in his congregation. The next morning he was passing his shop, and saw the man standing at the door. They recognized each other. "Good morning, Mr. Brown." "Good morning." "I saw you at our chapel last night." "Yes, I was there." "Ah! Mr. Brown, you do not believe those things." "No, sir, nor you either." "Sir, do you mean to insult me?" "No, I don't mean to insult you, but I mean to say, sir, that if I believed those things which you teach, and which you all profess to believe, I could not live as I am doing; I should feel that I must take everybody by the sleeve wherever I went, and tell them what I know and what I feel; as for my own life, I should be a very different man from you. You do not believe these things any more than I do." Well, that was a very rude way of giving a reason, but I am afraid it is a way to which many of us Christian people expose ourselves.

Thomas Binney

** **

31 I envy not the quality of the mind or intellect in others, nor genius, power, wit, or fancy; but if I could choose what would be most delightful and, I believe, most useful to me, I should prefer a religious belief to every other blessing; for it makes life a discipline of goodness, creates new hopes when all hopes vanish, awakens life even and death, makes an instrument of torture and of shame man's ladder of ascent to paradise, calls up the most delightful visions, the gladness of the blest, the security of everlasting joys, where the sensualist and the sceptic know only gloom, decay, annihilation, and despair.

Sir Humphry Davy

Belief and Life

32 It is recorded that a friend once said to Pascal: "I wish I had your belief, so that I might live your life." To which Pascal was swift to reply: "If you lived my life you would soon have my belief."

J. Trevor Davies

Belief and Unbelief

33 A fable about two frogs was born of Eastern literature. One lived all his life in a well. One day a frog whose home was in the sea came to his well. "Who are you! Where do you live?" the frog of the well inquired. "I am so-and-so, and my home is in the sea." "What is the sea? Where is it?" "It's a very large body of water and not far away." The frog of the well pointed to a board on which he sat, saying, "As big as this?" "Oh! much bigger." "Well, how much bigger?" "Why the sea in which I live is bigger than your entire well; it would make millions of wells such as yours." "Nonsense, nonsense; you are a deceiver and a falsifier. Get out of my well. I want nothing to do with any such frogs as you," the frog of the well shouted irately.

Only those that have seen something of the deeper things of life and the universe can understand in some measure the wonder which lies beyond. Let us not be like the frog, feeling secure in our own ignorance, for God's thoughts are not our thoughts nor His ways our ways. His foolishness is wiser than our wisdom and His weakness stronger than our strength. How mighty is our God! And the Word of the cross is the power of God. God offers you that power in the acceptance of Jesus Christ, for in Him we meet the Father.

W. Leslie Jenkins

Belief in God

34 Principal Cairns told of a confirmed law-breaker who was often in the hands of the police. The one redeeming feature of his dissolute life was love for his little girl, who was the image of her dead mother. Once, having committed burglary, he was sentenced to a fairly long term in prison. During his imprisonment his little girl died. On the day he came out he learned of her death. The blow shattered him. He was broken. He could not bring himself even to visit the home from which she had been taken. Suicide seemed the only escape. So he resolved to throw himself off one of the bridges of the Scottish capital. At midnight he stood on the parapet. He found himself climbing it. For no reason he could explain, as he said later, there flashed into his mind the words of the creed: "I believe in God the Father Almighty." He repeated it. He knew nothing of God but he did know something of fatherhood. "Why," he said, "if that is what God is, if God is like that then I can trust Him with my lassie—and myself." Death receded, life began anew. Heart-breaking loneliness and despair gave way before the Presence of Jesus who brings the Father near.

David A. MacLennan

Belief of Others

35   It is not safe to remove or meddle with the lower stages of man's development, even those that are imperfect, until they are superseded by something
better. It is not safe for a man, when he is perfect (perfect, that is, in the human
sense), to knock away the imperfect elements from beneath him, except by
putting in their places something better. For instance, it is a thousand times better that the Parsee should worship light than that you should satisfy him by
astronomical proofs that his gods are delusions, and so leave him with no God.
It is better that a heathen should have the restraint which comes from even
idolatrous worship, than that he should be left without idols and Godless. It is
a great deal better that a man should believe that the Church is the fountain of
authority, than that he should be made to disbelieve in the authority of the
Church without having taken in the greater authority under which the Church
itself is an institution. I never would say to a deep-hearted Catholic, praying to the
Virgin Mary, "That is an infatuation, a fiction." Until you can breathe into men
the conception that in Jesus Christ is all that tenderness of the mother-heart
which they long for, until you can preach to them the God that has in Himself
all these qualities which they seek in the Virgin Mary, it is better to let them
believe in her; but when they understand that Christ is a mother infinitely more
deep, and tender, and compassionate, and quick to hear, and ready to help, than
they ever conceived the Virgin Mary to be, then you may take her away indeed,
the Virgin Mary will die out of their thought then, and they will find in this
new conception what they sought for in the Virgin.

It is not safe to take away a man's view because it is inaccurate, unless you give
him a more accurate view. If you destroy a man's faith in those that serve him
intellectually and dialectically; if you destroy his faith in the priesthood, in
sacrifice, and in the system in which he has been brought up, in which his conscience has been trained, with which his associates have become interwoven, and
in which is enshrined his memory of father, and mother, and brothers, and
sisters, and neighbours, the tender thoughts of his childhood, and his early love;
if you destroy a man's faith in the Ritual, the Cathedral, and all those things
which are connected with the religion in which he has been reared, and if you
put nothing in its place, then, if you think you have done God good service, you
are mistaken; you have neither done God service, nor the man either. You have
destroyed the life that was in him, and left him a desert.

                                                            Henry Ward Beecher

Bereavement

36   It is said that a woman once went to Buddha, for her child had died, and asked that in some way he might restore it to life again. Said Buddha to her: "Take a bowl and go round the city, and beg a peppercorn from each house, only take none from any one who has experienced any suffering or bereavement." Away she went in the hope of filling her bowl and winning his blessing, but alas for her! When the night came on, not a single grain had she been able to collect. Such is the common lot.

George H. Abey

Bible

37   G. Ward Price, a correspondent of one of our London newspapers, once wrote from Johannesburg in South Africa to say that a saying was current among the Natives there which ran like this: "When you white men first came here, we had the land and you had the Bible. Now we have the Bible and you have the land."

H. Hodgkins

✳✳

38   In Dr. Sharp's *Life of David Livingstone* there is an incident recorded about the Makalilo natives. When they were taken to the coast and saw the Atlantic Ocean for the first time they expressed their feelings by saying, "We understood that the world had no end, but all at once the world said, 'I am finished. There is no more of me!'" Quite a number of people to-day seem to have that idea about the Bible; they imagine it is finished, out-of-date, superseded!

The remarkable thing is that the Dictators of the world, whether in Germany, Italy or Japan, have not shared this view. Indeed they have dreaded all Bible teaching because they came to realize that the message and influence and precepts of the Word of God were in direct opposition to their program! Even the Atheist and agnostic have to admit the ethical value of the Bible while they may deny the God it proclaims. A company of infidels, including Voltaire, were discussing their theories around the table one day when Voltaire said suddenly, "Hush, gentlemen—till the servants are gone. If they believed as we do, none of our lives would be safe!"

Harold T. Barrow

✳✳

39   The German poet Heine, who has been described as the German Byron, an unbelieving Jew, and an incurable cynic, on one occasion picked up a Bible, and spent the day in reading it. At the end of the day he exclaimed: "What a book! vast and wide as the world; rooted in the abysses of creation and towering up beyond the blue secrets of heaven! Sunrise and sunset, birth and death, promise and fulfilment, the whole drama of humanity, are in this book!"

                                                              Robert F. Horton

✳✳

40   Sir Isaac Newton accounted "the Scriptures of God the most sublime philosophy." "If there is anybody," said Professor Huxley, "more objectionable than the orthodox bibliolator it is the heterodox Philistine who can discover in a literature, which in some respects has no superior, nothing but a subject for scoffing, and an occasion for the display of his conceited ignoránce of the debt he owes to former generations."

According to Renan, the Bible is the great book of consolation for humanity. "It responds," says Carlyle, "to whatever is deepest in man's heart." After a visit to the great German scholar Ewald, Dean Stanley wrote, "It is impossible to forget the enthusiasm with which he grasped the New Testament, and exclaimed, 'In this little Book is contained all the wisdom of the world.' "

When Bishop Watson published his *Apology for the Bible,* George III remarked that he did not know that the Bible wanted any apology. Andrew Jackson, President of the United States, was of the same opinion. On his death-bed he pointed to the Bible, and said to his physician, "That Book, sir, is the rock on which our Republic rests."

But individuals as well as States have to rest at last upon "the impregnable rock of Holy Scripture." Here is something to which I ask the attention of my younger hearers. Not long before George Peabody's death he sent a boy in his office for a New Testament. The boy let it drop, and the old man said, "You carry that Book lightly in your youth, my lad, but when you are as old as I am it must carry you."

                                                              E. J. Hardy

Bible, and Sin

41   The Bible never attempts to gloss over or explain away sin. Its method is far different from that of many modern novelists. When Alexander, King of Macedon, one of the few world conquerors, had his portrait taken, it is said that he sat with his face resting on his fingers, as though in profound thought, but really that he might hide an ugly scar. Oliver Cromwell's wart-disfigured face is famous. We are reminded, too, that it was the fashion in olden times, when an ox was led out for sacrifice to Jupiter, to chalk over the dark spots, and so give the offering a false show of unblemished whiteness. But the Bible throws away the chalk: it keeps the sitter's fingers off the scars. It paints the full face with flawless detail, wart and all; beauty and blotches, saintliness and scars, all and in all: for instance: the face of Abraham, the friend of God, is still marred by the deep lines engraved upon it by the falsehoods told to Pharaoh in Egypt. No one looks at the countenance of Jacob without detecting traces of his trickery. Peter's denial of his Master is as indelibly inscribed as the stain in Macbeth's conscience.   G. H. Clothier

Bible, Influence of

42   In 1790 the crew of the *Bounty* mutineered, mastered the vessel, and turned their officers adrift. Nine of the mutineers with six men and twelve women of Tahiti landed on this uninhabited shore known as Pitcairn's Island. One of them unhappily learned how to make spirits from an indigenous root, and then that little spot only seven miles in circumference became at once, in consequence of the drink, a hell upon earth. Drink changed this paradise into a scene of devilish orgies and bloody massacres, till, by the year 1800, ten years after their landing, all the Tahitian men and all the Englishmen but one perished. That one English survivor was named John Adams. He had found a Bible in the wreck of the *Bounty*. He read it, he was struck with remorse for his crimes, and from it he began to teach the Tahitian women and their children. He became the head of a patriarchal community who, though half-caste and the offspring of mutineers and murderers, became through the teaching of that single Book renowned throughout the world for the kindness and gentleness of their character, the simplicity and virtue of their lives.   F. W. Farrar

Bible, Survival of

43   It was Voltaire, the French sceptic, who wrote in his study in Paris: "I will go through the forest of the Scriptures and girdle all the trees, so that in one hundred years Christianity will be but a vanishing memory." But the very room in which he wrote those words was later purchased by the British and Foreign Bible Society, and was packed from floor to ceiling with Bibles.

                                                David John Donnan

Bible, Unquenchable Light

44   I have heard of a scientist who invented, several years ago, some new kind of light. Then to protect it from the wind and the storm—which was one chief

source of concern to him—he had put around it a guard of exceptional strength. But one night the fierceness of the tempest shattered the guard and left the light without defence. And the light went out? No, to the experimenter's astonishment it still burned on, with clear and steady radiance, as though all the winds of heaven were asleep. I think some of us have had an experience like that. We were very fearful for our Scriptures, and we fenced them round with Watson's *Institutes* or Paley's *Evidences,* or Butler's *Analogy.* But the weather has begun to tell badly on some of our defences. Nobody reads Watson now. I have heard even a Fernley lecturer speak slightlingly of Paley, and the great Butler himself, who some of his critics think is getting leaky in places. The Bible, however, is not at the mercy of our defences; it shines by its own quenchless light; and what the hand of God has kindled the breath of man shall not put out.

George Jackson

Blessing of God

45   A certain shepherd who lived not far away from the home of Sir Walter Scott told of the great novelist a very touching story. He said that Scott was the best-loved figure in all the Border country, and many of the farm-folk almost worshipped him. One day Sir Walter rode over to Ettrick on his horse Sibyl Grey, and called in to have dinner with the shepherd and his family. Before leaving Scott smiled affectionately upon the little daughter of the household, walked round to where she was sitting, took her up in his arms, kissed her and set her down again. Then he laid his hand on her head and said very earnestly and reverently, "God Almighty bless you, my dear child!" After a moment's silence Scott took his leave. The shepherd accompanied him to the stable to help him to saddle his horse, and upon returning to the family room he found his wife crying as though her heart would break.

"Why, whatever's the matter?" he inquired in surprise.

"Oh," she cried, "I would have given everything that I possess in this world—everything, everything. If only he had done the same to all the children!"

We all long to feel a blessing laid upon our life: and God does bless each and every child. It is we in our ignorance, our blindness, and our lack of understanding, that fail to realize that God is blessing us all the time.

Frederick H. Carr

Blindspots, Religious

46   We have travelled a long way from the mentality of John Newton, who wrote the lovely hymn, "How sweet the Name of Jesus sounds," and regarded himself as a Christian man even when he was captain of a slave ship. In one of his diaries he wrote, "I never knew sweeter or more frequent hours of divine communion than on my last voyage to Guinea." He was no hypocrite and in the strange providences of God, John Newton did much to destroy slavery. Under his mighty preaching Wilberforce was converted to Christianity. When that stern man read his Bible in his comfortable cabin, while beneath was a cargo of men whose flesh was torn by manacles and whose hearts were breaking for their native wilds, it never occurred to him that he was unchristian. He knew that Christianity implied humility before God; truthfulness perhaps, maybe personal purity, but not that it implied love for man, even the black man.

J. Richmond Morgan

Boredom

47   A British officer who had grown weary of an assignment in India was rebuked by a friend for his immoderate drinking. As the friend was talking with him the officer lifted his glass and said: "This is the swiftest road out of India that I know." For tens of thousands of people the uplifted glass is the only road they know out of boredom and insipidity; the only road that promises oblivion as an escape from their empty lives.

John Sutherland Bonnell

Brotherhood

48   In the old days of the Evangelical Revival there was a man who owned a number of slaves, who wrote a letter to another and said in it something like this: "I am beginning to see that even black people are among those for whom Christ died," and he said, prescient of what he perhaps did not realize, "It may seem to you a dangerous doctrine, but I do not think that the world will ever be very much better until it is acted upon." Now, is not that the very essence of our Gospel, is not that the message that we need to carry today to the ends of the earth—all these rivalries in Europe, all these suspicious peoples who are looking on at the welter there and wondering what they are going to get out of it? How are we ever going to heal the enmities caused by the war except on the basis of accepting the doctrine of Jesus Christ concerning men—that in Christ there is neither French, nor German, nor Russian, nor Italian, nor English, nor American, but that they are all one in Him?

W. B. Selbie

⁂

49   Let us consider an incident in North Africa which took place on Easter
Day during World War II. The account tells of a chaplain who, while cele-
brating Holy Communion on Easter Day, noticed a body of German prisoners
looking on. Inquiring through the C.O. as to whether any of them were desirous
of taking part in a Communion service he was told that many would like to do
so. The Germans themselves prepared a rough altar and about 120 joined in
the service. The service was in English and where necessary a German N.C.O.
explained the purport of the prayers to his fellow-prisoners. But here, as everywhere, the actions spoke for themselves and the men reverently made their
Easter Communion. Prayers were said for the brotherhood of man under Christ,
and the Germans, as they filed out, shook hands with the padre and thanked
him for this opportunity he had given them of making their Communion.
There the miracle lived again, Christ our Lord threw down the middle wall of
partition, proving that in Him there is "nor East nor West," but that "all are
one in Christ Jesus."   S. Myers

✳✳

50   I wish I could paint for you a picture of the Communion rail on a Sunday
evening during a Communion service in my old church in Madras. A converted
Buddhist and his family, a converted Brahmin, a young fellow who was born a
Mohammedan, a leper, a half-caste, a prosperous English business man, a
Dravidian student, a Syrian Christian, the colonel of the regiment in which I
served in the war, an Indian lawyer, a professor at the university. There they
kneel together at the feet of Jesus. I used to wonder, with some pride I am
afraid, whether there was a Communion rail like that in the world. I certainly
do not think there is any place in the world where those people would have knelt
together, touching one another, save at the feet of Jesus, who had broken down
all the barriers.

Leslie D. Weatherhead
From *Christian World Pulpit*, Vol. 129

Burdens

51   Addison's impressive essay, "The Mountain of Miseries," was suggested by
the saying of Socrates: "If all our misfortunes were laid in one common heap,
whence every one must take an equal portion, most people would be content to
take their own and depart." Addison pictures all the burdens of mankind thrown
down in a huge pile. One cast down his poverty, another flung down his job, a
third, after a great deal of puffing, threw down his burden which proved to be
his wife. When the mountain of miseries was complete each picked up some-

thing in exchange for what had been thrown down. A poor galley slave took up somebody's gout instead of his chains. A venerable grey-headed man exchanged his colic and griping pains for an undutiful son. We are not told what happened to the difficult wife. Addison does tell us, however, that the whole plan was a failure and led to bitter complaints. The poor mortals preferred their own burdens.   J. Leonard Clough

※ ※

52   I remember reading a study of the Empress Elizabeth of Austria, the beautiful wife of the unhappy Francis Joseph. She was a high-spirited woman of romantic aspirations, and would cheerfully have given her life for her husband. The one thing she could not do was to give her life to him—to stand by his side and endure, for his sake, the boredom and ceremony of the old Viennese Court. She spent her life in yachting or hunting or globe-trotting: anything rather than bear the commonplace burden of everyday life. It is a parable of much of the practical infidelity of our own time.   Ernest H. Jeffs

Busyness

53   In the Old Testament there is a story of a man who, during a battle, was put in charge of an important prisoner and told at all costs to keep him secure, but when the battle was ended and they came at last to relieve him of his charge he could only reply: "While I was busy here and there the prisoner escaped." That story might be applied to many of us and our good intentions. While we were busy here and there, often with trivialities and personal inclinations, the duties we really did mean to discharge, the opportunities we really did mean to improve, the good we really did mean to accomplish and the service we really did mean to render, slipped silently away beyond recapture. And so both we and the world, and so many people and good causes in the world have been made immeasurably poorer through our dalliance and neglect. By themselves good intentions are not enough. They are of little use either to ourselves or the things we sympathize with or believe in. They must be improved by action and clothed in deeds without which even the highest impulse and noblest purpose will soon fade and perish.   J. A. Figures

Busyness, and God

54   "How is the silent peace and reality of God to come to us who need it so dreadfully; and how are we to go to Him in this distracting rush and tangle of things which make our daily lives?" Evelyn Underhill put that question to us at

an unforgettable service in my church in Birmingham some years ago, and it is even more pertinent today than when it was first spoken. Her answer to it is pertinent too. "I think," she said, "the answer to the problem is, that we have so to learn God, that the rush and tangle itself becomes our meeting-place with Him, and the very substance of a life of prayer."

James MacKay

Calvary

55   You may remember that Studdert Kennedy stumbled over an "undersized, underfed German boy, with a wound in his stomach and a hole in his head" and he saw another Calvary. "From that moment on I have never seen the world as anything but a Crucifix. I see the Cross set up in every slum, in every filthy overcrowded quarter, in every vulgar flaring street that speaks of luxury and waste of life. I see Him staring up at me from the pages of the newspaper that tells of a tortured, lost, bewildered world."

David A. MacLennan

Calvary, Triumph of

56   A man doesn't go to Gethsemane lightly. He doesn't put up a cross for collateral when what he says is guesswork! All through this story there is sweat on God's forehead—and the rippling of muscles that ache under the skin! If there is a word on His lips about forgiveness, He means it: by all His fasting and temptation He means it. "God, His mark." If there is a word about the victory He can give you: the soul He can make of you poor and prodigal as you are, He means it!—by all His agony and bloody sweat He means it! If there is a word there about His companionship on the loneliest of ways: by His Cross and Passion: by His death and burial He means it! Whether the Cross seemed like a victory that first Good Friday or not, it seals yours when you take Him at His word! "God, His mark." I wish you'd look up and claim it! Talk about the triumph of Calvary! I don't care what your circumstances have been, or what you've been either—been or done! for that matter—I don't care: not when God dares you with His own signature, to be one of His redeemed!

Paul E. Scherer

Character

57   Sir Archibald Geikie relates that when one of the holy or pilgrim wells of Scotland was cleared out, among the stuff which had gathered at the bottom of

the pool a large number of copper coins was found, some of them extending in date back to the times of the Stuarts. The surfaces of the coins had in many cases been dissolved to such an extent as to reduce the metal to little more than the thinness of writing paper. Yet so persistent was the internal structure super-induced by the act of minting that, even in this attenuated condition, the obverse and reverse could still be deciphered. Is not this a figure of the persistence of divine characters in men who have suffered the deepest debasement? Minted in the image of the King, the soul deeply fallen, corroded by vice, foul with sensualities, still retains somewhat of its royal qualities and superscription. It is the hope and glory of the Church to seek and to save that which was lost.

W. L. Watkinson

✳✳

58   D. L. Moody, the American evangelist, used to say that "character is what a man or woman is in the dark," when there's no one looking, no one listening. It is the thought, the desire, the intention that counts in the sight of God, because, "As a man thinketh in his heart, so is he." Our true character is determined not by our achievements but by our desires; not by our actual accomplishments but by our ideals. "Out of the heart," said our Lord, "proceed evil thoughts, murders, thefts, blasphemies."

G. H. Clothier

✳✳

59   Ruskin has a story of a statue in a Venetian church. The side which could be seen was elaborately chiselled, but the side to the wall was rough and un-wrought. Says Ruskin, "This lying monument is true in its testimony to the character of the sculptor. He was banished from Venice for forgery in 1847." If we play the fool, we must pay the bill. A worker in the Portsmouth dockyard said that the disaster of the war years made it impossible to believe that God lives. My reply was that it would have been difficult to believe in God if men and nations could ignore God's laws with impunity and get away with it.

J. Leonard Clough

✳✳

60   During the Revolutionary War, neither Joseph Reed nor Benedict Arnold went after the offer of British gold; it came to them both; Reed spurned the bribe as if it were poison; Arnold, at the sound of the jingling gold, caught at the glittering bribe, and it burned him to a cinder.

Theodore L. Cuyler

✳✳

Charity Begins at Home

61   One day, a minister in the course of his visiting was about to enter a house when he heard husband and wife quarrelling within. He hesitated. Should he call another time? On a sudden impulse, he knocked at the door. The angry voices ceased. He was cordially received. The husband, no doubt thinking that the parson's visit called for some pious talk, began to comment about the poor state of the world and the failure of the nations to live in peace. He said that if only the nations were Christians, all problems would be solved. The minister agreed, but he ventured to suggest that "first charity should begin at home" . . . that there was little likelihood of its being expressed elsewhere if it did not begin at home. That "went home"!   T. H. Mather

Cheerfulness

62   Life is like the ancient shield with two sides, one of gold and one of silver. The two knights fell out and fought as to which was right, one contending that the shield was gold and the other as stoutly asserting that it was silver. After both were worn out in the contest, they decided to look at the shield itself, and, lo, both were right. So it is in life. There is a bright side and a dark side. It is merely a question of which one prefers.

Let us cultivate the habit of looking at the bright side. Some one expressed an aversion to calling on Mrs. ——, and said: "She wails so much; but I understand she wails less now. Probably her health is better." "Her health is better," was the reply, "because she wails less." It is not a question of what to think about. There are plenty of things over which to worry. There are problems of sorrow and sufferings and pain and sin sufficient to drive us crazy if we allow them. It is rather a question of what we will think about. He is wise who counts his blessings.

The best way of all is the method Dr. Chalmers used to commend when he spoke of "the expulsive power of a new affection." It is the method of crowding out the gloom with the light. The way the seven devils were kept out of the cleansed house of the man in the parable, was by the angel who took up his abode in the house.   James I. Vance

Child, Influence of

63   In Bret Harte's story of "The Luck of Roaring Camp," he describes a camp of gold diggers. Some of them were fugitives from justice, some were drunkards

and gamblers. Even in a district where a reputation for evil was hard to make, Roaring Camp was famous for its crimes. Into that camp a woman strayed, gave birth to a child and died. The child lived and then the change began. In the presence of this helpless child rough men shed their roughness and became strangely tender. The cabin in which the child lay was first boarded and papered, then instead of the usual untidiness it was kept scrupulously clean. Flowers were planted around it, and a new sense of beauty was born in the camp, and spread to other cabins. Shouting and yelling were not permitted. Profanity was strictly forbidden. And after the day's work men formed the habit of lounging in to see the little one, and to hold him in their arms.

David Ramsay

Children, Teaching

64   It is a tragic thing when children are deprived of the knowledge of God. There can be no worse deprivation than for a child to go out into the world without a knowledge of God, and a sense of God which alone can give rest and direction. I do not suppose there are many parents who think that children should be left to form their own judgement about religion, to choose a religion of their own. I heard an interesting story the other day about some people who brought up their child on this principle. When he was about nine or ten he showed curious nervous symptoms, and in the end they decided to take him to a psychologist, a lady who understood the child mind. She had several interviews with him and she said afterwards to the parents, "You have brought up your child without any religion; and he has got a religion of his own; it is a primitive religion; for him the whole place is full of evil spirits; he sees them everywhere, and his life is a torment." The truth of the matter is that the human heart will not tolerate forever an empty shrine. If God does not fill the heart of man something else will—there will be the worship of money, of power, the attraction of some other authority.

James Reid

Choice

65   God comes to every one of you, saying, "Choose what I shall give thee." Goethe said that he admired the man who knew precisely what he aimed at in life. God wishes you at the commencement of your career to come up to the height of a great choice. "What shall I give thee?" You must choose; your refusal to choose is itself a choice, and it is this liberty to choose your own aim in life, and at last your own destiny, that makes life so serious. You must choose

between religion and irreligion; one of them must be right. Religion, to say the least, with hope of its truth, with no fear of its safety; irreligion, with constant doubt of its truth and constant fear of its safety—you must choose between them; and if you choose aright it will be well for you. You have read Carlyle's description of the Sphinx sitting by the wayside propounding her riddles to every one that passed; and if the passer-by answered correctly it was well for him, but if he did not answer the riddle he was destroyed on the spot. I have watched young men and others, and I say that life comes to every man in this world with its riddle, and if he answers it aright it is well with him, but if he tries to go on neglecting the commandments of the Giver of life; if he tries to go on living in his own way, and not in God's way, life to him will be a thing of loss, and he will become an object to be wept over. "There is no peace, saith my God, to the wicked."   Herber Evans

Christ

66   I have myself had the tremendous privilege of preaching about Christ in India to men who, I was told, had never heard Him preached before. When the meaning and import of my poor words about Him were received by them, it seemed to me as though their faces lit up, as faces light up at the recognition of a friend. And I was not surprised when I read of a fine old Hindu to whom an Indian missionary expounded the simple gospel of Christ, that the man turned to the missionary and said words which have often made me ponder: "Sir, I have known Him all my life, and now you have told me His name." As though the old man felt that there should be someone who, in his humanity, personified all the ideals of the Hindu, and when he heard about Jesus knew his dream was true. He belongs to them: He is theirs, raceless, eternal, divine.

Leslie D. Weatherhead
From *Christian World Pulpit*, Vol. 129

✳✳

67   In one of his essays Hazlitt tells us how, when Charles Lamb and some of his literary friends were amusing themselves by imagining how they would act and how they would be moved if some of the great dead kings of literature should appear then and there before them, at last one said, "What would each of you do should Jesus Christ appear?" A sudden solemnity fell on all that literary company. And finally Charles Lamb, falling into that stammering way he always had when his emotions were deeply stirred, replied, reverently, "If Shakespeare should come amongst us we should all rise; but if He should appear, we should all kneel." And no one in that company said him nay. It is the inevi-

table posture of us all; before the Master of our soul and our destiny we must fall in homage and in worship as to no other in this world; He stands by Himself.   William Watson

* *

68 In "Ecce Homo" the writer mentions one or two points of resemblance between Socrates and Jesus Christ, and then one or two points of difference. He says: "Both were teachers, both were prodigiously influential, both suffered martyrdom. . . . Both Socrates and Jesus Christ uttered remarkable thoughts and lived remarkable lives." Now comes the supreme point of difference. "But Socrates holds his place in history by his thoughts and not his life; Christ by His life and not by His thoughts."   John W. Veevers

* *

69 Modern science began with Darwin and his theory of evolution. It is significant, therefore, that in the village where he lived he opened a room for the people. When Fegan, the Evangelical and founder of children's homes, moved into the village, he gave him that room. A year later he wrote to him: "Your services have done more for the village in a few months than all our efforts for many years. We have never been able to reclaim a drunkard, but through your services I do not think there is a drunkard left in the village. Science has its place in life, but only Christ can save."   E. Aldom French

* *

70 Heinrich Heine, that brilliant writer, born a Jew, forsook his ancestral religion, and gave himself to a life in which temperament was law. In his later years, suffering from a paralyzing affection of the spinal cord, one eye sightless, and the other eyelid paralyzed so that it had to be held up whenever he wanted to see, Heine made his painful way through the noisy revolutionary excitement of Paris. His distressed spirit craved a last sight of the famous statue of the Venus of Milo—armless when found on the Island of Melos, and left unrestored by its French owners. Let Heine relate his own experience. "With great labour I dragged myself as far as the Louvre, and I nearly broke down as I entered the lofty hall, where the ever-blessed goddess of Beauty, our beloved Lady of Milo, stands on her pedestal. I lay a long while at her feet, and wept so bitterly that even a stone must have pitied me: and the goddess did look down compassionately on me, but with so little comfort that it seemed as if she would say, 'Dost thou not see that I have no arms, and therefore cannot help thee?' "

No exhausted spirit has ever felt like that about our Lord. In our time of greatest need, things that have fascinated and helped in life—things like art,

science, literature, music—are not able to help or support us. They have no arms.
But God in Christ has arms—strong arms. "Behold, the Lord's hand is not
shortened that it cannot save." "Cast thy burden upon the Lord, and He will
sustain thee."

                                                                    Charles Kellett

✳✳

71   As a man, an actual historical personality, Jesus of Nazareth has so indelibly
impressed the conscience and so vividly touched the imagination of mankind that
to contemplate as a serious possibility either His dethronement, as it were, or His
fading from human memory is next door to impossible. If it were put as a question is put to a jury, the majority of mankind, those that is who are unembittered
by suffering, unwarped by passion, and uncorrupted by their early training,
would agree that alike in His person and in His precepts Jesus is unique. The
standards of conduct associated with His name are respected and honored far
beyond the confines of His Church, as the following incident attests. On one
occasion Hindu and Moslem counsel were appearing before an Indian judge.
One suddenly declared a certain piece of conduct to have been "un-Christlike."
The adjective at once laid its spell upon the court. It was felt that on that point
the last word had been spoken and nothing further was needed. The ethical
loftiness of Jesus was taken for granted.

    Testamentary evidence exists, furthermore, which seems to prove that for cer-
tain minds the fascination and the authority of Jesus do not decline with the
passing of the centuries. "What a relief it would be," writes George Tyrell to
F. von Hügel, "if one could conscientiously wash one's hands of the whole
concern. But then there is that strange man upon his cross who drives one back
again and again." A few decades earlier Renan was writing: "Whatever the unexpected phenomena of the future, Jesus will never be surpassed. His worship
will constantly renew its youth. All the ages will proclaim that amongst the
sons of men none has been born who is greater than Jesus."

                                                                    D. W. Langridge

✳✳

72   All the history of the world is, if you come to think about it, in the Judgement Hall at Jerusalem. Caiaphas with his fox face schemes for security. Pilate
blusters in power. Judas clasps his money to his uncertain heart, the ignorant
mob led by fools swings this way and that, whilst clowns plait a crown of thorns
and feel for a bag of nails. And at the day's end they went to their beds feeling
that they had done a good day's work and rid the world of a dreamer. But now,
under the test of time and silence, they all slink into the shadows as foolish,

gibbering ghosts, and Christ stands in increasing light as King of kings, and
Lord of lords.   McEwan Lawson

✳✳

73   The Russian novelist Dostoievsky, in a letter written from exile in Siberia,
wrote, while still a young man: "I am a child of this age, a child of unfaith and
scepticism and probably (indeed, I know it) shall remain so to the end of my
life. . . . And yet God gives me sometimes moments of perfect peace; in such
moments I love, and believe that I am loved; in such moments I have formulated
my creed, wherein all is clear and holy to me. This creed is extremely simple;
here it is: I believe that there is nothing lovelier, deeper, more sympathetic, more
rational, more manly and more perfect than the Saviour; I say to myself with
jealous love that not only is there no one else like Him, but that there could be
no one." These words were written in 1854. Some fourteen years later Amiel—
a very different type of man—wrote in his journal: "We may hold aloof from
the Churches and yet bow ourselves before Jesus. We may be suspicious of the
clergy and refuse to have anything to do with catechisms, and yet love the Holy
and the Just, who came to save and not to curse. Jesus will always supply us
with the best criticism of Christianity, and when Christianity has passed away
the religion of Jesus will survive."   J. C. Hardwick

✳✳

74   Herkomer was once asked the secret of his success as a painter, and his
reply was: "I look, I look, I look, I look!" And the secret of becoming like Christ
is to look, and keep on looking at Christ.   Joseph Reavley

✳✳

75   There came a little time ago into the study of a New York pastor a successful business man of that city. The pastor asked him the question of this text,
"What think ye of the Christ?" That man said with perfect frankness, "I suppose I never do think about Christ." Turning to him the pastor asked, "When
were you born?" He said, "In 1843." The pastor said, "Before Christ or after
Christ?" He was confused. The pastor spared him further questions. It is an
astounding thing that there can be found, in a land of civilization and culture
and Christianity, a man who has no definite conviction regarding Jesus Christ.
It is astounding that a man claiming the honors of average intelligence, and
especially of liberal culture, should have no definite convictions regarding Jesus
Christ. Such an admission argues some degree of mental vacuity and of moral
inanity. Here is a business man who writes business letters, and dates those
letters, and yet has no special thought of Jesus Christ, who has given the world

a new calendar. Here is a man who visits halls of statuary and observes the finest products of artistic genius in sculpture, and has no definite convictions regarding Jesus Christ. Take away from the halls of statuary all the figures suggested by the religion of Jesus Christ, and you make the most glorious halls of sculpture indescribably bare. Wander through galleries of paintings and observe that the religion, the life, the soul of Jesus Christ, has been the inspiration of the noblest works of art as depicted on immortal canvas, and then admit that you have no definite conviction regarding Jesus Christ. Listen to the greatest music of the world, Bach, Haydn, Handel, Mendelssohn, Mozart—the music that thrills the soul, that ennobles the heart, that inspires the life, all born out of the brain and heart of Jesus Christ—and then say you have no definite convictions about Christ.   R. S. MacArthur

✳✳

76   Claude G. Montefiore—a liberal Jew—says: "I cannot conceive of a time when the figure of Jesus will be no longer a star of first magnitude in the spiritual heavens—when He will be no longer regarded as one of the greatest religious heroes and teachers the world has seen." T. R. Glover—Public Orator in the University of Cambridge—says: "Why must we undertake to form a judgment on Jesus Christ? Why cannot we leave Him alone? Because we are confronted with an historical Christian Church. The whole Christian history is there with all the endless ramifications of the influence it has exerted upon mankind. We cannot cut ourselves off from the deepest force mankind has known—a factor as powerful in the present as in the past—and keep our manhood and womanhood undiminished."   Stanley A. Clark

✳✳

77   Carlyle in his history of the French Revolution tells of a band of students, all infidels, rushing into the Louvre, and throwing down every picture that was obnoxious to their ideas. They lifted their muskets to destroy the picture of Christ. A young officer shouted, "Halt! There is He who taught the Brotherhood of Man." They doffed their caps and acclaimed the picture, exclaiming, "Liberty, Equality, Fraternity."   W. G. Reekie

✳✳

78   C. F. Andrews tells of a poor Hindu woman whom he saw crawling on hands and knees along the ground. She was going to travel in that way for thousands of miles, seeking what she described as "a vision of IT"—a vision of a sacred flame coming forth from a holy mountain. Andrews says that a great longing came over him that not only that poor woman, but all India, might have

a vision, not a vision of IT, but a vision of HIM; not a vision of a flame of fire, but a vision of One whose heart was aflame with holy love.

G. Randall Jones

Christ, and Our Handicaps

79   It is said that the great violinist Paganini suffered the loss of one string after another till only one string was left. The audience twittered and laughed. The wonderful musician, stung to the quick, said, as he lifted his poor instrument to his chin: "See what Paganini and one string can do." Though all the world desert you, and everything seems wrong, see what Christ and one poor human soul can do. Christ and one make a majority. With Him you are on the winning side.   Thomas Cameron

Christ, Attraction to

80   There is a remarkable record of one of the sayings of Napoleon Bonaparte in St. Helena. He had been reading one morning the New Testament, and he said to one of his friends who came in, "I am much struck with the contrast between Christ's mode of gathering people to Himself and the way practised by Alexander the Great, by Julius Caesar, and by myself. The people have been gathered to us by fear; they were gathered to Christ by love. Alexander, Caesar, and I have been men of war, but Christ was the Prince of Peace. The people have been driven to us; they were drawn to Him. In our case there has been forced conscription; in His there was free obedience."

Robert F. Horton

Christ, Beauty of

81   A little girl sat upon her mother's knee, and as she looked up into her face she said: "Mummie, you've got the prettiest hair and the sweetest eyes that I have ever seen, and Mummie, yours in the kindest face in all the world. But, Mummie, why are your arms so ugly?" "Sit still, my dear," said the mother, "and I will tell you. When you were a baby I left the house for a few moments and went to see a friend. As I came back I saw flames leaping up and as I drew nearer I discovered that it was the house in which you were sleeping, for I had just tucked you up and kissed you 'goodnight.' I rushed into the burning building and lifted you out of your cot, then rushed with you into safety. You were safe, but I was terribly burned, and I suffered for several months. I got better, but I'm terribly scarred. I know, as you say, that my hands are very ugly." The little girl had never expected an explanation like this, and her little heart was hurt by the recital of the facts. The tears were streaming down her face as she looked once more into her mother's eyes and said: "Mummie, you've got the prettiest hair I've ever seen, and yours is the sweetest face, and your eyes are wonderful. But, Mummie, your hands and your arms are the most beautiful of all." Ah! that was the beauty which had sacrificed itself in service.

Was not God like that in Christ? His feet were tired as He constantly trod the path of service. His hands were always lifting heavy burdens from the lives of others. His life, beautiful at all times, was never so beautiful as when He gave it for others on the Cross. "And when we shall see Him, there is no beauty that we should desire Him." No beauty! Yes, the beauty which was sacrificed in service for us.   Ezra E. W. Ramm

Christ, Changing Power of

82   Henry Drummond at one of his student meetings in Edinburgh read a letter he had received from a man who had made shipwreck of his life, a letter of hopelessness and bitterness. It was signed with the Greek word for death, Thanatos. A year or two later Drummond was again speaking to the students and reminded them of the story of this man who had seemed to him to be utterly lost. But he said: "I have in my pocket tonight a letter from Thanatos, in which he says he is a changed man—a new creature in Christ Jesus."

                                                                           John Bishop

Christ, Choosing

83   I once saw a blood-stained card that had on its face the Christian Cross, and on its back the words of the Christian Endeavour Covenant which begins: "Trusting in the Lord Jesus Christ for strength, I promise Him that I will strive to do whatever he would have me do." That card was found on the headless body of a Chinese boy during the Boxer uprising in China. The lad was given his choice. His captors said, "Give the card and keep your head, or keep the card and give your head."   Daniel A. Poling

Christ, Coming of

84   Mazzini, the Italian patriot, after describing the cruelty and hopelessness of the world under the Roman Caesars, goes on to say: "He came, the Soul the most full of love, the most deeply inspired by God and the future that men have seen on earth—Jesus! He bent over the corpse of the dead world and whispered

a word of faith. Over the clay that had lost all of man but the movement and the form, He uttered words until then unknown—love, sacrifice, a heavenly origin. And the dead arose. A new life circulated through the clay which philosophy had tried in vain to reanimate. From that corpse rose the Christian world, the world of liberty and equality. From that clay arose the true man, the image of God, the precursor of humanity."

T. J. Lewis

Christ, Compassion of

85   There is a legend that one day in an Eastern street a number of people were gathered around the body of a dead dog. The dog in the East is not like our dog, a domestic pet, but is the scavenger of the street, and is despised even when alive. The bystanders were passing comments on this repulsive spectacle of the dead dog. "How revolting," said one. "Loathsome," said another. Then Jesus came by and said, "But see how white its teeth are."

John Bishop

Christ, Comprehending

86   When Daniel Webster was in his best moral state, and when he was in the prime of his manhood, he was one day dining with a company of literary gentlemen in the city of Boston. The company was composed of clergymen, lawyers, physicians, statesmen, merchants, and almost all classes of literary persons. During the dinner the conversation incidentally turned upon the subject of Christianity. Mr. Webster, as the occasion was in honor of him, was expected to take a leading part in the conversation, and he frankly stated as his religious sentiments his belief in the Divinity of Christ, and his dependence upon the atonement of the Saviour. A minister of very considerable literary reputation sat almost opposite him at the table, and he looked at him and said, "Mr. Webster, can you comprehend how Jesus Christ could be both God and man?" Mr. Webster, with one of those looks which no man can imitate, fixed his eye upon him, and promptly and emphatically said, "No, sir, I cannot comprehend it; and I would be ashamed to acknowledge Him as my Saviour if I could comprehend it. If I could comprehend Him, He could be no greater than myself, and such is my conviction of accountability to God, such is my sense of sinfulness before Him, and such is my knowledge of my own incapacity to recover myself, that I feel I need a superhuman Saviour."

Bishop Janes

Christ, Comradeship of

87   David Livingstone, having returned to England for a brief holiday, was
received by Queen Victoria and honored by many cities and universities. When
he visited Cambridge the huge Assembly Hall was crowded with undergradu-
ates. Usually, on such occasions as you know, pea-shooters and catcalls are much
in evidence, but when the vast audience looked at Livingstone, this small man,
prematurely old, with furrowed forehead and face like parchment, there was an
awesome silence—not catcalls, no pea-shooters. Then Livingstone spoke, very
simply and very quietly. "Gentlemen," he said, "shall I tell you what it was that
kept me true to my resolve through all those years in the Dark Continent? It was
the word of a Gentleman: 'Lo, I am with you always, even unto the end of the
world.' "

Yes, there Christ has been, down through the ages, above all friends and comrades, the greatest Personality of human life; the One who has never deserted or
failed those who put their trust in Him, and He says to each one of us: "Believe
in God, believe also in Me." "Stand fast in the faith; faith in an everloving
Father; faith in an ever present Saviour."

G. H. Clothier

Christ, Discipleship

88   When somebody tried to flatter George Washington at Valley Forge, he
asked, "Where do you stand with reference to the cause I represent?" When you
tell God you love Him, He asks where you stand with reference to Jesus Christ.

John Huxtable

Christ, Effect of

89   There is a story told of Pinel, the Frenchman, who was the pioneer of work
for the insane. In his time insane men and women who had lost their minds and
had become mentally weak were treated with cruelty. There was a sea captain
who for twenty years had been chained and placed in a dark cave. He had never
seen the sun during that time, he had never breathed the pure, fresh air of the
outdoor world. And Pinel went to see him. Pinel looked upon him and said
to him, "I am going to take your chain off of you." He said, "You dare not." "I
am going to, man." "You dare not." But Pinel unlocked the chains and took
him by the hand, led him through the dark cavern into God's pure sunshine,
and bade him look.

The man looked abroad on the world that had been unknown for twenty years, looked above at the sun shining in the blue heavens. The tears began streaming from his eyes, and he said, "Oh, it is beautiful, oh, it is wonderful." And, do you know, that is what Jesus Christ does to a man. Jesus Christ brings him out of the prison house, Jesus Christ takes away the shackles of his own incapacities, Jesus Christ removes away from him all the hindrances of his past and brings him out into the clear presence of God.

Joseph T. Kelly

Christ, Ethics of

90   Mr. G. K. Chesterton used to say that when you first look at "The Sermon on the Mount," it turns everything upside down, but later you discover that it turns everything right side up. Dean Inge says freely that if Christianity cannot hold us at the point of ethical conduct, then what is left is not worth fighting over. If the ethics of Christ is unworkable, then His Cross is a stark tragedy, a mocking mirage. We must start off at the Cross if we would travel upward to the ethical call of Christ.

E. L. Allen

Christ, Experience of

91   Dr. T. R. Glover has given it as his opinion that the history of Christianity gathers round the lives of four outstanding personalities—Paul, Augustine, Luther, Wesley. Whence did these radiant and consecrated souls draw their inspiration and receive their power to wield the mighty influence they did; not only upon their own times, but also upon the whole course of human history? Was it a mere accident, the casual casting up upon the flood of time of men of unusual spiritual vision and faith; or must we look deeper for the answer? Surely the reason of their mighty contribution to the cause of Christianity is to be found in the fact that they were in possession of a real, vital, conscious experience of Jesus Christ and His presence in their lives. They were more sure of Him than of anything else. The consequence was that they could speak with a note of conviction and authority that otherwise would have been impossible.

H. J. Dale

Christ, Face of

92   Dostoievsky, the Russian novelist, relates a vision he once had. It was in a little country church, with wax candles burning before the pictures of the saints, and the peasants bowing and swaying with the rhythm and the cadences of the

great Russian liturgy. "All at once a man came up from behind and stood beside me. I did not turn toward Him; but I felt that that man was Christ. I made an effort and looked at my neighbour. A face like every man's face. His eyes looked a little upward, quietly and intently, the hands folded and still; and the clothes on Him like every man's. 'What sort of Christ is this?' I thought. 'Such an ordinary man, it cannot be.' I turned away, but I had hardly turned my eyes from this ordinary man when I felt again that it was none other than Christ standing by me. Suddenly my heart sank and I came to myself. Only then did I realize that just such a face is the face of Christ, a face like all men's faces." Dostoievsky was right. Jesus was, and is, one of our ordinary folk; it were well for us had we that fine insight which should enable us to see Him in each other's face, and worship Him there.   Richard Roberts

Christ, Facing

93   There is a strange portrait of the face of Christ, painted by Gabriel Max in 1840. It shows the thorn-crowned head, but the eyes are closed. Underneath the face it is written: "If you watch the eyes which are shut, you will see them suddenly open." That is it; if you look upon Christ, He will look upon you. You may see the picture in a shop window, as I did in a shop in the Strand. But the people who looked into the window were for the most part concerned with the landscapes and the daughters of Eve; and the Christ remained blind. But when one man looked, then one man saw, and the eyes were opened, and for a moment the eyes looked out upon him. And so it is with the Gospels. Whether you see Him or not depends much upon the heart you bring. You must come with an open child-like heart ready to believe in the immensity of goodness He is able to reveal. You must bring your imagination and your lively fancy whereby you can get back to the days of His flesh. You must come, as Dr. Glover sought to make plain to us, with the earnest endeavour to see Him as His contemporaries saw Him; and as you thus read the records there will be moments which glow with the presence divine.   Ralph H. Turner

Christ, Following

94   Some years ago there passed away from us a great Englishman—Wilfred Grenfell. He was a doctor, and the glittering prizes of his profession were within his grasp. But he heard the call of Jesus Christ, and he went out to Labrador where, on the inhospitable shore of that barren land, he spent his life in ameliorating the lot of the people who live there. Did he ever regret his step? Towards the end of his life this is what he said: "Feeble and devious as my own foot-

steps have been since my decision to follow Jesus Christ, I believe more than ever that this is the only real adventure of life. No step in my life do I even compare with that in permanent satisfaction. One thing about which I never have any question is that the decision and the endeavour to follow Christ does for men what nothing else on earth can do for them."   James Colville

Christ, Gain with

95   One thousand eight hundred years ago an aged saint was being led to Rome by ten rough Roman soldiers, to be thrown to the wild beasts in the amphitheatre. Can you imagine anything more dreary and deplorable! Was he unhappy? Did he count cruelty and martyrdom as evil? No; in one of the seven letters that he wrote on his way he says: "Come fire and iron, come rattling of wild beasts, cutting and mangling and wrenching of my bones, come hacking of my limbs, come crushing of my whole body, come cruel tortures of the devil to assail me! Only be it mine to attain to Jesus Christ." What are those words of St. Ignatius but an echo of the Apostle's, "What things were gain to me, those I counted loss for Christ. Yea, doubtless, and I count all things but loss that I may win Christ."   F. W. Farrar

Christ, Genius of

96   Charles Dickens was the great master of the pathetic style, yet when the novelist was asked what was the most touching story in literature, he answered, "The story of the Prodigal Son." Coleridge took all knowledge to his province, and his conversation sparkled with jewels of thought. Yet, when asked for the richest passage in literature, he answered, "The Beatitudes." Edmund Kean was a great actor and artist, but there was one passage so full of tears that he thought no man could properly present it—the one beginning, "Come unto Me, all ye that labor and are heavy laden, and I will give you rest." From the viewpoint of the statesman, Burke said the most impressive political document on the rights of man was the Sermon on the Mount. It is a striking fact, too, that in all literature the sentence best loved by children is Christ's "Suffer little children to come unto Me"; the sentence best loved by the ages, "Let not your hearts be troubled"; the sentence best loved by all men, the one beginning, "For God so loved the world that He gave His only begotten Son." In hours of health and success men may love the majestic pages of Webster or the rhythmical beauties of Ruskin, but in the last hour scholars and statesmen alike exclaim, "Read me the words of Jesus Christ; they alone breathe the language of eternity!"
                                                       Newell Dwight Hillis

Christ, Imitation of

97   When Sadhu Sundar Singh was in London he called on a Christian lady. The maid who answered the door said to her mistress, "There is a gentleman at the door, ma'am. I can't make out his name, but he looks as if he might be Jesus Christ." Yes, he did, and he not only looked like the Master, but he lived like Him.

Ignatius Jones

Christ, Inevitable

98   Dr. F. W. Norwood was once travelling in a railway compartment where one of the passengers was holding forth on the subject of war and these other evils and asserting that we should never get rid of them, human nature being what it was. After listening for a while in silence, Dr. Norwood intervened and said, "My opinion would not weigh with you, sir, but I think you are going to have some serious controversy with Jesus Christ on this subject."

G. R. C. Fuller

Christ, Influence of

99   There is a very instructive story told of an English Earl, who had become an infidel, visiting the islands of Fiji, and speaking to one of the chiefs of the island he said, "You are a great chief, and it is a pity you have listened to missionaries who only want to get rich amongst you. No one nowadays believes in the Bible or listens to the story about Jesus Christ; people know better, and I am sorry that you are so foolish." The old chief's eyes kindled, and he said, "You see that stone yonder, that is where we used to smash out the brains of our victims; and you see that oven yonder, that is where we cooked the bodies of men and ate them at our feasts; and I can tell you," he added, "that but for these missionaries, and that old Book and Jesus Christ, and His great love which has changed us from savages into God's children, you would never go away from this island alive. We should have brained you and cooked you, and eaten you with great joy long ago." I think we can learn a little from the Fijian chief.

Robert F. Horton

**

100   Shortly before the death of Joseph Conrad, the novelist, Epstein was engaged in carving a bust of the noted novelist. The sculptor worked twenty-one

days at a stretch on this particular bust. At the end he said: "I was glad to spend twenty-one days of my life looking at Joseph Conrad."

When a man gazes on the face of Christ, trying to reproduce it indelibly in his heart, his life will become transformed and transfigured. His confession will be: "Once I was blind, now I see."

J. Lyle Rodger

Christ, Kingship of

101 I never can forget that greatest of all the queens, Victoria, and how on one occasion she was present at the rendering of the "Hallelujah Chorus." It is the custom of an English audience to rise while the "Hallelujah Chorus" is being rendered. All the people leapt to their feet, but Her Majesty sat still in her appointed place. The great chorus rolled on, "Hallelujah, for ever and ever, for ever and ever. King of kings, and Lord of lords. Hallelujah, King of kings"; and Her Majesty rose, and she never was so queenly as when in rising at that great challenge she flung her simple diadem at the feet of "Our Lord Jesus Christ."

Joseph Parker

Christ, Living

102 Stanley Jones tells us that once a Mohammedan taunted a Christian with the fact that whilst they had the Tomb of the Prophet as a place of pilgrimage, Christians did not know for sure where Jesus had been buried. Quickly came the Christian's reply: "We have no certain tomb because we have no corpse." Exactly! No tomb—no corpse; for we have the living Christ.

Michelangelo is recorded to have said to his fellow painters on one occasion: "Why do you paint Christ on the Cross so much? Christ suffering . . . Christ dying . . . Christ dead! Paint Him rather Risen! With His foot upon the riven rock—paint Him victorious and glorious! Paint Him the Conqueror of sin and death."

J. Trevor Davies

Christ, Our Guide

103 Augustine Sabatier makes this noble confession, which finds a responsive echo in every serious mind: "If," says he, "if wearied by the world of pleasure or of toil, I wish to find my soul again and live a deeper life, I can accept no other guide and master than Jesus Christ, because in Him alone optimism is without frivolity, and seriousness without despair." No truer words were ever penned by man.

D. Ewart James

Christ, Pity and

104   We might even succeed in working ourselves up to the point almost of tearfulness about this loneliness of Christ. How pathetic, how pitiful, this lonely Via Dolorosa of the Man of Sorrows! One has become uncomfortably aware of such an attitude in some of our hymns. We are so plainly being asked to pity Christ. I read these words recently in a religious book: "In all the pathos of the Gospel story there is nothing so infinitely touching as the ever-increasing loneliness of Christ." Pathos! Touching! I do not like those words. I set against them the noble protest of F. W. Robertson, in that famous sermon on "The Loneliness of Christ" to which my own thought owes so much: "There is a feeble sentimental way in which we view the Cross. We turn to the Cross, the agony and the loneliness, to touch soft feelings, to arouse compassion. You degrade that loneliness by your compassion. Compassion! Compassion for Him! Reverence, if you will, but no pity, please!" The danger is, of course, that when we pity Christ in His loneliness we merely project into Him something of our own disordered feelings. Our pity for Him, if we are not careful, is simply a disguised self-pity. It is ourselves for whom we are crying dolefully. Down in the subtle subconscious places of the mind we have presumed to see in this tremendous Christ a companion in distress with ourselves. We have even hugged the thought that we have never been properly understood, never properly appreciated as we deserved, never even had justice, never have been given by the cold world the friendship and understanding for which we hunger. We have been passed by, ignored, and have found ourselves often unaccountably disliked. The pathos of it, the pitifulness of it to ourselves. And here is Christ suffering the same thing. We will weep for Him, too. He joins us in the great class of the unappreciated.

Men and women, is that too harsh? Is it unworthy sarcasm? I know and you know the insidious subtlety of self-pity, the way in which it indulges itself almost without our knowing it. And I know that whatever the sublime personality of Christ was meant for, it was not meant for pity. If you pity Christ you have not seen Him; what is standing in the way of your seeing Him except your own clouded self-projecting mind?

H. H. Farmer

Christ, Presence of

105   Think of J. G. Paton when he buried his young wife in that savage island of the South Seas. "If it had not been for Jesus and the presence He vouchsafed me there, I should have gone mad and died beside that lonely grave." Missionaries have been able to face hostile crowds and preach Christ in the strength which the Ever-Present Christ has granted them. Some years ago Dr. O. S. Davis, of Chicago, had a severe illness, and for days lay on the border-line between time and eternity. He came back to life with a more vivid consciousness of Jesus Christ. "The reality of a living, present Christ I do surely know. . . . I have experienced an awareness of Christ, a certainty of His presence beside and within me, a conviction that the age-old 'mystic union' is true and possible today. . . . Once I stood on the edge of the abyss of doubt. It was the blackest moment of my life; and it passed in a moment, as I felt myself upborne and made superior to the hideous doubt by the strength and love of Christ."

J. Ireland Hasler

* *

106 That great Hindu saint, Sadhu Sundar Singh, is said by C. F. Andrews to have become deeply concerned at one time lest the feeling of deep intimacy with Christ that he possessed and which was the secret of his moral triumphs, should prove to be mere auto-suggestion, just the product of a kind of self-hypnosis, the working of some psychological power of his own. So distressed did he become by this idea that he determined to put it to the most thoroughgoing test that he could conceive. He fasted, in imitation of Christ, for forty days and forty nights in order to exhaust his own powers. He was picked up off the ground in a state of complete exhaustion, very near to death, by a wandering wood-cutter who nursed him back to life, but he had settled his problem. He declared that the sense of Christ's presence, instead of diminishing with his weakness, grew still more intimate and vivid and he knew he was dealing with objective reality.

Albert D. Belden

Christ, Problem of

107 You have problems about Christ. Well, of course you do; problems about the ancient documents where His life was recorded, about the stories of His birth, the miracles attributed to Him, the prescientific world-views He shared with His generation, the early Church's theological interpretations of Him— endless problems. And such is the capacity of the human mind to be obsessed with problems, even when dealing with something singularly beautiful, that there are many people today who never get any nearer to Christ than that. He is a problem.

Do we really mean that in His teachings of the good life, that go before us yet like a pillar of cloud by day and of fire by night, we can see nothing but problems? In that luminous personality that incarnated them and made those teachings beautiful, so that across the centuries men like George Matheson have said: "Son of Man, whenever I doubt of life, I think of Thee," do you see nothing but problems?

Harry Emerson Fosdick

Christ, Receiving

108 Said a lady once to Carlyle, bewailing the wickedness of the Jews in not receiving Christ, "How delighted we should have been to throw our doors open to Him and listen to His Divine precepts. Don't you think so, Mr. Carlyle?" "No, madam, I don't," said the sage. "I think that had He come very fashionably dressed, with plenty of money, preaching doctrines palatable to the higher orders, I might have had the honor of receiving from you a card of invitation on which was written, 'To meet our Saviour,' but if He had come uttering His sublime precepts and denouncing the Pharisees and associating with publicans and lower orders, as He did, you would have treated Him much as the Jews did, and have cried, 'Take Him to Newgate and hang Him!'"

R. Baldwin Brindley

Christ, Saving Power of

109 Lycurgus, the Spartan lawgiver, was once brutally assailed by a would-be assassin, who succeeded in maiming one of his eyes. He ordered the offender to be delivered up to him for punishment. This was done, and Lycurgus himself administered the chastisement, chastisement of a new and altogether unique kind. The penalty which he inflicted was the following: he instructed him, watched over him, weaned him from his old and bad habits, in short, made a good man of him. Such was the fruit of pardon! He then called his chariot, entered it with the man, went to the theatre, and said to the great crowd, "Spartans! I received this person from you malevolent, mischievous, cruel. I restore him to you a good citizen." In like manner, Christ receives us selfish towards our fellows and rebellious against God; but by the blessed, mighty nurture of His love He restores us to a condition in which we are right with our brethren and right with our infinite Father.

F. W. Farrar

Christ, Teaching of

110 The other day I heard two men of definite highbrow quality discussing the book in which Mr. R. S. Lambert describes his experiences with the British

Broadcasting Corporation. He tells how, at the interview prior to his appointment, he was asked in effect by Sir John Reith to state whether he held the
teaching of Christ to be of fundamental importance. To these two men this
seemed a ridiculous and even impertinent question. It, they felt, had nothing to
do with the B.B.C.; it was as fatuous as the once suggested proposal to introduce
some reference to Almighty God into the Covenant of the League of Nations.
Contemporary life has, as Studdert Kennedy put it, left Jesus at the street corner
in the rain. And, consequently, life has been all mist with no wind of the Spirit.
And, even in the ranks of Christians, people have either enshrined Christ in a
creed or have kept Him very definitely out of the inner circles of their life, and
held His Truth at arms' length in any discussion of political or economic adjustment; or they have allowed the wind of agnosticism to blow their flame of faith
flat. The total result has been a wild, darkened, blinded rush over a precipice
edge.

McEwan Lawson

Christ, the Centre

111   A man once came to Whistler and asked for his aid to hang up a new
and beautiful picture. The man complained that he could not fit the picture to
the room. After looking the matter over, Whistler exclaimed, "Man, you can't
fit that picture to the room; you must fit the room to the picture." When we
bring the pictures of life which Christ has painted, we find it does not fit this
modern world. The world must be remodelled to fit the picture.

R. Sirhowy Jones

Christ, the Difference He Makes

112   When Charles Lamb faced the heart-break of tragedy with his mother
and sister, he wrote to Coleridge: "Write me as religious a letter as possible."
Coleridge himself once said to John Stuart Blackie, "I am finding great comfort
in the prologue to the Gospel of John." The knowledge that Christ was before
all and over all, that He was doing the works which none other did, was his
comfort and his hope. This then is our hope that Christ is here. He is more than
a fading ideal of Palestinian memory. He has come, and He abides. He is with
us here in the confidence of His sovereign power. His kingship is His glory and
ours, because He raises us to kinship with Himself.

Henry Drummond begins his little book on *The Changed Life* by quoting
Huxley's somewhat pathetic words: "I protest that if some great power would
agree to make me always think what is true and do what is right on condition of

being turned into a sort of clock and wound up every morning, I should instantly close with the offer." And Drummond proceeds: "I propose to make that offer now. In all seriousness without being 'turned into a sort of clock,' the end can be attained."

Christ has come; Christ is here. The evidence of His presence is seen in transfigured lives and in transformed homes.   S. W. Hughes

Christ, the Intercessor

113   King Edward III, who was made furious by the dogged resistance of the people of Calais, when he laid siege to the place, was bent upon treating them with severity. After much entreaty to show them mercy from the noblest in his ranks, he ordered six of the principal citizens to be brought, each with a rope round his neck, so that upon them his wrath might fall. At this juncture, when all others had failed, his generous-hearted queen made herself famous. Queen Philippa had just arrived from England. Kneeling down before her consort, she said, with tears in her eyes: "Ah, gentle sire, I humbly pray, for the sake of the Holy Son of Mary, and your love for me, that you will have mercy on these six men."

It is a matter of history that she prevailed with the King, and the men were spared.

How forcibly does this remind us of the intercession of Jesus on behalf of the sinner. Others only plead to be denied, for there is only one successful mediator between God and man, the man Christ Jesus.   J. Jacques

Christ, the Refuge

114   When Richard Jefferies, our greatest naturalist, flung his earlier faith to the winds as something outworn, there grew within his darkening soul a deep contempt for the churches and everything religious. He prided himself on his intellectual progress beyond others who still believed what he called "myths and folklore." At the age of thirty-four he lay dying, and he became aware that he must seek deeper for spiritual comfort. He began an urgent return to the New Testament. "Read me the Gospel of Luke," he asked his wife, as his breath came faster. Then, as she read, he signalled her to stop. "These are the words of Jesus; they are true, and all my philosophy is hollow—it was my intellectual vanity." And so Richard Jefferies, the young prophet of English meadows and woodlands, returned to the faith from which he had broken away, and refound the lost Christ at the spot where he had parted company with Him.

Norman N. G. Cope

Christ, the Revelation of God

115   There was a terrifying play of Euripides which may well have been performed in Greek theatres in Galilee in Christ's time. It told of the warrior
Agamemnon coming home and then, because of his sin, being slaughtered by
his wife. But Jesus came telling of a Father who hurried out to find a foolish
son and bring him safely to his home. Indeed Jesus went further still, and taught
that if a man, or a community or a nation dies in compassionate self-sacrificial
service in order to bring the knowledge of the forgiveness and saving Love of
God to the world, they are living in the Divine Life and their glorious resurrection is inevitable. The result of this conviction meant that, while the world has
been saddened and terrified by death, Jesus strides through death's folds as men
walk through a meadow mist. As death draws nearer, He stands transformed as
the glory of an Unseen Love streams upon Him. And when the Jews and
Romans had done their best to rid the world of Him, His disciples proclaim
Him as risen triumphantly from the grave in world-conquering power.

McEwan Lawson

Christ, the Second Coming of

116   Some people lay great emphasis on Christ's second coming, and any of
you who may know the halo with which it edged the character of the late Dr.
Andrew Bonar will not need to have it proved to you how much this can affect
Christian life. An intimate friend of Mr. Moody, the evangelist, told me he once
heard him say that he had never known any one greatly blessed in his kind of
work who was not greatly under the influence of this doctrine.

There are some extravagances connected with the doctrine of the second
coming which make it difficult to some minds—and I confess to being one
myself—to rest upon it. But there is one feature of our Lord's second coming, at
all events, about which no one could have any doubt. He is the Judge of man
and He is coming to wind up the affairs of this present dispensation and appoint
men their station and degree in eternity according to their deeds. Now, I say,
that ought to be one of the powerful motives of Christian life and Christian
work. I daresay many of you remember a passage in the Epistle of St. Paul where
he is discoursing on the motives of Christian work and he places this before
them all, "We must all appear before the judgement-seat of Christ; that everyone
may receive the things done in his body according to what he hath done,
whether it be good or bad." What did he mean? He was thinking first of all
of his own accountability. At the judgement-seat he would have to give an

account of the charge put in his hands; but it seems to me that he was thinking more of those to whom he was preaching. They would be there on the Judgement Day, and they might turn and accuse him to his face, "If you had been more faithful, if you had not spared yourself, if you had urged us more powerfully and lovingly, we might not have been here in this condemnation." Is there anyone who knows salvation himself and has the opportunity of making it known to others to whom that ought not to be a powerful motive?

Well, my hearers, these are the three ways, I think, of thinking about Christ—as the Christ who was, the Christ who is, and the Christ who is to be; the Christ of Palestine, the Christ in Heaven, the Christ in the new Heaven and the new earth.

James Stalker

Christ, Unity in

117   Listen to this passage from the letter we received from that German woman, who is one of our fellow members of the Church of Christ—in Wolfstein in Germany:

"I personally owe you my quite special thanks, for on Christmas Eve I received from Pastor Schwartz a piece of chocolate from your Christmas parcels. With devotion and deepest emotion, I held the dainty present in my hands. My thoughts covered many miles to your Church in England. . . . I read the Christmas story in Luke, sang the old Christmas songs with harmonium accompaniment and thought prayerfully of the unknown brothers and sisters in England. It is indeed something precious that binds together the believers throughout the world. I would like to express it in three words: 'One in Christ.' "

Barnard R. H. Spaull

Christ, Work of

118   They say that there is a picture at Catterick Camp which shows a signaller lying dead in No Man's Land. A cable had been broken by shell-fire and he had been sent out to repair the cable and restore the broken communication. As he lies there cold in death, you can see that he has accomplished what he set out to do, for his stiff hands hold the broken cable ends together. Under that picture is but one word: "Through!"

John Huxtable

Christian, Duty of

119   Miss Barbara Ward has suggested that the only finally compulsive Christian activity in a world inured to horrors and cruelty as ours is, is for Christian folk to live openly as near to the angels as others have lived near to the devils.

S. Myers

Christian, Life of

120   A missionary colporteur found himself in an out-of-the-way Chinese town, and to the crowd that gathered round him, told the story of Jesus. As he proceeded he thought the interest of the people was unusually keen, and when he finished the head man said: "Yes, we know him, he used to live here." The missionary explained that he had been talking of one who lived in another century and in another town. Then they took him to the cemetery and showed him the grave of an English medical missionary, who a few years before had served and healed and died there. They had known Christ. He had touched them through the Gospel of that missionary's life.

J. Ireland Hasler

Christian, Proof of

121   Four things are necessary to constitute a Christian. Faith makes a Christian; life proves a Christian; trials confirm a Christian; and death crowns a Christian.

Hopfner

Christianity

122   One day I met a man and walked with him for a short distance on the street, and, after a moment's hesitation, I said to him, "My friend, why are you not a Christian?" And then it was his turn to be embarrassed. He paused and hesitated and stammered a little, and his feet pattered on the ground; and then he said, "Well, I will tell you honestly. It is because I am not man enough." That is the only real reason that I ever heard a man give for not being a Christian. To be lost is to be something less than a man; to be saved is to become a man in the largest sense.   B. Fay Mills

**

123   A correspondent wrote to Canon Liddon: "The only thing that now attaches me at all to Christianity is that it alone of the systems of thought with which I come into contact seems to give a working answer to two questions: 'Whence am I?' and 'Whither am I going?' All else is dark, all else at least uncertain."

E. J. Hardy

✳✳

124   St. Augustine says, very daringly, that Christ found Christianity in the world when He came; that it existed at the very earliest periods—having reference to the highest thinkers and the noblest natures of those periods; and that when He ordained it, it was called Christianity, the ethical part of it.

Henry Ward Beecher

✳✳

125   In common talk, Christ's words, "deny himself," mean to subtract from himself meat on Friday, tobacco in Lent, wine permanently; and the answer of the sum is conscious spirituality. That is not Christian arithmetic. Let us try to re-translate; and, if our words are a little more obviously Latin, the meaning may be clearer—negate self, delete it. Any printer will tell you what it means when in his proof he finds a line drawn through the word self, and in the margin the sign dele. That, I think, is what Christ means. A hair shirt will, I expect, always remind you of your body: the Christian life is to forget it in using it for Jesus. Mortification, fasting, and so on, reminds you of yourself: they are negative; and in both ways they are anti-Christian. The Christian life is positive, and happy in being centered in Christ, and forgetful of all but Him and His ideals.

A. Jeans Courtney

Christianity, Effect of

126   An orator in Hyde Park some time ago was putting the case for religion. An impatient man in the crowd interrupted and shouted, "Christianity has been in the world for two thousand years and look at the state of the world." "Yes," replied the orator in a flash, "and water has been the world for two million years, and look at the state of your face." If the world is wrong surely it is because the men and women in it are wrong. Salvation is available but it must be applied. It is neither desirable nor possible that every Christian should be an economist, or a politician, but it is vitally desirable and necessary that every economist and politician should become a Christian.

Edward Bragg

Christianity, Influence of

127   I remember as a young man, travelling in the Far East and standing in a
Taoist temple in Singapore. There I saw a Chinese woman, who was obviously
suffering from some disease. She went up to the altar, clapped her hands to
make sure that the gods were attending, and then she prayed. This done, she
picked up from the altar a divining-box full of sandalwood sticks. She shook
the box until one stick fell out. As she could not read, the characters on the stick
were meaningless to her, but she took her mystery to the priest who sat at a
little desk in a corner, and for twenty-five cents was ready to reveal to her the
fate the gods had prepared. Something in the remoteness of that scene from the
whole of my own experience affected me with the force of a revelation.

B. Ilfor Evans

Christianity, Practical

128   It is by doing good that you win men for Christ. Clifford Bozeat tells the
story of an American chaplain during the Civil War. He saw a wounded soldier
on the battle-field, and having his Bible under his arm, he stooped down and
said to the man, "Would you like me to read you something from the Bible?"
The wounded man said, "I am so thirsty I would rather have a drink of water."
After he had drunk it he said, "Could you lift my head and put something
under it?" The chaplain took off his overcoat and rolled it up, and lifting the
man's head, made the coat a pillow. "Now," said the man, "if I had something
over me. I am so cold." The chaplain took off his coat and covered the man.
Then the wounded man said, "For God's sake, man, if there is anything in that
Book that makes a man do for another what you have done for me, let me hear
it." Isn't that what the world is needing today—the practical expression of
Christianity? The emphasis of Jesus was always upon doing good.

Joseph Sherratt

Christianity, Proof of

129   I like the story of Zeno, the subtle Greek philosopher, who was once trying
to show that there is no such thing as motion; upon which Diogenes simply
got up and walked about! So when cynics sneer at Christianity and say it is all
moonshine, the best way to refute them and prove that it is more than a dream
is to carry it out in our daily life.

G. H. Clothier

Christianity, Reasonableness of

130   Romanes tells us that when he was a young man of thirty, in 1878, he did
not even examine the question of Christianity. He assumed—as I well recollect
many men of the time did—that Darwinism had disproved it, and that Biblical
criticism had discredited the Bible itself. Very different is the tale in 1894, where
Romanes says: "We now begin to see that Darwinism has had no greater effect
on Christianity than the doctrine of Copernicus about the solar system; and the
Biblical criticism which was so much dreaded has established rather than
weakened the truth of the Bible." He finds himself, therefore, ready to inquire
now, as it were, for the first time, impartially into the Christian doctrine, and
what does he conclude? He says: "The highest argument to me is the absence
from the biography of Christ of any doctrine which subsequent growth of
human knowledge, whether in natural science, ethics, political economy, or elsewhere, has had to discount."   Robert F. Horton

Christianity, Superiority of

131   Goethe, the most capacious and most cultivated mind of the nineteenth
century, said a notable thing concerning Christianity: "Though the intellectual
and spiritual culture of the world progresses, and the human mind expands as
much as it will, beyond the grandeurs and moral elevations of Christianity as it
sparkles and shines in the gospels the human mind will not advance." It is
therefore today, as it has been for twenty centuries, a question which no one can
evade. What is Christianity? Who was Christ? Each age has to give a different
answer and each phase of thought has to give a phrasing to its own answer, not
because the answer is essentially different, but because in face of new problems
and new modes of thinking, the old truth has to reshape itself in order to be
convincing.   Robert F. Horton

Christianity, Supreme

132   In the immediate vicinity of the most popular Buddhist temple in Tokyo
is the largest district of organized and governmentally licensed vice in the
empire, the famous Yoshiwara. That I might not have to take anybody's word
for it, under missionary guidance I went through that hideous place. My guide,
a Christian Japanese, said to us, "My heart breaks to show to you Americans the
shame of my people." "But," some one may say, "while it may not be governmentally licensed and so made respectable, you may see the same kind of thing

in Christian America." To which I answer: No! There is at least one thing in Yoshiwara which you cannot see in any similar place in America: a temple is there, a shrine dedicated to the business of the district. I saw it and stood before its altar. And once a year Buddhist priests, in ceremonial robes, go down to Yoshiwara to bless the place. Can you even imagine that in America? The only things remotely approaching it in Christendom, I think, are the Roman Catholic chapels to the Virgin Mary in connection with the Spanish bull rings, where the toreadors pray for success before they fight or receive the last rites of the Church if they are mortally hurt. Christianity blessing bull-fights is bad enough; Christianity blessing organized prostitution is incredible.

It was my privilege to know personally Baron Goto, the Mayor of Tokyo. I laid before him this problem and said, "Can it be that from all the millions of Buddhists in Japan there is no protest?" And he, although he is not a Christian, said, "Not one voice of urgent protest from all Buddhist Japan, but protests are coming now—altogether from the Christians." What kind of religion, then, do you really choose to have: a religion, however comfortable, that is "a device for giving peace of mind in the midst of conditions as they are," or a religion, however disturbing, that hates iniquity and loves righteousness, not simply in the secret chambers of man's heart, but in the organization of man's social life?

Harry Emerson Fosdick

Christmas

133   For most of us Christmas is the birthday of Christ. For the New Testament, and for the Church if we may judge from the choice of the Epistle and Gospel, it is rather the birthday of the Good News, of the Great Revelation.

Christ, Himself, did not begin to exist on the first Christmas Day. He was with God the Father from all eternity. The world was made through Him, and without Him nothing came into being. He was and is the brightness of the Father's glory, and upholds all things with the word of His power. He was in the world, as St. John tells us, long before the Incarnation. He came into His own many times in the earlier history. He was in a figure the spiritual rock that followed the Israelites in the wilderness. He is the Lamb slain before the foundation of the world.

The Great Revelation was made in the fullness of time—that is to say, at the earliest possible moment. The seed was sown as soon as it could take root. From that time it has been growing secretly. The leaven has been slowly working upon the lump. Its progress has been slow, terribly slow, like that of the great physical changes.

W. R. Inge

✳✳

134   There was once a German prince who wished to possess a Cremona violin; and he offered a princely sum to purchase it. For months he had no success. Then one day an old man appeared at the castle with a worn case under his arm. The servants at first refused to admit him to the prince, but at length they agreed to carry to their master the old man's message. This is what he told them to say, "Heaven's music is waiting at your door." So he was received by the prince. He drew from its shabby case a perfect violin, and created such marvellous music as to win the prince's ardent praise. He was offered any price he liked to name for his instrument, but the man shook his head. "The violin may only be yours," he said, "on condition that I pass my life within your house, and use the instrument every day." So the prince accepted the violin on those terms.

That story is a parable. We have been hearing again at Christmas-tide the music of heaven, proclaiming the Saviour's birth and love and abiding presence in hearts that welcome and trust Him. Shall we not receive the Master Musician into our hearts and homes, so that His beauty and joy may illuminate our lives? "In all thy ways, acknowledge Him, and He shall direct thy paths."

W. Francis Gibbons

✳✳

135   Christmas is pre-eminently the Festival of the Home. Following the kindly custom of our old Christian land the scattered members of countless families will draw together round the old hearth, which stands in the earliest memories of their childhood glowing with a fire, not of earth merely but of heaven, and remains through the years of manhood a sacred Symbol of Purity and Love: and the old will grow young again in the joy of children, and the children's young hearts will expand in that atmosphere of brightness and affection as fair blossoms in the sunshine of the spring; shall the troubled Christian mind find there, in the hallowed scenes of domestic life, some compensation for the affliction which the spectacle of our public life must cause?

If our Christmas Festival within the home is to carry the power and beauty of Christian witness, it must bear these two marks upon it. There must be worship, and there must be harmony. A merely secular holiday crowded with noisy pleasures is no fitting version of the Christian Festival. Worship stands in the forefront of this commemoration of Christ's birthday. Worship has a twofold aspect for the disciples of Christ. We come to the Lord's house, and, according to His commandment, gather round the Lord's Table to receive as it were from His own Hands the Sacraments of His Body and Blood; and we show kindness for His sake to His chosen representatives: the poor, the sick, the sorrowful. "Pure religion and undefiled before our God and Father is this, to visit the fatherless and widows in their affliction, and to keep himself unspotted from the world." This aspect of worship is symbolized by the custom of giving presents at Christmas-tide; but how sadly hollow has the symbol become! We give presents now not to the poor and sorrowful, who need our consolation, but to one another, the rich to the rich, the happy to the happy. I do not plead for what is called "indiscriminate alms giving." Nothing could well be farther than such conventional charity from the mind of Christ; but I am thinking of those needy and derelict persons, relatives or neighbours as the case may be, whom we know, whose desolation we are aware of, and who cannot give back to us what we can give to them. At Christmas-time the claims of kindred and friendship and neighbourhood ought surely to be generously and cheerfully recognized. Worship, then, in this two-fold sense which Christ has given it, must be the first mark of our Christmas Festival; and the other must not be lacking. With worship must be harmony. That is the order of the Angel's Song, "Glory to God in the highest, and on earth, peace." Christmas is pre-eminently the Festival of Reconciliation.

H. Hensley Henson

✳✳

136 Is not our awkwardness about expecting and receiving Christmas gifts a sort of parable or symbol of the lack of faith, the lurking unbelief in the won-der of a giving God, which is the supreme weakness of our modern religion? Because we do not really expect God's Christmas gifts, we only half-heartedly ask for them, and we often fail to recognize them when they are placed within our reach. We are overwhelmed by the misery and the chaos of the world, and have almost ceased to believe that it is in the power of men to set things right. Nor is it in the power of men alone—but we are thinking and talking as if men with God have no power to set things right.

Ernest H. Jeffs

✳✳

137 In his "Christmas Sermon," Robert Louis Stevenson says in his quaint way: "There is an idea abroad among moral people that they should make their neighbours good; one person I have to make good—myself. But my duty to my neighbour is much more nearly expressed by saying that I have to make him happy, if I may." A. H. Moncur Sime

✳✳

138 The real meaning of Christmas is inward and spiritual, and not to be identified with outward and material accompaniments. Essentially Christmas is the time when we should remember that "God so loved the world that He gave His only begotten Son." Christmas means the fulfillment of the hopes and prophecies of the ages; it means the coming into the life of humanity of the life of God, in order to reconcile the world unto Himself and to lift humanity on to the spiritual plane of thought and life. There is, therefore, a Christian reason for rejoicing and festivity; for "unto us is born a Saviour which is Christ the Lord." Any explanation of Christmas which leaves out of account these deeper meanings is sub-Christian. Mr. H. G. Wells may wish to banish Palestine from his plan of world-history. He may try to teach this pleasure-loving generation that "nothing began there; nothing was worked out there"; but at Christmas-time the eyes of the Christian world will still turn to Palestine, and modern shepherds and wise men will still say one to another: "Let us now go even unto Bethlehem," and, in spirit, they go to the stable, where the Saviour of mankind was born, and bow in wonder, love and praise. "Nothing began there"? Can any reputable historian speak of the persistence of the Christian Church through the centuries; its peaceful conquest by love of the Roman Empire; and its beneficent influence on successive generations of mankind, as nothing? Is it altogether negligible today? The Christian Church and the Christian Faith "began there." "Nothing was worked out there?" Why, the greatest of all problems was worked out there and fully demonstrated—the problem of how to live. We know, now, even if we do not always attain to that way of life. J. S. Mill admitted: "There is no better rule than so to live that Christ would approve your life." Why should Jesus be thus acclaimed as the supreme arbiter of the way of life, if His birth and life are without any importance to the world, as Mr. Wells suggests? Jean Paul Richter has a juster estimate of the real significance of what was "worked out there." He says: "Being holiest among the mighty and mightiest among the holy, He has lifted with His pierced hand empires off their hinges; has turned the stream of centuries out of its channels; and still governs the ages."

P. R. Southgate

✳✳

139   To human sense, what took place at Bethlehem may well have seemed at the time commonplace enough. An infant was born under circumstances of hardship—was laid in a wayside stall. To those who do not look closely at what was passing, it might have occurred that a like event had happened scores of times before and would often be repeated. Everybody then, depend upon it, did not hear the song of the angels or mark the bearing of the virgin mother or of her saintly spouse. The kingdom of God had entered into history, but, certainly, not with observation. Nay, more, even among the worshippers of

Christ the full meaning of His birth, as opening a new era in the history of the human race, was not at once, by any means, practically appreciated. For five centuries and a half, Christians still reckoned the years by the names of the old Roman consuls, or by the era of Diocletian, just like the pagans around them. It was in the year 541 of the Christian era that Dionysius the Little, a pious and learned person at Rome, first arranged the history of mankind around the most important event in its whole course—the birthday of Jesus Christ. Christendom at once recognized the justice of this way of reckoning time; and the attempts to supersede it, such as that which was made in France during the first revolution, have never had a serious chance of success. But how often do you and I use the phrase, "The year of our Lord," without reflecting that it proclaims the birth of Jesus Christ to be an event of such commanding importance that all else in human history, rightly understood, is merely relative to it—interesting only as it precedes or follows, as it leads up to or is derived from it. And yet, as I have said, five centuries and a half of the Christian ages passed before this was practically recognized. And so it has been ever since; so it is at this hour. Real importance is one thing, apparent importance is another.

Canon Liddon

**

140 Mr. Chesterton's hero in "Manalive" deliberately travelled around the world in order to discover his own suburban house and garden. In other words, he knew that the world-wide traveller is sure to find out, in the end, that there is nothing in all the world so fine and wonderful and precious as the simple and familiar things. When I think of the men and women who are far from home, and longing, above all things, to be home again, I am not thinking only of their natural desire for comfort and safety and reunion with those they love. I am thinking also of the cause which took them away from home. What is all this world-upheaval for if it is not for the re-establishment of the simple and innocent things of life, so scornfully belittled by the ambitious war-makers? Millions of men are locked in deadly combat around—what? A State, a policy, a party, a leader? No: around a little home—any little home in the world where there is a child to love, and plan for, and defend. That is really the final goal of all our imposing strategies for war and our impressive manifestos for peace. The Wise Men found that their star-led journey ended at a Manger and a Baby. This is more than a pretty legend or an impressive parable. It is the revelation of heaven's wisdom to the wise men of the world: the wisdom that teaches us to find God, not in the distant stars, but in all simple loving and giving. To offer your life as a gift, in that cause, is indeed to come to the

true home of the spirit of man—the home and resting-place of all men everywhere.   Ernest H. Jeffs

Church

141 Some of the happiest recollections of my boyhood center around an old
man who was a sign-writer. He used to work a great deal with gold leaf,
making signs for banks, solicitors' offices and other grand places where they
must have gold letters. Sometimes, which gave me a thrill of awe, he would
have to paint the name and age on a coffin-plate. The hair of his head was
white, like white wool, and he had a long white beard. He lingers on in my
memory, like one of Blake's mythical figures, his massive head bent over some
task, his fingers busy fashioning the letters. He used to paint the letters on
with some kind of size and then cut pieces of gold leaf and lay them on the
wet letters. When he thought the gold leaf had sufficiently adhered to the size,
he would take a ball of cotton-wool and rub it gently over his work until all
the loose pieces of gold leaf were gathered up and the letters stood out with
clear-cut edges. One day, just after he had finished wiping a sign he had
done, I said to him, "There must be a lot of gold leaf in that ball of cotton-
wool." "Yes," he said, "there is. When it is quite full, I shall burn the cotton-wool
and get the gold." He came, He created the Church to burn the world until
only the gold is left.   James MacKay

※※

142 Newell Dwight Hillis went to a mansion on a New York avenue to
conduct a funeral. The master of the house was nearing seventy years. Beside
him was the coffin of his dead daughter. On the other side was his chum, his
closest friend. Suddenly he broke into speech, and cried to his friend. "There
is nothing in these things. You and I have been living for a good time and
success. We have got everything we could during the week. We have played
poker on Saturday nights and spent Sundays in our automobile, in driving
and social pleasures. We have put the club and the bank first, and my son has
disgraced me with his shameless marriage, and now my daughter is dead. I
tell you, Fred, there is only one place to bring up a family, and that is the
Church. There is only one way to use Sunday for children, and this is to take
them to church. What with money and wine and poker, and pleasure all day
Sunday, my family has been ruined. People don't know what the result will be
till it comes, but I know." That was the opinion of a wealthy man of the world.
                                                                          A. E. Cooke

※※

143 A well-known labour leader, who incidentally was a lay preacher, once said to me, "There will never be a successful Revival on a large scale until the Church is big enough to repent."

R. A. West

✳✳

144 Mr. Ramsay Macdonald once said to a group of students: "The Church is the soul of the world. Its work is to purify and illumine. To create an atmosphere—a spring-time freshness in which right conduct will freely blossom." What the conscience is to the individual, so should the Church be to the State.

F. C. Bryan

✳✳

145 I like the little girl's description of a home: "Home is where mother is." The same applies to the House of God. A church is not just a building of bricks and mortar. A church is a company of people bound to each other and to God in fellowship and love. I would like to borrow the little girl's description and alter it a little: "The Church, the House of God, is where our Father is."

C. H. Gay

✳✳

146 The Church has a rock on which to stand: Jesus Christ her Lord. From Him she has the principles and the power that can lead the world back to sanity and peace. Other social groups, bound together by a common idea, might change the direction of mankind, as the Nazis and the Communists have done. Only the Church can save mankind. The Church is not a club or a hobby for those "who like that sort of thing." Its raison d'être is the salvation of the world. The world's greatest need today is a living Church. That need is greater now than at any other period in history. The Church, created and sustained by the mystic power of God, is the only salt the world has, and if it becomes insipid the world will fall into corruption. The Church is the world's one hope.

James MacKay

✳✳

147 George Bernard Shaw said, "If all the churches were closed, it would not be long before they would be opened with greater constituencies than ever." However, he goes on to say that "at present the Church has to make itself cheap in all sorts of ways, to induce people to attend its services and the cheaper it makes itself the less the people attend." Look at the authorized devices to which we resort in order to feed the fancy of the crowd. The basis of our appeals has been largely to the selfish rather than the sacrificial. Observe the church page in the Saturday issue of your newspaper and see a long list of expensive advertisements advising the people what they will gain if they attend such and such a church. "Come to this church and hear our high-priced choir sing about the poverty of the lowly Nazarene."

"Come to this church and hear the highest-paid preacher in the city solve the problems of the poor."

"Come to this church and hear Dr. Impudence who in half an hour will unravel the secrets of the divine plan which the Almighty has taken eternities to create, and is still creating."

"Come to this church and we will give you the best social contacts in the city—we'll give you movies—good ones, free."

When Jesus called people He said, "If any man will come after Me, let him take up his cross and follow Me."   J. Richmond Morgan

**

148 It has been grandly said by Pascal that the church and the churchyard contain the whole of man. In the church you see the dignity and excellence of man's soul—that soul which in the house and amid the sacred services of God kindles up and glows with the fire of devotion and aspires heavenward. In the churchyard we tread over the ruins of the mortal body, which is brittle as a vessel tempered of potter's clay, and which awaits the moment when the trump of the archangel thrilling through the vaults of the sepulchre shall give the signal for its resurrection in a spiritual and a glorified form.

Edward M. Goulbourn

**

149 "The Church," says John Henry Newman, "was framed for the express purpose of interfering (or, as irreligious men will say, meddling) with the world." The Church, therefore, must be so convincing in her witness, so faithful in the way of life she commends, that plain men cannot but be persuaded of the truth, power, and beauty of the gospel.   Thomas Long

**

150 In the Church now-a-days we are so pathetically anxious about numbers. Can he draw a crowd? is almost the first question pulpit committees ask. Can he fill the collection plates? is commonly enough the second. Jesus was anxious not about quantity but about quality.   Robert James McCracken

**

151 There is the story told about the wife of a young Norwegian pastor who was permitted to visit Bishop Berggrav on his birthday, he being at the time in a concentration camp. Into his captivity, she smuggled a cake of her own baking on which she had inscribed the words: ECCLESIA MILITANS, ECCLESIA TRIUMPHANS—A militant Church is a triumphant Church.

Robert James McCracken

Church, Failure of

152   There is an Eastern story of four brothers who decided to have a feast. As wine was rather expensive, they concluded that each one should bring an equal quantity and add it to the common stock. But one of the brothers thought he might escape making his contribution. He decided to bring water instead of wine. "It won't be noticed," he thought. But when, at the feast, the wine was poured out from the common stock, it wasn't wine after all, it was water. For all four brothers had thought alike. Each one had said: "Let the other do it." That story is a parable. In it you will find wrapped up the secret of the failure and inactivity of many a church.

Edward Bragg

Church, Glory of

153   "Right across the page of modern history there hangs the glory . . . the Christian Church." So R. A. Edwards starts his book *The City of God,* and he goes on: "Whichever way you look at it, the Church is one of the most striking phenomena in history." It would hardly be too much to say that it is the greatest marvel of all time.

E. Allan Matheson

Church, Influence of

154   We ought to bless our churches. We ought to think of them as the instrumentalities by which miracles are wrought—these miracles of regeneration. The example of consecrated men is better than all the books and precepts that the world contains, except, perhaps, this Book that I am touching, which seems something more than a book. It seems to contain something more than words and printed pages, because everything in it is so concrete, the men it speaks of are so real, and the truths it utters are so compelling. Read in this air they are familiar; but they are not redeeming words unless they vibrate beyond the walls of the churches and walk the streets and are seen in the households, and are translated into the public life of the community.

Woodrow Wilson

Church, Joining the

155   A recent writer on the American Civil War tells us that Jefferson Davis, President of the Confederate States, was baptized by a rector and received into the fellowship of a near-by church when the Union Army under McClellan was about twenty miles from Richmond, where Davis lived! It looked as if the city would be captured. He put off that decisive step until his enemy was twenty miles away. Then he ran for cover! He waited sixty years to do it. That was too late. Not too late for God to forgive sins, for it is never too late for that; but it was too late for the Christian religion to have the effects in his life that it might have had.   David A. MacLennan

Church, Membership in

156   Would it be possible and wise to set up an entirely new principle of admission to church membership—a principle based upon the candidate's future instead of upon his past? I have a vision of a church whose membership shall be recruited as men are recruited for an army: enlisted, that is to say, without reference to what they have been, but entirely with reference to what they pledge themselves, with God's help and the church's, to do. I do not say "to be"; it is the doing that is the all-important thing. A Christian is what he does. The candidate will not become a church member merely because he wants to associate with like-minded people, or because he wants to form the excellent habit of regular church-going. These, at all events, will be only secondary considerations. The candidate will enlist, in the most literal sense, for service, and for the discipline that fits and hardens a man for service. And as the years go by, his retention on the church roll will depend entirely upon his obedience and zeal in thus living his Christian belief.   Ernest H. Jeffs

Church, Stands for Eternal

157   One marvel in the New Testament never wears out—the wonder that those first Christians could believe as they did in the Church. That they could believe in God—one can understand that; that they could believe in Christ—that is not so strange. But that in the Roman world, with its immense and overbearing power, they could believe in that small struggling Christian community, is a marvel. In Ephesus, to which Paul wrote this letter, the Temple of Diana, one of the seven wonders of the ancient world, dominated the scene. How could they believe then, as they did, in that feeble, faulty Church? Yet

lately I read the story of the archaeologists trying to discover in Ephesus where it was that the Temple of Diana used to stand. For years they dug before at last they found a few of its foundation stones sunk in a swamp. My friends, there is something eternal for which the Church stands, against which "the gates of hell shall not prevail."   Harry Emerson Fosdick

Church, United

158   As Dr. Whale has lately reminded us: "Look where you will at any denomination; the elements are the same in every case. In each you cannot fail to see the Bible; the institutional church as a local fact—a gathered company of believers; a ministry duly ordained; the observance, every Lord's Day, of the Feast of the Saviour's Resurrection from the dead; the preaching of the Word; the administration of the sacraments; ecclesiastical discipline; Christian character and even sainthood; the most unchristian hypocrisies and sins. No church has a monopoly of these facts. You cannot put a denominational ring face around them." Whether you look to Canterbury or Constantinople, to Rome or Geneva, "you see the same marks of the Holy Catholic Church in each, the same lineaments of Him who is the Head of the whole body." The differences are real, even enormous, but the essential and creative factors are the same. For there is indeed one Spirit and one Body, as God is one, as the Word of grace and life is one. It is our highest privilege, as it is our greatest task, to be called into that great society of the redeemed on earth and in heaven: the church militant and triumphant.   Philip Lee Woolf

Church Attendance

159   It is said that some one said to Mr. Gladstone as he was coming from church, "I cannot understand how a man of your intellect can listen to such dull sermons." To which Mr. Gladstone replied, "I go to church because I love England." That statement is full of meaning to those who are wise to see it, but I believe that there is a higher thing and it is this: "I go to church because I love the world. There I hear a law that men should love one another with a love that stoops to the Cross." It is such a spirit that makes the Church glorious.   Harry Ingham

* *

160   In "Why Go to Church?" by "A London Journalist," a story is told of a young man who came to New York from the West to be married. He and his fiancée one day were out shopping. She stepped off the sidewalk and was

knocked down and killed. The young man became in consequence so infuriated with life that he determined to commit suicide. Happening to pass a church where Dr. J. A. Hutton was to preach, he saw that the subject announced was "The Breaking Point." Something drew the young man into the service. Among other things, Dr. Hutton said, "It is always possible to hold on a little longer. In a world like this, which is not forsaken by God, you never know what good is waiting round the corner." Those wise and healing words were heard and heeded by the young man. He found new hope, because he found Christ in the sanctuary.   Harold T. Barrow

Church Attendance, Aim of

161   Dr. Francis Peabody, in an address to ministers, remarked, "A preacher at Harvard University once said to me that he would stand on his head in the college pulpit if it would induce students to come to the chapel; to which I was forced to reply, 'You would succeed. They would come, and they would go away saying that they had seen the distinguished gentleman standing on his head. You would get just the results you sought, and no more.'" We cannot say anything worth listening to standing on our heads. Cheap sensationalism degrades the pulpit. We must not confuse accommodation with adaptation.

                                                                           F. I. Riches Lowe

Churches, Fellowship in

162   Several years ago Dr. James Hamilton reminded us that when the tide is out, and you walk along the sea-shore, you see a large number of pools, and in them are living creatures, fish, anemones, and animalculae, and the fish in this pool do not know of the existence of the fish in that; but when the tide comes rolling up around as amidst the thunder's roar, all these pools get merged into one great boundless ocean, and they have fellowship and intercourse one with the other. A bigoted church is a church when the tide is low, and a bigoted man one who is not moved by a love of Christ to exert his power.

                                                                                 E. R. Gange

Civic Life

163   Dr. Dale, to whom I can never sufficiently voice my own indebtedness and under whose influence I grew up as a lad, once at a great public meeting in Birmingham, where he had been speaking with Mr. John Bright, electrified thousands of people with this, which has come down in his biography. He said:

"All true civic life has its roots in the great Christian principle, the principle that Jesus Christ came into this world to look not on His own things, but also on the things of others." Let no man seek his own, but seek his neighbour's good.

C. Silvester Horne

Civilization

164   There is no more striking division between the civilization that once was, the civilization of Greece and Rome, and the civilization that now is, the civilization of England, of Europe, of this world, than this: the old was brilliant, but it was not kind; the new is at once brilliant and kind. There was little heart in Greece, which was the triumph of the unaided intellect. There is the heart today, though there be armaments too. Nothing is more striking than this fact, as I believe Dr. Martineau has pointed out as only he can. You must not look for a hospital in ancient Greece, you must never think of a leper asylum or a home for the feeble and the poor. Perhaps they soared higher than we have yet done. No doubt they did. They soared higher than we have yet done in the triumphs of the mind. They knew nothing at all about the achievements of the heart. Who has wrought the difference—I speak about the source and sanction of love? Who has wrought this advance, this achievement which marks out the new civilization as different from the old? The answer that you would all give me is Jesus Christ. Since Christ we see the triumphs of love. Christ has come not to preach to the mind, but first to the conscience; it satisfies then the questioning intellect and it releases the imprisoned affections. The world received His message gladly; the world responds to the love of Christ. Now is it indeed nineteen hundred years ago, and that message has power still with men because its source and sanction is in God?

R. J. Campbell

Comfort

165   A small boy, the child of Christian parents, once put his finger right on the spot. In swift succession two families of his acquaintance had each suffered tragedy and loss through the death of a dearly loved child. One family were Christian people belonging to the same church as his own parents, the others were unbelievers. The boy said to his father, speaking of the Christian family, "Of course, it's not so bad for the Johnsons; they know what to do." He realized that faith is not something that gives way at the first impact of trouble, but something that bears one up, when the need is greatest.

We have all known instances of this sustaining power of God in the time of distress. Again and again we have said, or heard others say, "I was given strength to help me then." And we know that it is true; we have found ourselves possessed of resources that have not been ours in the ordinary course of events. Our faith in God, far from collapsing, has lifted us up and carried us through the deep waters.   Frank Shield

** **

166   I would yield to none in my admiration of the splendid character and morality of Marcus Aurelius; but when Marcus Aurelius wants to comfort men in trouble, what has he to say? Only this he says: "Don't fret; don't fume; you will soon be at the end of it; think of the great men, think of Trajan, for instance, what a stir he made; how he troubled himself with the enemies in other nations, and now he is in the dust; don't worry yourselves; don't beat yourselves to pieces against these rocks; you will soon be dead." That was his own message. I turn from that to the glorious eleventh chapter in the Epistle to the Hebrews, where the writer wants to strengthen men who are fighting the Christian battle; and what does he tell them? He gives them a list of the heroes of faith in the olden time; and then he tells them that they form a cloud of witnesses.

Rhonda Williams

Commandments

167   At one of the places I have visited in the Isle of Wight, there is a much-frequented path along the cliff, close to the sea. A good, quick hedge lines this path to prevent people from going too near the edge of the precipice. At places the hedge is broken, but is set with strong stakes and thorn bushes to prevent children from getting over. If they try they hurt their hands and tear their clothes. Now, I maintain it is humanity and kindness that put those stakes and thorn bushes. The persons who put them have no pleasure in bleeding hands and legs; their pleasure is to prevent trespassing and accidents to human life. So God's commandments are for our good always.

E. W. Shalders

Commitment

168   The other day I was travelling in the South of France. When we were crossing the border the morning broke with a thunderstorm, with a lurid dawn in the East, such a morning as is described by Joel, "The day of the Lord cometh, for it is nigh at hand, a day of darkness and of gloominess, a day of clouds and

of thick darkness, as the morning spread upon the mountains." The great thunderstorm was crushing the dawn like some immense judgement of the Eastern horizon. I got out at the station and came back to the carriage in which I had been alone all night. There I found the figure of a tall young priest against all this lurid background. I entered into conversation with him, and he told me in a simple way how he had been given to the Lord at his birth and his baptism, and how when he was thirteen years of age he had been taken away from his mother to study his profession in a religious seminary in Paris, and he had not seen her for seven years; he was not twenty. He was now on a visit to her for two months, and he said it was the last he should ever pay, for he was going into the great Jesuit mission on the Congo. I said, "When will you be back again?" He replied, "Not long. We have buried fifteen altogether, and the average period of life there is two years." I had been speaking to him about his motive in choosing such a life, and as he left the carriage and grasped my hand he said, "The life which I now live in the flesh I live by the faith of the Son of God, who loved me and gave Himself for me."

G. Adam Smith

Compassion

169   "When in my hearing," writes Turgenev, the great Russian writer, "the rich Rothschild is praised, who gives away thousands from his huge income, whereby children are educated, the sick healed and old people taken care of, I am touched and praise such deeds. But in spite of my feeling and the praise I bestow, I cannot help calling to mind a poor peasant family who once received an orphaned relative into its miserable hut. 'If we take home little Katie,' said the wife, 'the last penny will go; we shan't be able any longer to buy even salt for our soup.' 'Well, then, we can eat it without salt,' said her husband." Turgenev concludes, "It is a far cry from Rothschild to that peasant."

R. Oswald Davies

Compassion, Divine

170   To the spiritual man or woman there is pain in the presence of sin. It is related of Henry Drummond that the burden which he met in the waywardness of men well-nigh crushed him. "One Sunday morning," writes a friend with whom he was staying, "I found him leaning, with his head bowed on the mantel-piece, looking into the fire. He raised a haggard, worn face, when I spoke to him, and asked him if he were very tired. 'No,' he said, 'I am sick with the sins of these men. How can God bear it?'" We turn from the disciple

of our Lord to the Lord Jesus Christ Himself. When He was approaching Jerusalem to die on the Cross, He beheld the City with its sins and sorrows and with its glory fading, and wept over it. We reverently ask, "Who can interpret the feelings of the world's Saviour? Who can enter into the mighty rush of Divine compassion which at that spectacle shook the Saviour's soul, as He gazed upon that proud city so soon to be reduced to ruin?" Can we wonder at that Divine sorrow?   Horace E. Hewitt

Complaint

171   There is a story of the man who was up to his neck in mud out in Mesopotamia during the war; he was having a terrible time; and the postman came bringing him a nagging letter from his wife in England; and it was almost more than he could bear. And he wrote back to her and asked her not to write that kind of letter again, and at the end he said: "Do let me enjoy this 'ere war in peace!" That is a joke that can be turned into a prayer. Life is pretty hard for most of us these days: it is a real struggle and a real warfare. And I know no modern prayer more simple and yet more sincere than this: "Let me enjoy this 'ere war in peace."   H. R. L. Sheppard

Confession, Secrets of

172   In the Middle Ages there was gathered together a great company of important Church and State officers to a council in a capital of Europe. At the banquet a famous cardinal was asked to respond to a toast in honour of the Roman Catholic Church. In his speech he referred to the responsible duties that sometimes rest upon the priestly calling. "My very first penitent," said he, "was a man guilty of murder." When he had finished, the door opened to admit a well-known duke. Learning that the cardinal had just spoken, he, when called to speak, made reference to the cardinal as his great friend. Bowing low before the cardinal and turning to the assembly, the duke said, "My lords and gentlemen, I have the honour of being the cardinal's first penitent and the first to receive absolution at his hands!" The consternation of all present can be well imagined. A great State and Church secret had been unwittingly revealed.

                                                                    T. J. Lewis

Conscience

173   In very many ways it is possible to sophisticate the conscience. The temptation is always present if we see no aim or end before us in moral action but the

comforting approval of a clear conscience, and face no judgement beyond that. There is a truth in the daring paradox of Dr. Albert Schweitzer that "A good conscience is an invention of the devil."

C. H. Dodd

✳✳

174 The conscience in man is his Holy of Holies. It is the self-registering thermometer of his soul. It is the candle of the Lord. It is the voice of God. No man dare say that he never hears it.

Sometimes it is a still small voice and scarcely audible, sometimes it sounds like a clap of thunder. To exaggerate its power is impossible. Somebody once sent to the "Conscience Fund" of the U.S. Treasury fifty thousand dollars in currency, and with it an unsigned letter acknowledging that the money had been stolen. When conscience becomes inflamed it gives the offender neither rest nor peace till he has made restitution. Think of the lengths to which it carried Zacchaeus: "The half of my goods I give to the poor; and if I have wrongfully exacted anything from any man, I restore it to him fourfold." Shakespeare, whose references to conscience are in all his plays, compares it to "a thousand swords." The theology of the nineteenth century made much of the terrors of hell. What if the essence of hell should be a potent conscience that will not be appeased or assuaged?

Robert James McCracken

✳✳

175 We are obliged to do a good deal more than "follow our conscience." We are obliged to enlighten it and to keep it enlightened. It is just as liable to failure as our sight, just as liable to error as an uninformed and uninstructed intelligence. So far from being infallible, its verdicts are the measure of our moral capacity. That is why conscience varies so from man to man. Only when we develop it by constant discipline does it pass from adolescence to maturity, from the little to the big, from the relative to the absolute, from the provisional to the permanent. It is the business of each of us to keep cleansing and strengthening our moral vision. The point has been well put by T. E. Jessop. "A person whose conscience tells him at fifty exactly what it told him at twenty has not grown up; he has kept his faculty of moral discernment out of the general development of his mind. We do not always learn the will of God by remembering what He told us yesterday, even when we are sure that we have heard Him rightly. Conscience is not memory. It is the power of discerning the moral relation of things." In other words it is the faculty by which we know God and His will. Unless it is educated it is liable to give wrong direc-

tions. And the way to educate it is to put it to school with the Light of the World.

Robert James McCracken

**

176 "Let your conscience be your guide" is a maxim that warrants scrutiny. Paul acted according to conscience when he persecuted the Christians. Jesus foresaw just such a situation: "The time will come when he that killeth you will think that he doeth God a service." A participator in the terrible massacre of the Huguenots on St. Bartholomew's Day said, "God was obliged to me that day." Some of the worst crimes of history have been perpetrated and then justified on the ground of obeying the dictates of conscience.

Robert James McCracken

**

177 Some years ago the *Glendale* was wrecked off the Mull of Kintyre. The circumstances were peculiar. The trustworthy captain knew every inch of the coast, and at first there seemed to be no explanation of the accident. At the inquiry it was found that a load of iron pillars, which the vessel was carrying, had been placed too near the compass, and had deflected it. This illustrates how a man may imagine that he is steering his life by reason and sound judgement. His logic may be accurate in its working, but all the while there may be something in his life which nullifies the guiding of the compass of his conscience. He may think that he is holding a true course, while he is heading straight for the rocks.

A. Jeans Courtney

**

178 The story is told of a Chinese emperor who desired to stop criticism of his acts. So he resorted to the simple expedient of chopping off the head of anyone who ventured to disagree with him. The result was complete unanimity of opinion! People held their tongues in order to keep their heads. And if I let my conscience know that every time it dares to challenge what I do, I will bury it out of sight or, so to speak, chop off its head, it will not be long before it adopts silence as the safer policy. Or, if I continually turn a deaf ear when my conscience bids me act, the day will soon come when it will cease to be prodigal of an advice that is not wanted, and let me go my own way. Honestly, what use do we make of our God-given reason? I know what use I make of it myself. I use it chiefly to provide reasons for what I want to do in pursuit of some private end I do not like to acknowledge. And a many may have his conscience so well disciplined and trained, that instead of blazing a trail before him, it is like a pet dog which just trots obediently at his heels and never so much as barks! "If, therefore, the light that is in thee be darkness, how great is the darkness!"

E. L. Allen

**

179   Carlyle, who disliked him exceedingly in his old age, unwittingly bore a glorious testimony to Mr. Gladstone's conscience in a conversation he had with Mr. Stead. "That Gladstone!" he said. "Ay, mon! What a conscience he has. There never was such a conscience as his. He bows down to it as if it were the very voice of God!"

Hugh Price Hughes

**

180   I am very much struck by one remark which Mr. Gladstone made to Mr. Stead. He had one grievance with the Anglican clergy whom he has so faithfully served. "I have one thing," he said, "against the clergy; I think they are not severe enough on their congregations. They do not sufficiently lay upon the souls and consciences of their hearers their moral obligations, and probe their hearts and bring their whole lives and actions to the bar of conscience. The clergy are afraid of dealing faithfully with their hearers."

Hugh Price Hughes

Consecration

181   In the year 1867, on his first visit to England, the late D. L. Moody, at the age of thirty, heard and marked these words: "The world has yet to see what God will do with, and through, and in, and by, the man who is fully and wholly consecrated to Him." He said to himself: "A man, not a great man, nor a learned man, nor a rich man, nor a sick man; nor an eloquent man, nor a 'smart' man, but simply 'a man.' I am a man, and it lies with the man himself whether he will, or will not, make that entire and full consecration. I will try my utmost to be that man."

Shortly after, on being introduced by a London friend to Mr. Bewley, of Dublin, the latter asked: "Is this young man all O and O?" The friend inquired: "What do you mean by 'O and O'?" "Is he out and out for Christ?" replied Mr. Bewley. From that moment the passion of D. L. Moody's life was to be Out and Out for Christ; and his work was the outcome of an Out and Out man.

John Macmillan

Consolation

182   Unbelief had at one time no purer and more unselfish apostle for its creedless creed than Felix Adler, of New York City. He attacked no man's brighter and happier faith; he sought to rob no man of his hope in God and in the eternal future; he believed in men, and with a hopeless heroism he pushed on his philanthropic work for men. But when Dr. Damrosch died, and the coffin lay before the vast audience which filled the Metropolitan Opera House from floor to dome, and Felix Adler was called upon to speak to the solemn and sorrowing hearts in that vast assembly, this was all his message: "I have come to lay upon this bier three wreaths. The wreath of success; he had just grasped it when death paralyzed his arm, and it dropped from his helpless hand. I pick it up and lay it on his bier. The wreath of fame: his name we will cherish though he is gone; he is no more, but the memory of his honoured life lives on. The wreath of an earthly immortality; we may not see his face again, but his influence survives, and shall reproduce his spirit in our earthly lives." I condense into a sentence an oration faultless in its rhetoric; but I believe I have preserved all the essential consolation which it contained. And it is but a barren consolation beside the promise: "In My Father's house are many mansions; I go and prepare a place for you, I will come again, that where I am there ye may be also"; or beside the triumphant welcome to a death no longer grim: "This corruptible must put on incorruption, and this mortal must put on immortality. Death is swallowed up in victory. O death, where is thy sting? O grave, where is thy victory?"

Lyman Abbott

Contentment

183   Count Tolstoy was persuaded when a boy that he was a Christian by birth. But that persuasion did not save him. In early middle life he was sunken in misery, sin and despair. He looked at all the cultured people about him. They were all much in his condition. Then he was struck by the fact that there was a depth of contentment and simple nobility in the uncultured, untutored, impoverished serfs the aristocrats despised. What had they he and the well-to-do had not? It was faith. So Tolstoy set himself to believe—to believe quite simply and whole-heartedly in Jesus. And he tells us that from that hour he began to live again. Ready to lose his life, he found it. Ready to give up what was counted joy by his class, he found a new and surpassing joy given him. Holding life, possessions, powers and position as not his own at all, but

belonging to God and humanity, he has become the most notable and far-influencing personality in the world.

Newton H. Marshall

Conversation

184   The sainted Robert Murray McCheyne of Dundee halted once at an engine house by a stone quarry, when the fireman was opening the furnace door to throw in some fresh coal. McCheyne, pointing into the bright, hot flame, said kindly to the man, "Does that fire remind you of anything?" The man could not shake off the solemn impression produced by the startling question. It led him to attend the house of God, and was a turning point in his spiritual history.

Theodore L. Cuyler

Conversion

185   I must quote to you the change which came to one of the most gifted and brilliant minds of the past century, John Ruskin. He wrote on Good Friday, 1852: "One day last week I began thinking over my past life, and what fruit I have had, and the joy of it which had passed away, and of the hard work of it, and I felt nothing but discomfort, for I saw that I have been always working for myself in one way or another. Then I thought of my investigations of the Bible, and found no comfort in that either. This was about 2 o'clock in the morning, so I considered that I had now neither pleasure in looking to my past life nor any hope, such as would be my comfort on a sick bed, of a future one, and I made up my mind that this would never do. So, after thinking, I resolved that at any rate I would act as if the Bible were true—that if it were not I would be at all events no worse off than I was before; that I should believe in Christ and take Him for my Master in whatever I did; that to disbelieve the Bible was quite as difficult as to believe it; and when I had done this I fell asleep. When I rose in the morning, though I was still unwell, I felt a peace and spirit in me that I had never known before."

Robert F. Horton

⁕⁕

186   Sadhu Sundar Singh was once in agony of soul, hesitating between his old religion and Christianity. He spent one night in reading, meditation and prayer. Just before dawn he became conscious of a bright cloud filling the room, and in the cloud he saw the radiant figure of Christ. It seemed to him that

Christ said: "Why do you oppose Me? I am your Saviour: I died on the Cross for you." And from that moment onwards Sundar Singh was the devoted follower of Christ. Years ago when I was walking down a street in Calcutta with a fellow-missionary, a gentleman passed us, driving in his dog-cart. My friend called my attention to him, and told me that that man had lived for years a godless life. One morning he entered a hotel for a drink. He was on the point of raising a glass of liquor to his lips when there appeared to him a vision of the pained face of Jesus Christ. He put the glass down and went away, and that incident was the beginning of a changed life.   J. Ireland Hasler

** **

187   A man is born again the moment he becomes conscious of his spiritual nature and begins to live in harmony with the dictates of his soul. On the day when Richard Mill first saw the light, he wrote in his diary these words: "Clang! Clang! Clang! went every bell in heaven, for Richard Mill was born again!"   James L. Gordon

** **

188   St. Augustine in his *Confessions* tells us that from boyhood up to mature manhood he had been base, deceptive, and, above all, he was so deeply stained and corrupted with all sorts of impurity that it seemed to him utterly impossible that he should ever live a chaste life. Yet God found him. God at last spoke in thunder to his heart in the sudden text, "Not in rioting and drunkenness, not in chambering and in wantonness, not in strife and envying. But put ye on the Lord Jesus Christ and make not provision for the flesh to fulfil the lusts thereof." St. Augustine was converted; he was born again. That miracle of God's grace restored to him the one heart and the right spirit within him, and henceforth for many years his life was that of a pure and holy saint of God.
                                                                   F. W. Farrar

** **

189   An eminent preacher (so the story goes—not always with the same preacher's name) was accosted in the street by a drunken man who insisted on shaking hands with him on the ground that "you converted me." There the story ends, in the popular and incomplete version. Now listen to Guinness Rogers:

"Dr. Raffles (the great Congregational preacher of Liverpool) used to tell of a man whom he met reeling in the streets of Liverpool, who came up to him and claimed acquaintance with him. 'Oh, Dr. Raffles, Dr. Raffles, I know you. I am one of your converts.' 'Yes,' said the Doctor to the poor, miserable drunkard; 'you look like one of *my* converts.'"

So a merely funny story becomes a striking religious one. Dr. Raffles himself, says Rogers, often used the story to enforce his idea about converts who "traced the work simply to men and forgot God."

✳✳

190   Accepting the whole idea of conversion, I used to suppose that when a man was converted once he was converted for all time. I knew that men after conversion had their struggles and doubts and temptations; and yet I supposed they walked in the high places of the earth always. I supposed that when a man was converted, if at any time he wanted to look into heaven, he had nothing to do but to turn round and look in; and that though it might sometimes be shut, there it was when he wanted it. I supposed that a converted man had the sense of salvation all the time; and all the more because I used to hear men say so. I have heard people speak from whose words you would think they abode in a state of translation. Everything was radiant in their language. Oh, the ecstasy which they poured out! But I did not see that they lived any better than other folks. Yet they had a certain sensuousness of spiritual experience, together with the gift of utterance; and they could represent that experience in glowing terms.

Now, according to my experience, and no doubt according to yours, I think, while in certain mercurial natures, and in certain conjunctions of circumstances, conversions into spiritual life, accompanied by joy and a heightened imagination, do produce powerful effects instantaneously upon men, yet such cases are exceptional. Ordinarily the beginning of a Christian life is as the light that shines brighter and brighter unto the perfect day. It is kindled from a spark. It becomes a slender flame. It widens and spreads and intensifies little by little, gradually.   Henry Ward Beecher

✳✳

191   I remember Russell Maltby, preaching in his inimitable way, holding two imaginary globes in his hands and pointing out how short a step it was from the one to the other; the world of the unsaved and the world of the saved—between which a man may pass in a single stride through the miracle of conversion.   Ernest H. Jeffs

Co-operation

192   Co-operation is essential to any organized existence at all, and the most rudimentary form of society is a co-operative one. But co-operation is not enough, since man may co-operate for evil as well as for good, though there

appears to be something in the nature of co-operation that is alien to evil. Co-operation for evil is a monstrous and perverted thing and cannot endure. Nevertheless, to develop the fullest potentialities of co-operation, we require brotherhood. That alone can prevent a privileged class within the nation or a privileged nation within the world usurping to itself a disproportionate share of the fruits of co-operative effort.

N. C. Raad

Courage

193   There is a little incident in the life of my dear old friend Admiral Foote, which I love to think of. Foote was my ideal hero in all respects; he never flinched or grew pale in the lips under any circumstances. When in the Eastern waters he invited the King of Siam to dine on board his man-of-war. He asked God's blessing before meat. The King said with some surprise, "This is just what the missionaries do." "Yes," replied our Christian sailor; "and I am a missionary too." Not one man in ten thousand would have said that before royalty. Foote's courage in resisting the drinking customs of the naval mess-rooms was as admirable as his courage "under fire" on the *Tennessee*.

Theodore L. Cuyler

✳✳

194   The fear of man often makes us cowards. The fear of God makes the righteous as bold as a lion. God's Word makes frequent mention of boldness; but never once uses it in the offensive sense that in modern times is often applied to it. Boldness in the Bible never signifies impudence or brazen effrontery.

Jesus was the meekest and gentlest of all beings, yet His courage never flinched. How He scathes the scoundrel of Pharisees with the lightnings of His invectives! His apostles were wonderfully calm and collected men. They never bluster. Stephen before the furious Sanhedrin, Peter confronting the rulers at Jerusalem, Paul on the castle stairs and in Nero's judgement-hall, are among the sublimest characters for moral courage in history. What models they were for us ministers of the Lord Jesus! Over and over again we read that they "spake the Word of God with boldness." They did it at the cost of their lives. Shame on us that we so often conceal, or else muffle, the edge of God's truth, when it is not a question of life, but merely one of popularity or pay! We always cheat ourselves when we play the coward, for nothing "pays" better in the long run than fidelity to conscience.

Theodore L. Cuyler

✳✳

195   You have often heard of Martin Luther's speech when they warned him not to go into Worms—"that he would go there if all the tiles on the roofs were devils." Yes, but he said something greater than that, and which is not often quoted. People are not so much afraid of devils, especially in that quantity— they seem to be too many to be up to much. They said, "You must not go, Martin Luther, because if you do, Duke George will arrest you on the road" (there are many persons much more afraid of Duke George than of the devil), but he said, "I tell you if it were to rain Duke Georges as hard as it could for nine days, I would go, in God's name."   C. H. Spurgeon

⁂

196   There is a fine story told of Robertson of Brighton. After a certain sermon a lady said to him, "You will get into trouble if you preach like that." "I don't care," was Robertson's reply. "Do you know," asked the lady solemnly, "where Don't Care came to?" F. W. Robertson replied, "Yes, I know, Don't Care came to the Cross." The strength of sin in the world is in the cowardice of men, yet deeper than the coward lies the hero in every man, and Christ's voice is sounding from the sea saying, "Come!" But if we are to walk those waters safely there is a condition to be fulfilled.   Albert D. Belden

Courage, for a Cause

197   When Sir Harry Vane was dragged to Tower Hill on a sled to execution, one of the multitude cried out to him, "You never sat on so glorious a seat"; and when Lord Russell, for freedom's sake, was driven to the scaffold, the multitude, says the historian, "imagined they saw Liberty seated by his side."

F. W. Farrar

Creation

198   In the year 1863 two great scientists, Lord Kelvin and Baron Liebig, were walking in the country and came to a glorious view, and they stopped to take it in. "Do you believe," asked Lord Kelvin, "that the grass and flowers which we see around us grew by mere chemical forces?" "No," answered Baron Liebig, "no more than I could believe that a book of botany describing them could grow by mere chemical forces. If you come on a book describing your conifers and all the trees in the glen, you wouldn't believe the book grew up by accident. 'No,' said Peter, 'a book requires a thinker behind it.' 'So does evolution,' I concluded. 'And the thinker's name is God.'"   A. Stanley Hill

⁂

199   Miss Maude Royden once went into a hall where Sir J. Arthur Thomson was lecturing with lantern slides. She entered at the moment in which he was showing on the screen what she thought at first was the rose window of a Gothic cathedral, it was so beautiful. But she learned from his words that it was a picture of a transverse section of the spine of a sea-urchin. Here is beauty, hidden away, perhaps never found; for how many such sights are given to us? But we do see enough to know that in overflowing love God created this world our home.

Ronald A. Ward

Creed

200   A certain seminary in New England was built upon an elaborate and minute theological creed, and the founders strictly and solemnly enjoined that every article of this creed should "forever remain entirely and identically the same without the least alteration, addition, or diminution." What a prodigious conviction of his own omniscience the man must have who could put such a provision into the charter of a theological seminary! Did these godly founders suppose that they knew all the theology that ever ought to exist, and that wisdom would die with them? What right had they to ordain that every scribe employed to teach the doctrine of the kingdom in that seminary should forever bring forth out of his treasure everything old and nothing new?

The value of historic creeds, or confessions of faith in guiding and steadying the movements of religious thought, no wise man will dispute; the folly of rashly casting them away has been, I trust, sufficiently demonstrated; nevertheless historic confessions must be historically interpreted; it is only by a large, free method of handling them that they are kept from being fetters to the life of faith.   Washington Gladden

✳✳

201   Bishop Wilberforce and Thomas Carlyle were out walking one day and discussing the death of their mutual friend, John Stirling. Carlyle suddenly turned to the Bishop and said: "Bishop, have you a creed?" "Yes," replied the Bishop, "and what is more, the older I grow the firmer that creed becomes beneath my feet. There is only one thing that staggers me." "What is it?" asked Carlyle. "The slow progress which that creed seems to make in the world." Carlyle remained silent for a while, and then said: "Ah, but if you have a creed, you can afford to wait."   H. Hodgkins

✳✳

202   Ralph Connor puts these words into the mouth of a converted lumberjack, replying to the chaff of his mates: "I haven't much of a creed; don't really know how much I believe. But I do know that good is good and bad is bad, and good and bad are not the same. And I know a man's a fool to follow the one and a wise man to follow the other, and," lowering his voice, "I believe God is at the back of a man who wants to get done with bad."

John W. A. Singleton

✳✳

203   The opposition that arose against Stephen, and that culminated in his being stoned to death, was not owing to the life that he led, but to the religious views or opinions that he held.

P. Robertson

Criticism, Effect of

204   I remember a man telling me how distressed his father was by his detachment from the old church of his boyhood days. "Had my father known the truth," he said, "my attitude today is the reflection of his attitude expressed every Sunday in biting criticism of the service we had just attended. He never had a kind word to say of the parson, the choir or the deacons."

R. Morton Stanley

Cross

205   Archimedes asked that he might get a point to stand on. That is something we all need: a place to stand on; a place from which we can see and act with the absolute assurance that here we begin with complete finality. And that, says the New Testament, is precisely what we have in the Cross, in the experience that Christ faced and dealt with in the climactic hours of His ministry. Luther said that we should begin with the wounds of Christ; the wounds or emblems of the sacrifice He offered in His death. And unless we do, unless we take the Cross as our starting-point, we cannot hope to understand either Christ or the gospel He came to make possible.

Henry Cook

✳✳

206   It is recorded that when Clovis heard the story of the Cross, he was moved with righteous indignation and leapt to his feet, brandishing his spear, and cried: "If I and my Franks had been there, it never would have happened!" If

they had been there, the Saviour would not have died, and the purposes of God, declared in the Scriptures, would not have been accomplished.

G. C. Edmonds

※ ※

207   D. L. Moody declared that the message which produced the most effective and abiding effect was the love of God in Christ revealed in the Cross. Dr. J. S. Whale has affirmed that the Cross reveals two things. He has expounded these with unforgettable lucidity and power. In the Cross God deals with sin. He condemns sin. He exposes sin. In the Cross of Jesus we see the length to which sin could go. In the Cross we see the overwhelming love of God for the sinful. "Herein is love, not that we loved God, but that He loved us, and sent His Son to be the propitiation for our sins."

J. G. Bowran

※ ※

208   My readers will recall the familiar story of the young soldier doomed to be shot by Cromwell's order, at the ringing of the curfew-bell. The maiden whom he was to wed climbs into the belfry and holds the tongue of the swinging bell, at the peril of her life. She descends from the tower, wounded and bleeding. When Cromwell demands why the bell was silent, she shows him her hands, all bruised and torn. "Go!" cries Cromwell. "Your lover shall live, and curfew shall not ring tonight." Whether this story be historically true or not, it is a beautiful parable of the Saviour's sufferings for the sinner's sake, and of His intercessions for the guilty. Jesus not only died in the sinner's stead; but pleads with the sinner to come, and through his atoning sacrifice to become reconciled to God.

Theodore L. Cuyler

※ ※

209   Bishop E. A. Burroughs, who was Bishop of Ripon and King's Chaplain during the last war, tells a story of two brothers who were in the same company in that war. In the front-line trench one brother saw the other blown to bits with a hand grenade. And the surviving brother went into the dug-out when it was all over, and, taking a sheet of notepaper, he drew a sunrise and a cross, and wrote beneath it, "God is love," and pinned the sheet of paper on the wall as a reminder to himself that there is a God and in Him suffering and death are not in vain. It is because of that cross of Christ that you can still believe that God is "the Eternal who deals in kindness, justice and goodness upon earth."

Barnard R. H. Spaull

※ ※

210   On the occasion of Victor Hugo's death, the French resolved to secularize the Pantheon. They removed the great gilt Cross which ornamented its cupola. A famous Christian orator, addressing a Parisian audience, uttered his protest against this act of spoliation. He did not carry the sympathies of his audience, and many who were present expressed their dissent. With some indignation he exclaimed: "You think to take away the Cross from the Pantheon." Immediately came the response: "We have taken it away." He replied: "I tell you you cannot take away the Cross from the Pantheon." Again they shouted: "It is taken away. Down with the priests." The speaker paused, and repeated his statement. The audience rose and yelled defiance. Waiting until the tumult subsided, he quietly explained: "You cannot take away the Cross from the Pantheon, for it is built in the form of a Cross, and when you have taken away the Cross there will be no Pantheon left."   J. G. Henderson

※※

211   In *The Durable Satisfactions of Life* there is a story told of an agnostic friend of Dr. Glover's who set out to save a drunkard, to prove that a man's habits could be changed without the help of religion. He admitted that it was a miserable job; that the man was so weak that he could not pass a public house. He described how he had to give him continual comradeship; take him for walks in his leisure time; sit up with him at nights. "I dare not leave him alone," he said, "but I am resolved to stick to him." Some months after Dr. Glover met him again and said to him, "What about your drunken friend?" "I was getting on fairly well, though it was desperately slow work," he replied, "when a lot of rough people with red jerseys arrived, and an atrocious brass band, and they made him kneel down and pray. And—well, anyhow he can walk by the pub now without help." Of course, that is the way of the Cross: "For the Word of the Cross . . . is the power of God."   W. Ridley Chesterton

※※

212   Dr. Donald Fraser once addressed an open-air meeting in Glasgow, and held up the cross on his watch chain and said: "Whenever I am depressed and my work is too much for me and my sky is dark, my hand has found the habit of straying to this symbol and it brings to me this message: the Cross is empty, and on the crest of that wave courage comes back to me."   John Bishop

※※

213   Do you remember that very pathetic yet very beautiful story of Charles and Mary Lamb? "Mary was subject to periodical attacks of mania, in one of which she lifted a knife and stabbed her mother to the heart. When the awful paroxysm was over she became rational and gentle again. Charles felt it his duty to devote his life to her guardianship, and sacrificing everything, even the prospect of marriage to the woman he loved, he consecrated himself to this one life-ministry and for thirty-eight years never flagged in his tenderness and devotion. Certain premonitions told them when another attack of madness was coming on, and then might be seen brother and sister walking hand in hand across the meadows on the way to the asylum, both weeping, both weighed down with an intolerable secret, both pilgrims on the Via Dolorosa of infinite sacrifice and sorrow, each clinging to the other with despairing love and the anguish of foreboding fear." There, indeed, was a Calvary, and there, indeed, was the filling up of the sufferings of Christ. It was a brother giving up his life for a sister.

George Barber

✳✳

214   You have heard of that relic of early Christianity, a stone dug out of the soil containing a rude drawing of One nailed to a cross, before which kneels a Roman soldier in the attitude of prayer, while underneath is the inscription "Alexamenes adores his God." That little drawing may be taken as a concentrated expression of the intense irony with which the doctrine of the cross was regarded by the heathen world in the early years of the Church. And the cross is still an offence. If there is any reason why the religion of Christ is unpopular, it lies here. Men like what brings them the honour of the world, and they know that the world delights to honour, not the man who carries a cross, but he who is loaded with gold. If much is said about the cross, even in Christian life, it is liable to be complacently ruled out as morbid and unpractical. Men are always talking about the Sermon on the Mount as their ideal, but they take the cross out of it first, and the Sermon is full of the cross. How many act as though they really believed that the meek inherit the earth, or that the Kingdom of God belongs to the poor in spirit? We are not surprised to find this spirit in the world, but it comes also into the Church, if we are not careful.   J. B. Stedeford

✳✳

215   When Henry Drummond was dying, his friend, Dr. Hugh Barbour, sang hymns for his comfort. Nothing seemed to satisfy him, until these lines were sung:

> I'm not ashamed to own my Lord,
>   Or to defend His cause,
> Maintain the honor of His word,
>   The glory of His Cross.

"Ah, Hugh!" he said. "There's nothing to beat that!"   J. G. Bowran

Cross, Failure or Defeat

216   Two thousand years ago a stark Cross was reared against an Eastern sky, with a man dying on it. Did ever any failure or defeat seem more complete than that? Since then proud empires have crumbled into ruins leaving nothing but a few mouldering stones in a field where rabbits breed and feed. But that Man lives on to haunt men's minds and consciences forever; as someone said recently: "That Man on the Cross is the bad conscience of 600,000,000 people who claim to worship Him." He lives on in the power of His Spirit of truth, love and sacrifice. That Spirit is the greatest uplifting, ennobling, recreative force mankind has ever known. We need that spirit today.

"Adolf Hitler has become so big, and Jesus Christ has become so small." So said a German boy about ten years ago. Since then Adolf Hitler and his thousand-year Reich have gone. Jesus Christ—that Man on the Cross—remains, alive forevermore. Still He weeps over the cities as He did over Jerusalem long ago: "O London, Paris, Moscow, Washington, hadst thou but known the things that belong to thy peace."

Norman P. Stead

Cross, Judgement of

217   Dr. A. J. Gossip says that the three crosses that were reared up that day on Calvary have become a kind of parable, for ever since, when Christ has become effective in a life, two others have been nailed down and left remorselessly to die. First the world, by which is meant things not evil in themselves, but which might hinder me from coming to Christ—my hobby, work, home, family. And second myself, by which is meant something evil, the lower part of my nature which has so often had me beaten in the past, and from which, in vain, I have tried to free myself. And the wonderful thing is that if I set up the Cross of Christ in my life, I not only find forgiveness for my sins and failures of the past, but I am able to crucify both the world and myself. Again I don't pretend to explain it, but if I set up the Cross in my life, judging all things by it, drawing power through it, daily seeking the Christ who died upon it, then I have deliverance both from the sin of the past and from its power to hold me.

Geoffrey Walker

Cross, Response to

218   There is the disturbing story told by C. E. Montague, of the little boy hearing for the first time of the Cross, his uncle giving out from the pulpit the terrible news, no doubt because there were so many people there who might at once rush to help. The boy wept at the rending tale of that kind, brave Man so cruelly hurt and even now feeling the pain; but the people around seemed strangely tranquil, and when they left church, walked away as if nothing had happened.

R. E. McIntyre

Cross, Why the

219   A book was published entitled *Why Was I Killed?* It is about a soldier who was killed in battle; and after his death he returns and is able to enter into the minds of various people and groups still in this life, to try to discover what his death means to each of them. Well, the Cross of Christ presents the biggest question mark in the world's history. Why did Christ die? Why was He killed? Men are always gathering round that Cross and staring at it in wonder: and the longer they look, the more their wonder grows.

H. H. G. MacMillan

Crucifixion

220   Do you remember the scene in the film, *The Life of Emile Zola?* In the court-room the judge has kept insisting that the Dreyfus case is closed. The defence may not bring forward this witness, may not submit that evidence, because the Dreyfus case is closed. Time and again during the hearing the assertion is made that the affair of Dreyfus is a closed case, but when the court rises Zola's lawyer looks up at the wall-painting of the Crucifixion above the judge's seat and quietly remarks that that also was once regarded as a closed case.

R. G. Martin

Danger

221   Here are the moving words of a major in North Africa in a letter home to his mother: "You will be pleased to hear I go to church regularly, and that a fortnight ago I went to Communion the first Sunday after the battle was over. . . . You don't tell people to go to church, they just go. If the people at home were half as keen as the people out here there wouldn't be enough churches. It's surprising but true, men you would never imagine would bother about religion go to church and worry about church services in case they miss them. . . . War may be a bad thing, but one thing it has done is that it turns all men sooner or later to the church."

R. Oswald Davies

Danger, Spiritual

222   Dr. Watkinson reminds us of a great French beauty who was one of the most renowned of her type of the Second Empire. When her beauty began to vanish her anguish of mind was intense, displaying itself in her actions and mode of life. She possessed a full-length picture of herself by a distinguished artist, painted in the hey-day of her loveliness. One day her friends noticed that it had disappeared from the walls of her drawing-room. The reason was that she had fretted over the fact that every day she was growing more and more unlike the exquisite creature portrayed on the canvas, which, in a final fit of anger and vexation, she had cut into strips with a pair of scissors. That loss of beauty, however, did not happen all at once. Little by little, bit by bit, did it fade, until one day, comparing herself with what she once was, she was overcome with despair at the tragic contrast. That is how life changes. Little by little, bit by bit, till, one day, we are surprised at the great change that has taken place. It was all so subtle, but it was all so very real.

And it is the same so often in Christian life and experience. The decay and the drift are so imperceptible. We find ourselves to begin with, not quite so keen in Christian activity as once we were. We find it harder to persuade ourselves to attend God's House, to participate in Communion or in mid-week service. We need more constraint to do God's work, and find it increasingly easy to make excuse to any call that may be made upon us for Christian service and duty. So it is that slowly and gently we drift, till, one day, we find ourselves without spiritual interest or response. We had drifted so subtly and imperceptibly that we had hardly been conscious of the drifting. And because drift can be like that, we need to pay the more earnest heed lest we are caught in the toils that rush us on to spiritual death and disaster.

Horace E. Hewitt

Darkness

223   No one, I think, will dispute that we live in a world of growing darkness. Sir Edward Grey sat at his desk in Downing Street late on a summer night in 1914 and as darkness enveloped the city outside and as the sands of peace were running out—those last fateful moments—he said with deep insight: "The lights are going out all over Europe."

Frederick C. Gill

Death

224   There was once a minister who was called upon to conduct the funeral service of a young girl, the only child of a professed agnostic. He knew very well what her father thought, for many a time he had received the full force of his arguments. But in this hour the father was a stricken man. And rising grandly to the occasion the minister said very simply to the friends gathered: "My friends, I do not know what you believed yesterday and I do not know what you may believe to-morrow, but for to-day we will believe in God."

Morley B. Simmons

✻✻

225   When I was a boy I used to hear that famous old Welsh preacher, Morlais Jones, of Lewisham. I will not deprecate my own day; but I sometimes think we have no preaching like his now. A little while ago I was looking through a volume of his sermons, and there was one—I forget the title—in which he was speaking of the gathering glory. He told how he had recently been on a voyage, and he described how the time was spent on deck; the games, the novel reading, all the various ways of getting through the day. Then, one morning, the man at the look-out cried: "Land ahead!" The deck games were all put away, the novels were thrown aside, and we were every one of us leaning over the hand-rail watching for the first glimpse of home, and the land where we should be. "The glory of the Lord shall be revealed." And when that day comes, what will all the roughness, and the trials of the way, seem to us but a tale that is told, and is thrown aside for the light of the everlasting day? There is no doubt of it, for the mouth of the Lord hath spoken.

A. T. S. James

✻✻

226   Let me quote that unfinished sentence which was found on Dr. Dale's study table when he died: "Unworldliness does not consist in the most rigid and conscientious observance of any external rules of conduct, but in the spirit and temper and in the habit of living created by the vision of God, by constant fellowship with Him, by a personal and vivid experience of the greatness of the Christian redemption, by the settled purpose to do the will of God always, at all costs, and by the power of the great hope, the full assurance, that after our mortal years are spent, there is a larger, fuller, richer life in" . . .

There the hand has ceased to write; but we cannot be far wrong if we venture to close the sentence with the words we have been thinking of today; for the hope of the unworldly passes beyond the tasks and trials of our few years here to a larger, fuller, richer life in Him whose "kingdom is not of this world."

Francis Paget

* *

227   When Xerxes, the Persian king, was marching with his immense army to invade Greece, he came to the Hellespont. There, before crossing into Macedonia, within sight of the blue waters of the Strait, he ordered a grand review of his troops. A throne was erected for the monarch on the hillside, and seating himself upon that marble chair, he surveyed his million soldiers in the fields below. With a proud smile he turned to his courtiers and confessed that he was the happiest man on earth. He truly had some cause for pride.

But ere long, the king's countenance changed, and those who stood by him saw the tears beginning to trickle down his cheeks. One of them asked him why his joy was so soon turned into sorrow, and the cause of this strange and unseasonable grief. "Alas!" said Xerxes, "I am thinking that of all this vast host, not one will be alive in a hundred years." It is with feelings very much akin that the preacher often enters a pulpit.

When one sees a church filled from Sunday to Sunday with a crowd of worshippers, one is most thankful and encouraged in the discharge of a great and responsible work. But sadness mingles with the joy, in that within a few years, comparatively, not one of us will be in our places here though others will fill the gaps. The Persian king anticipated that in a hundred years his vast army would be dissolved by death. He little knew what lay before him. Only a few months passed before that vast host was hacked to pieces at Thermopylae and Marathon, and the wretched survivors were straggling back again into Asia Minor as they best could. The king himself was glad to escape with a mere handful of followers, leaving behind him all his cherished possessions.

Alfred Thomas

* *

228   There is something strange and pathetic in a Hindu funeral. The shrouded corpse is placed on a rough bamboo bier, and as the bearers hurry with it to the burning ghat they chant this dirge: "God's the only Living One, and another soul has gone." The mortality of the human reminds them of the immortality of the Divine.   J. Ireland Hasler

* *

229   A remarkable statement is made by Jung on the personal aspect of belief in survival after death. Speaking as a scientist, Jung says bluntly, "We cannot

know whether anything happens to a person after he is dead. The answer is neither yes nor no." But he goes on to say that when he takes up his work as a physician he finds that he must give his patients a hope of life after death. They cannot do without it. "As a physician," he says, "I am convinced that it is hygienic—if I may use the word—to discover in death a goal towards which one can strive. . . . I therefore consider the religious teaching of a life hereafter consonant with the standpoint of psychic hygiene." We live more healthily and happily when we believe in life beyond death. Socially and personally this is true. It would be strange indeed if a lie worked better than the truth.

James MacKay

**

230   Do you remember that quaint answer that an ex-President of the United States, John Quincy Adams, gave, at the age of eighty, to a friend whom he met in a Boston street? The friend asked him: "How is John Quincy Adams to-day?" and the answer came: "Thank you, John Quincy Adams himself is well, quite well, I thank you. But the house in which he lives at present is becoming dilapidated. It is tottering upon the foundations. Time and the seasons have nearly destroyed it. Its roof is pretty well worn out. Its walls are much shattered, and it trembles with every wind. The old tenement is becoming uninhabitable, and I think John Quincy Adams will have to move out of it soon. But he himself is quite well, quite well."

Barnard R. H. Spaull

**

231   May I remind you of that simple illustration that is given to us in one of the books by Mr. Oliver Wendell Holmes. What he suggests is this. He says that a father ought to go to the school where he has left his boy, and go in suddenly some day, and take him by the hand, lead him out of the school, and say to him, "Now, my boy, the time of your education is over, you are coming out with me, and the wider world is just opening before you." The boy's heart begins to pound, his spirit to exult in the new freedom, the new prospects, and the new possibilities; then the father tells him that this moment is just like death, that death is the leaving of the old school, and passing out into the fuller life of the larger possibilities and opportunities in the life beyond. Ah! if you could believe that this life is your probation, your education, your preparation for the life that lies beyond, what a different thing some of you would be making of it to what you are making of it.

C. Silvester Horne

**

232   If you have read any of Stephen Graham's stories you may remember that in one of them he tells the story of a poor Russian peasant woman who was found sobbing on her husband's grave, a whole year after his death, clutching at the earth, pouring out her soul in sobs, telling him that he must come back, that she needed him, that the children needed him, that she could not live without him. It is an exaggerated reaction, but it is the far end of the road travelled by the person who never comes to terms with death.

Leslie D. Weatherhead
From Christian World Pulpit, Vol. 139

* *

233   The mother of Robert Louis Stevenson, after her son had decided to make his home in far-away Samoa, cut right adrift from all her moorings in Scotland and went out to make her home with her beloved boy. There she saw him pass away, and then she came back to Edinburgh to live with her sister. People marvelled at her quiet composure as she talked of the boy she had lost. "I have my precious memories left, and I feel I have much cause for thankfulness," she would say, "but still my heart cries out for my boy." Some three years after her return from Samoa she was seized with pneumonia. Her sister pictures the final scene: "About midnight I was told I might see her. Her dear hand was pushed out to clasp mine for the last time. Suddenly she said, 'There's Louis! I must go!'"

I shall never forget the talk I had with Sir Oliver Lodge at his home in Birmingham in October, 1915, during the first great war. Some time later, in an address given in a church in the heart of the city of London, I heard him say: "Death is a serious adventure, but it is not the end of anything. The spirit discards the body, and goes on without it. Personality, character, memory, affections, persist. We go on as we are when we leave the body. You carry with you your real self; nothing more, nothing less."   Henry J. Cowell

* *

234   Alfred Tennyson, whose attitude to the future life is indicated in "In Memoriam" and in "Crossing the Bar," once declared: "The life after death is the cardinal point of Christianity." Then there is the witness of F. C. Spurr: "The Testimony of Jesus Christ was that He came from the other world and was returning to it. While He was here He witnessed to that life beyond, and unless the whole of Christian experience and testimony for two thousand years has been an extraordinary myth and mockery He has been at work through the centuries and acting upon people with all the power of a living personality. For myself I am content with the witness of Jesus Christ. Death does not end all; it leads to further education, to fuller life and to higher service."

Edward Wilson of the Antarctic wrote to his wife: "We will all meet after death. My love for you is for ever." And F. B. Meyer told a friend: "My doctor says the end cannot be far away. I'll see you in the morning."

Henry J. Cowell

✳✳

235   Once the famous American evangelist, Mr. Moody, remarked in a sermon, "Some day you will read in the papers that D. L. Moody of East Northfield is dead. Don't you believe a word of it. At that moment I shall be more alive than now. I shall have gone up higher, that is all—out of this old clay tenement into a house that is immortal; a body that death cannot touch, that sin cannot taint, a body fashioned like unto His glorious body. That which is born of the flesh may die. That which is born of the spirit will live for ever." And that is the sure and blessed hope the Gospel inspires. "O death, where is thy sting? O grave, where is thy victory? Thanks be to God which giveth us the victory through our Lord Jesus Christ."

R. J. Anglin Johnson

✳✳

236   Archbishop Leighton in the seventeenth century tells us of a man who entered a church at Glasgow one day when the fifth chapter of Genesis was being read, of the patriarchs who lived for hundreds of years, and the man left the church that morning converted. Archbishop Leighton tells us that what converted him was the perpetual recurrence of the phrase, "And he died."

Robert F. Horton

Death, Anchor in

237   John Knox put grit into all of us. He taught that every man had access to God, with no priest and no Church between his soul and God. When he was dying he said to his wife: "Read where I first cast anchor." She knew what he meant, and she turned to the 17th chapter of John's Gospel and read: "This is life eternal to know Thee, the only true God, and Jesus Christ whom Thou hast sent." From the day that Knox commenced his Christian life, he had lived in the storm, and he had this as his anchor. And now as he is facing death he said to his wife: "I want to lay hold of that anchor as I face the last storm."

John Wilson

Death, Attitude Towards

238   Charles Lamb, in his essay on "New Year's Eve," says: "I care not to be carried away with the tide that smoothly bears human life to eternity. . . . I am in love with this green earth; the face of town and country; the unspeakable rural solitudes and the sweet security of streets. I would set up my tabernacle here." He was as reluctant as we are to look death in the face. We are in love with this life, perhaps in love with it too much; we are drunk with its elixir and forget that this earth is not our permanent abode. St. Paul said that our citizenship is in heaven and the first Lord Halifax said that you should live in the world so as it may hang about you like a loose garment.

H. Hodgkins

Death, Coming to Terms With

239   One day Philip de Neri was walking in the grounds of a great Continental university and he fell in with a young student who told him that he had come to the law-school there, attracted by its fame. Philip said: "When you have completed your studies, what do you intend to do?" "I shall take my doctor's degree." "And then?" asked Philip. "Then I shall have a number of difficult cases to deal with and shall call attention to myself by my eloquence and my learning, and gain a great reputation." "And then?" repeated Philip. "And then I shall be promoted to some high office and make money and grow rich." "And then?" "Then I shall live comfortably in wealth and dignity." "And then?" persisted Philip. "Then I suppose I shall die." Then Philip raised his voice and said, "And what then?" The young man made no answer. Hanging his head, he went thoughtfully away. That last question struck home, and he came to realize the utter futility of living for this world alone.

Death is the one future fact of which we are all certain, and it is wise for us to come to terms with it. Most of us give little thought to it except when it comes near to us or ours.

John Bishop

Death, Fear of

240   The fear of death rests like the shadow of a dark cloud upon many a soul. Count Tolstoy, speaking of his early married life, remarks, "Fate had given me all that could be desired: a fine family, a loving wife, universal fame, wealth, health—everything! If a fairy had come and offered to fulfil all my desires, I would not have known what to ask for, but the shadow of death was over all."

James L. Gordon

Debate

241   They tell the story of the visitor to the Sorbonne at Paris who was told that here the doctors had debated for 1,300 years. "Indeed," was the reply, "and pray, what have they settled?"

C. Silvester Horne

Debt

242   In a Tube near Whitechapel there entered a young airman who was badly burned. His once handsome face was now terribly disfigured; plastic surgery had done its best to rebuild the face, but the tightness of the replaced skin only added to the disfigurement. It was a face marred beyond most. The frail body, still of upright bearing, bore signs of strain and stress, or nervous suffering. He seemed to walk with an uncertain air, and sat as if he were a visitor from another world. An old lady sat looking at his sorrowful figure, as all did in the Tube train. Tears filled her eyes. Then as she got up to leave the carriage, she went to the Air Force lad, and placing her hand on his shoulder she said, "Thank you, son, I'll try to be a better woman. God bless you." Those scars were part of the price paid for her deliverance.

Norman Greenhalgh

Debtor

243   "I am a debtor." This is not a popular thing to say. It is not an easy thing to say. We like to claim credit for ourselves and we are not fond of acknowledging our indebtedness to others. One of the commonest forms of selfishness is just this kind of pride. We want to stand well in the eyes of the world. One man boasts that he is "self-made." Another courts praise for his achievements, "Alone I did it." How rarely a man acknowledges, "Of myself, I am nothing. Such as I am, I owe to others. That I have been able to do anything at all in my life is due to the heritage, the example, the help, given by other people."

Harold Derbyshire

Decision

244   In the old days of the Roman Empire there was constant trouble on one of the borders. The border tribes, though nominally at peace with Rome, were making raids into Roman territory, with the secret connivance of the chiefs.

Finally the Roman general called a conference of the tribal chiefs: and when they were all assembled on the open plain, he drew his sword, and marked a circle around them on the grass. Turning to them he said: Before you cross that circle, you must decide. If you want peace, let it be peace. If you want war, then war let it be.

In the same way, Christ may be drawing a circle around you. The time to decide has come, one way or the other. Delay is useless: decision is demanded. The way to conversion is open to each one of us. Christ is waiting for your answer.

H. V. Martin

Dedication

245 It is related that someone asked Quintin Hogg, the founder of the Polytechnic Institute in London, who had devoted a large fortune to the enterprise, how much it cost to build up such an institution. "Not very much," was Mr. Hogg's reply, "simply one man's life-blood."

R. C. Gillie

Democracy

246 There is a common belief among us that the democratic form of government is necessarily the best form, but if that claim is submitted without qualification it is a fallacy. Democracy can only justify itself if it is a disciplined democracy. Thomas Carlyle was right when he said that "the best form of government was any form of government by the best men." A dictatorship need not necessarily be condemned if the dictator is animated by high ideals. Cromwell was a dictator, and England has received a rich heritage because of his period of government. The final argument in favor of democracy is that it is a safer form of government than a dictatorship; but this presumes willing discipline on the part of its individual citizens, and it is our problem to ask ourselves to what extent we can claim at the present time to be a disciplined people.

Angus Watson

Denominationalism

247 Denominationalism only becomes a sin when we are Presbyterians or Anglicans or whatever it may be, first, and Christians second. Paul has no desire to shake the attachment of his converts to himself or of Apollos's to Apollos. A tie of this kind can be of great value. But it must not be allowed to interfere with the common attachment to Christ. Provided loyalty to Him is first secured, we can rejoice that others serve Him as we cannot, that others find Him where He is hidden from our eyes.

E. L. Allen

Despair

248   When Robert Louis Stevenson discovered himself in a despairing mood, he would laughingly say: "I must get out my wings."   H. G. Doel

∗∗

249   Lord Lothian, in the last speech he made before his lamented death, said: "The triumph of Hitler no doubt grew out of the despair that settled on Central Europe in the long years of war, defeat, inflation, revolutionary propaganda, and which grew out of the unemployment and frustration which followed from the absence of any real unity in Europe." Next, listen to Nicholas Berdyaev, described by the Archbishop of York as "one of the most important writers of the time." "The present catastrophe in the world was born, not of a joyful superabundance of creative force, but from man's profound unhappiness, his feeling of hopeless despair." Now listen to Peter Drucker in *The End of Economic Man:* "The despair of the masses is the key to the understanding of Fascism. No 'revolt of the mob,' no 'triumphs of unscrupulous propaganda,' but stark despair caused by the breakdown of the old order and the absence of a new one."   James MacKay

∗∗

250   God forbid that I should ever say an untrue or an unkind word about any of the sons of men—least of all that I should seem to tear aside with ruthless hand the veil that hides the secret place of sorrow! But the occurrence to which I am about to refer was not done in a corner, and I only bring to your mind what you all know when I mention the time when Colonel Ingersoll endeavoured to fulfil the promise he made to his brother, who was also his boyhood playmate, and pronounced his funeral address. It was in June, 1879. This brother had died in Washington, and Colonel Ingersoll stood by the coffin and tried to read his address. His voice became agitated, his form trembled, and his emotion overcame him. Finally, he put down the paper, and bowing himself upon the coffin, he gave vent to uncontrollable grief. When at last he was able to proceed he raised himself up, and among other words, he said these: "Whether in mid-ocean or 'mid the breakers of the farther shore, a wreck must mark at last the end of each and all; and every life, no matter if its every hour be filled with love, and every movement jewelled with a joy, will at the last become a tragedy as sad and dark and deep as can be woven of the warp and woof of mystery and death.

". . . Life is a dark and barren vale between the cold and ice-clad peaks of two eternities. We strive in vain to look beyond the heights. We lift our wailing voices in the silence of the night, and hear no answer but the bitter echo of our cry." Could ever words more sadly hopeless have been uttered at a time like that? And then he added what to me were the most pathetic words of all—something about "hope trying to see a star, and listening for the rustle of angels' wings."

B. Fay Mills

✳✳

251   Somebody has said that we are living in a world today which is certain only of its uncertainties. In his novel, *The Uncertain Trumpet,* A. S. M. Hutchinson describes a girl named Rhoda, who throws herself unreservedly into the work of an East End parish. One day the priest of the parish says to her: "Rhoda, I notice that you are not so much living for this work as by it. Tell me, as you look out on life, what do you see?" And this is Rhoda's answer: "I see a great big question mark!" Those words aptly describe the mood today of many people, and especially of many young people. Not that this attitude of questioning, of fierce criticism, is to be entirely deplored. It is far better for us to test our opinions and beliefs in the crucible of our own experience than to accept them, at second-hand value, from other people. But the plain fact is that when every allowance has been made for the value of healthy criticism, the world cannot live on questions. "Who will show us any good?" If that is the last word, it is a very dismal and depressing word. It is a question which connotes despair.

But thank God that is not the last word. The question of the cynic is answered by the prayer of the saint. "There be many that say, Who will show us any good? Lord, lift Thou up the light of Thy countenance upon us."

W. Francis Gibbons

Disappointment

252   Near San Francisco is Leland Stanford University. Stanford was governor of California. He was a very wealthy man and he had one son called Leland Stanford, junior. The parents wanted to give all that the new world could offer to the lad, so while he was very young they took him to Italy. There, at the age of nine, the only son was stricken with a malady from which he died. What happened? Mr. and Mrs. Stanford went back to California broken-hearted. They said, "All our hopes and dreams are represented by mouldering dust. Leland, junior, has gone; the only thing to do is to make all the children of California our children." So they built and endowed the famous Leland Stanford Junior University. I think Mr. Stanford, when he died, left a sum of money estimated at twenty-two million dollars for the endowment of that university, so that it might be possible for every boy and girl in America, and particularly in California, without respect to class, to have the opportunity of enjoying a university education. That is the boon afforded largely through the beneficence of the man who was inspired to a great service by a deep and bitter disappointment. Had Leland Stanford, junior, lived, we should not have seen thousands of the pick of the West enjoying the privilege of a university education in the most delightful part of California. As we look back over the years and think of all that has happened, how often we can see that God utilizes the dark days as well as the bright ones in working out His plans in our lives.

William C. Poole

Discipleship

253 When Garibaldi published that famous proclamation to his soldiers after the storming of Rome, "Soldiers! I have nothing to offer you but hunger, thirst, hardship, death. Let all who love their country follow me!" he knew many a gallant youth would follow him, accepting hunger, and thirst, and death. And you will accept the call of your Master, Christ.   F. W. Farrar

* *

254 When the Japanese invaded the Gilbert Islands in the Pacific they found a young English missionary there. He had been given the opportunity to leave the Islands when danger threatened, but he determined to remain with the native Christians and share their hardships and seek to comfort them in their tribulations. There came a day when the Japanese guards put down on the ground in front of the young missionary the Union Jack and ordered him to walk over it. He refused, but instead walked around the flag. Once again they commanded him to walk over the flag of freedom and honour, but this time they threatened Alfred Sadd with death if he refused. With set face, calm and unafraid, young Alfred Sadd quietly walked around the flag, and within a few seconds he was put to death by the brutal Japanese. He was loyal to his earthly King, and as a missionary of the Cross of Christ he was loyal to the King of Kings. He had crowned Jesus Christ as King on the throne of his own life, and he gave that young life—young and strong and free—in the service of others, seeking by his witness and his example to extend Christ's Kingdom.

Harold T. Barrow

* *

255   There is one sure way to be unworried and unalarmed; one sure way to keep men and women of widely differing theological opinions united in the fellowship of Christ; one sure way of judging whether a preacher is or is not being disloyal to his ordination vows; one sure way of combining the lighted mind with the warmed heart, and of changing the phrases of religion without giving up one single grain of the peace and comfort and joy of religion. It is the one sure way, and, as I believe, the only way. It is to concentrate all the time upon the word Discipleship. It is to believe that all the different forms of Christianity are more or less unimportant variants of the Christianity which means simply following Christ.

What form of Christianity, from that of a scholar and scientist like Bishop Barnes to that of the most unlettered local preacher, does not really begin and end with following Christ—which means trying to live in Christ's way, upheld by the belief that Christ's way of life is the one authentic picture we have of the nature and the will of God?

Ernest H. Jeffs

Doctrine

256   One great secret of R. W. Dale's power as a preacher is that he put his pulpit first and gave his best hours to preparation for it. He was a doctrinal preacher. In the preface to his volume of sermons on *Christian Doctrine* he tells an interesting story about himself. Three or four years after he had settled in Carrs Lane he met another Congregational minister in the streets of Birmingham, a Welshman, who said to him: "I hear that you are preaching doctrinal sermons to your congregation. They will not stand it." To which Dale promptly replied: "They will have to stand it." They did stand it, and liked it, and the result was a congregation which for robust and masculine Christian intelligence was perhaps unrivalled in England.   John Bishop

✸✸

257   Dorothy L. Sayers in a little book about Christianity called *The Greatest Drama Ever Staged* writes, "We are constantly assured that the churches are empty because preachers insist too much upon doctrine—'dull dogma' as people call it. The fact is the precise opposite. It is the neglect of dogma that makes for dullness. The Christian faith is the most exciting drama that ever staggered the imagination of man—and the dogma is the drama. The drama is summarized quite clearly in the creeds of the Church, and if we think it dull it is because we have never really read those amazing documents, or have recited them so often and so mechanically as to have lost all sense of their meaning." Yes, those

words from a secular writer rebuke us. The Church of today has travelled too far along the road of theological vagueness and doctrinal ambiguity. We must return to the verities of the faith, Christ's revelation, redemption and resurrection. "They continued steadfastly in the apostle's doctrine."

W. Francis Gibbons

Door, Christ the

258   It is told of Sir Isaac Newton that he had a favorite cat which he liked to have with him always in his study. This cat had a kitten; and Sir Isaac used to be sometimes troubled when he heard the two mewing on the wrong side of the door, wanting to come in. So in an absent mood of mind he ordered a carpenter to make two holes in the door, a big one for the mother cat, and a smaller one for the kitten. He did not realize at the moment, till the astonished carpenter explained to him that one hole would suffice for both, that the kitten could go in at the same door as its mother. Now, the moral of the homely story is that there are not two doors to religion, one for parents and another for children, one for grownups and another for young people. Jesus is the door for all.   Hugh MacMillen

Doubt

259   Doubt can never prevent a first-hand experience of Christ. To insist on a crystal-clear solution of doubts before the hand can be struck in a compact of loyalty is to be less than candid. Jesus did not lay down any such terms. In an impassioned speech to the students of the university, President Harper, of Chicago, said long ago, "Why didn't some one tell me that I can become a Christian and settle the doubts afterwards?" When the mind of the disciple runs into the mind of Christ, as two globules of mercury run together, doubts lose their independent significance.

This is scepticism sure enough. To attempt to explain it away is gratuitous. We do no good decorating it with fine phrases and plausible apologies. Thomas was, through and through, a thoroughgoing sceptic. But Thomas was religious. His immaturity of brain was constantly outrun by his precocity of heart. His faith went deeper than his beliefs.   Miles H. Krumbine

Drink, Effect of

260   Mr. Hamilton Fyfe, the editor of one of London's great newspapers, wrote, "Since the beginning of the year five men of my acquaintance and all more or less in the public eye, have died at an early age from the effects of drink. Three were connected with newspapers, one was a brilliant writer, and the fifth was a prominent lawyer. Five out of one's acquaintance in half a year! What is the number all told? You can't check it by official returns. Death certificates never say, 'Cause of death—drink!' "

Plato used to counsel drunkards to look in a mirror, that they might never so disgrace themselves again. The Spartans taught their children temperance by the cruel method of making their slaves drunk, and pointing to the disgusting spectacle.

P. Burnell

Duty

261   Michael Gareth Llewellyn in his book of reminiscences, *Sand in the Glass*, tells this moving story of a sheep-dog. Taffy was the faithful companion of Shon the shepherd, and when his beloved master died Taffy followed the cortège to the little graveyard on the hill. "The funeral dispersed, the sexton filled the shallow grave, but Taffy would not follow Shon's son when he was the last of the family to leave that sad resting-place of his father. "Let him be," said one of the farmers, "he will run home when he is hungry."

But Taffy did not come home. Day and night he lay on that grave and would not be comforted. For a whole week he lay there, pining for his dead master. In the spring Welsh mountain sheep often tend to stray into the villages. From Hafod Olaf to the village was five miles, but that spring, for the first time within living memory, sheep from this farm strayed into the village, and of all places, into the churchyard. Past their late owner's grave they strayed. Taffy knew them at once. He sat up. His professional instincts were aroused. Though tired and exhausted, he shepherded the straying sheep along the road to Hafod Olaf. Safe to the fold there he brought them. Taffy had at last come home. And it was duty that had brought him home. Duty is the pathway to God.

R. Oswald Davies

✳✳

262   General Lee, perhaps the greatest general in America's history, was condemned by a fateful choice to be the leader of a lost cause. While in the early prime of life, before the rains came, he wrote to a student who had failed at West Point: "For I consider the character of no man affected by a want of success, provided he has made an honest effort to succeed." Several years ago it was my privilege to stand on the spot under a tree near Appomattox Court-house where General Lee sat on horse-back that fateful day when the rains came, the torrential rains of unconditional surrender. He said as he sat there, "There is nothing left me to do but to go see General Grant, and I would rather die a thousand deaths." Casting his eye over the bloody fields as the fog was lifting he muttered, as though tempted to a desperate act, "How easily I could be rid of this, and be at rest! I have only to ride along the line and all will be over." But he pulled himself together and said with a deep sigh, "But it is our duty to live."

John W. McKelvey

✳✳

263 Dr. Fairbairn loved to tell his students a fine story of Dr. Dale. The source of it, I believe, was Prof. Dale. The son said: "I never admired my father more than when I heard him preach the Sunday before my sister died. On the Sunday we knew there was no hope, but father preached in the chapel, and never by word or look or tone would the stranger have known what was upon his heart." It would be a poor and easy explanation to say it was acting. The greatest preaching is never acting. What was it then? I think it was such a sense of duty, such a realization of other men's needs, such a sympathy with those who had come with their own thoughts and joys and sorrows, that made the strong, unselfish man think of them before he thought of himself. I can't think he forgot his sorrow, though I can believe he forgot himself, and that the trouble was, in a sense, lost in that general forgetfulness. But where had he learned to do his duty so nobly that day? Surely in that school of experience wherein he had squandered none of life's hard lessons, but had used them, and from them had found the large heart which his people felt, and the manly self-control which his son admired.

George E. Darlaston

Duty to Fellow-Men

264 The lives and experience of the servants of God demonstrate beyond any doubt that the sovereign remedy for apathy is a divine enthusiasm for humanity. This is well illustrated by the story of the French king of old, who, satiated by an endless round of pleasure and frivolity, was at length persuaded by a Christian courtier to visit the hovels of the poor and sick within a stone's throw of his palace. From that day a new light shone in his soul, a new interest blossomed in his life. Man's duty to God can only be rendered in so far as each man is striving to fulfil his duty towards his fellow-man. The two duties are indissolubly linked the one with the other.

Cecil H. S. Willson

Dying

265   They say that when Paganini, the great violinist, lay dying, he turned to
his son, who was sitting and watching him, and whispered the words: "Draw
back the curtains: the moon is shining on the sea!" Yes, and if we will believe
in Christ, and trust Him, it can be like that for us too. Not the end of the
brave story; not the cruel annihilation of all we have longed and hoped for,
not that, but: "Draw back the curtains; the moon is shining on the sea!" and
the way will be open, across the gleaming waters, to life, and light, and joy!

A. E. Gould

Earthquake

266   It is very difficult to realize that Christians today are the lineal successors
of the handful of early pioneers who, it was said, "turned the world upside
down." Dr. Leslie Weatherhead has referred to an invitation once given by
the Archbishop of Canterbury to some clergy to spend a quiet day in considering their problems together. One clergyman wrote back and said, "Your Grace,
in my village we do not need a quiet day, we need an earthquake."

J. Noel Thompson

Easter

267   We read that in the cities of Russia, at the beginning of every Easter
Day, when the sun is just rising, men and women go about the streets greeting
each other with the information, "Christ is risen." Every man knows it. But
all these are illustrations of how a man, when his heart is full of a thing, wants
to tell it to his brethren. He does not care if the brother knows it already. He
goes and tells it to him again. And so, when the truth of Christ's Gospel shall
come so home to each and every one of us that all men shall be filled with the
glad intelligence and tell the story of how men are living in the freedom of
their heavenly Father, it shall not be needful to have a revival of religion.

Phillips Brooks

✳✳

268   There is a word of wisdom in the message which Sir Oliver Lodge stated
that he received from his son, Raymond, who was killed in the first world war;
"Never visit my grave. I am not there." Then there is that striking passage in
the *Confessions* of St. Augustine which is also calculated to comfort the yearn-

ing hearts of mourners. I refer to the conversation which Augustine had with his mother, Monica. At first she was very anxious that her body should be laid in the place which she had prepared for herself by the body of her husband. He was buried in Africa and she was passing away in Italy. But as the end of her life drew near, she ceased to have any anxiety in the matter and said to her son, "Lay this body anywhere, let not the care for that in any way disquiet you." When asked whether she was afraid to leave her body so far from her own city, she replied, "Nothing is far to God." May this too be the affirmation of many a grief-stricken heart—"Nothing is far to God."

                                                                        Philip W. Lilley

                                        ✳✳

269   A man was looking in a shop window at a beautiful picture of the Crucifixion. Standing next to him was a ragged little street urchin who was rapt in contemplation of the picture. Wondering if the boy really understood it, the man asked: "Sonny, what does it mean?" "Doncha know?" he answered. "That there man is Jesus and them others is Roman soldiers, and the woman what's cryin' is His mother, and—they killed Him." The man turned away, and in a moment heard pattering footsteps behind him. The little street arab said breathlessly: "Say, mister, I forgot to tell you, but He rose again!"

                                                                        T. Wilkinson Riddle

Education

270   Christian faith gives moral worth and direction to all human energies. The Duke of Wellington was not wrong when he declared: "If you divorce education from religion you will produce a race of clever devils." Indeed, if detached from religion, education is ultimately perilous, for it creates weapons that destroy when unwisely directed.   W. Erskine Blackburn

Effort

271   Robert Browning tells of a famous Italian musician who, to please a certain public, wrote an inferior jingling work, which he conducted. In his heart he was ashamed of it, but he needed money and the public gave him that. One night, after the audience had cheered his performance, and flung flowers at him, he looked around, beaming, only to see sitting in a private box, the master, Rossini. His eyes fell and his color rose. The mob applauded while the master had condemned the cheap and unworthy work.

                                                                        Frederick C. Spurr

Egoism

272 "The course you propose," said Prince Metternich to Napoleon, "would cost the lives of a hundred thousand men." "A hundred thousand men!" answered Napoleon. "What are a hundred thousand men to me?" Prince Metternich walked to the window, flung it wide open, and said, "Sire, I let all the world know that you express this atrocious sentiment!"

There you have this egoism on a colossal scale. Yet a man need not be a Napoleon to sacrifice the good of hundreds, to sell the fate of his country to the satisfaction of himself, his party, or his class.

F. W. Farrar

Emotions

273 William James says, "Refuse to express a passion and it dies." Power unused is power wasted. Emotion unexpressed will soon become incapable of expression. Love without works is mere sentiment. A Lancashire lad going to his mother and throwing his arms around her neck exclaimed, "Mother, I love you so much I would die for you." The mother replied, "Lad, I don't want you to die for me, but I wish you would come in a little earlier at night time." Love without works is mere sentiment. G. Cadbury once said, "If I want to know whether a man is truly changed in aim, desire and purpose, I do not go to the church of which he is a member, but to the home in which he lives. There I discover whether his professions are turned into realities." The author of *The Roots of Methodism* gives great prominence to these words, "He felt his heart strangely warmed." This is a reference to a great emotional experience in the life of John Wesley. But more wonderful is this fact, that John Wesley kept his heart warm for more than fifty years. He did not allow that warmth to degenerate into grey ashes. He carried the warmth of his Aldersgate experience throughout England, and by his spiritual zeal he helped to save England from the destructive power of a seething revolutionary spirit. He kept his heart warm. He harnessed his emotions.

J. C. Mitchell

Employee

274 I remember once in my life seeing an advertisement that went thus: "A clerk wanted, a free thinker preferred." I do not know what kind of business they did in that office, and I do not know what was the upshot of that advertisement, but I always remember it. It was striking! I had never seen it before, and I have never seen it since; so that it is somewhat uncommon. Now, I say today without the least fear of contradiction, that in the great business world where there is no regard at all paid by masters to any practical religious consideration, nine hundred and ninety-nine out of every thousand of them would decline that advertisement. In literature unbelief is splendid. It is the sign of a noble, intellectual independence. But it is altogether changed when you come into the practical world, for mind, masters would be very shy, as a general rule, indeed very shy, at taking their servants from an infidel club, and taking with those servants loose views on property and marriage, and the rest that, as a general rule, go with atheistic conceptions. No, no, the men of the world know the difference of things, and, as a rule, although a man has no religion himself, I believe few people will question it, he would rather, as a rule, that his servants were true Christians and remained in fellowship with the Christian Church. "Their rock is not as our Rock, our enemies themselves being judges."

W. L. Watkinson

Encouragement

275 Encourage your minister. There are times when the most buoyant sink into despondency, when a great chilly mist creeps over the soul of those who have the largest happiness in the service of God, and they feel as if all their strength was gone. Not very long ago—if I may venture once more to speak of myself—one of these evil moods was upon me; but as I was passing along one of the streets of Birmingham a poor but decently dressed woman, laden with parcels, stopped me and said, "God bless you, Dr. Dale!" Her face was unknown to me. I said, "Thank you. What is your name?" "Never mind my name," was the answer; "but if you only knew how you have made me feel hundreds of times, and what a happy home you have given me! God bless you!" she said. The mist broke, the sunlight came, I breathed the free air of the mountains of God.

R. W. Dale

Enthusiasm

276 Carlyle's last message whispered to a friend was, "Give yourself royally." It is royal giving that Christ asks today—royal giving of Christian personalities. Oh, surely you will from this day forward be enthusiastic in your religion. Some may wish to shine but not to burn. The will o' the wisp shines without burning, but it is a false light. Be not afraid to be enthusiastic. Aristotle said, "No great genius was ever without some mixture of madness." It is not polished

Erasmus, but rough, red-hot Martin Luther that made the Protestant Reformation. Among the last words of Joseph Parker in the City Temple, London, are these, "As long as the Church of God is one of many institutions, she will have her little day. She will die and that will be all; but just as soon as she gets the Spirit of Jesus Christ, until the world thinks she has gone stark mad, then we shall begin to take this old planet for Christ."   Josiah Sibley

⁕⁕

277   When Savonarola preached in the Duomo at Florence the whole city was stirred with a mighty enthusiasm, and the citizens chanted through the streets: "Jesus is King!" It was a brief enthusiasm, you say, because Savonarola was only a single man; but, depend upon it, it is these enthusiasms of corporate life which make the growth and education of men, and where men are so situated that they can never be touched by such enthusiasm the individual natures become proportionally starved and killed.

Robert F. Horton

Environment

278   In one of his books Studdert Kennedy imagines a book of Browning's poems in the hands of different creatures or people. The chimpanzee "sees the book, claws at it, smells it, tries to eat it, tears it in pieces and throws it away." The boy of ten uses it as a stand to put his toy engine on. "The unenlightened stockbroker of forty" uses it to prop up the leg of a wobbly table that he writes his letters on. Finally there is "the one who knows." "He sits rapt and silent, and very happy, his body upon the earth, his soul in another world." The wealth is there, but it must be appropriated. There must for life be traffic with environment.

Hugh W. Theobald

Equality

279   George Bernard Shaw has pointed out that it is ridiculous for a father to tell his son that when he has a pen and paper before him he has equality of opportunity with George Bernard Shaw. Heredity, talent, and opportunity tend to limit our human freedom.

Eternal, Importance of

280   On the triple doorway of a great cathedral in Milan, Italy, there are three inscriptions spanning the archway. Over one is carved a beautiful wreath of roses, and underneath are the words: "All that which pleases is but for a moment." Over another is sculptured a cross, upon which we read: "All that which troubles is but for a moment." But underneath the great central entrance of the main aisle is the inscription: "That only is important which is eternal."

F. B. Meyer

Eternal Life

281   Eternal life does not mean merely long life hereafter. It means something more. Eternal life no doubt would not be a very satisfying thing to think of, if it did not contain within itself the idea of unending life. But to confuse the notion of unending life with the eternal life is to confuse a lower thing with a higher thing. Some of you may know those notable words in the Book of Wisdom which distinguish between life as mere time and life as quality of living. The words are these: "Old age standeth not in length of time; but understanding is grey hairs unto men, and an unspotted life is ripe old age." That is very much the same as George Macdonald wrote when he said: "Life is measured by intensity, not by how-much of a crawling clock." And in this connection you might note that the longevity of a Methuselah is never held up in the Bible as a subject of reasonable envy. There is nothing in merely a prolonged existence more satisfying than in expanding to a great size or growing upwards to a vast stature. With a great many people the problem is not how to get more time, but how to kill the time they have. On the other hand, the Bible ideal of life turns not on quantity, but on quality of life. "This is the life eternal, that they may know Thee, the only true God, and Jesus Christ whom Thou hast sent." And so eternal life is not necessarily a thing of the hereafter. It may, and it should, begin here; and therefore the question for each of us to ask himself in this connection is not, shall I live again after I die? but am I alive today? And that is the question which in order that we may answer we are called into fellowship with Christ.

J. A. F. Gregg

Eternity

282   Years ago a bishop told a story of a missionary and his little son. They left Central Africa for England, being the only survivors of four adults who had gone out to Africa at the call of Christ. With health broken, this missionary and his boy travelled across the African plain in an old broken-down wagon. Then they embarked for England. After a few hours on the sea they endured a terrible storm. The waves and the wind combined to make the noise as of an earthquake and the boat trembled from stem to stern. During a lull in the storm, the missionary comforted the cold and frightened child. Presently the lad said to his father, "Father, when shall we have a home that will not shake?"

William Walton

**

283   When Raphael was dead the last picture which he had painted was the Transfiguration, and they carried it at the head of the procession at his burial. That picture said nothing. It did nothing. It returned from his tomb, and was hung upon the wall. And in its muteness, its inactivity, simply because it was full of the majesty and beauty of the Saviour, that picture has thrown a regent influence out. Dead though it be, and painted on canvas, it has penetrated every generous soul. It has gone from nation to nation; for beauty speaks in every language. Its silence has been more than all the eloquence of the Forum; and the joy and peace that it has given, what tongue can tell? God knows, and I could form some slight conception of it as now and then I have glanced at the work of some great artist that has lifted me out of time, and into the real life of eternity.

F. R. Barry

Evangelism

284   There is a story told of a man who was traveling the country selling bacon-slicing machines. Going into a shop in a small country village, he placed his sample on the counter, and gave the grocer a demonstration.

"Isn't it a wonderful machine?" he asked.

"Yes, it is."

"It would be a marvellous investment, don't you think?"

"Yes."

"And a great time-saver?"

"Yes."

"Don't you think every grocer ought to have one?"

"Yes."

"You realize what an advantage it would be both to yourself and your customer if you had one?"

"Yes."

"Well, why don't you buy it?"

"Well," said the grocer, "why don't you ask me to?"

Now, isn't it just there that so much of our Christian preaching and witness misses the mark? We talk, and describe, and illustrate and philosophize, but how often do we drive home that direct, personal challenge, "What think ye of Christ?" "Are you for us or against us?" If we are truly to prepare the way of the Lord, there must be this direct, determined, purposeful dynamic about all our Christian living, service and witness.

John B. Nettleship

✳✳

285   "I have never heard anyone preach like you," said a gay and fashionable woman to the pastor of one of the New York churches. "You preach as if you cared for my soul as my mother used to do, and I must stop my gay life or stop coming here." Then when the pastor leads the church must follow. Dr. Van Dyke has truly said: "There is needed not only a pastor who will draw but a Church that will hold." Another great American divine has said: "Only a saving Church is worth saving. And only a saving Church will be saved." When the elder Beecher was preaching in Park Street, Boston, some one asked him why it was that his church was so splendidly successful. "Why," said he, "I preach on Sabbath, and then I have four hundred and fifty members who go out on Monday to preach the same Gospel every week." If a man has the real Gospel he will want to preach it. And if a man thinks he has religion and has no impulse to give it to others, he has a false brand and needs to get it changed.

Dr. Dawson tells of a prisoner condemned to be hung. A minister went to see him, and when he told him the good news of salvation, the prisoner said to him, "Do you believe that?" "Believe it? Yes," replied the minister. "Well," said the criminal, "if I believed that I would go across England on my hands and knees, on broken glass, if I could bring the news to any needy heart." That is what a criminal said. What are we saying? What are we doing? We know the thought of God. We know the heart of Christ. We know the needs of the world.

George Ernest Raitt

✳✳

286   I remember hearing about a minister in the north who one evening found one man in his parish lying drunk by the wayside. He remonstrated with him and the man asked, "What can I do?" The minister replied, "Come to the Church"; and then came the shrewd statement, "Do the sheep look for the shepherd?" The first practical note is that of seeking them.

James Marshall

✳✳

287   George Macleod tells us a Clydeside near-Communist once said to him:
"You folk have got it; if only you knew that you had it, and if only you knew
how to begin to say it."

R. Wragge Morley

Evil

288   In his apology *On Being No Longer a Rationalist*, Dr. C. E. Joad has
described how he was led to take, as he puts it, "my first downward step on the
slippery slope that leads to heaven." The war came, he writes, and "for the
first time in my life the existence of evil made its impact upon me as a positive
and obtrusive fact. All my life it had been staring me in the face; now it hit
me in the face. . . . I now found myself quite unable to write off what I had
better call man's 'sinfulness,' and have done with it, as a mere by-product of
circumstance." Is such an experience unique?

"If a way to the Better there be, it exacts a full look at the Worst." More than
the "positive and obtrusive fact" of evil stares us in the face. Nietzsche has a
deep saying that modern man can rightly be accused of "blunting the edge of
all Christian terminology." How otherwise can we explain that "Christ made
too real becomes the unreal Christ"? Have we not here One who from His
Cross should stir up the labyrinthine depths of the human soul? Is it strange
that here Nietzsche should be a better guide than those who use the name of
Christ to humanize the wheels of earthly circumstance? "Never, anywhere,"
he writes of "God on the Cross," "has there been seen a like audacity in
making an inversion, never anything so frightful, so question provoking, so
question deserving as this formula; it means the inversion of all the values
of antiquity."

A. B. Lavelle

Evil, Overcoming

289   A conceited young fellow wants to paint the portrait of his mother.
With ill-prepared canvas, and with much conceit, he makes a portrait that he
thinks to be wonderfully like her. He is very proud of it. He sets it on the
table of his studio. Conceive that someone, an artist rare, or one following the
photographer's art, shall have, with exquisite pains, really brought out the
likeness of the mother, so that everyone who sees it thinks at first that it is
she herself. He says not a word, but goes and puts it by the side of the other,
and leaves. The young man comes back. He is so happy. He thinks he is Titian,
or his grandson, and he pictures in his mind what he will become when he gets

a little more cultivation. On going into his studio he looks—and throws the picture he has painted under the table. There has not been a word said to him but there was the exquisite likeness of his mother put beside his, and his looked so hateful that he would not have anything to do with it.

By the side of a bad deed put a beautiful deed. By the side of a wrong put the characteristic right. Leave them alone. They will fight with each other, and the beautiful and the good will overcome the evil. Overcome evil with good.

Henry Ward Beecher

Evil, Return for

290   In the early days of the Society of Friends, a Quaker was riding one day across a lonely moor when he heard behind him the sound of a horse's hoofs. Another moment, and a highwayman drew up beside him, held a pistol to his head, and demanded his money or his life. Without a word, the Quaker took out his purse and handed it over. "That's a fine beast," said the highwayman, looking at the other's horse. "Get down!" Without a word, the Quaker dismounted and the robber got up in his place. He was turning the horses' heads to ride away, when the Quaker stepped in his path, seized the horse's bridle and began to address the rider. How could he, a man made in the image of God, be content with this life of violence and crime; let him be warned and repent while there yet was time. In a flash the pistol was out again and pointed at the speaker's head. "You coward," hissed the highwayman, "you let me take your money and your horse without lifting a finger, and now you want to preach to me! Another word and I shoot you where you stand!" The Quaker smiled and looked without flinching down the gleaming barrel. "Friend," he said quietly, "I would not risk my life to save either purse or horse but I would gladly lay it down now if by so doing I could save you!" The man's hand dropped with the pistol in it, he sprang off the horse, flung the purse to the ground with the words: "If that's the kind of man you are, I will take nothing from you," and rode away.

E. L. Allen

Experience

291   There lived in Scotland about a century ago a man of saintly character, Thomas Erskine, minister of the parish of Linlathen. "All religion," he would affirm when speaking of God and our mode of addressing Him, "is in the change from He to Thou. It is a mere abstraction as long as it is He: Only with the Thou we know God." His biographer tells how one day, meeting a

shepherd on the hills, in a tone which combined in an extraordinary fashion sweetness and authority, Erskine put the unlooked for question, "Do you know the Father?" The shepherd, with all the native reserve of the Scot, was completely taken aback and answered nothing. But something about the question and about the personality of the questioner made so deep and abiding an impression that he could not evade the issue with which he was there and then confronted. Meeting Erskine many years after, he recognized him at once and said, "I know the Father now."

Robert James McCracken

Eyes, New

292   When Christ comes into a soul's life He shows him many things he had not seen before. Everything seems transfigured with new meaning. He is like the lad of whom the Bishop of London told. He had fallen in love with a young woman, and had been accepted by her. As he walked along one day with a friend, he exclaimed: "And I used to think Stepney an ugly place." The love that filled his heart had opened his eyes to see beauty in even the most sordid part of a great city. A Christian sees with new eyes. His vision, which heretofore had been focused upon himself, is now turned out upon others.

Stuart Nye Hutchison

Failure

293   Some years ago Sir Arthur Quiller-Couch, the distinguished writer and man of letters, was presiding at a meeting of the Cornishmen's Society in London. During the evening he told a very interesting personal reminiscence. "Just on forty years ago," he said, "at a certain university I went in for an examination and before going into the examination hall I bought a cork penholder which cost the modest sum of 1½ d. When the results came out I discovered that I had not done too well. So I went for my 1½ d. penholder and holding it in my hand and looking straight at it I said, 'Now, my boy, you and I have somehow or other to redeem this.' With that penholder I have written every one of my books and I have it here for my notes tonight."

A. Stanley Hill

✷✷

294   Huss died at the stake of Constance. Did he fail? He paved the way for Luther. Tyndale, the translator of the Bible, was strangled at Vilvorde, and

then burned, and at the stake he prayed, "O Lord, open the King of England's eyes!" Did he fail? The very next year Henry VIII had issued his order that the Bible should be published through all England and placed in every church for the free use of the people. Ah, my friends, do not, whatever happens to you, be discouraged; never give up work, never despair. There is no such thing as failure to the sons and servants of God.   F. W. Farrar

Faith

295 In the biography of Hudson Taylor there is a revealing passage. In a letter written to a friend, and dated November 18, 1870, Taylor tells this story. He had been reading in his New Testament in the original Greek. He was reading the Gospel according to St. Mark, when, suddenly and strangely, his attention was arrested by a short sentence of three brief words. He turned to his King James edition of the English New Testament and read the familiar words, "Have faith in God," but in the Greek original there was a thought, an insight, which the authorized version had failed to render. For this is how Taylor read it: "Hold to the faithfulness of God." The discovery, he said, lit up many of the dark places of his own thinking. It gave him a big lift. And so it should; for such is the basis of true faith.   Hobart D. McKeehan

✳✳

296 Your faith is a vote. My faith in Christ is a vote for Him. When I say I believe in God I do not mean that I have absolute mathematical demonstration that a Being, having the qualities attributed to God, exists. I do not know; I would require to be omniscient in order to be quite sure of that on the intellectual plane. But you never can be certain of anything that you believe. That is why we speak of dead certainties. All certainties are dead. I don't believe a man ever lost his faith, but many a man has lost his certainties and has been the better for it. Your faith is your vote.   John A. Hutton

✳✳

297 Mr. Gladstone all his life has been so brave and outspoken a Christian that there is no doubt as to his creed. In an interview which he had with Mr. Stead—the last important interview, I believe, he ever had with Mr. Stead—the conversation was closed by the following question, which Mr. Stead addressed to the veteran statesman: "What do you regard as the greatest hope for the future of the human race?" Mr. Gladstone hesitated a moment, gathered himself together, and then said deliberately, "I should say we must look for that to the maintenance of faith in the invisible. That is the great hope of the future. It is the mainstay of civilization, and by that I mean a living faith in a personal God. After sixty years of public life I hold more strongly than ever to this conviction, deepened and strengthened by long experience, of the reality and the nearness and the personality of God." In front of his bed where he died, always before him, there was an illuminated text with these words, "Thou wilt keep him in perfect peace whose mind is stayed on Thee." That is the secret of his peaceful and triumphant death. He recently wrote to a young American inquirer the following words: "All I write and all I think and all I hope is based upon the divinity of our Lord, the one central hope of our poor wayward race."   Hugh Price Hughes

✳✳

298   The well-worn story of the French soldier who obtained his captaincy by just believing the Emperor's word is a fine illustration of the "faith" necessary for salvation. The Emperor's horse had bolted with him. An ordinary soldier stepped from the ranks, seized its bridle and stopped it. "Thanks, captain," said the Emperor to him. "Of which regiment, sire?" was the soldier's prompt question. "Of my Guards," came the reply. And we read that the soldier with nothing but the word of the Emperor as guarantee, at once made his way into a group of officers, confident of his right to the privileges belonging to the rank of captain, because the Emperor had called him by that title. And surely you and I ought to believe the Word of our God concerning us.

Ernest E. Newell

✳✳

299   Not long ago I read a description of two very ancient charts, dating back to the time of Henry V's navigators. With all their brawn and stamina those intrepid men had scarcely shaken themselves free of the pitiful superstitions which characterized their age. This fact their handiwork revealed; for on those charts there were vast unexplored wastes over which the geographers had written the weird legends, "Here be dragons," "Here be demons," "Here be sirens." But the second of those documents had passed through the hands of that valiant master-mariner and man of God, Sir John Franklin. The mystery of those unknown regions was no clearer to him than to his fellow-navigators; there was an entire hemisphere into which he had never penetrated. But Franklin knew the experience of the psalmist, and, scoring out those superstitious comments, he had boldly written in their place, "Here is God."

Edward Beal

✳✳

300   The Dutch have a legend about a spider. It was a respectable, well-behaved spider, and it lived high up under the rafters of a barn. One day, looking down into the barn, it said to itself, "I wonder what things are like down there," and, being quite adventurous, it dropped on the end of its long, slender, strong thread until it came to rest on a beam many feet below. It liked the look of its new surroundings, so it spread its web and set up home. There it lived as the long days went by. It caught flies and grew fat and prosperous. Then, one day long after, it noticed the long, slender, strong thread running up into the darkness high above. It was puzzled, and said, "I wonder what that's for. It serves no purpose that I can see. I can do without it." So it broke it: and its little home and its little world collapsed.

R. W. Hugh Jones

✳✳

301   G. K. Chesterton has an amusing note on the Unitarian church that became an Ethical Society in order to get the services of a certain Dr. Stanton Coit. "God Almighty was dropped out of the whole business, as a concession to Dr. Stanton Coit. It generally felt, apparently, that it would be really rather churlish not to meet him on a little thing like that." A little later the Ethical Society diminished rather sadly in numbers: Dr. Stanton Coit was losing his grip and a lot of his followers had "gone off to listen to Maude Royden." Chesterton sums up, not unfairly, as follows: "So that the truly astonishing history of this school of thought, if we regard it as a school of thought, was as follows. They began by believing in the Creation but not in the Incarnation. For the sake of Dr. Coit they ceased to believe in the Creation. And for the sake of Miss Royden they agreed to believe in the Creation and the Incarnation as well. The truth of the matter is, I imagine, that these particular people never did believe or disbelieve in anything. They liked to go and hear stimulating lecturers."

James MacKay

Faith, Child-like

302   I remember a little lad about two years old who came one day to his father in the garden with a dead bird in his hand and with eyes full of tenderness and utter confidence he looked up into his father's face and said, "Mend it, daddy!" Have we got in our view of God that child's expectancy, that utter confidence in God's power to mend all broken things—including ourselves? It is that we want to get back to. He never dreamed his father would not want to do it; it seemed so obvious that a love like his own would be in his father's

heart. He had the faith that the biggest thing in his own little heart would be at the center of his universe. He never dreamed that his father could not do it. And Jesus said: "Of such is the kingdom of heaven."

James Reid

Faith in God

303   Mr. Eric Fenby, in his book on Delius, says: "If Delius had understood contemplation in this traditional and Dionysian sense [he refers to the contemplation of Christian mystics], what a musician we should have had! He would have been unquestionably the greatest composer of his generation, and the most inspiring composer who ever put pen to paper. With what serenity he sang of the loveliness that is fast passing away before our eyes, of creaturely happiness shortlived, never more to return. But we need to forget the misery of this our exile, and be made mindful of the happiness which is our destiny. With what serenity would he have sung had he beheld 'God in all things, without distinction, in a simple setting, in the divine brightness'! He had no faith in God, no faith in his fellow-men, only a proud and simple faith in himself. All through his self-guided life he was blind to what he was doing, blind in the highest sense of the word, directing his untiring energy to the worship of Pure Beauty as a supreme end in itself, instead of to that end of ends which is God." For my part, though others will disagree, I must range myself alongside Mr. Fenby, for no experience can truly satisfy me if it shuts God out. We cannot, therefore, remain in the loft with the plotters of Beauty.

O. J. Beard

Faith, Meaning of

304   Often when we speak of faith we mean some form of wishful thinking, a kind of belief that we shall muddle through, like Julian Huxley's "My final belief is in life." But life is in Hitler and Huxley, in lions and rats, in horses and toads. What can faith in life mean? But "to have Christian faith," as Karl Barth says, "means to live as a man who is faced by Jesus Christ." And that can mean the making of all things new.

James MacKay

Faith, Path to

305   George Matheson of Innellan tells us: "At one time, with a great thrill of horror, I found myself an absolute atheist. After being ordained at Innellan,

I believed nothing: neither God nor immortality. I tendered my resignation to the Presbytery, but to their honour they would not accept it, even though a Highland Presbytery. They said I was a young man, and would change. I have changed." And Matheson lived through the darkness and was able to write these unforgettable words:

> O Light that followest all my way.
>   I yield my flickering torch to Thee;
> My heart restores its borrowed ray.
>   That in thy sunshine's blaze its day
>   May brighter, fairer be.

John A. McFadden

Faith, Prime Need

306   It is difficult to see any end to our troubles unless mankind can recover its sense of the sacred. "The fear of the Lord is the beginning of wisdom." This is borne out by the sayings of many great thinkers. For instance, Dr. C. G. Jung, one of the greatest living psychologists, says that "modern man, having put material security, general welfare, and humaneness in place of faith in a most high Father, finds that all these have now gone by the board."

H. W. Theobald

Faith, Seeking

307   Negley Farson in one of his books tells how he, in company with other journalists, once visited a conference of young men. They were divided into groups to discuss such questions as "Do you believe in the omnipotence of God?" At the end of the day the score of each group was chalked on a blackboard by a professor who was a picture of collegiate efficiency. It seemed even to the onlookers that he was analyzing God with a piece of chalk and a slide-rule. In the middle of all this a wounded ex-officer sprang to his feet and cried, "Stop! This is hideous. You must not talk of God like this. This is blasphemy. The way to Christ is not through gymnasiums and shower-baths. No! No! I tell you. You must read the Bible—the words of Christ Himself. Oh God!" He sank down as though ashamed of the scene he had made. Afterwards that group of sceptical journalists admitted to one another that they had each wanted to walk over and put an arm around that man in whose figure they saw a hunger and thirst for a real faith.

Graham W. Hughes

Faithfulness

308   Some years ago a humble funeral procession entered the churchyard of
the Old Grey Friars, at Edinburgh, and the chief mourner who followed the
hearse was the dead man's dog. After the funeral was over all the poor man's
human friends went home; but the dog would not leave his master's grave.
Day after day people tried in vain to lure it away; but it would not leave the
spot. They fed it there; and there, by its master's grave, for fourteen years the
dog lived, and died in the year 1878; and on the spot a noble lady has raised
a little monument, which you may still see as the monument which marks
the burial place of "Bobby, the Faithful Dog."   F. W. Farrar

Faithfulness to Duty

309   That was the splendid example set by St. Ambrose. Theodocius was a
great, and in many respects a good, Emperor; but in a fierce outburst of passion
he had led his soldiers into the amphitheatre of Thessalonica, and had slain
some five thousand or six thousand human beings, the innocent no less than
the guilty, in indiscriminate massacre. Courtiers said nothing; the world said
nothing; civil rulers said nothing; then it was that St. Ambrose stood forth
like the incarnate conscience of mankind. For eight months he excluded the
Emperor from the cathedral, and when he came at Christmas-tide to the
Communion he met him at the door, and, in spite of purple and diadem and
praetorian guards, he forbade him to enter till he had laid aside the insignia of a
guilty royalty, and, prostrate, with tears, upon the pavement, had performed a
penance as public as his crime. You all know Rubens's splendid picture of the
scene in which St. Ambrose, in golden cope and jewelled mitre, is almost
as magnificent as Theodocius himself. The reality was very different. Ambrose
was not a man to care for such gilded gewgaws as copes and mitres—mitres
were not heard of until centuries later—but, for all that, Ambrose, in his simple
dress and his humble poverty, was brave enough to tell the truth.

F. W. Farrar

Family

310   I remember a Chinese Christian woman telling me that in her judgement the most important thing that our Lord ever said was that "A man who
married should 'leave his father and mother and cleave to his wife.'" This
saying is a quotation from the Book of Genesis (2:24), but our Lord gave it a
new depth and urgency by His recalling and repeating it. Somewhat puzzled,

I considered for a while, and then asked the woman why she thought it such a tremendously important saying. She looked at me with shining eyes (and I shall never forget the expression on her face), saying, "Don't you see that in these words our Lord struck at the very heart of the worst tyranny in the world?" And in a flash I realized the often appalling hardship of home life in that great Eastern country, especially though not solely for the women. It is the humanity and sanity of Christian teaching that constantly strikes one when travelling in countries uninfluenced or practically uninfluenced by it.

Maude Royden Shaw

Fatherhood

311   I saw once, years ago, in an Assize Court, a scene that can never be erased from the memory. A public school boy, of good family, was arraigned on a criminal charge. He had fallen into bad society, and inflicted sorrow on his old home. Without retiring the jury found him guilty. Asked the usual question, "Have you anything to say why sentence should not be passed upon you?" the young fellow hung his head. At that moment a white-haired man rose and said, "I am his father. May I be allowed to stand in the dock with him while sentence is passed?" Permission was given . . . the father who wouldn't even then despair of his son. I knew then a little of what God felt.

Frederick C. Spurr

Fatherhood of God

312   Mr. Paton in his last book, *A Faith for the World,* tells a story of a woman in India who was being taught the Lord's Prayer. She got as far as the invocation "Our Father . . .," and then she said to the missionary who was teaching her, "Is that true?" He assured her that it was. Then she said, "I don't think I need to learn any more." That word "Father" changed everything for her. It brought her into a world where hate and fear were banished, and love was all in all, and that outlook changed everything. Let us get fresh hold of it—this is the basic fact about the world in which we live, whether people realize it or not. The world is God's and He is the Father. This day is a day of good tidings.

James Reid

Fear

313   You remember well the story of the Swiss martyr who was tied to the stake, and the faggots were about him, and one who had to carry out the

execution of his sentence said he felt sorry he had to burn him; and he said, "Sir, I know it is not you, it is the other men who are mine enemies; but would you come here and put your ear close against my heart: hear how it beats. There," said he, "am I not more calm than you are?" And he that had to put him to death confessed that he it was whose heart was fluttering; but the child of God, even between the jaws of death, was calm and still, and so will God keep you in perfect peace, if you put your trust in Him, and do not turn aside to crooked ways; for if you do, He will lead you forth with the workers of iniquity.   C. H. Spurgeon

✶✶

314   Mrs. St. John Ervine has an unforgettable character portrait of a Mr. Timms, a clerk in a large London office. "The life of Mr. Timms revolved continually around the thought: Supposing that one day he should be unable to work, what should become of him? He would awaken at night, crying out in fear because of some horrible dream in which he saw himself dismissed from the service of his employers for one reason or another. The same terror was his evil genius by day. So as the years passed the despotism of this fear took heavy toll of the best possibilities of his life. Something inside of him would urge the quest of adventures. 'Do something to show that you are alive,' it would say, and the fear of endangering his position by some time yielding to one of these moods added another to his many terrors. He thought of marriage, 'and the thing inside' kept saying, 'Risk it, man, risk it!' But the thought of the possibility of getting sick and out of employment with a wife and perhaps a family to support, drove him back to the dreariness of his dingy bed-sitting-room. Finally, the inevitable comes; he loses his position and his savings rapidly dwindle. Sickness overtakes him and the doctor's verdict is that he has only a short time to live. The doctor is amazed at the calm which the announcement brings. 'Thank God,' said Mr. Timms to himself. 'I am safe now.' In three months he was dead." It is a pathetic picture of a man vanquished in his fight against fear.   David A. MacLennan

✶✶

315   The other evening, reading a book, I came upon a passage which, in the light of current events, makes for melancholy reflection. It was a book written in 1902 by George Coe, and this, with special reference to the achievements of science, is what he was affirming: "Men have ceased to be afraid. We have our own unsolved problems, as our fathers did, but they awaken little mystic presentiment, and no fear. We do not catch our breath at the thought of what may be, but boldly take to pieces every new phenomenon certain in advance

that it harbours no hobgoblins." The atomic bomb has put an end to all such sentiments. Two world wars in twenty-five years, with a third on the near horizon, have awakened the profoundest misgiving and apprehension. Everywhere there are people who are fretful, nervous, depressed, irritable, sleepless, physically under par, and the basic reason is because they are the victims of fear.

Robert James McCracken

✳✳

316   An amusing story is told of a member of a Bomb Demolition Squad who, having entered the hole already dug, was about to place the lifting tackle around a 1,000 lb. bomb, when he suddenly called to his comrades, "Pull me out quick." Upon his reaching the top they asked anxiously, "What's up? Is it about to go off?" "I don't know about that," he said. "There's a rat down here, and I can't bear rats." He wasn't afraid of the bomb, but he was nervous of a rat.

A. E. Bristow

Fear and Christ

317   Jesus came into a world of fear. He brought the light of the love of God into the darkness. "Fear not, little flock." Today, as nineteen centuries ago, that power is still operative. Writes Dr. Schweitzer from Africa: "Redemption through Jesus is experienced by him [the Negro] as a twofold liberation: his view of the world is purged of the previously dominant element of fear, and it becomes ethical instead of unethical." On the edge of the primeval forest where Dr. Schweitzer reproduces the cures of the Great Physician, or in the crowded ways of men where we live, what think you, can we dispense with that kind of religion?

David A. MacLennan

Fear in Advent Story

318   There is a curious lack of emphasis whenever the Advent Story is told. One hears of the shepherds, the star, the magi, and the manger—all set in so beautiful and peaceful a setting that the idea of terror seems ruled out! Yet although this Child of Bethlehem was destined to be the Prince of Peace, the first emotion aroused by the proclamation of His Advent was that of fear.

The shepherds of these times usually led quiet and lonely lives. They were very largely unaffected by the stirring events of the outside world: so that it is not a very remarkable thing, on the face of it, that as they were watching their flocks during the long night of the winter solstice they were startled by a sudden apparition, a bright light and angel voices in the sky. Little wonder surely that they were "sore afraid"! This, however, would hardly account for the emphatic expression: "they feared with a great fear." The first effect of the Advent news was then that those who heard it "were," as Moffatt puts it, "terribly afraid."

Moreover, there was a deeper and more reasoned fear in the heart of another. This time it is a king. "When Herod the king heard it, he was troubled." Was there ever in history a more amazing thing than this? A despotic king trembling because of the birth of an unknown child. Wickedness, however, always trembles in the presence of righteousness.

Nor was this fear confined to the king alone. "All Jerusalem [was troubled] with him." The Jews trembled because of what the fear of the king might bring forth; they had good cause, for we now know that the massacre of the Innocents was the outcome.

F. W. Aveling

Fear of God

319   The real trouble running through masses and classes alike, which is collective only because it is personal, is that crowds of people have ceased to believe that they have anything more vital to save than their own skin. Dr. Dale knew what he meant when in a bitter moment he said, "Nobody is afraid of God now." I am not sure whether, in what is called a religious assembly, a man today does not speak somewhat with a foreign accent who maintains that the problem of sin, of personal guilt and failure, is the first and worst and nearest of all problems for each man of us and for society.

Ambrose Shepherd

Fellowship

320   You remember the relationships between Emerson and Carlyle, those two great thinkers, so different in some ways, so similar in others, who lived their lives with the Atlantic rolling between them, and met, if I remember rightly, only once. The biographer of one of them was there when the long-anticipated meeting between the two men, who had admired one another at a distance for years, took place in Carlyle's home. According to his story they sat the whole evening one on each side of the fire-place and never said a word. When it was time for Emerson to go Carlyle conducted him to the door and parted from him with these words, "Aye, mon, we've had a grand time!" How odd that

sounds to those of us whose fellowship depends upon chatter. How silly it seems to those of us who feel how much we would like to have said, how much we would have tried to put into an hour of what we had thought in common through the years. Oh, but their fellowship was deeper than that. They lived with the Atlantic between them, but they could dispense with words, mind to mind, heart to heart, because they really knew one another.

W. E. Sangster

**

321 I have often told the story of a girl who met a perplexing problem in life. She was a packer in a warehouse and was asked to put one faulty pair of stockings in each packet of twenty. Her conscience was troubled, and she told her friends in the Bible Class that she did not feel that, as a Christian, she could do it. But she had a widowed mother solely dependent on her. This group prayed with her, and then told her that if she felt that her present work was contrary to the will of Christ, she should refuse to do it, and then come to them and tell them what had happened. She was at once dismissed, and then her friends said: "Do not tell your mother; but we will all share so that you still take home the same amount of money each week until you get a new job."

Now, is that characteristic of Christian fellowship, or is it not? If so, what are we doing about it? I think that a man who is up against some moral problem in business or any other part of his life ought to be able to feel that he can put that problem before friends in his own church, knowing that they will pray with him, seek the guidance of God on it, and thus be spiritually strengthened. I think that is good New Testament teaching. In this fellowship we ought to be able to identify ourselves with the needs and sufferings of our brethren. And if a brother falls we ought not to point the finger of scorn at him and spread tittle-tattle, but to redeem him from his failure and build him up in love.

S. Maurice Watts

Fidelity, Compensations of

322 Bernard Shaw in *The Showing Up of Blanco Posnet* drives home a lesson. Posnet, the thief of horses, goes soft when a mother's plea for him to fetch a doctor for her sick child is reinforced by the touch of baby fingers round his neck, and he exclaims, "Gosh, when I think I might have been safe and fifty miles away now with that horse; and here I am waiting to be hung and filled with lead! What came to me? He means to win the deal and you can't stop Him." There are amazing compensations, happiness too deep to be expressed, in taking the high road, but it is a hazardous journey, and that the Master knew right well, and when we enter a treacherous patch of the road we do well to remember He too walked that way.

R. Morton Stanley

Forgiveness

323   Moffat Gautry tells the story of an old saint who lay dying in an Oxford village. For over eighty years she had been travelling to the Celestial City, and now at the last her face grew bright with the prospect of heaven's approaching glory. An Anglo-Catholic priest, under the entire misapprehension that none of his parishioners could find access to the city unless he unlocked the gate, paid her a visit. "Madam," he said, "I have come to grant you absolution," and she, in her simplicity not knowing the meaning of the word, inquired, "What is that?" "I have come to forgive your sins," was the reply. "May I look into your hands?" she said. Gazing for a moment into the hands of the priest, she turned and looked him squarely in the face, and said, "Sir! You are an impostor." "Impostor!" the scandalized cleric protested. "Yes, sir, an impostor. The man who forgives my sins has a nail-print in His palm." The wonder of those nail-print hands was very real to the old saint.

J. W. Price

✳✳

324   In Victor Whitechurch's forbidding book, *The Locum Tenens*, we have an unforgettable refusal of forgiveness. It is the tale of a husband deeply wronged by his wife, whom he passionately loved. He visits her quite accidentally after an absence of more than twenty years and finds her dying. She craves for forgiveness. "Henry," she said, "I am dying." The husband raised his head almost imperceptibly, but that was all the movement he made. "You . . . you . . . you loved me once," she said, chokingly. He stood unmoved and aloof from her who sought what only he could give her—forgiveness. "It is because I am dying. I ask, I suppose, too hard a thing. You cannot, oh, you cannot forgive!" He straightened himself, but remained silent. He did not look down at her again or so much as turn his head. He kept it averted from her as he quickly crossed the sick-room, opened the door and vanished. Poor soul, she watched him to the last, her eyes a-starting from her head, her hands clutching each other convulsively; but he had gone never to return. What an answer to such an impassioned appeal, an appeal that proved to be love's last!

J. G. McKenzie

✳✳

325   The story is told that once, as a young man, Charles Spurgeon was preaching about the martyr Stephen. His sermon was suddenly interrupted by a question from an unbeliever, who shouted: "What did God do to help Stephen when he was being stoned to death?" That was a shrewd thrust. What did God do? He did not turn the stones aside. He did not carry Stephen away to safety. Spurgeon had an answer, indeed THE answer, ready. He replied, "God enabled Stephen to pray, 'Lord, lay not this sin to their charge.'" God delivered Stephen in his distress by giving him grace to forgive and to die in glowing, joyful faith.   H. W. Theobald

✳✳

326   There was a man in Japan in 1918—Ishii by name—who had committed almost every crime known to men: murders, some of them of the most brutal kind, robberies and assaults of all kinds, made up the awful sum of his record; if ever there were a hardened and hopeless criminal here was one. Yet some one saw beyond the surface appearance to the reality that was there; and while he was in prison, awaiting his trial for the murder to which he had confessed, two frail women, English missionaries, visited that man, sent him a New Testament, and told him of Christ. And as he sat in his lonely cell, he was suddenly smitten to the heart as he read the story of the Crucifixion, and in particular the prayer from the Cross, "Father, forgive them, they know not what they do." There is no other way adequate to describe what happened than to say that he was completely and utterly transformed. The warders and the Governor, Mr. Shirosuke Arima, and several other people who came into contact with him in prison were amazed at the real saintliness of that man's life. He wrote the story of his life—though he was an uneducated man—and it has been translated into English. When some one with very great influence in the highest quarters in Tokyo asked him if he would like to be given a fresh chance, he insisted that he ought to accept the responsibility that came to him on account of his crimes and of the laws of the land, and declared that his only desire now was to be with God, believing that his soul would enter into the rest of pardon. After he was executed on August 17, 1918, the Buddhist chaplain who was with him told the story of his end thus: "Many who die on the scaffold face death with a firm resolution to win a good name for themselves at the end. But Ishii's fortitude was far different from that. He had not the slightest appearance of desiring to win a good name or of merely enduring the inevitable. With humility and great earnestness he seemed to see nothing but the glory of the heavenly world to which he was returning when he had cast off the heavy load of his sins; just as one turns with great longing to his own native home. Among the officials who stood by and saw the clear colour of his face and the courage with which he bore himself,

there was no one but involuntarily paid him respect and honour. On the very scaffold, when in a moment his life was to disappear like a dewdrop, he uttered those last words of his: 'My soul, purified, today returns to the City of God.'"

Barnard R. H. Spaull

✳✳

327   In one of his books the late President Hyde wrote of a physician whom he knew in our American Andover. As a youth, Hyde sought this physician's counsel again and again, and grew to look upon him as a master. The physician had a wild son, who one morning was found dead on a railway track. Apparently he had been killed by an on-coming engine. The doctor, being a scientific man, did not take appearances for facts, and examined his son's body. On the throat he found marks of hard-pressed fingers. He then knew that the boy had been strangled, and that the body had been thrown upon the track to hide the crime. A day or two later he met in the street a man whom he looked through and through. That night the man, knowing that he was discovered, came to the doctor's office. He began to confess. The doctor stopped him. "I know all about it," he said; "you needn't say another word." "Then," said the wretched man, "what are you going to do about it?" "Only one thing," answered the doctor: "I ask you to promise me that for the rest of your life you will say every day, from your heart, the Lord's Prayer." The man was amazed. He went out of the doctor's office that night a redeemed, because a forgiven, man.

Charles Lewis Slattery

✳✳

328   There is a novel by a Norwegian author, Johann Bojer, called *The Great Hunger*. It tells of a poor Norwegian lad, Peer Holm, who, by dint of hard labour, became a great engineer, and made a huge fortune in Africa. He was an orphan and, during the years of struggle, lived with his little sister. She fell suddenly ill and died, and though he advanced rapidly from one position to another there remained a great unsatisfied hunger in his soul. After his great success in Africa he returns to his native land, marries, and settles down. But soon his speculations begin to go wrong and in time every penny of his fortune vanishes. After much poverty and many wanderings he is reduced to being a kind of local blacksmith in a poor village; but the brazier, already settled there, is afraid that the newcomer may snatch his daily bread from him. Both Peer and the brazier are on the last confines of poverty, and there is not a living for two in the village, so they become bitter enemies. Amid all his bitterness and despair Peer has one hope and comfort, his wife Merle, and his little daughter Asta. The brazier and he quarrel bitterly; the storm passes, and then the whirlwind comes. Peer tells it in his own words: "A couple of days later I was standing at the forge, when I heard a shriek from my wife. I rushed out—what could be the matter? Merle was down by the fence already and all at once I saw what it was—there was Asta lying on the ground under the body of a great beast, the brazier's dog.

"And then? Well, Merle tells me it was I that tore the thing away from the little bundle of clothes beneath it, and carried our little girl home. A doctor is often a good refuge in trouble, but though he may sew up a ragged tear in a child's throat it does not follow that it will help much. There was a mother, though, that would not let him go—that cried and prayed and clung about him, begging him to try once more if nothing could be done. And when at last he was gone, she was always for going after him again, and grovelled on the floor, and tore her hair—could not, would not believe what she knew was true."

So all night mother and father sat in silence, terribly alone, by the bed of a slaughtered child. There was no sound save an occasional sob from the heart-broken mother. It seemed as though they sat alone in a dead world, as though they had been actors in a drama upon a brilliantly lit stage and then the lights had suddenly gone out, and they were alone in the darkness with no audience, no fellow-actors, and no director. In bitterness of soul the father explored to the last promontories of existence, and seemed to find nothing beyond but the utter darkness of eternal night. A terrible hatred surged within him against the brazier who had set his dog upon a defenceless child. He seemed alone in the dark with his hate—nothing more.

It was early spring and the brazier had sown his little patch of ground with corn, but the frosts had come and had nipped the early shoots, so there could be no harvest for him. He had no more seed. In his extremity he tried to beg some in the days which followed, but the neighbours remembered the death of Asta and drove him with curses from their doors. Surely the vengeance of God was being wreaked about him! "Ah!" thought the neighbours, as they slammed the door in the brazier's face, "God has His own way of punishing the sinner," and as they returned to their cosy fires they felt better for that thought. It seemed truly religious.

One night, some time after little Asta was laid to rest, Peer Holm felt unable to sleep. A vague purpose seemed to be forming itself in his mind, even though all his nature cried out against the thing he dreamt of. He rose and dressed slowly, but still some purpose kept struggling within him. Merle's quick ear caught the sound of his movements. At that moment the clock struck two. "Where are you going?" asked Merle. He hesitated to reply because he could scarcely say. It was all so vague. "I want to see if we haven't a half-bushel of barley left," he answered.

"Barley—what do you want with barley in the middle of the night?" she inquired.

Then the purpose grew clear to him. "I want to sow the brazier's plot with it," he said, almost ashamed of the thought, as though it were treachery to her. "It's best to do it now," he went on, "so that nobody will know it was me." She sat up and stared at him in amazement. "What!" she exclaimed. "His—the brazier's?" "Yes," said Peer. Then he searched round for a reason for this impulse he could not explain. "Yes, it won't do us any good, you know, to see his bit of field lying bare all summer."

Fate had been cruel to Peer. All his past experiences should have driven him to bitterness and revenge; but a new spirit was born within him as he stood naked on the shattered ruins of his fortunes. He passed out into the cold and silent night. This is how he describes his emotions. "The spark of eternity was once more aglow in me, and said, 'Let there be light.' And more and more it came to me that it is man himself that must create the divine in heaven and earth—that that is his triumph over the dead omnipotence of the universe. Therefore I went out and sowed the corn in my enemy's field, that God might exist."

John K. Elliott

** **

329   You remember the incident recorded in the life of Martin Luther; how the poor monk in his cell, visited in his visions at night in the dreams which possessed him, visited by his great arch-enemy, and yours and mine, the tempter brought to him great rolls which he bade him read, and he saw in his dream that these contained the record of his own life, and that they were written with his own hand. And said the tempter to him: "Is that true, did you write it?" And the poor stricken monk had to confess it was all true; and scroll after scroll was unrolled, and the same confession was perforce wrung from him. And then the evil one prepared to take his departure, having brought the poor stricken monk down to the lowest depths of abject misery; and then there came upon him in his vision, like a flash, that upon which his whole soul was saved, and he turned to the tempter and said, "It is true, every word of it, but write across it all: 'The blood of Jesus Christ, God's Son, cleanseth us from all sin.'"

J. Stuart Holden

Forgiveness, Disposition to

330   You say that the desert is a desert because no rain falls upon it; but that is only half the truth. No rain falls upon it because it is a desert. The heated air rushing up from the arid surface disperses the vapours that would descend in rain. Some moisture there must be on earth, else there cannot be rain from heaven. So in your heart this forgiving disposition must be, else you cannot rejoice in the fullness of God's forgiving grace.

Washington Gladden

Fortitude

331   I remember the story told by Florence Nightingale of a man in a hospital who had to undergo the operation of having his leg off without an anaesthetic. "You'll try and be as brave as you can, my child," she said. And he answered, "Give me that stick," and he put the knob in his mouth, and never uttered a single word. When it was all over, and the stick taken out, the knob of the stick was reduced to a pulp by the clenching of the teeth. That is the sort of fortitude with which we ought to bear pain.

L. H. Burrows

Freedom

332   What a fool a man would be who took a sailing ship out on to the great ocean and said: "I am not going to be a bond slave to a pilot or a compass or a chart. I am free to sail the seas." I think the ocean would laugh at such folly, and the end of that voyage would be at the bottom of the sea, and it would be a short voyage. When he is enslaved by the compass, and the chart, and the stars, and the pilot who stands at his side and tells him when to change direction, when to drop anchor, when to let sail down, and when to pull sail up, then he finds he is free.

Leslie D. Weatherhead
From *Christian World Pulpit,* Vol. 130

** **

333   E. P. Dickie tells the story of a slave trading vessel which was returning from Africa with its cargo of "black ivory." Two hundred slaves were packed together under the decks. One of them was a great chief, who lay in the hold plotting revenge for this deadly insult. His opportunity came. When the guards had grown careless he overpowered the sailor who had the key for the irons which chained them. Quietly he released the other slaves and at a given signal they rushed on the deck, overpowered the crew, murdered them and threw their bodies overboard. They were free. But there was something they had forgotten. None of them knew anything about the sailing ship. They had seen the sailors watching the compass, but to them the compass was like a god or devil. They

thought they might persuade it to guide them home, if they fell down and worshipped it. But the compass was useless to them because they knew nothing of the great magnetic forces which the compass obeys. You see, the slaves got their freedom and power, but power without the right direction leads inevitably to disaster.

Harry Allen

**

334   We are advancing in our present legislation towards the Servile State against which Hilaire Belloc warned us twenty-five years ago. We are to be fed, and educated, and "directed," and conscripted, but we are not to be free. A bleak outlook!

Angus Watson

**

335   In *Freedom and the Spirit* Berdyaev tells us that he found Christ through freedom. "I have come to Christ through liberty and through an intimate experience of the paths of freedom. My Christian faith is not a faith based on habit or tradition. . . . Freedom has brought me to Christ and I know of no other path leading to Him. . . . No one who has left a Christianity based on authority can return to anything but a Christianity which is free."

D. R. Davies

**

336   In the slave market of New Orleans, before Abraham Lincoln's slave emancipation, there was put up for auction one day a beautiful mulatto girl. The usual traders, as they made their bids, were startled by a strange voice, strong and decisive, which came from the edge of the crowd. Then the bids went on again and rose higher and higher until at fourteen hundred and fifty dollars the stranger got the girl. He turned out to be a man from the North, and the girl did not like the idea of becoming his slave. The next morning he called at the house where she was. With a sad voice she said: "Sir, I am ready to go with you." "But," said the stranger, "I don't want you to go with me. I bought you that you might be free; look over this," and he handed to her the paper of her freedom. "You bought me," she exclaimed, "that I might be free! Am I really free? Can I do as I please with myself?" "Yes," he answered, "you are free; you can do just as you please with yourself." "Then, sir," came the reply, her voice broken with sobs of joy, "won't you let me go with you and serve you for the rest of my life?" That surely was a natural thing. She had been made the servant of liberty. And Jesus Christ makes us His servants by setting us free.

A. Burt Taylor

Friend

337   You remember that epitaph over the grave of John Howard in far distant Russia. Oh, would you not like to have that epitaph over your grave? I can conceive no epitaph more desirable. It is put upon that stone by the Russian people who buried him there: "Whosoever thou art, thou standest by the grave of thy friend."   Robert F. Horton

Friend, Christ the

338   About the year A.D. 120 Pliny, the Roman governor of Bithynia, was trying to root out the Christians. "I will banish thee," he said to one whom he was trying, but the reply came: "Thou canst not, for the whole world is my Father's house." "I will slay thee," said the governor, and the answer was made: "Thou canst not, for my life is hid with Christ in God." "I will take away thy treasures"; and again the reply came: "Thou canst not, for my treasure is in heaven." "I will drive thee away from men and thou wilt have no friend left." But the Christian still said: "Thou canst not, for I have a friend from whom thou canst never separate me."

The world can never be too much for men and women like that.
                                                                Eric O. A. Brampton

Friend, True

339   I think General Grant one of the most magnanimous men that we have ever had, and I was very much struck with an instance of his magnanimity. When Conkling precipitated himself from the Senate, it was very much against General Grant's judgement, and that was known, and yet he attempted in every way to befriend Mr. Conkling, and shield him to such an extent that everybody thought he was on his side, and a man expostulated with him and said: "General Grant, how is it? You don't believe that he did right." "No, sir, I don't." "How is it, then, that you are on his side now?" His reply was worthy to be written in letters of gold: "When is the time to show a man's self friendly, except when his friend has made a mistake? That is not the time to leave a man when he has made a blunder or a mistake." That is one of those unimpeachable moral principles that address themselves to the universal conscience. Stand by a man who is your friend. Stand by him in his adversity, if you don't stand by him at any other time or anywhere else.

                                                                M. D. Butler

Friends

340   When Columba settled in the Isle of Iona life was rude enough in Scotland. It was in no sense a nation; there were only a great number of clans, always at war with one another. Pillage and licence were rampant. The result was that many refugees from violence and fugitives from justice came from far and near seeking sanctuary in the sacred isle. To these refugees Columba appointed monks, who were responsible for their religious guidance and help, and these monks were called Soul-Friends. It is a beautiful and most suggestive name, and one can hardly hear it without being conscious of a certain thrill. A Soul-Friend—what a wonderful thing it is to stand to anyone in such a relation! What a gift for God it is to have one who is in very truth a Soul-Friend!

A. Morris Moodie

Friendship

341   A perplexed youth once sought an interview with Phillips Brooks, the great American Christian. When the long-anticipated day arrived he spent a radiant hour with Phillips Brooks. He came out from it transfigured, feeling the joy of living. Later he realized he had forgotten to ask the question which had baffled him. He said, however, "I did not care. What I needed was not the solution of a special problem, but the contagion of a triumph spirit."

J. Leonard Clough

✳✳

342   Samuel Johnson once said to Sir Joshua Reynolds: "If a man does not make new acquaintances as he advances through life, he will soon find himself alone. A man, sir, should keep his friendships in constant repair." And a greater than Johnson says: "Thine own friend, and thy father's friend, forsake not."

James L. Elderdice

✳✳

343   Flattery is the poison of friendship, because it is false, and it has always been counted one of the greatest gains of friendship that one friend can, without offence, tell the other his faults.   James Stalker

✳✳

344   Kagawa, that amazing Christian teacher and saint of Japan, once revealed the value of friendship to some of his fellow-students. Once in the theological

college he criticized the members of the staff for having dismissed a student wrongly. He and four others were to be expelled from the college for having so criticized the staff. As he went to the principal for the final handshake before leaving, Kagawa said to him, "Christianity is a religion of love and a theological college should be a school of love. A school of love should guide a mistaken student. As God never abandons anyone, so a college ought never to drive a student away. Please forgive and reinstate the other four students and let the sentence of expulsion fall upon me alone." All were reinstated.

J. E. Evans

Frustration

345   There is preserved in the crypt of St. Paul's Cathedral a plan of a church that was never built. It is the plan of the cathedral that the great architect, Sir Christopher Wren, had in mind and heart for the great city of London, but which the conditions and straitened circumstances of the time prevented him from seeing erected, and it is said that the great architect used to sigh bitterly at the contrast between the model which the heavenly genius within him saw and planned, and the actual structure, huge and magnificent though it is, which the stinted means and stinted imagination of that age compelled him to build. He was not able to build according to the pattern showed to him in the mount.

Henry Thomas

**

346   Everyone knows something of the life of St. Francis of Assisi. He chose to be a monk, devoting his life to religious interests at a time when celibacy was a much-insisted-upon requirement. While St. Francis gave his life to that work he was in love with a very beautiful girl. He felt he never could go on to do the bigger work that was calling him till he made some final settlement regarding the appeal this pure and beautiful woman made in his life.

The story is told that many years afterwards, when he had gone into the ministry, though he tried to forget, this thing still followed him. He could not escape from the witchery and the charm this woman had flung over his life. But one night the monks saw him go out into the snow bare-headed. Out of the snow he made a woman, and out of the snow he made some little children and for one blissful hour he enjoyed in rapture the thought of what might have been. Then he resolutely turned his back on it and went into the monastery, and, as some one has said—I think it is Mr. Boreham—he really had conducted his own funeral. There comes a time in our lives when we have got to do that. There comes a time when our selection of something as between two competing interests is going to bring us a most poignant twinge of disappointment. But when the time has passed and the awful strain has successfully been borne we can say, "In the year that King Uzziah died I saw the Lord. In the year in which I sustained that awful family loss I saw the Lord. In the year in which I suffered that shattering business catastrophe I saw the Lord. In the year in which I underwent an experience in my professional life that almost smote me to death, I saw the Lord."   William C. Poole

✳✳

347   The picture of Moses, at the point of death, gazing at the Promised Land to which, through the long, arduous years he had led his beloved people, but into which he himself was never to enter, has always laid hold of the imagination of mankind. The simplicity and reticence of the Scripture words assist the powerful impression which is made. There is no attempt to match tragic words to a tragic happening, still less to draw an edifying moral. We are simply led into the presence of the old man as he sits on the mountain-top, conscious that the end is very near, and that the fruit of all his anguish and labour is to be plucked and enjoyed by another, and there we are left. We will not attempt to probe his thoughts, for he has been a giant among men, with the cords of destiny running through his fingers, and we are so small. We can only feel, somewhat inarticulately perhaps, that here is summed up all the tragic element, all the element of frustration and disappointment in life, which neither the great nor small amongst us ever escapes. There is, indeed, something of great art in the stark simplicity of God's irrevocable word to him: "I have caused thee to see it with thine eyes, but thou shalt not go over thither." For, as in all great arts, a universal truth of life is here seized upon, and expressed in a single sublime instance of it.

H. H. Farmer

Fullness of Time

348   The teaching and writings of the ancient Gentile world were, all unconsciously, pointers to Christ. Men were still exclaiming with Job in agony, "Oh that I knew where I might find Him!" It is true that "the world by wisdom knew not God." The world by its own efforts failed to find the truth, and the thinkers of ancient Greece failed to solve the problems of life. St. Paul's message to the Athenians, on Mars Hill, was: "Whom ye ignorantly worship, Him declare I unto you." The Stoics, philosophers like Seneca, Epictetus and Marcus Aurelius, "Seekers after God," as Dean Farrar called them, express thoughts of moral purity, not unworthy of the New Testament, and their teaching contributed to the preparation for the coming of Christ. Greece with its refined

tastes and beauty, and Rome with its austere discipline and physical strength, were stepping-stones towards the truth which Christ was to bring.

G. H. Clothier

Future

349   The heathen mind is not sure about the future; when Paulinus came to Northumbria and stood before the King and his thanes, and the question of the introduction of Christianity was being considered, you remember that an old thane rose up and said, "Sire, the life of man is like the flight of a bird through your hall, which, when it comes out of the storm, and rain, flies for a little through this lighted space and then goes out again into the storm and darkness beyond. But whence it comes and whither it goes we know not, and if this new religion can teach us, then let us listen to it." That has always been the thought of man, "Whither do I go?"

Those of you who have visited the catacombs of Rome, who have lit the torches and gone down into the pagan catacombs and have wandered through those subterranean passages, will often have looked up and seen the inscription over the ashes of the dead: "Vale, vale, in eternum"—an eternal farewell.

F. B. Meyer

Gambling

350   In William Blake's wonderful picture of the Crucifixion he represents Christ on the cross and behind the cross are the soldiers casting the dice to determine which of them shall have the seamless robe. Those gamblers behind the cross are in Blake's treatment of them the perfect incarnation of evil, while Christ upon the cross is the incarnation of good. You cannot imagine the two reversed. You cannot imagine Christ gambling any more than you can imagine the gamblers dying for the salvation of the world. Bring it to that test. It is the safest test I know in all other matters, the only way that quickly responds to our inquiry. Our moral arguments may easily deceive us, our casuistry is often quite misleading, but here is a test which quickly answers our question. You want to act in such a way in every condition of life that you can say: "Christ would do this if He were in my position." There is the simple law for us, the infallible law which keeps us in the right way, which takes us to the right goal; what Christ would do, what Christ would approve. That is the answer to the question: Is it right to gamble? Would Christ gamble? No.

Robert F. Horton

Genius

351   Sir Joshua Reynolds, being asked his opinion of a painting, said, after a long look: "Well, it is a very fine painting—colours are excellent, grouping admirable—a very fine work, sir; but yet, somehow, it wants—that!" and a snap of the fingers accompanied the word.

Llewellyn H. Parsons

Giving

352   I remember Dr. John Wilson, the Spurgeon of Woolwich, telling me a little story once. A minister in that district was building a new church and was anxious to open it quite free from debt. A little boy, quite poor, in the Sunday-school was anxious to help so he wrote a letter like this: "Dear Minister, I am glad that you are building a new church, and you want to open it without any debt. I am sending you one penny towards the cost." Then he put at the bottom of the letter these words, "P.S. If you want any more, let me know. Yours truly, Johnny."

J. Westbury-Jones

Giving, from Love

353   Dr. Newton tells the story of a blind girl who came to her minister with a one pound note for foreign missions. He refused to take it, telling her that it was too much for one in her condition and circumstances to give. Her answer was an index of the love that throbbed within her. "Please, sir," she said, "I can afford it better than the girls who can see, for they require to spend money on light in the long, dark evenings; but I can make my baskets without light, and I have saved this." Yes, my young friends, if you have love for Jesus it will find an outlet.

T. C. Hill

God

354   An old historian tells us that at one time a dismal plague visited Athens, and as none of the city's gods seemed able to avert its ravages, Epimenides turned loose a number of sheep and wherever any one of these animals rested an altar was erected to an unknown God; the people evidently feeling that their fate was in the hands of one who was not usually worshipped in their temples

and wanting to invoke his help. There is a lot of pathos in that. Is it not a true and vivid picture of human life? We feel we are in the presence of a power and mystery which we cannot understand or control. Everybody is seeking after that.   Thomas Phillips

✳✳

355   Dr. Fosdick tells a story about Edwin Booth, the great American actor. A clergyman wanted to attend a performance at his theatre, but he was afraid that some of his congregation might not like it if they saw him, so he asked Booth if he could arrange for him to enter by a side door. Booth's answer was a stern rebuke to the parson. "There is no door in my theatre," he said, "through which God may not enter!" What a tremendous claim to make! Can you and I make such a claim about our working days, our leisure, our home life? "No door through which God may not enter."   Harold Derbyshire

✳✳

356   Augustine has said, "I have looked through many of the heathen writers and have found many jewels in Cicero and in Herodotus." Yet says he, "I never found anything like 'Come unto Me all ye that labour and are heavy laden and I will give you rest.'"   F. B. Meyer

✳✳

357   I have no doubt we are all familiar with the story of Helen Keller, the poor girl who was deaf and dumb and blind from early days. A living death you would say. But there was a clever brain and a beautiful soul beyond the darkness and the silence. And you all know the wonderful story of how communication was established with her by the sense of touch, and she was trained in all the knowledge and culture of the day. And at last the time came when communication was so perfected that it was thought possible to lead her into the knowledge of things spiritual. A well-known minister was entrusted with the charge of telling her the story of God's revelation of love in Jesus Christ. But when he had finished, to the surprise of all present, the answer came back across that lonely isolation in which she dwelt, "I knew all this before, but I did not know His Name."

Donald Davidson

God, Calling

358   There is a story told of two men upon the Niagara River, a few years ago. They were going on toward the Rapids. The oars were lying in the boat, and

they were drinking, and talking, and having a jolly time. Some one on the shore saw their danger, and shouted to them to turn back; but they laughed at his fears and went on. A little farther down some one else saw them and warned them; but one of them held up his bottle and shook it at him, and told him what a grand time they were having. They didn't believe the warning; they didn't believe the Rapids were anywhere near them. They had drunk too much and were intoxicated with liquour. Ah! many a soul is intoxicated with this world's affairs and his plans here below. Well, it wasn't long before some one else saw their danger, and he warned them. But the men went on. And at last one of them said, "I hear the Rapids!" And they seized the oars and pulled against the current; but it was too late. They pulled and pulled; but it was too late. They could not pull against that awful current; and in a few minutes they went over the cataract and into the jaws of death, and lost their lives because they would not take the warning. So God calls upon you to seek His kingdom; and tells you if you will seek Him with all your heart you will find Him.

D. L. Moody

God, Caricature of

359 I remember the daughter of one of our former Colonial statesmen being tormented in her mind by the ugly and almost wicked cartoons the newspaper men used to make of her father in their criticism of his policy. One day, having reached the end of her patience, she took a real photograph from the wall, hastened to the newspaper office and thrust it before their eyes to show them what her father was really like.

I am afraid we, too, have often been not even caricatures of our Lord.

Norman N. G. Cope

God, Escape from

360 "I went to Africa," confessed John Newton, "that I might be able to sin to my heart's content." And there in Africa he lived the life of a pagan till Christ laid hold of him. "I was a wild beast on the coast of Africa till the Lord caught and tamed me," he wrote afterwards. Not till he was mastered by Christ did he enter into the fullness of life.   R. T. Cameron

God, Experience of

361 You have no doubt heard of the boy who was flying his kite and succeeded in letting it fly out of sight. A gentleman passing inquired, "What are you doing, my boy?" "I am flying my kite, sir," he answered. "But you must be mistaken," said the gentleman, "I cannot see any kite." "No more can I," said the boy, "but I know it's there, because I can feel it pull." No man hath seen God at any time, but every man some day will feel the "pull" of the infinite Spirit, and know that there is a God.

J. Tolefree Parr

God, Fatherhood of

362   Jesus teaches us, when we pray, to say "Our Father." He could have made no greater revelation of the character of God. The Mohammedan has ninety-nine names for God, but "Father" is not even one of them.

George W. Shelton

God, Finding

363   The late Dr. J. C. Carlile of Folkestone, who was one of our best-known British preachers and editor of *The Baptist Times*, used to tell of a millionaire, known to him, who, during the last war, lost nearly all his money and was compelled to live upon an amount which he had settled upon his wife for pin money. "I was going to console with him when he said: 'No, don't sympathize with me on my losses; congratulate me upon my gains; I have lost the money and found God.'"

G. H. Clothier

God, Greatness of

364   We launched the *Queen Mary*. Oh, we felt awfully proud of that. Really it is rather like a little boy pushing a penny Woolworth boat along a path. In one respect, at any rate, it is like that. We get very excited about it; the papers are full of it; when the vessel arrives at New York, New York goes mad as only New York can. And the other day God launched a new planet and nobody will know anything about it for twenty million years.

Leslie D. Weatherhead
From *Christian World Pulpit*, Vol. 130

God, Hunger for

365   Rudyard Kipling was once lying seriously ill with typhoid fever, and in his delirium he talked and talked and mumbled to himself. One morning the

nurse leaned over him and said: "Mr. Kipling, what do you want?" He opened his eyes and said feebly: "I want God."

In the restlessness of your life, in the fever of life's cares, demands, pleasures, interests, your soul is saying that. If only you would sit down quietly and listen to your own heart you would hear your real self refusing to be deceived, refusing to be suppressed, saying, "I want God."

If the spiritual urge for God within us is not satisfied, the whole of our inner life is out of gear. Your motor car can't make any progress until you put it in gear, no matter how fast you accelerate your engine. Until you do this first thing in life, get right with God, all the hurry and activity of your life will never give you happiness, peace with yourself and other people.

You remember how Mr. H. G. Wells put it in the words of Mr. Britling: "Religion is the first and last thing, and until a man has found God, and been found by God, he begins at no beginning, he works to no end. He may have his friendships, his partial loyalties, his scraps of honor. But all these fall into place only with God."   Harold Bickley

God, Inescapable

366   When men say they have finished with God, God has not finished with them, and in the end they are always brought face to face with reality. Do you remember that story they used to tell us when we were little children of the little Dutch boy going home from school one afternoon and finding a hole in the stone wall that kept out the ocean, and he knew the danger that if the hole got bigger the wall would go down, and the tide would flow in: and with great courage he put his hand in the hole, and that little child's hand held back the ocean. His mother waited for him in vain, and when at last they found him he was nearly exhausted, and they said to him, "You saved Holland." The frail hand of man's will can hold back the tides of God's desire, and the ocean of His Spirit. But it will be only for a time. You cannot fight against God and win. Do you remember that in the history of the Dutch people their salvation came in that day when they broke down the dykes, and let in the ocean that they had kept out for so long? You are holding back the infinite God, and your salvation will begin when you let in what you have kept out so long. Do not hide under any excuses: you must at some time or another come to terms with God and with eternal realities.

Leslie D. Weatherhead
From *Christian World Pulpit*, Vol. 128

✳✳

367 A man said to me, "There is always one way out. I can take a knife and cut my throat." I said, "Before the knife is out of your hand you will be looking into the face of God." One who felt the need of getting away on a cruise, when he reached the Mediterranean realized that he had taken all his worries with him. "If I take the wings of the morning . . . even there shall Thy hand lead me, and Thy right hand shall hold me." This is what Francis Thompson tried to say to us in that poem of his when he made it appear as though the soul were running away from a hound, the Hound of Heaven.

> I fled Him down the nights and down the days
> I fled Him down the arches of the years
> I fled Him down the labyrinthine ways
> Of my own mind: and in the midst of tears,
> I hid from Him, and under running laughter
> > Up vistaed slopes I sped
> > And shot, precipitated
> Adown titanic glooms of chasmed fears
> From those strong feet that followed, followed after.

Leslie D. Weatherhead
From *Christian World Pulpit*, Vol. 128

God, Interest in

368 Mr. Crabb Robinson tells how once he was in the Lake Country, near Grasmere (the very village where William Wordsworth lived), and met a seemingly intelligent gentleman (also an inhabitant of those parts) who asked him: "Is it true, as I have heard, that Mr. Wordsworth ever wrote verses?" Perhaps people said of Jesus: "Is it true, as I have heard, that He gabbles a good deal about God?"
George A. Buttrick

God, Knowing

369 Justin Martyr asks, "Can a man know God as he can know arithmetic or astronomy?" and answers, "Assuredly not!" Clement of Alexandria says the process of theology with regard to its doctrine of God is negative and agnostic, setting forth what God is not, rather than what He is. Tertullian confesses the unsearchable nature of the Great Being, though he feels that he is brought into living relation with "the human God, who had revealed Himself in His Son." Augustine affirms that the power adequately to name God is not attainable by men in this earthly life.

John Clifford

God, Living

370   Many will remember the incident during the American Civil War when things were going badly for the North. A meeting was being held in Washington at the time news of a most serious defeat for the northern forces reached the capital. Frederick Douglass, the slave orator, was speaking. When the news reached the platform and Douglass heard it, he gave way to despair and burst into tears. The news passed from seat to seat, and the audience was gripped with fear. But in the back gallery was one old Negro woman who, when she saw the meeting falling into something like panic and even Douglass in despair, cried out with a hint of reproach in her tone: "Frederick Douglass, God is not dead!"

David A. MacLennan

God, Meaning of

371   Professor D. N. Baillie has written, "It requires all the training of a religious home, all the fellowship of religious people, all the worship of the Church, woven into life itself, to show what the word 'God' means."

C. Sidney Hall

God, Mindful

372   The first child of Dr. Martineau, the eminent Unitarian minister, died in infancy and was buried in the French cemetery in Dublin. Before they quitted Ireland for Liverpool, the father and mother paid a farewell visit to the grave of their first-born. The years went by and in the course of them Mrs. Martineau died. At the age of eighty-seven, Martineau was a lonely old man. But when he was attending the tercentenary of Dublin University he stole away from the brilliant public function to stand once more by the tiny grave that held the dust of his first-born child. No other living soul recalled that little one's smile or remembered where the child was sleeping. But the father knew and the little buried hands held his heart. And just as the great Dr. Martineau was mindful of his little one, so the God and Father of our Lord Jesus Christ, despite the inconceivable and illimitable vastness of His works, is mindful of each one of us. "The very hairs of our heads are numbered by Him; our most trivial moments are watched by Him; asleep or awake, in sickness or in health, we are never out of His sight." Every day and hour and moment He contemplates us with a love that passeth knowledge. And as St. Paul once said, "He

leaves not Himself without witness, in that He does good and gives us rain from heaven and fruitful seasons, filling our lives with food and gladness." To Him, therefore, it behooves us to give continual thanks, submitting ourselves wholly to His will and pleasure, and studying to serve Him in true holiness and righteousness all our days.   R. J. Anglin Johnson

God, Nature of

373   When Goethe was a very little child—only six years of age—his mind was greatly disturbed by the earthquake that happened at Lisbon in the year 1755. The reports of the calamity came to him with such a vivid sense of dread that his very soul seemed to be singed by the breath of the volcanic fire. The disfigurement of beautiful forms of nature and art, the gratuitous destruction of property, the wholesale sacrifice of thousands of human lives—the daring violence of the whole tragedy so overwhelmed him that his childish heart cried out in helpless despair. Can the God of the Lisbon earthquake be a good and merciful God? The child-soul saw the flame of nature's wrath, and trembled and was afraid. "The Lord was not in the earthquake"—that was the strange thing to the ancient prophet. The Lord was in the earthquake—that became the strange thing to Goethe.

The supplementary and corrective half of this problem is given by Charles Kingsley in his romance of *Two Years Ago*. In the presence of a terrible epidemic, which filled a town with unutterable grief and misery—"a banquet of Beelzebub"—the hero and heroine calm their alarmed faith by the thought that the God who permits such sorrows must be a very good God. The broken hearts of the world testify to the infiniteness of the pity of God. A God whose love could be less than the sum of all pain would be an impossible God. The world is very dark; therefore God is light. The world is very tired and heavy-laden; therefore God is rest. The world is a "universe of death"; therefore God is life. The world is very sinful and sorely stricken; therefore God is love. The world's stormy midnight, the world's depth of despair, the world's walk in the wintry gloom of the grave, this is both a prayer to the Father of lights and a proof of His goodness. He would not permit His creation to sink so low, unless His pity went lower still. The anguish of Calvary lies deeper down than any human pain, and explains all lesser depths.

Henry Ward Beecher

✳✳

374   Once F. W. H. Myers, a Victorian thinker who passed through faith to scepticism and then to a kind of faith through spiritualism, was asked what

question he would ask the Sphinx if he could be sure of an answer. He replied, "I would ask, Is the Universe friendly?" For us Jesus gives the answer. When the disciples came closest to Him, they saw not wrath or judgement or darkness, but "love to the end," love as wide as the Universe, love deeper even than man's iniquity. Such is the love of God the Father Almighty.

H. W. Theobald

✳ ✳

375   The Bishop of Bedford told me a story the other day about a man who was known in that part of the East End where the Bishop happened to be preaching that day as an infidel lecturer, and after the service was over he came up to the vicar's wife and said: "I never heard of a God like that." She said something about its being the true God. He did not presume to say about that; "but," he said, "I never spoke against a God like that and I never would speak against a God like that," and the end of it was that he said he could not hold up his face to those to whom he had been in the habit of talking as he had, and he left the place. That is not a second-hand story. What does it mean? Why, that there is a great deal said about God that is as false as Satan, and that the wrong presentation of God is the very thing that has set men to deny Him.

George MacDonald

God, Need of

376   Leslie Stephen, the father of Virginia Woolf, was a man who had felt the full force of religious difficulties and had renounced the Christian faith altogether. Writing to his friend Lowell, when his wife died, he began a sentence, "I thank—," and recollecting that he had no one to whom he could think himself indebted for the dear companion of his heart and his own affection for her, he continued: "I thank—something—that I loved her as heartily as I know how to love." And here is a more modern example: Katherine Mansfield, writing to her friend D. H. Lawrence from Switzerland, said, "God is now gone for all of us. Yet we must believe; and not only that—we must carry our weakness and our sin and our devilishness to some one." Katherine Mansfield had struggled hard after a satisfying religious relationship, but she had to admit failure and suggested that the only thing left was love between lovers. But she suddenly broke off almost in despair and confessed: "But oh, it is no good." Of course not. However beautiful and wonderful an experience it is to love and be loved, we only court disillusionment when we think that, in a world in which death holds sway, it is enough.

D. Myrddin Davies

God, Picture of

377   A little girl was busy one day with pencil and paper. "What are you doing?" asked her mother. "I'm making a picture of God," she replied. "Nay," said the shocked mother, "you can't do that. You have never seen God. Nobody has ever seen God. Nobody knows what God is like." The maiden was in no wise abashed. Licking her pencil and bending over her task, she replied: "They will know when I've finished this."

That little girl was not doing an outrageous thing, as her mother seemed to think; she was obeying, in her own way, a universal instinct. For men in all ages have made pictures of God. This is what an idol is—an image or picture of God. In practice men have always come to worship their idols; but in theory God is worshipped in or through the idol. Even a savage knows that God is a Spirit. But spirit is so intangible. He wants something to worship that he can see. And so he makes this image—the crude representation of his idea of God—and when he has made it he thinks that the Spirit comes and dwells in it, and he worships it as God.

                                                                                E. B. Storr

God, Place of

378   Not so long ago, in order to advertise a revival meeting which was being held in a Highland town, a Scotch newspaper adopted an arresting procedure. In large letters the editor invited his readers to look on the back page, and there splashed in much larger letters was added: "Is this where you are putting God?"

                                                                            Cyril Brailsford

God, Presence of

379   F. W. Boreham tells of a Scotsman who, being very ill, was visited by his minister. As the latter sat down he noticed a chair drawn close to the bed as if some one had recently been sitting there. The minister, by way of introduction, said: "Well, Donald, I see I am not your first visitor today." The Scotsman looked surprised, and the minister indicated the chair. "Ah," said Donald, "I'll tell you about that chair. Years ago I found it impossible to pray. Often I fell asleep on my knees I was so tired, if I was awake my thoughts wandered, so I spoke to my minister of those days and he told me not to worry, but just to sit down and place a chair opposite, and imagine Jesus sitting there

and talk to him as I would talk to a friend. I have been doing that ever since, so now you know the meaning of that chair." Some days later the daughter of the invalid visited the minister. Amid tears she intimated that her father had passed on. She said: "I did not think the end was so near. He was sleeping quite comfortably and I went to lie down. When I returned he was dead. He had not moved except that his hand was stretched out resting in the empty chair by his bed. I think you will understand."   Charles E. Garritt

※※

380   A story is told of that famous surgeon, the late Lord Moynihan. One day he was invited to operate before a group of distinguished doctors. Afterwards one of them expressed his admiration and surprise that the surgeon could do his work so calmly and well, undisturbed by the onlookers. "When I operate," he said, "there are just three people in the theatre—the patient and myself." "But that is only two," said the other. "Who is the third?" "God," was the reply.
                                                                    W. Francis Gibbons

※※

381   Here is Gipsy Smith writing to a friend: "What can you see in me? I honestly feel ashamed of myself and want to hide away somewhere. It is a good thing I know my heart and also my limitations better than anybody or my head might be turned. But you know me better than anybody else, I think, for you have seen me under all sorts of circumstances, and how you have patience with me I don't know. There is One Who knows me even better and in spite of all my unworthiness and my sin He never lets me go."

Can you and I say anything of that kind? Alongside that testimony of Gipsy Smith put this one of General Dobbie, the heroic defender of Malta during those terrible days of concentrated enemy attack. The general tells us that he first trusted Christ when a boy at school, and that for him it was a real and final transaction. "I owe everything to Him who loved me and gave Himself for me," he says. He goes on to say that he would not dream of facing life in the army or out of it without Christ.   N. H. Fisher

God, Response to

382   They tell a story of Ole Bull and Ericsson his bosom friend—Ole Bull marvellous in his love and mastery of music, Ericsson marvellous in his inventive skill and power, yet Ericsson without any ear for music, as was supposed. Again and again Ole Bull tried to arouse his friend, inviting him to his entertainments, striving to get him to listen to music, but he always refused,

until one day Ole Bull took down his violin to the office of his friend and said, "Ericsson, here is my violin, something is the matter with it. Have you a workman in the shop that can put it right?" Ericsson gave it over, on account of his friendship, to one of his men, and in a little while the instrument was brought back. Then Ole Bull, not only with that marvellous skill of his, but with a marvellous intuition of the capacities of his friend, drew the bow across the violin, and began to send forth some of those marvellous notes of which he was capable, until the doors and the passage-ways were filled with workmen flocking from all parts of the factory to listen to the master. And Ericsson then finally cried out, "Ole, Ole, I've an ear for music after all." And so God tries to draw out, to find the hidden thing in you and me, the capacity for great things that is inherited, maybe, that we have not recognized, the capacity for holy living, the capacity for response to Himself, and He touches this spring and that spring and the other, until the man suddenly rises to this great fact, he reaches the place where he says, "I ought, I ought, and therefore I can."

Joseph T. Kelly

God, Search for

383 We ought either to be sure beyond all doubt that there is no chance of knowing God; or else we should search for Him with all the heart, and follow on, and still on—till we know Whom we have believed and are persuaded that He is able and willing to take care of every thought and purpose, every prayer and deed we commit to Him, against the day of eternal manifestation.

John Clifford

God, Serving

384 In the war of 1861 a timid supporter said to Lincoln that he hoped the Lord would be on the side of the North. Lincoln replied, "About that I am not at all concerned; but only that we should be on the side of the Lord."

John Clifford

God, Sovereignty of

385 When Abraham Lincoln was lying dead and the great crowd of people in New York were in despair at having lost their national faith for a moment, a young man stood out among them, who turned out to be Garfield who afterwards became President, and said, "Fellow-citizens, God reigns! God reigns!"

C. Silvester Horne

God, the Creator

386   As Napoleon was blazing his trail to his throne he sought to conquer Egypt. Along with him as assistants he had some of the ablest engineers and scientists of France. It was natural that they should talk about the land of the Nile, and the part that religion had played in it. It was agreed that religion had coloured and carved the history of Egypt, but that religion after all was only legend and humbug. That, indeed, was the case of all religions. It couldn't be otherwise, seeing that even God was a myth. So they talked, beneath the starry heavens, these thinkers of France. They were atheists, as indeed so many of their fellow-countrymen were at the time. But their leader did not share their views. He listened very quietly to all they had to say. He did not challenge them or seek to refute their arguments. But as he rose to leave the company to seek his own tent he lifted his hand and pointed to the silent sentinel star that shone so brilliantly through the deep black sky: "Very ingenious, Messieurs," he said, "but who made all that?"

J. Allardyce

God, Thirst for

387   George Borrow wandered into the fields of Wales and fell into conversation with a group of gypsies. He did not talk to them of religion, yet all unknowingly the virtue went out of him; so that when he made as if to go they besought him, saying: "Oh, it was kind of you to come . . . that you might bring us God." He made it clear that he was neither priest nor minister, but they entreated him the more: "Oh, sir, do give us God." Such is the age-long cry that the world lifts to its pulpits: "Oh, sir, do give us God."

George A. Buttrick

God, View of

388   I wonder if our view of God has not been affected of late years by the pruning knife of our criticism. Have we not been so anxious to show what God is not that we have missed something of what God is? We have been laying the ax to the root of the trees so busily that we have not realized that no one cuts down a jungle except to plant a field. We have forgotten, have we not, that every big theological idea, however wrong it may seem, had its roots in a valid experience which we have got to recover in some truer form. The only excuse for breaking the earthen vessels that hold the treasure is to find some-

thing larger, something more adequate to hold the wealth of the Eternal riches. Horace Bushnell passed through this critical stage in his day, and after he had become a minister some one met him and said: "Dr. Bushnell, you do not believe the Westminster Confession, do you?" "Yes," he said, "I do." "But you do not believe the Thirty-nine Articles, do you?" "Yes," he said, "I do." "But surely you do not accept the Augsburg Confession, do you?" "Now stop," he said, "or mention them altogether. I believe all that and a good deal more." Of course he was not speaking of the meticulous articles of the creed. He was demanding for himself a view of God that was big enough to hold all the amplitude of a grace that was beyond conceiving, exceeding abundantly beyond what he could ask or think.   James Reid

Gods, False

389   O Pan, you god of the Greeks, when you played your pipes you lured so many along the path that seemed the way of happiness as they danced away towards Arcady! O Mars, you god of the Romans, you brought that ancient Empire to world domination, and men thought you knew the way to self-realization! Nor were all the false gods in the distant past. Hitler beguiled young men of Christian families, made them forswear their Christian faith, led them back towards paganism and towards a darkness deeper than death. Karl Marx, we read your stinging words, and millions have followed you because they thought you knew the way and were, indeed, the light of the world. But now we turn and look at Ancient Greece and Rome. We contemplate modern Germany and Russia, and we know that, like the will-o'-the-wisp, you led men into a morass, and the end was darkness and fear.

Leslie D. Weatherhead
From *Christian World,* Dec. 21, 1950

Goodness

390   The essence of goodness is not conformity to a pattern but a disposition and dedication to meet every new situation in the finest spirit and best way we know. Admiral Byrd has told us what was his final test for choosing men to accompany him into the Antarctic. It was not intellectual ability nor physical endurance nor technical skill, important as all these were. The final test was a man's disposition. Would he be inclined to respond to what was most needed in any situation on that voyage of discovery, regardless of his own convenience?

Ralph W. Sockman

✳✳

391   A few days before the end of his life Sir Walter Scott is reported to have said to his son-in-law and biographer Lockhart, "Lockhart, I may have but a few minutes to speak to you. My dear, be a good man; be virtuous; be religious; be a good man; nothing else will give you any comfort when you come to lie here."

J. Yielder

Goodness, Christian

392   This victorious goodness: this goodness which wins over your enemy instead of driving him away, which wins him over when he is unmoved by all your texts and your apologetics: is not easy to define, and yet it is unmistakable when you see it and touch it. The hardest thing about it to describe is this: he convinces the man he is trying to win, and yet he never uses the argument, "See, I am better than you." It is not because of a studied humility that he never uses that argument; it is because he thinks it is just bad tactics. The point is that the question never arises in his own mind. He is not trying to make the other man as good as he. He is trying to win him to Christ, with whom alone the other man must come to terms on the question of his own goodness or badness. Besides, the very essence of Christian goodness is that it is not conscious and studied goodness at all. It is love. It is simply the continuation of Christ's yearning love for the world, His saving pity for that blindness of the world which is taking men to the edge of a precipice from which their bodies and souls alike may be plunged into ruin. The good Christian is better than other men—he is better than other good men—because he loves the world more.

Ernest H. Jeffs

Good News

393   I once heard of an old mother whose son had been reported missing. She entered into that dreadful ordeal which thousands have known, when the heart trembles between hope and despair, when days pass into weeks, and weeks drag into months of long suspense. One day, whilst she was sitting in the company of one or two acquaintances, two letters came. The letters lay in her lap while she continued her conversation. After about two hours, she opened them. One was a message to say that her son was alive; he was a prisoner of war and well. And the poor mother wept and laughed and sobbed, "Why, I have been holding this good news in my hand for the last two hours, and never knew it!"

How many souls are passing through a similar experience! God's glorious news has come to them. It is there to have, at their heart's door; but they do not heed it; they do not read it. It is May, God's sweet May—and they are blind!

Frederick H. Carr

Gospel

394   More than a quarter of a century ago, Prebendary F. S. Webster, of All Souls, Langham Place, asked a question which was to mark a crisis in all my thought of preaching: "What happens when you go into a pulpit? Do you give the people good news or good advice?" Ever since, I have been trying, all too imperfectly, to give them good news—the good news of Christ Jesus, who abolished death, and brought life and immortality to light through the Gospel.

T. Wilkinson Riddle

Gospel, Enduring

395   When Dr. John Clifford had completed sixty years of ministry I heard him say: "It has never occurred to me that there is any narrowness about the Gospel. I believe that life is a whole thing. I preach politics, civics, art, science, literature, as all affected by and included in religion. Circumstances have changed, methods of thought have changed, but I have never seen any occasion or reason to change the Gospel it has been my joy and privilege to preach for all these years. In the seventies and eighties, a time of great unsettlement and unrest, from twenty to thirty young men and women would find their way from all parts of London to my vestry at Westbourne Park on Friday nights, seeking counsel in their perplexity and bewilderment. I glorify Him who has privileged me to preach this Gospel and to see such results from its being preached."

Dr. Clifford's active pastorate at Westbourne Park closed on the last Sunday in August, 1915. At the evening service on that day every seat was occupied, while numbers stood at the doors. He chose as his topic "The Unique and Abiding Charm of Jesus." "It has been my joy," he said, "to tell men about this Jesus and to have seen what He has done in and through this Church. In this building men and women looked Him in the face and fell in love with Him."

Henry J. Cowell

Gospel, Enthusiasm for

396   John McNeill, the well-known Scottish preacher, was addressing a crowded audience not long ago in a certain place, and he was speaking quite

rightly, by way of criticizing certain men in the world of business, men who will forgive excitement of any kind, so long as it is not excitement on the question of the Gospel. Said Mr. McNeill, "I was reading in the newspaper the other day, and I read the market column and saw the statement 'pig iron excited.'" That to the commercial world is an ordinary thing. "But," he said, "while pig iron may be excited with impunity, if a man gets excited about the things of eternity, about the love of God to man, then that of all things to the cynical man today is the least excusable."

Archibald Lamont

Gospel, Hardened to

397   Some years ago a North American Indian, after hearing the story of the Crucifixion, became a Christian; full of his new-found joy, he determined to tell everybody he came in contact with that Christ is able to save the uttermost. One morning, when doing his rounds, the first man he came in contact with was an Englishman, and the Red Indian convert greeted him with the words, "Has my brother white man heard the good news?" He replied, "No; has there been a vein of gold found, or a herd of buffaloes seen?" The convert said, "No, better than that." Then he said, "Jesus died for sinners and for me." The Englishman turned away in disgust: "Oh, I have heard that for years in the Old Country." Here, then, we have a case of man being like Judas, Gospel-hardened; and is it not so today? There are thousands living in a Christian land, with Christian means of grace, hearing the Gospel preached at almost every street corner, yet it seems to make no impression on them. They are Gospel-hardened. But though Judas was Gospel-hardened, yet on that night of the betrayal he might have been saved had he asked for pardon.

George Barratt

Gospel, Inexhaustible

398   For thirteen years I preached to my beloved people at Newcastle. I gave them upwards of two thousand sermons on salvation—for I never preach about anything else. I went back the other night to preach to my own folk, and as I went up the pulpit steps I was overwhelmed with the thought, not that it was difficult to find anything new to say, but with the thought that I had left so much unsaid.

A. T. Guttery

Gospel, Power of

399   A story is told of the Japanese sculptor Nobumichi Inouye, who received
a commission to carve a four foot high crucifix for a Christian church. Not
being a Christian himself, he found this a difficult work to undertake. He began
by studying the story of the Passion, and in this way he hoped to work out his
own conception of Christ on the Cross. The final result was not only a beautiful
piece of sculpture, but a sculptor who became a convinced Christian.

R. Beverley Large

✸✸

400   Rev. T. Dalington, who has worked under the auspices of the China
Inland Mission for more than twenty years, tells very remarkable stories of
changed lives. One day brigands attacked the town in which he was working
and where he had built up a Christian congregation. To show that they would
stand no nonsense they killed a number of children who were playing in the
street. Then they proclaimed martial law; no one was to leave his house. That
night the missionary went into the church, threw open the doors and invited
the brigands to enter. They did so with threats and cursing, but beckoning for
silence, he read to them in their own dialect the story of the Passion and Death
of our Lord. They had never heard it before. They listened wrapped in silence.
He invited them to come the following night and promised to read the same
passage.

The following night the same thing happened, and it went on through the
week. Feeling that the Holy Spirit had been moving in their hearts, the
missionary asked those who wished to accept this Christ as their Saviour to
come forward and kneel down. Thirteen of those men murderers, and some of
them cannibals: men who had killed people, cut out their hearts and eaten
them, came forward with tears in their eyes and accepted Jesus Christ as their
Saviour.

W. Eddleston

Gospels, Not Legends

401   As a literary historian, I am perfectly convinced that whatever else the
Gospels are they are not legends. I have read a great deal of legend and I am
quite clear that it is not the same sort of thing. For one thing the Gospels are not
good enough to be legends; they are not artistic enough.

C. S. Lewis

Gossip

402   We read in the book of Numbers that the camp of Israel had gone on steadily from the Red Sea on its march to the Land of Promise, when without apparent cause it suddenly stopped, the pillar of the cloud stood still and the journey was arrested at Hazeroth. All were looking anxiously for the cause of this: and what was it? Moses had married an Ethiopian woman against the wishes of Aaron and Miriam, who went about with stories of gossip and scandal with the intention of doing harm to the chosen leader of God's people in Israel and setting public opinion against him. The cloud stood still at the touch of God's hand and Miriam was smitten with leprosy.   James Weller

Government

403   Some time ago a Czechoslovakian girl skater, in the world championship class, said she liked the freedom of England so much that she would stay in England and not return to Czechoslovakia. Immediately an official of the Czechoslovak Embassy said: "She has permission to stay here for a program of skating exhibitions. When these are completed she will return home." Just like that! For all the world as if the feet she skates with are not her own! No doubt he keeps them in a drawer in his office, prepares them and lends them to her. We are not so very far from having a political party capable of believing that it has lent to God the sun and the moon and the rain for strictly limited purposes, and that if this use is not on party lines the loan may be withdrawn without notice.   C. A. Rowlands

Grace

404   Mr. Watts-Ditchfield, a well-known Anglican missionary, tells in one of his books of a visit he paid to a woman who was very much in need of religion. When he called she was at the wash-tub. He said something to her about the higher life, and she replied: "Yes, I know all about that: I was converted in Manchester twenty years ago." Immediately after he said: "I am surprised to see you washing these clothes again, because it is only a week or so since they were last cleaned." "Well," she said, "if I did not wash them over and over again they would soon be past wearing." Watts-Ditchfield replied: "What must your heart be like if it has not been cleaned for twenty years?"
                                                              John Bishop

✳✳

405   There was a great painter a few years ago who was painting a picture, which I believe afterwards became a notable one. He wanted to give a picture of the present-day aspect of life in London, and on his canvas he wanted to represent the various forms of life in the great busy metropolis. He was looking about to get a good specimen of a little London street arab—you know the little specimen, all alive, dirty, in rags, but with a lot of sharpness. And at last he got just the sort of boy he wanted in the gutter. "My boy," he said to him; "my boy, would you like to earn sixpence?" "What," he said, "a tanner? Yes, I would like a tanner." "Well, here is my card. You come just as you are tomorrow at nine o'clock to this address, when you shall have a tanner."

The little boy thought he had never got sixpence so cheap before. "Yes, sir," he said; "I'll be there." At nine o'clock to the stroke he was pulling the bell of the painter's studio. The maid who answered the door came and said, "There is a little boy, sir; wants to see you." The painter had forgotten all about what had happened. He had many other things to think about. "A little boy," he said. "What sort of little boy?" "Well, sir, he is a very respectable little boy; his face is nice and clean and his clothes are neat, though he is very poor."

"Tell him to come in," said the painter, and the little boy of the day before stood before him. But his face was clean, his hair was brushed, and his mother, who had thought there was a good opening for the boy, had sewn together his rags. When he stood before the painter he said, "Where is that tanner you promised me?" "Do you remember what I told you?" asked the painter. "Yes, sir." "Are you sure?" "Yes, sir, you told me to come at nine o'clock and here I am plump on time. It has just gone nine." "But I wanted you just as you were. If you had come just as you were you would have got the sixpence, but as you are not as you were I will not have you." I do not know whether the painter gave the boy the tanner or not, but I should have done so had it been me. The boy did not suit because he had come clean when the painter had said, "Come as you are."

Now, God wants you just as you are. He wants to put you into redemption; He wants to show you what His precious blood can do in washing your sins away. He wants to show what His grace can do in restoring you. He can wash you white as snow.   W. E. Burroughs

✳✳

406   A man is never so truly and intensely himself as when he is most possessed by God. It is impossible to say where, in the spiritual life, the human will leaves off and Divine grace begins.

                                                                    W. R. Inge

Grace of God

407   "Grace," says Dr. Jowett, "is an energy: not a mere sentiment: not a mere thought of the Almighty: not even a word of the Almighty. It is as real an energy as the energy of electricity. It is a Divine energy: it is the energy of the Divine affection rolling in plenteousness towards the shores of human need." That is a fine explanation, especially those last words: "it is the energy of the Divine affection rolling in plenteousness towards the shores of human need"! That is exactly what it is. Helpless in sin, wallowing in iniquity, grace came, like some great ocean, rolling in in plenteousness, covering and cancelling my need. Ruined in the tumble of the world, fallen in its power, grace came—a mightier something—to rescue and to save! "Grace abounding—grace abundant —grace to COVER all my sin"! Hence, as the Apostle puts it elsewhere: "where sin abounded, grace did much more abound." Where there were "the shores of human need," created by sin and iniquity, the Divine affection did much more abound, rolling in, in ample plenteousness, answering the deepest requirements and the deepest needs.   A. Russell Tomlin

❊❊

408   Gipsy Smith tells a very striking story. It has to do with a crowd of gipsies who, having picked fruit for a farmer on the banks of the Medway, were detailed to another field for a similar purpose, a mile away. To reach this field they made use of a wagon, drawn by a team of young farm horses. When, however, they got round the bend of the country lane, they saw the wooden bridge suspended over the Medway, and the river in flood, the water being so high that it was over the roadway of the bridge. Before it could be avoided the horses had made a plunge, the wheels of the wagon had crashed into the side of the old wooden structure, and every soul had been thrown into the water.

One of the gipsies pulled up from the stream a little, and feeling solid ground, threw off his coat, strained his eyes, and there caught sight of his mother. There she was, struggling in the stream. Plunging in, he got hold of her, whilst she got hold of him, both seeking to save each other. Then he shouted, "Mother, let go, and I'll save you!" For all that, however, the struggling went on, till, at length, the mother finally sank.

When the day of the burial came, the poor lad so forgot everything, even the clergyman conducting the service, that he made his way down into the grave, and got down on his knees beside the coffin, and, laying his head upon it, groaned out in agony these words: "Mother, mother, mother! I tried to save you, but you would not let me!" So, in like manner, God has done His best to save us! By grace, He has provided the great salvation. He has done His part. He can do no more. It just rests with us to accept it—to accept this greatest of offers, by the very simplest of means. "Salvation—through faith!" And that is the wonderful story—the wonderful Gospel of the grace of God in Jesus Christ, for the rescue and redemption of sinful man.

A. Russell Tomlin

** **

409   Boyesen says that when he returned to Norway after many years he was met at the pier by the man he used to be, and that his Lost Self would hardly speak to him, remarked that he affected a foreign accent, and reproached him for turning from the old ways. But the good grace of God will make us worthy of that lost self with whom we lived in the days when life was new and the heart was pure. It seems impossible, but it is true.

Joseph Fort Newton

Gratitude

410   A few years ago a boat was wrecked in a storm off Evanston, in America. In Northwestern University the students formed themselves to rescue the drowning passengers. One of the students, Edward Spencer, saved seventeen people from that sinking ship, and when he was being carried exhausted to his room, he asked, "Did I do my best? Do you think I did my best?"

Dr. Torrey was telling this incident at a meeting in Los Angeles and a man in the audience called out that Edward Spencer was present. Dr. Torrey invited Spencer up on the platform and an old man with white hair slowly climbed the steps amid loud applause. Dr. Torrey asked him if anything in particular stood out in his memory of so gallant a rescue. Spencer replied: "Only this, sir. Of the seventeen people I saved not one of them ever thanked me."

R. F. J. Charlish

** **

411   Some men were talking about causes of gratitude. One said, "Well, I, for one, am grateful to Mrs. Wendt, an old school-teacher, who thirty years ago went out of her way to introduce me to Tennyson." Asked a listener, "Does this Mrs. Wendt know that she made such a contribution to your life?" "I'm afraid not. I've never taken the trouble to tell her." "Then why don't you write her?" He did. The letter was forwarded. Then this note came in return, written in the feeble scrawl of an old woman. It began:

"My dear Willie . . ."

That in itself was enough to warm his heart. Here was a man of fifty, fat and bald, addressed as "Willie." He read on:

"I can't tell you how much your note meant to me. I am in my eighties, living alone in a small room, cooking my own meals, lonely and like the last leaf of fall lingering behind. You will be interested to know that I taught school for fifty years and yours is the first note of appreciation I ever received. It came on a blue, cold morning, and it cheered me as nothing has in years."

David A. MacLennan

✳✳

412   If one should give me a dish of sand and tell me there were particles of iron in it, I might feel for them with the finger in vain. But let me take a magnet and sweep through it, and how would that draw to itself the most invisible particles by the mere power of attraction! The unthankful heart, like my finger in the sand, discovers no mercies. But let the thankful heart sweep through the day, and as the magnet finds the iron, so it will find, in every hour, some heavenly blessings—only the iron in God's sand is gold.

O. W. Holmes

Gratitude and Service

413   Gratitude, rightly understood, can be the inspiration to a dedicated life of self-forgetting service. Witness the example of Dr. Albert Schweitzer who, speaking of the reasons that led him to offer himself for the ministry of healing in Africa, says: "It became steadily clearer to me that I had not the inward right to take as a matter of course my happy youth, my good health, and my power to work. Out of the depths of my feeling of happiness there grew up gradually within me an understanding of the saying of Jesus that we must not treat our lives as being for ourselves alone. Whoever is spared personal pain must feel himself called to help in diminishing the pain of others."

G. R. C. Fuller

Greatness in Service

414   Greatness does not consist in being served, but in serving. That was the message of Jesus, and it melts all our false ideals and our pride. The wife of President Hayes, when her husband was governor of Ohio, saw a crowd on the street jeering a drunken woman. She stopped the carriage, and took the woman in beside her, and drove off. That act glorified her. Or take the story of the Glasgow policeman who noticed a poor woman picking up some things

from the pavement, and demanded to see what they were. Uncovering her basket she showed him pieces of broken glass, and said, "I thought I would take it out of the way of the bairns' feet."

R. P. Anderson

Greed

415   Tolstoy, the famous Russian writer, has a story of a Russian peasant named Pakhom, who lived with his wife in humble, yet comfortable, circumstances. One day he conceived a great envy for some of his wealthy acquaintances and resolved that he too would have more land. "Only give me more land and I fear no man, no, not even the devil himself."

As time went on he found frequent opportunities for improving his position, and wherever he went good fortune attended his labours and his harvests were consistently good. But still he was not satisfied. "Too little land" was his invariable complaint. Then, one day, he heard tidings that made his heart throb with joy, that in the country of the Bashkirs you could buy as much land as you wished, and that for a song, provided you first humoured the peasants with suitable gifts. He was assured that this was really so, but there was a strange custom among these people.

The prospective buyer was required to put down his money in a bag at an appointed place, and from that place he would start to walk at sunrise, and all the land he staked off during the day would be his providing he arrived back at the starting-place by sunset.

Pakhom saw in this custom an unprecedented prospect of wealth, and having set down his purse, he began to walk. He went off at high speed and, scarcely stopping to eat or rest, he walked through the sweltering afternoon. On and on he went. Yes, he would take in that piece of rich land, and that, and that. By and by, he thought he had better direct his course for the starting-point again. He was very fatigued. His feet ached. His heart throbbed. But he must redeem his pledge.

The sun now was hastening to set, and he broke into a run, and just as the sun dipped out of sight he reached the goal of desire. He fell prostrate, blood running from his mouth. He lay there dead. The land that was to bring him wealth and prosperity claimed him as its victim. How Jesus urged men to beware of covetousness! "For what is a man profited if he shall gain the whole world and lose his own soul?"

S. H. Hedley Perry

＊＊

416   A few years ago a missionary was standing near a bunch of trees watching a number of monkeys jumping gaily from one branch to another. He was deeply interested. Along came a dark-skinned boy, and seeing the missionary was interested, he said to him: "Would you like me to catch one of those monkeys for you?"

"Yes," replied the missionary, "I would like to own a monkey for about one hour. Of course I would not like to keep it fastened in a cage, or tied to a chain or a rope; just keep it for one hour."

"Right," said the boy, "I will catch one for you." He hurried off. In a few minutes he returned, carrying a big pumpkin under his arm. Taking a knife from his pocket, he began to take a lot of the inside of the pumpkin away. Then he got a tin just big enough to pass through the hole in the pumpkin. This tin rattled inside the pumpkin. Then a piece of rope was fastened to the pumpkin, and to a tree. The boy and the missionary went some distance away. The missionary was greatly excited, wondering what would happen.

Within a few minutes several of the monkeys left the trees and came down to view the pumpkin. One monkey lifted it and shook it, and hearing something rattle inside was curious to know what it was: not only to feel it but have it if possible. These monkeys had plenty to eat, but they were not satisfied. One monkey wanted this tin and decided to have it. He laid hold of it and would not let go. The hole in the pumpkin was not big enough for the hand and the tin to come out. So while this greedy monkey was tugging at the tin, trying to get it out, the boy went along and caught the monkey without any trouble. You see this monkey, because of its greedy spirit, lost its freedom, spoiled its joy of jumping from branch to branch. Greed is one of the things that can spoil a life.   J. C. Mitchell

Growing Old

417   In that dreadful month of Britain's catastrophe, June, 1940, Winston Churchill flew to Tours, in France, and returning called a special session of the British War Cabinet. As Brigadier Bishop, who was there, reports, he announced to his dismayed ministers that France was on the verge of caving in and asking Hitler for his terms. He painted the situation in the grimmest colours. He reviewed the desperate military and political outlook and summed it up by saying, "We are now facing Germany completely isolated. We are alone." Then in the awful silence that followed he looked up and said, "I find it rather inspiring." To a student of human nature one of the most impressive facts in that scene is that Winston Churchill was then sixty-six years old.

Harry Emerson Fosdick

Growth

418   I heard of a boy who recently won a prize for drawing at a Sunday-school exhibition. When some one was congratulating him on having done such a good drawing he said, "That isn't my best drawing." "Why didn't you exhibit your best?" he was asked. "Oh," he replied, "my best drawing isn't drawn yet." That boy was by way of becoming a real artist. So it may be with us, if we let our eye of faith rest on the promise of God, the gift of the Holy Spirit, and not on the meagre successes and the frequent failures of the past.

John Bishop

Guidance

419   A tribute and testimony to God's guidance in life comes from Sir William Dobbie, who was Governor of Malta during the trying months of its siege. He tells how, at the age of fourteen, he came into a new relationship with God through Jesus Christ, and from then on he was conscious of God guiding his life. He also firmly believes that God intervened in the Battle of Malta. The air-craft carrier *Illustrious* had limped into Malta badly damaged by bombing. The German planes continued their attacks on the ship as she lay in dock. The dockyard officials estimated that it would require four days free from bombing to get the ship seaworthy enough to leave port. Sir William and some others joined in prayer that the ship might be saved. The planes still came over, but not one bomb hit the ship, and at dusk on the fourth day the *Illustrious* sailed for Alexandria, which she reached without mishap. Some people might call that a coincidence. But not Sir William Dobbie. He declares: "Humanly speaking, the chances of the *Illustrious* getting away from Malta were negligible, but the impossible happened, and we watched a miracle being enacted before our eyes." He is a convinced believer in the power of prayer and the guidance of God.   Adam Jack

⁂

420   Robertson of Brighton was destined for the Army. His father, his grand-father, his brothers were all soldiers. What more natural than that he should wish to follow in the family tradition! He applied for a commission, but there was inexplicable delay. Meanwhile others voices were urging him into the Church. So he went to Cambridge to take Holy Orders. Five days after this, too late, the commission came through. Yet in the view of that amazing ministry who would dare to say that God was not in that delay? Robertson was guided of God into the ministry. The Psalmist found out the secret. "In all thy ways acknowledge Him and He shall direct thy paths."

Edmund B. Potts

Handicaps

421   When Beethoven was thirty-two years old he set down on paper one of the saddest documents ever written. It was a will, or at least he called it a will, drawn in favour of his brothers, Karl and Johann. Most of it deals, not with the settlement of his property, but with the squaring of his grudge against life: "For six years I have been a hopeless case, cheated year by year by the hope of improvement. I am deaf. How can I endure an infirmity in the one sense which should have been more perfect in me than in others? . . . A little more and I would have put an end to my life—this wretched existence!" Then with a burst of feeling he adds: "O Providence, grant me at last but one day of pure joy; it is so long since real joy echoed in my heart."

That was in the year 1802. Twenty-four years later Beethoven was standing in the Karntertheater in Vienna. A vast audience had risen to applaud him, shouting their delight at the first performance of the Ninth Symphony, at the end of which the chorus joins with the orchestra, singing the composer's version of Schiller's "Ode to Joy." It was a veritable outpouring of exuberance in song. But the great composer stood silently turning the leaves of his score. Not a single sound could he hear of their glad applause.

Twenty-four years after his bitter complaint against life, he was able to compose a symphony symbolizing the spirit of joy. It was not because his deafness was cured. He was, in fact, more completely cut off than ever from the world of sound. It was not what happened to him that had turned for the better. It was what had happened within him that made the difference.

Theodore C. Hume

Handicaps, Overcoming

422   In Kobe, Japan, the outcast son of a Japanese official joined a voluntary Bible class to study Christianity. Deeply dissatisfied with national conditions and his inherited religion, he listened to the story told by Dr. Myers, the American missionary. "Gradually the story of Jesus, the Carpenter of Nazareth who poured out His life for the poor, gripped the heart of this young idealist." When he informed his uncle of his decision to become a follower of the strange Galilean, his uncle drove him out penniless as an insane dreamer and devotee of an impossible cult.

Despite the care of his missionary friend who had taken him into his home, the young Japanese contracted tuberculosis. He resolved on a desperate venture. If he had only a short time to live, he would live a life to the full. He would have his fling—for Christ and His cause in the midst of the greatest human need and misery he could find. When asked why he chose the slums of Kobe, he said: "I thought that I had only a few years to live and I wanted to do all I could in that short time for the people who needed me most."

In a district inundated again and again by floods of disease, he lived and laboured for a thing not seen with the eyes. He was arrested for "dangerous thoughts" by a government which later pleaded for his service on behalf of the nation. Despite physicians' protests—"there is not a sound organ in his body," declares an associate—he leads his crusade on behalf of a Christianized Japan, promoting trade unions, co-operative societies and a proletarian political party. Kagawa has been captured by the spirit and dreams of a young man who lived in a tiny corner of the Roman Empire nineteen hundred years ago.

David A. MacLennan

Happiness

423   In his enchanting fantasy, *The Blue Bird*, Maurice Maeterlinck relates how his dream children, Mytyl and Tyltyl, set off in search of the "Blue Bird of Happiness," which, however, eludes all their seeking, till at last they discover it in their own peasant home, and in the simple pleasures they enjoyed there—bread, fire and water, and the friendship of their cat and dog. It is a play that may be profitably re-read today, when citizens the world over are searching vainly for the elusive Blue Bird. The quest is an eternal one, for back to the story of the Garden of Eden, men and women have ceaselessly sought for, and pursued, the state of mind that we call happiness, in spite of the truth that the philosophers throughout the ages have warned us of its uncertain existence. Strangely enough, the Bible does not once contain the word "happiness," although it says that "the people are happy who have God as their Lord." Certainly comparatively few there be who seek for their felicity from that source.   Angus Watson

** **

424   Have you heard the story of Bismarck's Best Cigar? The Iron General, at the close of a stern conflict, sat down on the battle-field to smoke his last cigar. Just as he was about to light the match he noticed a poor wounded soldier lying near his feet, who was looking up at the cigar with wistful eyes. Immediately Bismarck lit the cigar, gave it to the wounded soldier and, after

watching him enjoy smoking it, he said: "That was the best cigar I ever had." It was the "best" because it gave him happiness by giving happiness to some one else.   Thomas Calvert

* *

425   Let me relate a story told by General Bramwell Booth. "I was once travelling by train," he says, "with Cecil Rhodes. My father was in the next carriage. Rhodes and I were alone. Struck by his depression and gloom, and hopeful for him, because of his interest in our work, I said to him: 'Mr. Rhodes, are you a happy man?' He threw himself back in his seat, looked at me with that extraordinary stare of his, and exclaimed: 'Happy? I happy? Good God, no!' And then, when I spoke to him of the only rest for the human spirit he said to me: 'I would give all I possess to believe what that old man in the next carriage believes.' I shall never forget the tragedy," said Bramwell Booth, "the utter tragedy of his voice, as long as I live." Yes: Cecil Rhodes had gathered many goodly pearls—fame, wealth, honor, power—but he had not found the Pearl of Great Price. Only when we have found Christ are we at rest, for "none but Christ can satisfy."

G. H. Clothier

Happiness, Road to

426   Professor Edgar S. Brightman, of Boston University, said to a group of high-school students recently: "Everybody wants something. The practical man is the man who knows how to get what he wants. The philosopher is the man who knows what man ought to want. The ideal man is the man who knows how to get what he ought to want."

John W. McKelvey

Happiness, Springs of

427   L. H. Myers, in his recent and delightful novel, *The Root and the Flower,* makes one of his characters, an Indian Christian, say to another Indian who was not a Christian and who felt that he had not reached the meaning of life: "Your business now, surely, is to look, not for happiness but for something deeper out of which happiness will spring." That is exactly what we have to do. It is worse than useless for us to keep asking ourselves: "Am I happy?" We must look for something deep out of which happiness will spring.

Howard L. Philp

Hate

428   It is told of Leonardo da Vinci, that when he was painting that picture
which stands perhaps among the best known in the world, the great picture,
wonderful for all its marvellous skill—the picture of the Last Supper—he had
a bitter quarrel with one of his contemporaries, and he thought that he would
strike a lasting blow at him, and that he would show what he thought of the
fellow by painting his face in that picture for the face of Judas Iscariot. And so
he did. The enemy whom he hated he set in the picture as Judas Iscariot, that
men might know what he thought of him. And then he worked on at his
picture until he came to paint the central figure—till he came to paint the face
of our Lord; and he tried and tried again but he never could satisfy himself
with it. Always it was at fault. Always it was clearly behind what he wanted
to get. Meanwhile there had been growing in his heart some sense of shame
at what he had done towards his enemy—some sense of uneasiness at treating a
man like that, however much he hated him. This feeling grew and grew in
him as he worked on, until at last he got quite ashamed and made up his mind
that he had done a wrong; and so at last he sponged out the face of Judas
Iscariot. He took it right out of the picture, and that night he saw in a dream
that face of our Lord which he has sketched and painted in the picture. There
were the lineaments and the look that he had been longing to sketch. There
they were. He could now portray the face of Christ because he had put away
bitterness out of his heart, and had made at least one step towards being in
charity with all men.

                                                                    Francis Paget

Hatred

429   "Class consciousness" is a Marxian word much in the mouths of men
who seek to create a new order of society by the suppression of every class but
that which comes under the technical definition of the "workers." "Class
consciousness," as commonly used, is a synonym for "class hatred." Hatred is
explosive, disruptive, destructive. It poisons the mind and heart of the hater.
It can only pull down. It is love that builds up. What the world most sorely
needs for "the healing of the nations," and the healing of the warring "classes"
alike is not "class consciousness" but "Christ consciousness."

                                                                    Ernest H. Jeffs

Healing

430   Let me tell you what happened to me not long ago. I found myself in the company of some men who were listening to an address by Dr. Richard C. Cabot on the subject of psychotherapy. When he had finished his address, one of the men said to him, "Dr. Cabot, that kind of thing may be possible in the case of nervous disorders; but you would not say, would you, that organic disease like cancer, for example, could be cured in that way?" And Dr. Cabot answered: "I have never heard of a case of cancer being cured in that way. But I would like to say this: I have never yet found myself in the presence of any disease which I myself feel unable to cure, or which I have never heard of any one else curing in that way, without saying to myself: 'if there were some one here who had one hundred times the personality that we have, that disease might be cured in that way.'" Now, right here lies the ground of reasonable belief that all the healing of Jesus was done in that way. There is no mathematics that can calculate the magnitude of the personality of Jesus Christ. And in proportion to the magnitude of His personality, lies the entire credibility of the effect of the impact of that personality upon the bodies of men.

Raymond Calkins

✳✳

431   There was a distinguished doctor in the medical faculty of Trinity College, Dublin, half a century ago, who used to begin his winter course of lectures in this way: "Gentlemen, you will soon be leaving these halls of learning for the larger practice of medicine. When you do you will meet two main classes of patients: those who get better by themselves and those who might have got better if the doctor had not interfered." Professorial jokes are a time-honoured institution, and yet I discern behind the Professor's facetiousness a genuine humility. No man has been long in the practice of medicine without realizing his limitations. He can do much but there is more to be done. Healing is of God. Of recent years a great new branch of that tree whose leaves are "for the healing of the nations" has been studied very earnestly—the branch called "psychiatry"—the healing of the mind. It is not enough to attend to the patient's bodily ailments; for real healing the mind and the spirit must be brought in too. And it is here that the power of religion has been recognized. All true healing is of God.

W. J. Priestley

Heaven

432   John Baillie in his great book *And the Life Everlasting* tells of his revolt against some of the hymns he used to sing as a boy so disparaging of our earthly life.

> I'm but a stranger here,
> Heaven is my home;
> Earth is a desert drear,
> Heaven is my home.

"I felt that something noble and beautiful was being defamed. Earth a dreary desert, yes, I know better now than I did then how often and for how many people it can be just that. But I am sure this is not the whole truth about it. It is also a garden of delights. It is also a field for heroes. And if no view can be true which forgets its gall and its weariness, neither can any be true which forgets its laughter and its glory." How true that is and how finely said! And yet for man with eternity set in his heart, how short are our days and how quickly do they fly!

                                                                    K. L. Parry

**

433   A woman once asked George MacDonald: "Are you quite sure that in heaven I will know my husband?" to which George MacDonald replied: "Madam, do you think we shall be greater fools in heaven than we are here?"

                                                                    Norman MacLean

**

434   There is a story of a minister who preached a sermon on "Heaven." Meeting one of his hard-headed deacons on the street the next day, the deacon said: "Dominie, you preached a fine sermon on 'Heaven.' You told me all about heaven, but you did not tell me where heaven is."

"Well," said the pastor, "I am glad of the opportunity of telling you this morning. I have just come from the hill yonder. In that cottage there is a member of your Church who is extremely poor; she is sick in bed with fever. Now, if you will go down in town and buy five dollars' worth of provisions for her, then go up there and say, 'My sister, I have bought these nice provisions in the name of our Lord and Saviour'; and furthermore, if you ask for her Bible and read the twenty-third Psalm, and then if you will get down on your knees and pray—if you do not see heaven before you get through, I will pay the bill."

The next morning the deacon said: "Pastor, I saw heaven yesterday, and I spent fifteen minutes there as certainly as you are a living man."

Frederick F. Shannon

Hell

435   I believe that when the physical life ceases—to put it personally, if it should chance that one of you should die to-night and your breath cease and your body lie cold in death, immediately you—the person—will find yourself in another atmosphere, but still living, and you will be there exactly what you are as you sit in the pew there; all the passions, all the tendencies, all the ideals, all the virtues, all the vices, all the glory, all the shame, that are in you, will be there in you still. And I have no hesitation in saying that should you be a bad man full of malignant passion, selfish, cruel, debauched, when that little tie of the body is loosened and the spirit is out in the world beyond, it will be in torment indescribable, and that it is in allusion to that, that our Lord used the strange expression about the rich man in the parable: "In hell he lifted up his eyes, being in torment."

Robert F. Horton

Heresy

436   The heresies of yesterday have a strange way of becoming the beliefs of tomorrow. No less an orthodox believer than A. B. Bruce said that the hope of Christianity is heresy. We know what he meant. He didn't mean that heresy is always the truth. He meant that God has yet more light to break forth from his word. Forms of faith change . . . faith abides. Theories about Jesus alter, but Christ remains the same yesterday, to-day and for ever. What makes a man a heretic is not incorrect belief according to the accepted standards of Church faith, but incorrect life according to the spirit of Christ. Not disagreement with a generally approved religious theory, but lack of Christ's love in daily living.

Harold Bickley

Heritage

437   Dr. A. J. Gossip tells of the shock he experienced when passing a shell-hole in Flanders to come suddenly upon the body of a Highland soldier laddie lying supine upon the earth. He was young, handsome and dear to some mother's heart. But his open eyes seemed to gaze into the onlooker's soul with mingled challenge and reproach. Dr. Gossip finds this memory, though sad and harrowing, an unending source of inspiration to live worthily of those "who had done their work and held their peace and had no fear to die."

Alfred Thomas

** **

438 A king of France discovered an ancient man engaged unremittingly in the planting of date kernels. "Why," he asked the man, "do you sow the seeds of a tree of such tardy growth, seeing that the dates will not ripen till a hundred years be passed?" The answer was, "Am I not eating the fruit of trees planted by my forefathers who took thought for those who were to come? And shall not I do like unto them?"

H. Bulcock

** **

439 Do you remember that story of how David in the heat of battle longed for water from the well of Bethlehem where he had drunk as a lad? At the wish, strong men sprang to arms, cut their way through the enemy, and brought him what he desired. It was only common water, but when he took it into his hands he could not drink it. The devotion and hazard of those men had made it for him a sacred thing, and he poured it out as an offering before God. So much that we take for granted would be seen on examination to be a privilege secured at great cost by those who went before us.   E. L. Allen

Heroes, Anonymous

440 When, at the end of the first world war, an unknown soldier was laid to rest in Paris amid all the pageantry that the state could provide, we dismissed this at first as a display of sentimentality permissible perhaps for Frenchmen but not conceivable in ourselves. But on reflection we decided to follow their example and to install a nameless victim of the war among the men and women whom the nation holds in honor. We did that, I take it, because we had come to see that wars are won and events decided, not only by statesmen doing their work in the sight of the public, but also by unknown and forgotten, quite ordinary men and women. Just as a charitable society has two sets of contributors, those who give their names and those who do not, so the roll of the heroes who have served the triumph of God's Kingdom will include its anonymous victors.

E. L. Allen

History

441 "What is history," asked Napoleon I, "but a fiction agreed upon?" "Don't read me history," said Sir Robert Walpole, for twenty-one years Prime Minister of England, "for I know that this cannot be true." The answer to such remarks is, that history may be uncertain in thousands of minor details, but it is not uncertain in its wider issues. History is like a battle; it sways to and fro; it is full of shocks and flank movements, retreats and advances, rout and resistance, utterly confusing to those who take part in it. Nevertheless, we know in the evening which side has won or lost.

F. W. Farrar

History, Lessons of

442   Professor Charles Beard, the historian, once said that there were four lessons of history. (1) Whom the Gods would destroy they first make mad with power. (2) The mills of God grind slowly, but they grind exceedingly small. (3) The bee fertilizes the flower it robs. (4) When it is dark enough you can see the stars. Our only hope is that the power behind things is set on righteousness: that the constitution of the world is opposed to evil; that this is no haphazard place where anything may happen, but that to sin is to fling ourselves against the powers that be. That is the settled basis on which we build our thinking. A great nation wrongs the world and we appeal to God with confidence and live through dark days unafraid, because He is on the throne. Much is amiss in the earth, and when nothing happens we boldly claim all eternity and say that if things do not right themselves here, then there must be something beyond this world where evil goes down, and good comes to its own.

John Bishop

History, Reading of

443   The gospel has put into men's hands the clue to history. In *The Bible Today*, Dr. Dodd has recently declared that this is the problem of our time, and he has expounded Professor Toynbee's analysis of the various attitudes to events which are continually recurring in human thought and which are presented as the choice before this age. They are:

(1) Archaism, an attempt to idealize the past and to restore it. Such is the attitude of Fascism.

(2) Futurism, which is born of despair of the present and insists that the present order must be swept away before Utopia can be established. Such an attitude is held by Marxism.

(3) Detachment, an endeavour to contract out of the historical situation altogether; and this characterizes modern forms of mysticism.

(4) Transfiguration, which is the endeavour to see the total situation and

ourselves as a part of it, and by bringing it into the light of some great purpose
and truth to transform it.   Leslie E. Cooke

Holiness

444   "What a comfort," wrote a soldier from the hospital at Scutari with
reference to Florence Nightingale, "it was to see her even pass. She would speak
to one and nod and smile to as many more; but she could not do it to all, you
know. We lay there by hundreds; but we could kiss her shadow as it fell and
lay our heads on the pillow again content." "Before she came," recorded another,
"there was cursing and swearing, but after that it was holy as a church." The
magic of her presence was felt in the dreaded room where operations were performed. When the maimed soldier saw her nerving herself with compressed
lips to undergo the pain of witnessing pain, he took heart of grace and gave himself into the surgeon's hands; and when the dying soldier saw her pen transmit
to paper his final messages for mother or wife or sweetheart, and heard from
her lips a verse of Scripture appropriate to his case or a stanza of one of her
favourite hymns, "his last faltering accents whispered praise." She unconsciously
imparted to the sufferers a new conception of God; and in the hearts of the
survivors there was enshrined down to their latest day "the lady with the lamp,"
idealized and invested not merely with angelic, but with even Divine, attributes.
                                                                      John Macmillan

✳✷

445   A certain preacher has recently said, "I was speaking on a platform one
night, and a 'cello, strung just as the musician had set it down, was standing
behind me, and as I spoke I could hear it answer. Every tone of my voice was
taken up by the tense strings of the musical instrument, which repeated behind
me the thing I was saying to the audience." The man who has the right tone
lives the Christ life and has in him the mind that was also in Christ Jesus.

                                                                         D. L. Moody

Holy Spirit

446   Dr. Brunner has voiced the conviction that we have shifted from the New
Testament centre of gravity. The chronic weakness, the spiritual poverty of
the Church is in his opinion due to our lack of apprehension of the New Testament witness to the Holy Spirit. Where the Spirit comes, he declares, things
happen which do not occur elsewhere and otherwise.   W. E. Farndale

✳✷

447   John Robinson was the minister of the Independent or Separatist church at Leyden in Holland, from 1609 to 1625. He, and those to whom he ministered, were exiles from their native England, from where they had been driven by the persecution of James I. But his persecuting hand followed even there, and so it was that on the 16th September, 1620, the *Mayflower*, a small vessel of 180 tons, with 104 men, women and children aboard, left for America, to arrive some 65 days later. We speak of them with admiration as the Pilgrim Fathers, and honour them for their love of, and fight for, freedom to worship. The epic story of the *Mayflower,* and the significance of its perilous journey should be known by every free churchman.

It was with historic words that John Robinson bade farewell to his people, and the latter part of that message—"the Lord had more light and truth yet to break forth out of His Holy Word"—has been quoted so often as though it might be from Holy Scripture itself.   W. J. Peacock

Home

448   Mr. John R. Mott tells us that in examining the biographies of 128 ministers, covering a period of 500 years, he found that all but nine of them came from homes favourable to the work. A hundred of these men were among the leaders. Does that signify anything? The old Scotch proverb has it that "An ounce of mother is worth a pound of clergy." "Every day of my life," said the mother of Hugh Price Hughes, "I have prayed that he might do a good and great work, and be aided in the doing of it." When he had decided to be a Methodist preacher, and had written his father that he believed it was the will of God for him, the reply was: "I would rather you were a Methodist preacher than Lord Chancellor of England."   R. O. Armstrong

✳✳

449   In the life of Principal Rainy there is an illuminating incident. He was the storm centre of theological controversy. A friend said, "How is it you can keep sweet and calm in the midst of such a storm?" Rainy replied, "I'm very happy at home."   J. C. Carlile

Home Life, Impress of

450   On the great Antarctic ice barrier, when the bergs break off and float away towards the warmer water, the young penguins often remain on the floating ice. What pain and terror to witness the parting of the ways between the old and the young; but the young birds can swim; they learn the power and function of their gifts only when put to the supreme tests, and when danger rises they drop into the water, and the homing instinct brings them back home.

So shall it be with our children. We older folk remain on the firm barrier of safe and wise tradition; but see our children floating away upon a dangerous floe. Yet they have in them undiscovered powers, they can breast the waves of danger when put on their mettle, and deep within them lies the impress of their home life; they too have the homing instinct, and eventually will turn back home.   Harris E. Kirk

Honesty

451   I do not adopt all Darwin's positions, but I have profound admiration for his honesty and courage. He, as you will remember, affirmed that the folk of Tierra del Fuego were so debased that it was impossible to civilize them. When in later years he revisited the island and found that Christian missionaries had settled there, preached and practised the gospel and civilized the people, he publicly withdrew his statement and sent a cheque to the missionary society concerned. But that only illustrates the habit of his life.

Darwin and his son and Romanes spent an evening together. In response to a remark Darwin said that he had never experienced the emotion of reverence awakened by beautiful scenery so much as when standing on the slopes of the Cordilleras. After he had retired Darwin came down in his dressing-gown and slippers in order to say that on reflection he had remembered that the beauty of the forests of Brazil had stirred him to greater emotion, and he could not sleep till he had corrected his previous statement. For, said he to Romanes and his son, "It might conceivably affect your conclusions." He would work for months in order to establish a theory, and then give up the whole thing because one little insect he was watching by its acts exploded his theory.

Contrast that with Haeckel. Fifty years ago scientists were reading his works. Twenty-five years ago we were all reading popular editions of his *Riddle of the Universe*. You never hear of it or him now. Why? Because in order to buttress a theory of his he used the photoplates of one thing and called it another in the illustrated edition of that once famous work.

Darwin could climb down and he lives; Haeckel would not climb down and he is dead and buried.   F. J. Miles

Hope

452   It is said that Harlan Page once went through his Sunday-school to get the spiritual census of both the teachers and the scholars. Coming to one of the teachers, he inquired, "Shall I put you down as having a hope in Christ?" The teacher replied, "No." "Then," said Mr. Page, very tenderly, "I will put you down as having no hope." He closed his little memorandum book and left him. Those two solemn words, "no hope," rang in the unconverted teacher's mind, and the Holy Spirit gave him no rest until he found a hope at the cross of Christ.   Theodore L. Cuyler

＊＊

453   There once was a terrible accident in one of the great coal mines in Pennsylvania. Hundreds of men worked day and night till they fell with exhaustion. Women were carried away unconscious. Girls fainted with the horror of it; there were fathers and brothers and husbands down there. And a wire trembled up from the President at the White House: "Is there any hope for the men?" The answer shivered back to the White House: "No hope." This world of ours was suffering sorrow and shame because of sin, and it seemed as if there was no hope for man. Then the glad message vibrated from Calvary's hill through the whole earth: "There is hope for all."   Evangeline Booth

＊＊

454   I was talking two nights ago to a doctor who is on the staff of our clinic here and whose practice in Harley Street, I am afraid, has come to an end for the time being. He told me how his two little children dashed into the room from the darkened streets and said, "Daddy, until the streets were darkened we never saw the stars!" Well, there are stars of hope and truth and love and kindness and serenity. They have always been shining in His sky. Perhaps now that the world is so dark we shall see them a little better. And remember, those stars will never fade until the dawn of God's eternal heaven.

Leslie D. Weatherhead
From *Christian World*, Vol. 136

Hope for World

455   Professor Joad, in the final section of his latest book, *A Young Soldier's Search for a New World,* gives two sign-posts for the future. First, we must find some means for putting an end to war, for unless that is done everything will be in vain. Second, there must be a spiritual revival, without which there is indeed no hope for the world. Is there then no hope for the world? Is there to be no end of war? Are the nations of the world to be for ever at strife? Is it the inevitable fate of humanity to go back into barbarism and despair? Is there no source from which spiritual renewal and revival can come? The answer to all such

questions is contained in the "saying concerning this Child," who was born to usher in the golden age when there shall be "peace on earth, goodwill among men."

R. Sirhowy Jones

Human Nature

456   One of the leading educators of the United States has come back from a prolonged stay in China. A high-minded gentleman of finely tempered intelligence, he is not a Christian. He habitually treats religion as a negligible affair. But before he left the Far East, he did make a confession to a friend of mine. "I have been taking too much for granted in the United States," he said; "I have been taking it for granted that human nature can always be counted on to act in certain ways, but I find that it cannot, except among people who have had a long Christian tradition."

Harry Emerson Fosdick

✳✳

457   A physiognomist, closely scanning the face of Socrates, pronounced him to be a bad man. He even went so far as to specify his vices and faults. "Proud, crabbed, lustful," were the charges brought against him. The Athenians laughed this to scorn. What could be more absurd? Everybody knew its falsity. The distinguished sage was the exact opposite of the description. To their amazement, however, Socrates hushed them, and declared that no calumny had been uttered. "What he has said," he remarked, "accurately describes my nature, but by philosophy I have controlled and conquered it."

T. R. Stevenson

✳✳

458   In 1666, when the Great Fire destroyed so much of London, Sir Christopher Wren appealed to the authorities that no longer should there be those dark, narrow, festering, beastly lanes where noisome pestilences could gather and sweep away their population. He pleaded that a new London should be built with fine broad streets and avenues and squares—squares that would be lungs for the city. And they listened—but nothing was done!

In one of Dostoievsky's great novels there is a picture which I should like to leave with you. I cannot give you it adequately; there is not time, and I have not the power. The old fable ran, you know, that Jesus Christ came back to earth, and in the novel there is a picture of Him in a city square, healing the sick as before, raising the dead, going about doing good. Suddenly the cathedral doors slide back, and the Grand Inquisitor, a man of ninety, who the day before had sent a score of heretics to the stake, walks into the market-place. He sees what is going on, and immediately he has this Heretic arrested and thrust into a cell. At midnight the old inquisitor goes into the cell and has an interview with the Master. I will not try to reproduce the scene, but in the end the old inquisitor says: "To-morrow I shall have you burned." And Christ rises, crosses the cell, and kisses the old man on his bloodless lips, until the old man cries, "I cannot bear it," and throws open the cell door and says to his august prisoner, "Go," and Christ moves out into the darkness and is seen no more. Then Dostoievsky writes down these two sentences: "But he did not alter his opinion. He did not change his practice."

That is not the kind of end to the story we should have liked, but oh, men and women, that is human nature.

Leslie D. Weatherhead

From *Christian World Pulpit*, Vol. 134

Humility

459   We know that William Carey would deprecate our thinking of him, for humility was among his outstanding characteristics. We recall that death-bed scene when the eager young Scottish missionary, Alexander Duff, paid one of his visits to the sick chamber at Serampore. Towards its close, Carey said, "Dr. Duff, you have been speaking about Dr. Carey. When I am gone, do not speak about William Carey, speak only of William Carey's Saviour."

H. L. Hemmens

Humility, Secret of

460   There is a lovely story told of the saintly scholar Bengel, who lived in the eighteenth century. His students, we are told, marvelled at the great intellectuality, humility and Christ-likeness that blended in such beauty in the old man. One night, one of them, eager to learn the secret, concealed himself in the professor's room. There he waited hour after hour, and he thought how weary the old scholar would be after his long evening's work in the class-room. At length, however, he heard his step in the hall and waited breathlessly to learn the coveted secret. The old man came in, changed his shoes, and sitting down at the study table, opened his well-thumbed Bible, and began reading leisurely page by page. For half an hour he read, three quarters of an hour, an hour and more, and then, leaning his head upon his hands for a few minutes in silence, he said in the simplest and most familiar way, "Well, Lord Jesus, we're on the same terms. Good night."

H. G. Doel

Humour

461   Robert Hall was conspicuous for the blending in his fine nature of the pathos and the humour that we speak of, a sad, glad man, much given to laughter, soon moved also to tears. On one occasion, he having preached at a chapel anniversary a most solemn and pathetic discourse, and being followed in the evening by a "serious" brother, when the day's work was done, was as witty as he was wise, mirthful, and jocund, and the cause of wit also in others. The "serious" brother at length remonstrated. "Mr. Hall, I am surprised at you, sir, after the solemn sermon you preached this morning, that you should trifle now as you do." "Are you, sir," replied Mr. Hall; "shall I tell you the difference between you and me, sir? You talk your nonsense in the pulpit, I talk mine out of it."

J. W. Lance

Humour in Pulpit

462   Spurgeon was full of common sense and, of course, he had a great wit. You remember the three young fellows who went to the Tabernacle and did not take off their hats. It was at the time when there was a good deal of society mocking and jeering at Spurgeon. There were caricatures of him and wild stories about his extravagances which you cannot see in any of his sermons, because they are sternly chaste. So three young fellows, of the jolly kind, as they called them then, thought they would go to the Metropolitan Tabernacle to show these people what they thought of them. This was not a place of worship, it was a sort of music-hall. They went there, and kept on their hats.

The officials went up to them and said: "Won't you take your hats off, gentlemen?" They said: "No, this is not a place of worship." Spurgeon started preaching, and he began to say a word about the virtue of Christian forbearance. He said: "The other day I went to a Jewish synagogue, and out of respect to the building I took off my hat. But then I saw that everybody else kept his hat on. Then I realized that was their method of paying respect to the sanctity of that building. Well now," he continued, "I appeal to those three young Jews to return that compliment!" If the people had started howling at these three young rascals they would have persisted, but they could not stand the laughter of the Metropolitan Tabernacle, which would have resounded throughout London the following day, and their hats were soon off.

David Lloyd George

Humour, Use of

463 One of the elements in Lincoln's greatness was his ability to distribute his burdens by bringing his emotions into play. He said: "With the fearful strain that is on me night and day, if I did not laugh I should die." It was difficult for others to understand that quality in him. On a certain day Lincoln came to a Cabinet meeting, and asked if they had seen the new volume by Artemus Ward. He read aloud to them from it. Secretary of War Stanton, as usual, was very critical of the President. But in a few moments Lincoln closed the book, and took from his hat a folded paper. He read them the first draft of the Emancipation Proclamation. Lincoln demonstrated the importance of balance. He explained his point of view as follows:

"Sometimes the telling of a good story or the listening to one lightens the load of sorrow and suffering that one in my position has to bear; but it is a mistake to think that I am a humourist, or tell stories for the laugh that is in them."

David John Donnan

Hymns

464 Look at a modern hymn; it is, as a rule, full of man, full of his wants, of his aspirations, of his anticipations, of his hopes, of his fears, full of his religious self, if you will, but still full of self. But read an ancient hymn: It is, as a rule, full of God, of His awful nature, of His wonderful attributes; it is full of the Eternal Son, of His acts, of His sufferings, of His triumphs, of His majesty.

Canon Liddon

Hypocrisy

465 A young man once said to Professor Henry Drummond, "Do you see that elderly gentleman? He is the founder of our infidel club." "What!" said Drummond. "Is not that man an elder in the Church?" "But still, he is the founder of our infidel club. Everybody in the village knows what a humbug he is; and so we will have nothing to do with religion."   A. M. McIver

Ideals

466 I read once of a mother praying at the bedside of her child when she heard the voices of angels. "I am health," one said; "whomsoever I touch shall never know pain." "I am wealth," said another; "whomsoever I touch shall never know want." The third angel said, "I am fame; whomsoever I touch shall be renowned." "I am power," cried the fourth; "whomsoever I touch shall have dominion." The fifth angel said, "I am wisdom; whomsoever I touch shall have knowledge." "I am love," another said; "whomsoever I touch shall win the world's affection." The seventh angel said, "I am none of these; whomsoever I touch shall have high ideals." The mother, with out-stretched arms, exclaimed: "Oh, you with the high ideals, touch my child!"   John Bryant

Ignorance, Spiritual

467   Admiral Sir Geoffrey Layton, Commander-in-Chief at Portsmouth, said recently that he had found that among men of eighteen or nineteen years who were entering the Navy only 65 per cent knew the significance of Good Friday and only 45 per cent the significance of Easter. It is a sad business when we come to take as a matter of course the great Christian festivals, especially Good Friday and Easter Day. These two days are the greatest days in the Christian year. On these days man's redemption was wrought. On these days the way was open for man to fulfil the purpose for which he was born.   J. Calvert Cariss

Immortality

468   Emerson tells of two members of the United States Senate who used every opportunity of leisure to discuss speculative subjects. After a time one of them retired, and the two did not meet for twenty-five years. Then one of them asked, "Any light, Albert?" "None," was the reply. After a pause the other inquired, "Any light, Lewis?" and again the answer was "None." Their life was spent in the attempt to resolve the problem of mystery, yet its solution had evaded them. But the Christian hope is that in the life to be mystery shall have vanished in perfect and full-orbed knowledge. "Now we see through a glass, darkly"; true!—"but then face to face." "Now I know in part"; true!—"but then shall I know even as also I am known."   H. S. Seekings

※※

469   When Livingstone was in Central Africa he asked the natives what became of their noble river. They had no conception of the sea, and after they had mused over it awhile they said they supposed it was lost in the sand. Now what becomes of this other great river, the river of human life? Oh! how it does rush day by day through the streets of this great city, through the streets of the world. And what is going to become of it, this mystic river of human life, of its bubble cities, its jewelled thoughts, its musical language, its shell histories—

what becomes of it all, what significance is there in it? Oh! says the sceptic, the parson and the undertaker and the sexton, they see the last of it under the sun. I tell you that this race is never going to sit down to any rational satisfaction with that creed. Where do you get your great hope from? The Gospel brought life and immortality to light. And I say to you, don't you be ashamed of the doctrines of the future.   W. L. Watkinson

✳✳

470   Professor Huxley gives his opinion of Tennyson in a letter. He says that Tennyson comprehended science, its spirit, its significance better than any poet since Lucretius. He said that he had followed its findings, sympathized with its aims, given delicate expression to its accomplishments. He says Tennyson is the greatest scientific poet that this world has known for two thousand years—since Lucretius.

Very well, what about Tennyson? Here, the very man who is the poet of science according to Professor Huxley, who is a reliable witness on such a subject, here the greatest poet of science is at the same time the poet of immortality. That man, that poet, your own laureate, who studied biology and astronomy and geology, who had entered into all the peculiarities of the scientific spirit and aim, wrote the one poem of your generation that will not perish, the poem of immortality, and when that great man came to lay his noble head upon a dying pillow he breathed out the last aspiration of his noble soul in the hope that when he had crossed the bar, he would meet his Pilot face to face. So don't you be shy about the doctrine of immortality. If you feel a bit uneasy about it get behind Tennyson; nay, take your stand with St. Paul; nay, take your stand with Him who spake as never man spake, and who declared unto you that if there is not another world He would have told you. "I go to prepare a place for you."   W. L. Watkinson

✳✳

471   For half a century, I have been writing my thoughts, history, philosophy, drama, poetry, romance, satire, ode and song. I have tried all, but I feel that I have not said a thousandth part of what is in me. When I go down to the grave I can say with others, I have finished my work, but I cannot say, I have finished my life.   Victor Hugo

✳✳

472   I cannot understand how anyone can believe in a loving God and yet not believe—I will dare to say, not make his faith in God conditional upon believing—in reunion after death with those he has loved and lost. You may call this sentimentalism if you like. I can only say that I cannot believe in a

loving God who could implant in the human heart the passion and tenderness of human love and yet say in the end, "This is of no importance to my eternal purpose, and I have nothing to say to you when your baby dies but that you must get over it as best you can." I leave it there: or, rather, I leave it by saying that I believe in reunion after death because I believe in a loving God. "Proofs" are nothing here. The two beliefs stand or fall together.

                                                        Ernest H. Jeffs

**

473   Anatole France thought he was saying a clever thing when he made fun of the simple old countrywoman who clung to the thought of her own immortality. "Tell her she will live a million years but must die at last—she will still be inconsolable!" Of course she will be. She does not want a million years of eating and drinking. What she wants, though she cannot express her thought, is some assurance that she was created for something more than eating and drinking. In her heart and mind and soul she challenges God Himself to justify her instinct and her claim to live while He lives, and, as she shares His labours and sufferings in time, to share His victory in eternity. "Because I live, ye shall live also."   Ernest H. Jeffs

**

474   Napoleon found an artist once painting a picture, and asked him, "Whom are you painting that for?" And he, drawing himself up proudly, replied, "I am painting it for immortality, sir." "How long will your canvas last?" asked the Emperor. "It has been skilfully prepared; it will last at least a thousand years." Napoleon shrugged his shoulders: "Now we see what an artist's idea of immortality is."   Lyman Abbott

**

475   Dr. John A. Hutton has said that we have fallen away from the richness of the Christian anticipation of the future because we have allowed ourselves "to speak of the immortality of the soul, which is not the Christian doctrine." The immortality of the soul is not a Christian doctrine at all. Barbarians hold it, Hindus, Confucians, every tribe and every nation. The "distinctive Christian doctrine" is not that the soul is immortal but that the body rises from the dead.
                                                        A. H. Selway

Immortality, Impersonal

476   There are some who believe in a fantastic kind of impersonal immortality. They believe, as Julian Huxley puts it, "that spiritual or mental activity

is not lost, but all of it returns, in some way not yet understood, to a store or pool of spiritual reality which is the non-material counterpart of energy." But, apart from the fact that we have no experience of spiritual activity apart from personality, that sort of evaporation of spiritual energy from personality, so that it may be stored in some unimaginable celestial tank, is too far-fetched ever to commend itself as an explanation of what happens at death.

With Henry Jones, "I turn my back on metaphors that lower spirit to the level of things of sense." For surely Julian Huxley's idea of impersonal immortality does that, and, in doing so, destroys values that seem to us to be the very highest we know. I have listened many times to Julian Huxley's fascinating lectures. I know of no other person like him. And if all that makes him Julian Huxley were lost, if nothing continued but his spiritual activity, whatever that vague phrase could mean, then something of unique value would be lost. And that theory involves the complete denial of God the Father. For a father does not love the sum total of the mental activity of his children and seek to decant it into a tank; he loves John and Mary and Peter, even though the mental activity of Peter may be scarcely noticeable. And if he loses one, nothing can make up for the loss of that one. It is useless to tell him that the amount of mind-stuff in the pool has not fallen perceptibly. He is not thinking in terms of mind-stuff. He has lost John, and a million million others will not make up for John. That is the very essence of the Christian gospel—the value of the individual to God. He loved me, and gave Himself for me! Death will never conquer that love.

James MacKay

Incarnation

477   There is a story of a little girl who was being put to bed one night and she was afraid of the dark. "Do not be afraid," said her mother, "God is with you." "I know," said the little girl, "but I want some one with a face." Pass from that childish story to the words of Paul Elmer More, one of the greatest scholars and the most eminent literary critic America has ever produced. After working his way from a position of complete scepticism to a position where he saw that "the ideals and standards by which men live must have a place in the structure of the Universe," and then to the position that they must exist in the mind of a Person, and finally to the position that such a Person could not for ever remain silent, he said: "My longing for some audible voice out of the infinite silence rose to a pitch of torture. To be satisfied, I must see face to face. I must, as it were, handle and feel."

This aching desire to hear a voice and this longing to see a face are both met in the Christian revelation of God to the world. In the Person of Jesus Christ, who came into the world at Bethlehem on the first Christmas morning so long ago, we believe we see the face, the character of God; and in the voice of Jesus Christ we believe we hear the authentic utterance of God.

James Colville

**

478 I do not know what an angel is. I do not know how an angel manifests himself in this world. I do not know how a light that does not come from a material source shines into human minds. I do not even know how the light that has come from the sun this morning has reached my mind through my nerves, carrying with it the picture of those exquisite frosty trees. I cannot explain how the Angels manifested themselves to the Shepherds. I cannot explain how the Babe was conceived by the Holy Ghost. But I believe in both because I believe in a real Incarnation of God in Jesus Christ. I believe in an Incarnation because nothing else explains Jesus Christ to me. The Guiding Star, the Angels, the journeying Magi, the worshipping Shepherds harmonize with and emphasize that conception so perfectly that I cannot believe they have been invented.

James MacKay

Indifference, Social

479 One day, as Louis XV was hunting in the woods away from the guilty palace of Versailles, he met a ragged peasant with a coffin. "What did the man die of?" asked the king. "Of hunger," said the serf, and the king gave his steed the spur. When Foulon was asked how the overtaxed people were to live, he brutally answered: "Let them eat grass." When the mob, maddened into wild beasts, caught him in the streets of Paris, they hung him, and stuck his head upon a pike, his mouth filled with grass, amidst sounds as of Tophet from a grass-eating people.

F. W. Farrar

Indolence

480 A distinguished Swiss theologian has written: "If you ask me which is the real hereditary sin of human nature, do you imagine I shall answer pride, or luxury, or ambition, or egotism? No; I shall say indolence. He who conquers indolence will conquer almost everything."

Horace E. Hewitt

Inferiority, Accepting

481   A tense, screwed-up, strained, striving, hysterical, never-are-but-ever-about-to-be kind of personality is not much to be desired. Better an honest and cheerful realist in this matter of spiritual achievement than a neurotic idealist. "Everything, except God," says Mr. C. S. Lewis, expounding a much neglected principle, the principle of hierarchy, "has some natural inferior." This is well worth pondering. It is better for many of us to be cheerful and useful turnips than to pose all our lives as luxurious vines about to be.

D. W. Langridge

Influence

482   Dick Sheppard has told the story of his first attempt to serve in the East End of London. He was a cock-sure University student, full of zeal to set the world aright. He was given the job of trying to redeem a hopeless drunkard. He talked to him as well as he could, but seemed to make no impression. But one day when he called, he discovered that the man had signed the pledge, and was keeping it.

A parish clergyman, Strickland, whose congregation was sparse, who had no reputation as a preacher, called upon him. He was shy. For long periods the two would sit in the room together, not saying a word. But when he had gone, the man said to his wife: "It's just as though Jesus Christ had been sitting in that chair." It was the sheer influence of goodness that had brought the change.

John Bishop

✳✳

483   One of the most thrilling and dramatic chapters in the history of astronomy has to do with the discovery of the planet Neptune. It came about like this. As early as 1690 Uranus had been sighted and it was observed at intervals thereafter over a period of a hundred years. But there was something puzzling to the astronomers in these appearances of Uranus. The planet seemed to be behaving most peculiarly. About its movements there was a curious eccentricity for which the astronomers found it difficult to assign a cause. After much hard thinking, they concluded that there was only one way in which to account for these aberrations, and that was to postulate the existence of another planet, then unknown, which was supposed to be exerting a gravitational pull upon Uranus. So it transpired. Stronger telescopes were constructed and, when turned to the sky, they brought within range of human vision the sparkling beauty of Neptune. Thus the seeming eccentricity of Uranus was explained by the existence and attractive power of this great heavenly body.

Ian Macpherson

＊＊

484 Quintin Hogg was a merchant prince who lived in London and who gave his fortune and service to the boys of the London streets. Among them was Jem Nichols whom Hogg had rescued from the mud and given a chance to achieve character. A long while after Quintin Hogg had died, a friend met Jem Nichols going straight in spite of many difficulties. When this friend asked him how he was able to do it, Jem brought out of his pocket a tattered photograph, saying as he did so: "Whenever I am tempted I just take this out of my pocket and look at it. His face is such a wonderful help." What a steadying influence the confidence of others in us has upon our own self-control!

Harold W. Ruopp

＊＊

485 A certain plain, modest, old-fashioned schoolmaster, named John Trebonius, always took off his hat in the presence of his scholars. "For, who knows," said he, "there may be among my pupils a great poet, or a great preacher, or a great philosopher!" And as a matter of fact, he had in his class a chubby little boy whose name was Martin Luther—so called by his parents for having been born on the eve of St. Martin. Martin Luther's tutors were many—yet not any of them are known to fame, and John Trebonius is remembered, not for anything he said, but for something he did and his explanation of it. To the simple removal of that man's hat, I suggest, we may owe the Reformation!   W. Stuart Scott

＊＊

486 Here is John Egglen. He is the deacon of an out-of-the-way church in the oldest city in England—Colchester. He wakes up on a winter Sunday morning. The date is January 6th, 1850. It is snowing hard. Should he or should he not attempt the journey to church? He thinks to himself: "Well, if the deacons do not go, how can they expect the people to go?"—and, although it means a tramp of over a mile to the church, he ventures out, and arrives on the stroke of eleven o'clock. He is met in the vestibule by a brother deacon, who says to him: "We are in a fix, Brother Egglen, I must say. The preacher hasn't turned up! There are only thirteen people in the church. What are we going to do? Cancel the service?" "Good gracious, no!" replies Brother Egglen. "It is quite understandable why the preacher has not got here; the snow-drifts are six feet deep between here and Kelvedon. I will take the service myself.

I expect everybody present belongs to the church, so they will excuse any mistakes on my part." "Of course, Brother Egglen!" says the deacon. "I think they are all our own people, save one—a boy sitting under the gallery. He is a stranger, but as he is only a boy, he really doesn't matter. But, do you think you ought to bother? All told, there are only thirteen!" "Well," said John Egglen. "Our Lord had only twelve! If He thought it worth while to deliver immortal discourses to them, I must not think it worthless to address thirteen!"

I need scarcely tell you—for the name Colchester will have given you the clue—that the "boy sitting under the gallery" was Charles Haddon Spurgeon. When John Egglen, insignificant deacon of an unimportant church, looked at that boy and said pointedly: "Young man, you look pretty miserable! And you will always be miserable—miserable in life, miserable in death—if you do not obey this text: 'Look unto me and be ye saved, all the ends of the earth!' But if you will 'look' this moment you will be saved." "And I looked," said Spurgeon, "until I could almost have looked my eyes away; and in heaven I will look still, in joy unutterable!"

So we owe his remarkable, world resounding ministry to a man who, Spurgeon says, "was really stupid as you would say. He was obliged to stick to his text for the simple reason that he had nothing else to say. He did not even pronounce the words rightly, and in about ten minutes he got to the end of his tether. But when he addressed me, shouting as only a Primitive Methodist can: 'Young man, look to Jesus! Look, look, look!' I did, and then, and there, the cloud on my heart lifted, the darkness rolled away, and that moment I saw the sun." There is, so far as I know, no monument in existence to John Egglen; but who can deny that he was the wire through whom came the power which in Spurgeon's ministry electrified the world?   W. Stuart Scott

※※

487   Dwight Moody had a brother, and after his own conversion he earnestly pleaded with him, until the brother also yielded himself to Christ and became such an earnest worker that he was the means of leading a number of his friends at his home into the kingdom. And then this brother died and was buried. A few years ago, as I spent a day in Northfield and was driven through its beautiful streets by one of the old residents, I said, "I wish you would tell me something about Mr. Moody that may not be generally known." And as we passed the old white church he said, "I remember his brother's funeral." He said that there were a number of ministers in the pulpit, and that after they had finished the usual service and the coffin-lid was about to be put in its place, Mr. Moody arose, and stepping forward from the seat where he had been sitting, with a shining face, he laid one hand upon the coffin, and then lifting

the other he poured out such a stream of thanksgiving unto God for the life that was gone, and for the wonderful comfort and joy and hope that came to him in Jesus Christ, that it was said by this onlooker that it almost seemed as if the heavens were opened and they could see the angels of God ascending and descending upon the Son of man.

At last he ceased, the coffin-lid was placed in its position, and the body was carried out and laid in the grave. On one side of the sepulchre stood fifty young men, many of them led to Christ through the influence of this one who was gone, and they held in their hands beautiful white flowers, which they cast down upon the coffin in token of the glorious resurrection. And on the other side of the grave stood Mr. Moody; and he said that as he stood there and thought of how his brother, being dead, was yet speaking, he felt that if he were silent the very stones would cry out, and he cried with a loud voice, "Glory to God! Glory be to God! O death, where is thy sting? O grave, where is thy victory?"   B. Fay Mills

※※

488   Dr. Charles Brown has told us that when he was a youth a noteworthy incident took place between him and his minister. He was then at Birmingham, and Rev. George Jarman was the pastor of the church. Under his direction a lay preachers' class was started for the men of the district, and Rev. Henry Platten was entrusted with the care of these young men, who included Charles Brown. The teacher soon discovered that in Charles he had someone above the average, and on one memorable night he put his hand on his shoulder and said to him, "Have you ever thought of the ministry as your vocation?" And from that hour he was placed under the guidance of his own minister. Writing later, Dr. Brown said of his minister: "He was never a great preacher; indeed I often found myself straying to other churches not infrequently because his sermons were tedious. But he was a great pastor and a true friend. I thank God for the memory of him."   William Mudd

※※

489   The influence of Christian writers is seen in an interesting light, in the way in which one book becomes the parent of another through successive generations. About the close of Queen Elizabeth's reign, a Puritan minister, called Edmund Bunny, met with a book written by a Jesuit priest, named Parsons; and, excluding the Popery, he recast the book and published it with a new title. A copy came into the hands of Richard Baxter, then a boy in Shropshire; and its earnest appeals led to his conversion. He grew to manhood, became a laborious preacher of the Gospel, and a voluminous writer. Among other books, he wrote the *Call to the Unconverted,* twenty thousand copies of which are said to have been sold in a single year. Twenty-five years after Baxter's death a copy of this book fell in the way of Philip Doddridge, a youth at St. Alban's, and brought him to God. He became a Christian minister and author, writing, in addition to other works, *The Rise and Progress of Religion in the Soul,* which has been translated into several languages, and made useful to many souls.

Thirty-three years after the death of Doddridge, William Wilberforce was setting out on a journey to the South of France, and, at the suggestion of a friend, took a copy of this book to read on the journey. The perusal of it led to his consecration to Christ. He found time, amid all his political and philanthropic duties, to write his *Practical View of Christianity,* a work which has passed through more than one hundred editions, and which, among the upper classes of society especially, has been a powerful leaven of righteousness. When Leigh Richmond was a young curate in the Isle of Wight, still ignorant of the Gospel, a college friend sent him a copy of Wilberforce's book. He began to read it, and could not leave off till he came to the end. The result he thus describes:—"To the unsought and unexpected introduction of Mr. Wilberforce's book, I owe, through God's mercy, the first sacred impression which I ever received as to the spiritual nature of the Gospel system." Another copy of the same work taught Dr. Chalmers the way of salvation, and made him such a distinguished preacher of Christ's Gospel. Leigh Richmond, as you know, afterwards wrote the touching story of "The Dairyman's Daughter"; and Dr. Chalmers preached and published some of the ablest and most effective sermons of the age. Who knows how this genealogy may lengthen as time goes on; and what other books may trace back their ancestry to the copy of *Bunny's Resolution,* lent to Richard Baxter's father.   William Walters

* *

490 To maintain the sanctity of the home and the meaning of the marriage vows means undeviating loyalty of the highest order. And yet, notwithstanding the difficulties and trials involved, life lived in harmony with this law of honour rings true and that is the final test. No better example is afforded than the chaste and noble life of Alice Freeman Palmer. This remarkable woman, elected president of Wellesley College at twenty-seven years of age, resigning her office when she married Dr. George Herbert Palmer, Professor of Philosophy at Harvard, devoted her life with conspicuous ardour and success to the development of Christian womanhood throughout our land. So profound was her influence upon the women of America in particular that when she died the nation was swept with universal sorrow. After her death Professor Palmer

received, among innumerable messages of condolence, a letter from a farmer's wife. This plain woman of the soil wrote: "I remember your wife for many things. The last remembrance is as I remember kneeling at the Communion table. I cherish her chaste and noble character so deeply that I have cut her picture from the newspaper and placed it on the wall by the breakfast table, and every day I look at her picture and say within my soul, 'I'll be a better woman because you lived.'" There was no doubt that the religion of Alice Freeman Palmer rang true.   John W. McKelvey

* *

491   R. L. Stevenson tells a story of a young traveller who stayed for a little while in a house surrounded by beautiful scenery. In the room where he slept there was hanging on the wall the picture of a very beautiful, but very licentious woman. He was conscious of the evil in the face, but it had a strange fascination for him. It was the last thing he saw before he went to sleep, and the first thing on which his eyes alighted when he awoke in the morning. He realized that it was gradually absorbing his thoughts throughout the day. And then one day the daughter of the house, who had been away from home, came back. They passed on the stairs and it was a case of love at first sight. When the young man went to his room that night he looked up at the picture and smiled. It had lost its power and influence.   George Fairfoot

Influence Conditioned by Humility

492   Hankey told how in pre-war days, in settlement work in London, he had made little impression until one day he dressed in workman's attire and spent a night in a casual ward. This seemed to catch the imagination of those he sought to influence, that anyone possessed of comfort should voluntarily deprive himself, even for a time, of what he possessed, and Hankey wrote, "If ever you get a chance of sharing men's privations and dangers when you are not obliged to, or of showing humility in practical ways, that will be of more influence than anything else. If ever you have ways of showing that you are willing to share the often hard and sometimes humiliating lot of men, it is that which will give you power over them, just as it is the Cross of Christ and the spitting and the mocking and the scourging and the degradation of His exposure in dying that gives Him power far more than the Sermon on the Mount." Donald Hankey was an officer before the Great War. He surrendered his commission and entered the ranks as a private. He was promoted to sergeant, but felt he was losing his influence and again surrendered rank.

                                                                       Archibald Chisholm

Influence, Immortal

493   The artist Wilkie visited the Escurial to see Titian's picture of the Last Supper. An old Jeronomite stood by and said, "I have sat in sight of that picture nearly threescore years. The visitors have come and looked and wondered and gone their way. My companions have dropped off one by one; but these remain— these painted men. They are the true realities; we are but shadows." This is the solemn truth. Titian dies, but his work remains. Influence is immortal. We are but shadows, the sun sets and we are gone; but our works do follow us.

J. Burrell

Influence of Hymns

494   There is an account of two American sailors. An old man and a young man were drinking and gambling in a Chinese port, and as the elder man was just shuffling the cards the younger man, unconsciously to himself, began to hum a tune, and under his breath to sing the words:

> "One sweetly solemn thought
> Comes to me o'er and o'er;
> I am nearer home today
> Than e'er I've been before."

The older man stopped, threw down the cards and said, "What is that you are humming?" "I don't know," said the boy. "I don't know that I was humming anything." "Yes, you were, it was:

> "One sweetly solemn thought
> Comes to me o'er and o'er;
> I am nearer home today
> Than e'er I've been before."

"Oh," said the boy, "is that it?" "Yes." "I learned that in Sunday-school." "Come, Harry," said the older man, "here is what I owe you—here is what I have won from you. As God sees me I have played the last game and drunk the last bottle. I have misled you, Harry. Give me your hand, my boy, and promise me that this day you will quit this infernal business." That little hymn, written in the unconscious heart of the Sunday-school boy, was the direct means of reclaiming both these gamblers and of bringing them back into the ways of virtue and sobriety.

R. F. Horton

Influence, Unconscious

495   When Stephen uttered his prayer for the forgiveness of his enemies,
a young man, Saul of Tarsus, was standing by. He was deeply impressed by
what he heard, the impression culminating in his conversion and in his becoming the great apostle to the Gentiles. "If Stephen had not prayed," said Augustine, "the Church would not have had Paul." There is force in the suggestion,
and it reminds us of the power of unconscious influence inherent in us all. "Let
us go down to the town and preach," said St. Francis of Assisi to a young monk
in a certain monastery. The novice, delighted at being singled out to be the
companion of St. Francis, obeyed with enthusiasm. They passed through the
principal streets; turned down many of the by-ways and alleys; made their
way out to some of the suburbs and at length returned by a circuitous route to
the monastery gate. As they approached it, the younger man reminded Francis
of his original intention. "You have forgotten, Father," he said, "that we went
down to the town to preach." "My son," replied St. Francis, "we have preached;
we were preaching while we were walking. We have been seen by many; our
behaviour has been closely watched; it was thus that we preached our morning
sermon." There may be a touch of exaggeration in that. Yet as Stephen in his
death preached a powerful sermon by which Paul was won for the Christian
faith, so are we all preaching by our lives. It is as the Scripture says, "No man
liveth unto himself." Even when we are least aware of it, each one of us by
our unconscious influence is helping those around us either up to heaven or
down to hell.

                                                        R. J. Anglin Johnson

Ingratitude

496   I have lost two friends by helping them to considerable positions in life.
I was able to do a favor for them at a certain time in life, and I have not got the
friends I had before. We do not quarrel, but they are not as near as they were.
Does not that sound cynical? It is a fact of life many of you know. That is how
we treat God. We pray for what we want, but we do not come back to thank
him. It is the sign of a shallow nature. In life, as we know, ingratitude is the un-
failing mark of a narrow soul. No great mind is ever ungrateful, and if we can't
be grateful in other respects we can at any rate be grateful to God. And genuine
Christianity has always this vital throb of praise.

                                                            James Moffatt

Inspiration

497   Dr. Horace Bushnell, of Hartford, was the most brilliant genius that the American pulpit has seen during this century, and his hard common sense kept him from being a mystic. During the fifteenth year of his ministry he had a marvellous revelation, enabling him to spiritually discern spiritual things. "On an early morning of February, 1848, his wife awoke to hear that the light they had waited for had risen indeed. She asked, 'What have you seen?' He replied, 'The Gospel!' It had come to him, not as something reasoned out, but as an inspiration—a revelation from the mind of God Himself." This new and glorious conception of Jesus Christ lifted Bushnell into a higher life, gave him new insight and power, and shaped all the remaining years of his quickening and extraordinary ministry.   Theodore L. Cuyler

❋ ❋

498   George Frederick Handel did much of his work in the service of an earthly monarch—the Elector of Hanover, who later became George I of England. He dedicated to this sovereign, for example, the beautiful "Water Music" which is often heard in symphony programs. But when Handel wrote his greatest work, *The Messiah,* no earthly king could draw forth the inspiration needed for such a composition. Of the writing of the "Hallelujah Chorus" he said: "I did think I did see all heaven before me, and the great God Himself."

David John Donnan

❋ ❋

499   In one of the cities of eastern France stands the statue of a Negro by the great sculptor, Bartholdi. On the face is an expression of wistful sadness. One day a German boy, named Albert Schweitzer, stood before that statue. He had been looking forward to a brilliant career in music. But as he looked into that sorrow-riven face above him, he was moved with compassion and, leaving the high place which might have been his at home, he went out to Africa to give himself to the redemption of the Negro race.   Stuart Nye Hutchison

Interests

500   Dr. H. E. Fosdick tells of taking a ride in a bus in New York and overhearing two people's conversation. In half an hour's ride they gave their fellow-passengers a résumé of their characters. "They loved to play bridge, and played it a lot and gambled at it. One of them had trouble at home because of the gambling. They loved musical comedies and the talkies, and became excited in their admiration of the actors and actresses. They loved dancing, and when not at bridge parties that was their chief diversion." So they went on, and he listened to hear if any other interest of a higher kind would be revealed, but no, this was their all. With those things they had struck bottom.

J. E. Evans

Invitation

501   I am told that in the deserts when a caravan has exhausted all its water and they are all thirsty and ready to die, they will send a camel on ahead, a swift dromedary, and the man rides as fast as he can go, and then at a distance they send a second just to keep in sight of the first, and when these two have ridden till they are almost out of sight they send a third, and then another, and they go speeding over the desert, the camel's instinct leading it towards the wells. And when the first man on the camel reaches the water, he leaps from the camel, stoops down, drinks and makes sure it is there, and having refreshed himself, he turns back on the camel, and calls out "Come!" and he that is nearest behind takes up the note and says "Come!" and he that is still behind cries "Come!" till the whole desert echoes with the sound of "Come!" and they hasten with all their might to drink. The Spirit and the Bride have found the living water, and they say: "Come! and let him that heareth say Come, and whosoever will, let him come and take of the water of life freely."

C. H. Spurgeon

Jesus, Influence of

502   One comes back from the Far East estimating, as he never could have estimated before, the incalculable difference that the influence of Jesus has made in Western life. There may be some of you who are not Christians. I propose to you this simple test: go to the wide areas of the world where the Gospel has not come; see if you can find one spot on the planet outside the range of the influence of Jesus where you would be willing to settle down and make your home and rear your children; see if a Christian church spire does not look good to you when you come back; see if you can say that there is not something, however difficult to locate and define, which has happened to the hearts of men, their ideals and purposes, their capacities and spiritual powers, where the influence of Jesus has come. As for me, with all my discontent about American Christianity, this needs in all honesty to be said at the beginning: coming back from the Far East, any kind of Christian church looks very good to me.

Harry Emerson Fosdick

Jesus, Moral Splendour of

503   A half-tipsy working-man in London, Mr. Silvester Horne tells us, was interrupting him while he was preaching in the open air in a London park on "What think ye of Christ?" At the close of the meeting the man tried to get into argument with the preacher. "What," he said, "about the Archbishop of Canterbury, with his ten thousand pounds a year?" "My man," said the preacher, "my text does not say what think ye about the Archbishop of Canterbury, but what think ye of Christ?"

"Well, but," went on the man, "what about the Pope of Rome, with his hundred thousand pounds a year?" "My man," said the preacher, "my text does not say what think ye of the Pope of Rome, but what think ye of Christ?" "Oh, if that is what you are at, sir," said the man, seeing the preacher's meaning even with his muddled brain, and reverently taking off his cap, "if that is what you are at, sir, I will take off my cap to that." Here was the testimony of even a poor, half-tipsy man to the moral splendour of Jesus Christ.

William Stoddart

Journalism

504   G. K. Chesterton wrote: "Journalism as a picture of life must be consistently and systematically false, because it is always a description of exceptional things." You cannot have all the houses that are not burgled mentioned, nor all the couples that are not divorced. The vast mass of mankind get on much better with their wives and neighbours than anyone would suppose from reading those highly picturesque and fallacious sheets which come to us every morning.

C. Walter Rose

Joy

505   St. Paul spoke of himself as "sorrowful, yet always rejoicing." And Jesus went to the Cross for the joy that was set before Him. One of the distinctive marks of many people today is that they have no conception, still less experience, of a joy that can deepen in silence and even in sorrow. Dr. Reid tells how it was said of W. E. Gladstone's daughter that she was "so happy she could afford to be serious." "Some people," adds Dr. Reid, "cannot afford to be serious, for the moment they are serious they come face to face with the spectre of their own unhappiness."

Frederic Greeves

Judgement

506 Daniel Webster met with a company of gentlemen of large intelligence
and of high station in one of the hotels in New York, and to that great genius,
the interpreter of the American Constitution, the man of the largest brain of
his time, some one said: "Mr. Webster, what is the greatest thought that you
ever had?" He looked around the company before he spoke, and then he asked,
"Are these all friends?" They said, "Yes, sir; they are all your friends." Then
said Daniel Webster, "The greatest thought that ever came to me was my
personal responsibility to Almighty God."   J. J. Muir

✳✳

507 Oh, what a change it will be for you and me when we do not stand in
the light of each other's appreciation, and are not appraised by the measurements
that men apply to us; when we are not so good as we seem to be, and are worse,
a great deal, in some things than we seemed to be. What a judgement that
will be, when all hearts shall be unclosed, and we shall stand naked and open
before Him with whom we have to do, and God shall say to the highest and
the proudest: "Men knew you, and I never knew you"; and when He shall
call up the poorest and lowest, and say: "Come ye blessed, inherit the kingdom."

An eminent minister in England, Baxter, said: "When I get to heaven I
think I shall be surprised to see how many men there are there that I never
expected to see in heaven; next I shall be surprised to see how many are
absent whom I thought surely I should meet there; and, lastly, and greatest of
all, I shall be surprised to find that I am there myself."

Henry Ward Beecher

Judgement of God

508 You remember the story of Lady Asquith's famous question to Benjamin
Jowett: "Dr. Jowett, what do you think of God?" "Madam," came the reply,
"the important thing is not what I think of God, but what He thinks of me."

G. Holland Williams

Judging Others

509 Well would it be for some of us when sitting in judgement even upon
the most abandoned characters of our acquaintance to remember the well-known
incident in the life of John Bradford. When he saw a man passing to execution

to atone for some great offence, he exclaimed, with an outburst of humility and true Christian love, "There goes John Bradford, but for the grace of God."

James Weller

Justice of God

510 T. H. Huxley in a letter to Charles Kingsley in 1860 says: "I am no optimist, but I have the firmest belief that· the Divine Government is wholly just. The more I know intimately of the lives of other men, the more obvious it is to me that the wicked does not flourish nor is the righteous punished. The ledger of the Almighty is strictly kept and every one of us has the balance of his operations paid over to him at the end of every minute of his existence."

John Bishop

Justification

511 There is a sentence of John Calvin which is sound theology and true experience: "Partial justification is of no good; it only produces misery." To get rid of our bondage and fear we must see God drawing near, in his unutterable love and fullness, and displacing everything, not only our guilt and sin, but even our righteousness and penitence and faith: compelling us to forget everything but the wonder of His grace, and annihilating by His glory every shred of sin and self. Then, as the waters are cradled on their ocean bed, as the mountains rest on their unyielding sockets, as a child nestles in its mother's bosom, so shall we rest our whole support on the everlasting arms of the Almighty God.

Thomas Phillips

Justification by Faith

512 Carlyle said the greatest moment in the modern history of man was Luther at the Diet of Worms. You remember Luther in the monastery at Erfurt had reduced himself by his misery and despair almost to death itself, when the Vicar-General visited him, and said, "Luther, repeat the creed," and when Luther came to the line, "I believe in the forgiveness of sins" he realized that his sins were included there, and relief came to him. And then he was summoned to Rome, and he climbed the stairs of St. John's Church.

I have seen long processions of people there, climbing those steps on their hands and knees hoping thereby to obtain forgiveness of sins. And as Luther was thus climbing these stairs there was flashed in upon him, by the light of the Spirit of God, the words: "The just shall live by faith," and he sprang to his feet, and said: "I defy all those who deny that a man is saved by faith." He realized that it was the doctrine that brought light and liberty and joy and power to all who accepted it.

You and I know what it is to be justified by faith, to be forgiven, to be accepted of God, and to experience joy and peace in believing. It was that doctrine that brought Luther to the Diet of Worms. That was a great moment: with all the power of the Church, and all the power of the world on one side, and he, standing alone, on the other. "Recant, and you are forgiven: fail to recant, and death." Luther begged for time to consider, and the next day, after a night of prayer he was himself again, yea, more than himself. "Convince me," he said, "by plain reason, or by this Word of God, and I will recant."

John Wilson

Kindness

513   Most of us know John Ruskin's fairy story of the *King of the Golden River*. It tells of the two wicked brothers who went up the mountain carrying water of magical power with which they hoped to change the stream into molten gold. They passed a little child lying on a rock parched with thirst, and begging for water; but each of them went on without pity. Coming to the river, they fell into the gorge, and were changed appropriately into two hard black rocks, called "The Black Brothers." Gluck, their gentle younger brother, came to the child, and gave him the last few drops of water in his flask, whereupon the child arose, and became fresh and beautiful, and began running down the mountain; and as Gluck watched him his golden head seemed like a star lessening in the distance. That is the used opportunity for doing good, the chance taken for pity or kindness. It passes, but not like a shadow—rather like an angel who does not forget, like a star that always shines in the sky of our past.

John Murphy

King, Christ the

514   Three centuries ago the Spaniards were besieging the little town of St. Quentin, on the frontier of France. Its ramparts were in ruins, fever and famine were decimating its defenders, treason was gliding among its terrified population. One day the Spaniards shot over the walls a shower of arrows to which were attached little slips of parchments, promising the inhabitants that if they would surrender, their lives and property should be spared. Now, the governor of the town was the great leader of the Huguenots, Gaspard de Coligni.

As his sole answer he took a piece of parchment, tied it to a javelin, wrote on it the two words, *Regem habemus*—"We have a king"—and hurled it back into the camp of the enemy. There was his sole answer to all their threats and all their seductions. Now, that was true loyalty—loyalty in imminent peril, loyalty ready to sacrifice all. But who was that king for whom, amid sword and flame, amid fever and famine, Coligni was defending those breached and battered walls? It was the weak and miserable Henry II of France, whose son, Charles IX, was afterwards guilty of the murder of Coligni and the infamous massacre of St. Bartholomew.

Have you a king? Is Christ your King? Ah, if He be He is not a feeble, corrupt, false, treacherous man like Coligni's master, but a King who loves you, who died for you, who pleads with you even now on the right hand of the Majesty on High. Are you loyal to Him as Coligni was to the wretched Henry II? Are you loyal at all—much more would you be loyal to Christ, even unto death? If so, what will you do for Him? That is the test.

F. W. Farrar

King, Leaving Out the

515   I once saw in the Berlin Art Gallery a picture of Menzel, an unfinished picture of Frederick the Great, talking to his generals. There is a small bare patch in the centre of the picture, where a charcoal outline indicates the artist's intentions. He has painted in all the generals, but the King he has left to the last. It is so like life for most people. They put in all the generals, and leave the King to the last, with a hope that grows more faint that some day they will put the King in the centre. Poor Menzel died before he finished the picture.

Sidney H. Price

Kingdom of God

516   Said Sir Wilfred Grenfell: "As I see the Christ, He teaches that the task of making life worth living is not a loafer's job." The slacker is not only miserable hereafter, but harmful and foolish here and now. Life is like Labrador, a Labourer's Land. It is intended to produce that which no loafer's land ever anywhere can produce, the character of the sons of God. Can anyone desire a world better suited for that task?

H. W. Theobald

＊＊

517   Not very long ago I came across these words of personal testimony by Frederic Denison Maurice: "All my religious consciousness became centred

in the welfare of humanity; in activities tending towards the realization of the Kingdom of God. In this aspiration towards the welfare of humanity I found complete satisfaction."

Likewise I found these words written by Dr. John Oman: "The way of living in the Kingdom is to pray for the true worship, the true consecration, the true use of material things by subordination to the spiritual, forgiveness as we exercise the forgiving of our Father among our fellows, and meeting trial and temptation by having nothing in us to which the prince of this world might appeal."

Henry J. Cowell

Kingdom of God, Expedient

518   I was in Blantyre during my Presidency, and I took the opportunity of going to see the Livingstone memorial. There are stained-glass windows, and in two of them there are extracts, one from a letter written by Livingstone, and one from his diary. One was written earlier in his life, and it was this: "I will place no value on anything I possess, or expect to possess, except in relation to the Kingdom of God." There is no harm in possessing, or in expecting to possess, so long as you value it for what it can do for the Kingdom of God.

The other extract was written two days after he had parted with Stanley. Livingstone was lost for many years while in Africa, and a great New York paper sent Stanley to find him. You know the story how at last this American found the British missionary. Livingstone was sick and ill, and Stanley wanted him to leave Africa, but Livingstone refused. "No," he said, "I must finish my work." And he did finish it. Shortly after Stanley left him he wrote these words in his diary: "My Jesus, my Lord, my Life, my All, I again dedicate my whole life to Thee." He was thinking only of his work, and of the dark-skinned people of Africa. "It shall not be so among you," said Jesus. "But whosoever will be great among you let him be your minister, and whosoever will be chief among you, let him be your servant; even as the Son of man came not to be ministered unto, but to minister, and to give His life a ransom for many." Jesus comes and He asks us for the surrender of our whole lives to Him, then He can use us.   Gilbert Laws

Knowledge

519   One recollects Henry Drummond's story of the librarian of Edinburgh University who wanted more room for books and asked the professor of a certain scientific subject which books on his subject were no longer needed.

The reply was: "Take every book more than ten years old and put it in the cellar." But why were the text-books of ten years ago out of date? They were based on the "facts" that were then known—yes, but as our knowledge grows, as our facts accumulate, it becomes evident that the knowledge based on the facts known to us at any one time is partial, incomplete. We know in part; when that which is more complete comes then that which is in part shall be done away.

H. Bulcock

Labour Movement

520   In England, the labour movement owes its inspiration much less to Marx's economic theories than to the Sermon on the Mount, and it is to the same source that we may trace back the humanitarian impulses which are active today amid the devastation, misery, and hunger which war has left behind it.

E. L. Allen

Language

521   There is no reason why when you have at your service the noblest language for an orator that was ever spoken by the human race, you should be satisfied with the threadbare phrases, the tawdry tarnished finery, the patched and ragged garments of a small vocabulary like that of the stock of a second-hand clothes shop, with which half-educated declaimers are content to cover the nakedness of their thoughts.

R. W. Dale

Laymen

522   Years ago a little child lived in a stableyard in South London. He played in mean streets till he was old enough to be employed as an errand-boy delivering papers. Eventually he became one of the world's greatest scientists. The wisest men of his day consulted him, learned societies showered their honours upon him. But every other Sunday, for twenty-seven years, he preached to a little congregation the unsearchable riches of the love of God in Jesus Christ. His name was Michael Faraday, and this is how he spoke of himself and of his work: "All my life, I struggle to bring every thought into captivity to the obedience of Christ."

G. Holland Williams

Learning

523   Hugh Bourne was once asked why he wrote a grammar. He replied, "To learn by." It is said of a certain professor that whenever he wished to acquire more knowledge of a science he wrote a book on it. The head of a Cambridge college was once asked to recommend a tutor. His reply was, "Take a pupil." There is much sound wisdom here, for the principle of the harvest field operates with regard to our knowledge. Knowledge scattered becomes knowledge multiplied.

Arthur Wood

Lent, Challenge of

524   A call for a week of self-denial in Paris some years ago was accompanied by an extract from a letter by Wilfred Monod, running thus:—

"How is it that Protestants have produced, on a man like Père Gratry, the impression which he formulates as follows? 'Protestantism is, in essence, the abolition of sacrifice. To abolish abstinence and fasting; to abolish the necessity of good works, effort, struggle, virtue; to shut up sacrifice in Jesus alone and not let it pass to us; no more to say, as St. Paul did, I fill up what is wanting in the suffering of Christ, but rather to say to Jesus on his Cross, Suffer alone, O Lord—there is Protestantism.'"

Of course, sacrifice means more than doing without food, and it is going too far to say that Protestantism abolishes good works, efforts, virtue; but the latter part of the statement is only too true. Both in theory and in practice we have shut up sacrifice in Jesus alone, holding that the merit of His suffering is imputed to us without sharing His suffering. Not so St. Paul, whose passion it was to be a partaker of the fellowship of the sufferings of Christ, if so that he might win the high prize of the life eternal. St. Bernard, not less than Wesley, taught the goodly gospel of free grace, but he did not feel that it exempted him from a habit of austere living. Nor did Wesley, who fasted every Friday as long as he lived, and partook of the Holy Communion fifteen times in the last six weeks of his life, because he needed such aids in the practice of salvation. Neither of these masters of the spiritual life neglected the stern culture of the soul, as so many of us are wont to do, under the notion that the virtues are gifts and not trophies. Père Gratry was right in pointing this out as a grave defect in our teaching, and even more so in our practice, of the religious life.

If this is true of Protestantism in general, I fear it is still more true of that wing of it which calls itself, not always truly, liberal.

Here, at least, I may be permitted to speak frankly and to the point, applying my words more severely to myself than to any other. If I allow myself to be called a liberal Christian, it is not because I like defining my Christianity by an adjective—for I do not. But I somehow got the idea that this movement meant that a man is free to be a Christian, not that he holds his Christianity loosely, if not lightly. It had come to me that a liberal is one who has the same charity towards the past as towards the present, and is as willing to listen to St. Bernard as to Bernard Shaw. At any rate, it had been told me that the liberal pulpit rejected certain dogmas about Christ, and I thought that was because it wanted Christ brought nearer to us—with the demand which I knew would plague me with an unsatisfiable passion to be more like Him. Some of us thought it was discontented with doctrines of the atonement, because it wanted the reality—that we are called to be crucified with Christ, that He may rise in us. We thought it held the gospel of salvation which bids a man be willing to stand naked before the Awful Holiness, seeking "purity rather than peace," as Newman made his motto. Were we mistaken? If so, then liberalism shall know me no longer, for who teaches an easy gospel teaches a gospel of perdition, whose end is death.   Joseph Fort Newton

Liberty, Conditioned

525   There's a lovely passage in Rabindranath Tagore, in which he bids us look at a violin string, lying on a table. It is free to move in any direction we choose. But it is not free to sing. Take it up and bind it in the violin, and when it is bound, its music can be evoked. When it is gripped it is free to sing. And the law that runs everywhere, comes to its climax in religion. Jesus offers to all men complete liberty, liberty throughout the entire structure of human society. But it is always a liberty that is conditioned by an inward loyalty. He says: "The spirit of the Lord is upon me, because He hath anointed me . . . to preach deliverance to the captives." He also says, "Follow Me."

G. Oswald Cornish

Life

526   Rough and hard was the life-struggle of Martin Luther; fierce the words that he had to utter—words which are half battles, words which smote like lightning when he set his face as a flint against wrong and lies; yet the strong fighter never lost the natural tenderness of his heart towards all God's creatures. He once saved a hare which fled to him from the hunters, and he saw in it the image of a poor human soul chased by Satan. "That little fellow," he said,

when he saw a bird going to roost, "has had its supper, and is now going to sleep, quite secure and content, like David; it abides under the shadow of Almighty, and lets God take care of it. How glad are the little birds," he said, "singing so deliciously, and hopping from branch to branch! We might well take off our hats to them, and say: 'My dear Sir Doctor, I have not learnt thy art of trustfulness. Thou sleepest all night without care in thy little nest; thou risest in the morning, and praisest God, and seekest thy daily food. Why cannot I, poor fool that I am, feel that I am thus like these living saints in fulness of content?' There go our preachers," he said, as he watched the cattle going to pasture—"our preachers who daily preach to us faith in God." And when his footsteps frightened the birds who were building their nests in his garden, he said: "Ah, dear little bird! fly not from me; from my heart I wish thee well, if thou couldst only believe it; but just so do we distrust our dear Lord; who, nevertheless, gives us nothing but good."   F. W. Farrar

** **

527   Old Methuselah lived for 900 years, and never said a word worth putting down in the Bible. He lived for nine centuries and never did a single act worth reporting. He vegetated like a tree that was not living. Jesus Christ was only here for three years of public life and His name has gone through the earth, filled heaven with its praise, and His deeds shall be spoken of throughout the ages of eternity. Only three years! Life is yours to fill it with helpfulness, with kindness to act your part so that you can look back upon it with pleasure, not with remorse, saying with Lord Byron, "It is not anything that I have done that troubles me, but it is what I might have been." Ah, well thou mightest have said that with thy brilliant genius—what thou mightest have been! How the saying seems to toll the knell of a lost opportunity. Life is yours to fill it as Christ filled it with noble deeds of help to others, and then you can say when it comes to its close, "It is finished."   Herber Evans

Life, a Prelude

528   Liszt, at the head of one of his preludes, wrote, "What is life but a series of preludes to that great unknown song of which death writes the first solemn note?"   Douglas A. Smith

Life, Ampler

529   Michelangelo, it is said, passing one day through the room where his pupils were busy, noticed a design of noble conception which an inexperi-

enced hand was drawing within lines too narrow and cramped; the great artist took up the pencil, and wrote over the design the single word "Ampler," and went his way. Is not that the word which the Divine Master might write over many of our lives—Ampler? Our canvas is too narrow. Our worldly space of effort and achievement is too limited for the design of which our souls have dreamed and which our hearts love. Religion is ampler life. In Christ's service we shall find amplest life.   Newman Smyth

Life, Finding by Losing

530   You, perhaps, remember the old story of Pope Innocent IV and Thomas Aquinas, who were standing together as the bags of treasure were carried in through the gates of the Lateran. "You see," observed the Pope, with a smile, "the day is past when the Church could say, 'Silver and gold have I none!'" "Yes, Holy Father," was the reply from the saint, "and the day is past when the Church could say to the lame man, 'Rise and walk!'" When the Church's life is lived on the plane of ease, and comfort, and bloodless service, she has no power to fertilize the dry and barren places of the earth. When the Church becomes sacrificial she becomes impressive. The sacrificial things in history are the influential things today. It is the men and the women who give away their being, the bleeding folk, who are our present inheritance. The woman who gave the two mites still works as a factor in the life of the race. Sir John Kelynge—have you ever heard of him?—the brutal, cynical justice who thrust John Bunyan for twelve years into Bedford gaol, his very name is now a conundrum. John Bunyan, the sacrificial martyr, is still fertilizing the field of common life with energies of rich inspiration. The finders have lost. The apparent losers are at the winning-post! The sacrificial are the triumphant. "They loved not their lives unto the death, and they overcame by the blood of the Lamb." A sacrificial Church would speedily conquer the world! "He that findeth his life shall lose it; and he that loseth his life for My sake shall find it."   J. H. Jowett

Life, God's Use of

531   Beethoven, it is said, after he became deaf, would sit and play on the old, worn-out harpsichord that had long been unfit for use, and suppose that he was playing matchless harmonies. The instrument was so poor that not one chord in five responded. Here was one that gave forth some sound, and there was another; but even they were out of harmony. And I sometimes think God plays on a poor harpsichord when He takes this world to evolve the melodies

of Divine love, so few chords respond at all, and so utterly inadequate are those
that do respond to illustrate this crowning attribute of the mind.

Henry Ward Beecher

Life, Greatest Lesson of

532   A friend of mine in the North of England conceived the happy idea of
writing to a number of famous people asking them to answer the question,
"What is the greatest lesson life has taught you?" Amongst those to whom this
inquiry was addressed were Sir Oliver Lodge, Miss Maude Royden, the late
Dr. R. F. Horton, and Lord Baden-Powell. Being busy people, they all of them
found time for a courteous reply, and the answers are especially interesting,
remembering the personalities concerned and the character of their replies.

Sir Oliver Lodge replied, "The greatest lesson life has taught me is the reality
of the spiritual world." This testimony has its own peculiar value coming from
one of the most outstanding scientists of our day. Miss Maude Royden replied,
"The greatest lesson life has taught me is that all things can work together
for good to them that love Christ." There is a pathetic interest attached to this
reply, remembering Miss Royden's physical debility and constant suffering,
for there is another side to the fame and glory of the most popular woman
preacher in England.

Dr. R. F. Horton, then minister of one of the wealthiest congregations in
London, and accustomed to meet with people of considerable means, replied,
"The greatest lesson life has taught me is that people who set their mind and
heart upon riches are equally disappointed whether they get them or whether
they do not."

And Lord Baden-Powell, known the wide world over as the hero of Mafeking
and the founder of the Boy Scout Movement, replied, "The greatest lesson life
has taught me is that the only way to true happiness is the way of Jesus Christ,
to follow Him and to do His will."   A. A. Lee

Life, Length of

533   Did you notice in the paper recently that a Russian scientist, Dr.
Bogomolets, had died? Only about a month before, he had announced the
discovery of a wonderful serum, which would enable people to live for a
hundred and fifty years. It was most unfortunate that the man who discovered
that serum should die at sixty-four!   A. E. Gould

✳✳

534 It is not the length of a man's life that matters, but what he does with it. It is not how long he lives, but how he lives, that counts. The poet Keats died in his youth, and yet he gave to the world for all time some of the loveliest poetry the tongue of man can recite. A greater than Keats died on a lonely Cross when He was only thirty-three, after putting all eternity into three brief years. Some men have lived to be a hundred and when they have gone to whatever reward was coming to them the world has been none the poorer for their departure. Others have been spared only a quarter or half that time, and mankind has been all the happier, all the richer and better, for their stay here on the earth. You can't take a measuring-line to a human life. Its length you can calculate but its value belongs to the eternities.

Graham W. Hughes

Life, Meaning of

535 First: life means to me an unceasing gratitude to God who gave it. There is no day of my existence on which I forget to give thanks to that Eternal power who, out of an unconscious Past, beneficently called me into the Present of this world—a world so lovely in its natural beauty that we can imagine nothing lovelier—save heaven. Secondly: life means to me a glorious opportunity of which no moment should be wasted—a way of spiritual progress —a time in which to make use of all the best powers which Nature and education have bestowed upon me—a little space wherein to perform as many kind actions as possible, and to say as many kind words as I can to my fellow-creatures who are journeying with me along the same road onward—and upward. Thirdly: life means to me not only the blessing of itself, but the promise of a higher life—and I live it joyously, devoutly, hopefully and lovingly—accepting it, as a divinely appointed schooling, which when it shall arrive at what is called the "end," will have placed me happily at a new beginning.

G. H. Clothier

Life, Partnership in

536 Towards the end of his life W. T. Stead, the great journalist, abandoned a lucrative position on the press for conscientious reasons. A friend asked him, "Can you afford to do this?" "Well," said Stead, "you see, I have a very wealthy partner." "Who is he?" asked the friend in surprise. "God Almighty," was the reply.

Norman Castles

Life, Purpose of

537   When Julia Ward Howe was ninety years of age, she was asked to "express the aim of life." A moment was given to thought, and then she answered:

"To learn; to teach; to serve; to enjoy."

Writing at the age of eighty, in *Stepping Westward,* her daughter, Laura E. Richards, said:

"This utterance comes more deeply home to me with every year; I realize more and more how these four aspects of life are linked together; how, whenever I have tried to teach I have been the chief learner; and whenever I have tried to serve, the chief pleasure has been mine."

David A. MacLennan

Life, Roots of

538   In Professor Gilbert Murray's admirable book, *Greek Studies,* he tells us of an occasion when two members of the House of Commons were once discussing why it was that Mr. Gladstone, when compared with such highly able and industrious colleagues as Joseph Chamberlain and Sir Charles Dilke, seemed to tower above them by a sort of "greatness" of mind and character. Why was Mr. Gladstone such a great man, and the other two men with all their energy and ability much lesser men? One of the members of the House of Commons in this discussion said: "One thing is that Mr. Gladstone spends his spare time reading Homer and Plato and Dante and the Bible, whereas Dilke and Chamberlain mostly read Bluebooks." Mr. Gladstone fed his mind and soul on the mental and spiritual treasures of our ancient civilizations. He looked after the roots of his mental and spiritual life, whereas Chamberlain and Dilke looked after the fruits.

H. Hodgkins

Life, Success in

539   John Roach, the great ship-builder, was in many respects a noble man; he had built more ships than any other American, but he had built no ship that could carry him across the eternal sea, and when he came to the close of his life, the last week upon earth, he sent for a minister and said, "I want to be baptized and received into the Christian church before I die." I want something better than that.

I want something better than mere bravery ever brought to me. General Grant was not a coward, and yet you may remember that several months before he died his physicians thought that he was passing away, and Dr. Newman baptized him. And then afterward, to the surprise of all his attendants, he somewhat recovered his strength and lingered for several months. Bishop Newman told me that he said to him during that time, "I wish I could live at least a year in health and strength, that I might be a consistent member of the Church of Christ."

I want something better than purely intellectual endowment or culture ever gave to man. Aaron Burr was one of the most intellectual Americans and one of the most debased. He is said to have been the most brilliant student that ever studied in the College of New Jersey at Princeton, but he lived a sinful, selfish life and died a miserable death. Lord Byron had the most brilliant brain of any man of his generation; it seemed to be able to shoot off sparks of fire without effort; and yet this brilliant man, who was known throughout the world when he was thirty, was a decrepit, prematurely old man at thirty-six, and spent the last days of his life in writing words like these:

> My days are in the yellow leaf,
>   The fruit, the flower of life are gone;
> The worm, the canker, and the grief
>   Are mine alone.

I want something better than that. I would like to have a "leaf that shall not wither," and be able to "bring forth fruit in old age." I should like to be able to say, as did that hero of the early Christian era, "I have fought a good fight, I have finished my course, I have kept the faith; henceforth there is laid up for me a crown of righteousness, which the Lord, the righteous Judge, shall give me at that day."   B. Fay Mills

Light

540   When O. Henry, the American short-story writer, lay dying of tuberculosis in his poor lodgings, those beside him could see the end coming. One of them, moved by some feeling of reverence, stepped to the flaring gas-jets and began to lower the flame. The dying man lifted his hand in weak protest, and whispered: "No, don't turn out the light; I'm afraid to go home in the dark."   A. E. Gould

**

541   I remember reading of an Australian bush preacher who went to a little church in the bush to preach. It was dusk when he arrived and the place was without light and he wondered what to do about it. Presently he saw twinkling lights moving about through the bush. His congregation was arriving. Each person carried a hurricane lamp, and as they came in they placed their lamps upon a shelf around the chapel wall, and soon the whole place was flooded with light. Each had contributed light that had dispelled the darkness.

"Ye are the light of the world," said Jesus to His disciples, and as we each carry the light of Christ out into the world, into our little bit of the world, so shall we help to dispel its darkness and correct its false theories of life. In the Name that is above every name all the false theories of life are corrected, and God's way of life for men is clearly revealed.   Wilfred J. T. Brown

⁂

542   "Play the man," said Latimer to Ridley, when they were perishing in the flames. "We are lighting a candle in this country today that by the grace of God shall never be put out." That's where your Protestantism comes in. The condemnation of Roman Catholicism is that everything it touches withers. Latimer and Ridley lit that candle for you. Mind that you take care of it. There has been a great deal of thimblerigging for some generations now with that candle. Mind you keep it burning. I went into a house the other day, and I saw a figure on the mantelpiece. It was a candle extinguisher in the shape of a monk. Ah, the man that made that did not make a toy—he made a magnificent symbol. You have got it all there! Mind and take care of that candle! It is the golden light of your guidance, the torch of your illumination, the star of your hope. Mind you take care of it. "And thou mayest add thereto." If you are a parasite you will live upon what your patriotic ancestors did; if you are a patriot you will make your own little contribution to the new and perfect civilization.

                                                                    W. L. Watkinson

Light, Minding the

543   Many will know the famous story of Mrs. Katie Walker and the Robbins Reef Lighthouse in New York Harbor. Her husband was the keeper of the lighthouse, and was stricken with serious illness, which necessitated his removal to the hospital on Staten Island. Mrs. Walker remained on Robbins Reef to do his work. One dark day the message came that he had entered into the Land where the Lamb is the Light thereof. "We buried him," said Mrs. Walker, "in the cemetery on the hill over there. Every morning I stand at this porthole and look in the direction of his grave. Sometimes the hills are green, sometimes they are brown, sometimes they are white with snow. But they always have a message for me. Something I heard my husband say more often than anything else. Just

three words—'Mind the light!'" "The fire shall ever be burning on the altar;
it shall never go out."   David A. MacLennan

Limitations

544   You have all heard of the celebrated mathematician who, after reading
Paradise Lost, asked what it proved. Why, it proved that there was a cell lacking in his brain, and that as soon as he stepped off his own proper ground he
gave himself away. He proved that a man may be a mathematician, and not a
poet. You have heard of Sir Humphry Davy, when he went to Paris and walked
through the magnificent galleries of that famous city, how that the only observation he was known to make was that it was the grandest collection of frames he
had ever seen, showing that a man may be magnificent in a science and blind in
art. Turner, the great painter, was a master when he sought to transfigure the
canvas, but he had got the notion, unhappily, that he was a poet also; and I need
not tell you that his poetry is not immortal. "One science does one genius fit,"
and if a man attempts to jump out of his skin, and do something which God
Almighty never meant him to do, he makes poor work of it. And that is the first
thing we have to feel in life, the limitations which it has pleased God here and
now to fix in our very constitution. We have but limited power, facility, aptitude,
resource, and as soon as ever we want to do something that we were never
destined to do, heaven shows us unmistakably, "Nevertheless, thou shalt not
build the house."   W. L. Watkinson

Literacy

545   Little over a hundred years ago (1817) John Smith, the missionary, went
to Demerara. When he arrived the Governor of the colony said to him: "If ever
you teach a Negro to read, and I hear of it, I will banish you from the colony
immediately." He taught them to read, and died in a felon's prison for it. The
trouble arose because the Demerara planters knew and publicly said that "it is
impossible to teach slaves to read without making them free," or, as a contemporary newspaper put it, "either Christianity or slavery must fall."
                                                                    E. Allan Matheson

Living, Shallow

546   Some years ago there emigrated from North Carolina to Oklahoma in
the United States of America a man and a woman who bought a little farm and
settled on it. They found it pretty heavy going. The soil was not very produc-

tive. And the yield at harvest time hardly justified the labour that they had expended upon it. Then one day some business men came along and asked the good woman of the house for a drink of water from her well. Of course she gave it them, as anyone would have done in the circumstances. But she was rather surprised to find one of them put some of it in a bottle before they went away. And it was not till much later when they came back and made a miserable offer for the farm, and she and her husband had gladly accepted the money, that she found there was a rich oil-well beneath the ground of the farm where they had spent the best years of their lives. It is often thus, friend, I fear, that many people, even Christian people, live their lives. They live on the surface. They never penetrate below. They are utterly ignorant of the good things which God has given them richly to enjoy. They have not learned the precious truth which is written in Holy Writ for our learning: "The word is nigh thee, in thy mouth, and in thy heart."

Frank Y. Leggatt

Loneliness

547 Loneliness can sap the last vestige of a man's moral and religious strength. When the small ship in which Sir Ernest Shackleton had attempted to reach the South Pole was wrecked, he with two other men set out in an open boat in an endeavour to cross the South Atlantic and obtain help from South Georgia. These three men spent sixteen terrible days on the open sea, and when at last they reached land they still had thirty-six hours of marching and climbing over mountain and ice. The last part of their brave adventure was the worst. They were tired of trudging in the desolate wastes. But when those men came to talk over their experience what a wonderful thing they discovered! Shackleton had recorded it thus: "I know that during that long march of thirty-six hours . . . it often seemed to me that we were four, not three. And Worsley and Crean had the same idea." What a wonderful thing—the invisible companion!

Harry B. Miner

✳✳

548 When Rupert Brooke sailed from Liverpool to America in 1913 there was nobody to see him off. So he gave sixpence to a little urchin playing around the docks and asked him to wave his handkerchief to him till the vessel was in midstream. The ache of loneliness was behind that request. When everybody else had friends to wish them Godspeed, the one man who was alone could not escape his loneliness and clutched at the mercenary friendship of a ragged boy, who kept the contact by straining his eyes over the widening water and waving till his new-found friend was out of sight. The last comment made by the lonely man on the ship was "I had my sixpennyworth."   John Bishop

※ ※

549   In 1920 there died a woman who was described as the loneliest woman in the world. I refer to Mrs. Christina Forsyth. For thirty years she lived, the only white woman, in an African village. For thirty years this brave white woman was living alone among black heathen people to win them for her Lord and Master.

Some one, during a conversation, spoke to her about the awful loneliness of her life, and she replied: "I am never alone."

J. C. Mitchell

Looking Back

550   Near the end of his life Alexander Maclaren was talking with an old friend who spoke of days past when life was in front of them. Maclaren got up and with gleaming eyes said: "Life fronts us now: it is not behind us but before."   John Bishop

※ ※

551   Speaking to the students at Edinburgh, Nansen said: "I have always thought that the much praised line of retreat is a snare for people who wish to reach their goal. Let me tell you one secret of such so-called success as there may have been in my life, and here I believe I give you really good advice. It was to burn my boats and demolish my bridges behind me, then one loses no time in looking behind when one should have quite enough to do in looking ahead, and then there is no choice for you or your men, but forward. You have to do or die."

John W. A. Singleton

Love

552   Explorers once came upon an Egyptian tomb which had remained closed and silent for some three thousand years. They opened and entered it and found within the exquisitely carved sarcophagus of a little child. Upon it was inscribed these words: "O my life, my love, my little one, would God I had died for thee!" The two Englishmen silently uncovered their heads, and with tears dimming their eyes crept from the darkness of the tomb into the light. Reverently they sealed up the tomb once more and left love and death to their eternal vigil. The

very spirit of love survived in that place of silent death. How old is love! How it clings through the years, through the centuries.   J. Trevor Davies

❋❋

553   The poet, Edwin Markham, was persuaded by some of his friends to put the savings of a lifetime into some very unsound investments. The day came when he was informed that he had lost all. At first he strongly resented and felt bitter over the matter, but not for long: his fundamental Christian attitude asserted itself. He took a sheet of paper and idly drew two circles, and then almost before he knew it he wrote his famous quatrain "Outwitted":

> He drew a circle that shut me out—
> Heretic, rebel, a thing to flout,
> But love and I had the wit to win:
> We drew a circle that took him in.

That is the way of Christ; it is the big vision that will take in—everybody.
                                                                          A. E. Willmott

❋❋

554   A good many years ago Dr. W. Russell Maltby knew a working-man in the North of England whose wife, soon after her marriage, drifted into vicious ways, and went rapidly from bad to worse. He came home one Sunday evening to find, as he had done a dozen times before, that she had gone on a new debauch. He knew in what condition she would return, after two or three days of nameless life. He sat down in the cheerless home to look the truth in the face and to find what he must do. The worst had happened too often to leave him much hope of amendment, and he saw in part what might be in store for him. He made his choice to hold by his wife to the end and to keep a home for her who would not make one for him. Now that a new and terrible meaning had passed into the words, "For better, for worse," he reaffirmed his marriage vow. Later, when some one who knew both intimately, ventured to commiserate him, he answered, "Not a word! She is my wife; I loved her when she was a girl in our village, and I shall love her as long as there is breath in my body." She did not mend, and died in his house in a shameful condition, with his hands spread over her in pity and in prayer to the last.   Johnstone G. Patrick

❋❋

555   Bishop Polk of Louisiana, who was in a slave-owning tradition, went to see a dying slave. He asked him if there was something he could do. "Yes," said the slave, "you can lie beside me and put your arm round me, just as you used to do in bygone days when we were lads together playing beneath the walnut

trees." And Bishop Polk put his arm around him, and the old slave smiled his way into eternity. To learn of love like this is to learn of those whose love is an approximation to the Master's love—a touching of the Saviour's garment. A poor widow contributed to the Dorpation branch of the Russian Bible Society a rouble. Some one told her it was rather too much for a poor widow. She replied very simply, "Love is not afraid of giving too much." God's love is a boundless love. His giving is an illimitable giving. May we all in our lives experience the thrill of loving as He loved.   T. R. Griffin

※※

556   Many years ago, in 1928, I was told of the dreadful suffering of wounded Chinese soldiers who had been brought back from some battle between the then powerful War Lords, laid out on the station platform, and left there throughout a cruelly cold autumn night. Many of them were found dead in the morning: the others were removed to hospital. I asked eagerly who was responsible for taking pity on them at last, and was told that it was a philanthropic Buddhist society. I suppose my interlocutor read my feelings in my face, for he said, "You wish it had been a Christian society?" And I admitted that I did. He said, "You needn't mind; it is only the impact of Christian teaching on Chinese life that has created a Buddhist philanthropic society at all."   Maude Royden Shaw

※※

557   The ethic that is based entirely upon the commandment "Thou shalt love" is the supreme ethic because it never allows the practiser of it to be comfortable. The very essence of Christian love is that it is for ever restless and unappeased. A man's conscience may be appeased when, conceiving Christianity to be a list of rules, he can look back at the day's end and say "I have kept all the rules. I have done all the 'Thou shalt nots.'" A man's conscience can never be appeased when the very seat of it is in his heart and his spirit; when it does not "love" because he is good, but is good because he loves. His love can never be satisfied so long as he knows there is a single sorrow in the world, a single injustice, which he has not been able, or has not done his best, to remove or to lessen.   Ernest H. Jeffs

※※

558   Henry George and Cardinal Manning had a great conversation, and it culminated in a spiritual conversation. Manning made his confession to Henry George in these words: "I love men because Jesus loved them." Henry George replied: "And I love Jesus because He loved men." It does not matter which way you put it, but somehow, inextricably blended together, there is the love of

Christ and the love of men. No man can love Christ who does not love man in Christ's name for Christ's nature, and no man who truly loves men but must love the Christ, who came as the great representative of our manhood.

C. Silvester Horne

** **

559   G. R. Sims, in a sweet little poem, tells of a London slum girl whose father was a drunkard, and whose mother was slowly dying. Sally, only eight years old, was given a fairy's part in the winter pantomime at Drury Lane. She held in her hand a silver wand, and when she waved it and recited certain lines the scene was suddenly changed from one of gloom to one of beauty and brightness. Sally thought that it was really her wand that caused the change, and she longed to be able to wave it over her dying mother that she might see the splendours thus created. One night she took the wand home. The home was only a cellar in a tenement. Her mother lay asleep on a wretched bed. Moving quietly to the bedside, Sally raised her wand and waved it, and recited her magic lines. And the transformation was wrought, though not as Sally expected it; for when her mother awoke it was in the land of eternal day.

There is a magic wand which converts hovels into homes, and touches the drabbest conditions into beauty—and its name is Love.   E. B. Storr

Love, Craving for

560   Once when Thomas Carlyle was holding forth at great length in his living room before a distinguished visitor, with his wife Jane Welsh listening attentively, he paused in his pontifical monologue. Turning to his devoted and long-suffering wife he said, "Jane, don't breathe so loud." Not long afterwards Jane stopped breathing altogether. When Carlyle read her private journal, he discovered that his failure in kindness hurt her mortally. She died of emotional starvation; she craved and was denied love and considerateness. "If I had only known," moaned the miserable philosopher. But he should have known.

David A. MacLennan

Love, Divine

561   Divine Love is seeking those of us who are half-healed, and that Christ wants, for our sakes and for the sake of the world, to touch our eyes for the second time. There is an old chestnut of a story of a man travelling in an American railway compartment with an overdressed and excessively nervous young man. The young fellow was rather like Mr. Toots in *Dombey and Son,* who, as G. K. Chesterton puts it, had learned to smoke before he had learned to spell. He kept lighting a cigarette and then crushing it out, opening a magazine, reading a page or two, and then looking out of the window. He explained that he had left home to make a fortune, and had not succeeded. He had written to ask whether he might come back, and then he had sent off another letter to say that he was definitely returning home, and asking, if it were all right, that they would hang a couple of handkerchiefs on the garden apple-tree which stood near the line. And now he was wondering whether the handkerchiefs would be there. So as the train drew nearer and sounded its horn for his home station, the incredible young man closed his eyes in agitation and suspense and the stranger had to watch. And as the train swung round the bend there was the apple-tree down by the line festooned with handkerchiefs. That home love is a reflection of the love of God, and if we have been a disciple on crutches, and have in this reeling world found faith in the love of God incredibly difficult, a compassion for the world can bring the healing of Divine compassion very near to us.

McEwan Lawson

Love, God Is

562   George Eliot has left on record that when she was a little girl she was so terrified by a teaching that God is vengeful that she used to pray to Jesus at night for His protection against God! Supporters of this view must surely have forgotten the saying of St. Paul, "God commandeth His love towards us in that while we were yet sinners, Christ died for the ungodly," or his other word, "God was in Christ reconciling the world to Himself."

Albert D. Belden

Love in Preaching

563   I have seen people preach the doctrine of election as if they wanted some Arminian to come and fight over it. That is not the way in which the Master tells us to do it—in such a spirit that we seem to want to make a wrangling, Irish fight over it. No, no, no. Go to Christ for truth and you will preach it strongly, honestly, openly, positively, but you will always preach it with love.

C. H. Spurgeon

Love of Christ

564   Dr. John Macbeath, in one of his books, has a beautiful story of two little girls who are standing on the deck of a liner in mid-ocean, looking out to sea.

"What a wonderful day!" exclaims the elder girl. "Look at the horizon." There is a baffled expression on the face of the little companion as she replies: "What is the horizon? Where is it?" "See," answers the older one, pointing with her finger. "See, where the sea seems to meet the sky, and the sky seems to meet the sea; that is the horizon, and when you get there there is another one and then another one, and then another one. You never really come to it. It's always further on."

Ah, that is the love of Christ. There is no end to it. It is always further on. Further than life, further than death. It is always further on. And yet the miracle is that it is here now for anyone who would grasp it.   R. B. Owen

Love of God

565   In his life of Edward Irving, Mr. Oliphant tells us how he once went to visit a young man in Glasgow who was dying of consumption. When he entered the room, the great preacher went up to the bedside and looking into the face of the patient said softly: "George, God loves you; be assured of this, God loves you." After the visitor had left, the young man's sister came in and found her brother in a tearful ecstasy not to be described. "What do you think, Mr. Irving says God loves me," said the dying lad, overwhelmed with the joy of that great discovery which had brought glory into the chamber of death.

John Bishop

✳✳

566   I once heard Archdeacon Wilberforce describe the finding in Pompeii of a little invalid child which had lain buried in the volcanic ashes for nearly two thousand years. The mother, who was a woman of noble family, had plenty of chance to escape and save herself, but she had gone back to rescue this helpless deformed boy, and through all these years the mother's arm has lain there underneath this little child she died to save, a mute and yet tender token of deathless love. So, in greater fashion, through the confusions of the world, the din and noise of our busy and material lives, the darkness and mystery of time and space, the everlasting arms of the love of God are underneath us, and He is with us in our pains, and our struggles, and our follies, striving to put His image on us and to make us in fact children of God.   Rufus M. Jones

✳✳

567   In a very low district of a very great city I found a man standing in a wretched hovel that had been ordered by the Municipal Authorities to be pulled down. He was a rich man, well known for his public work, his public services;

he had spent his whole life working for others. I asked him what he was doing there. He said: "I come here once every twelve months. In this doorway, which is now tumbled down, fifty years ago I stood a child nine years old, with my little sister aged four, by one hand, and a little brother, aged six, by the other. I do not know who my father was, and I cannot remember my mother. We were left there, and I realized that we were alone in the world. I said in that doorway the only words I knew that had to do with God: 'Our Father which art in heaven'; and I walked out with my little sister and brother, without a farthing, without hope. You know what I am now. My prayer, poor as it was, was answered, and I will come here every twelve months until this place is pulled down, for fear that I should forget the love of God."

William Foxley Norris

✳✳

568   At the time when Luther was having his Bible printed in Germany, pieces of the printer's work were allowed to fall carelessly on the floor of the shop. One day the printer's daughter picked up a piece of paper on which she found the words "God so loved the world that He gave." What followed had not yet been printed. Up to this time she had been taught that God was to be feared. The thought that God so loved the world that He gave was a new idea of God to her, and it made life seem joyous. Her mother asked her the cause of her happiness. Putting her hand into her pocket she handed out the crumpled piece of paper. Her mother read it and said: "God so loved the world that He gave. What was it that He gave?" The child was perplexed for a moment and then said: "I do not know what it was that He gave, but if He loved us well enough to give us anything, we need not be afraid of Him."

John Bishop

Love, Power of

569   Hadfield, in his book, *The Psychology of Power*, tells of an explosion in a munitions factory at midnight. A woman, whose husband and son were working at that factory, heard the explosion, rose from bed, and ran seven miles to the scene. It was the love in her heart that gave her the power to do the seemingly impossible.   George Fairfoot

Love, Redeeming

570   I have been told that every foot of cordage which belongs to the Royal Navy has one little strand of red thread running through it. And the Bible also has its little strand of red thread which runs through the whole of it from beginning to end—the story of redeeming Love. It tells us of "the Seed of the Woman" that shall crush the serpent's head; of the "Seed of Abraham" in whom all the nations shall be blessed; of One who shall sit on David's throne and reign for ever. In Isaiah we read of the "Man of Sorrows," "despised and rejected of men." And we have here, too, the Gospel story of His birth in Bethlehem, His Crucifixion on Calvary, His glorious resurrection and ascension, and the assertion that He shall judge the world and reign as King and Lord of all for ever and for ever.

G. E. Prideaux

Love, Sacrificial

571   You remember the story of Tygranes, a prince or petty king in Armenia, whose land was conquered by Cyrus. He and his wife were conducted into the presence of the conqueror, and the sentence of death was pronounced according to the barbarous custom of the time. Tygranes, however, pleaded with Cyrus that if necessary he might be exposed to double suffering and torture, in addition to his death, if only his wife might be spared and set free; and Cyrus was so pleased with the man's sincerity and earnestness that he pardoned them both. When outside the royal pavilion, Tygranes asked his wife what she thought of Cyrus, and she replied: "Indeed, I have no thought for him at all; I thought only of the man who said he was prepared to bear the torture and agony of death for me." Suppose after that Tygranes had been suddenly elevated to a front place in the world, and that all men had done him honour, don't you think she would have prided herself on a tie between him and her which no one else could emulate? Would she not say: "That man whom they admire loves me, and gave, or offered to give, himself for me." There is no man or woman in this audience who may not look on Jesus Christ in that way.

F. B. Meyer

Love to Christ, Expression of

572   Dr. Parker once had gone to have a holiday somewhere, and he had, as he often had, a little child, child of his heart, with him when he went walking in the fields; and the little one bruised herself in trying to do something to please the Doctor. She ran and gathered him a posy—daisies and buttercups and what not—and she embarrassed the Doctor by the frequency with which she ran after him and pressed a fresh handful of flowers upon him. When he had told so much, the Doctor paused and looked us in the face, and said, "Did I need

them? No. Did I want them? Yes." God does not need the best of us. He can manage without us; it pleased Him to use us. There is responsibility in possession. What you have is His, what you are is His. If you have a love to Christ which is expressing itself as it ought to do in the fruits of the Spirit, love, joy, peace, they are yours and they are not yours; there are people hungry for them; bring them in, keep them in, make them strong; let them feel the power of God by what you are and by what you know.   R. J. Campbell

Love Towards Christ

573   In *The Life and Letters of Gertrude Bell*, the authoress tells how—in her presence on one occasion—an Arab Chieftain inquired of a Christian missionary why he regarded Jesus as a revelation of God. And when the interview was over, the Chieftain—half in complaint and half in admiration—turned to Miss Bell and said: "I wanted the reply of the learned, but when your missionary friend speaks of Jesus, he talks like a lover." That remark goes to the core of our Christian faith.   Leyton Richards

Love, True

574   A young fellow in the Army confided to his padre that he never went about with another girl if he was within fifty miles of home. So! His loyalty went fifty miles. Beyond that it broke down under the strain. But true love will go further.   E. Neville Martin

Loyalty

575   Long ago a Cavalier soldier had sold much of his property and given a great deal of his money to the Royalist cause. Then he was killed in a battle against the Roundheads. His friends paid tribute to his memory in these words, "He served King Charles with a constant, dangerous and expensive loyalty." It is to the same type of self-denying service that we are called, though for a King and a Cause greater by far. Freely we have received, freely we must give, not grudgingly or of necessity, for God loves a hilarious giver.

Robert James McCracken

Loyalty to God

576   Philip Inman tells the story of a man who visited his imbecile wife every week for over fifteen years, but each time he was met with just a vacant stare.

She never recognized him. This is what he said on one of those visits: "I have visited her every week for over fifteen years and she has always been the same. But I shall never fail to come while my legs can carry me. One day I hope, if only for a few minutes, she will be as she used to be. Her reason went when that cursed war robbed us of the last of our five boys." Such is the loyalty that man gives to man. Why should it be a burden to honour our obligation to God?

                                                                            H. G. Davis

Magnanimity

577   The magnanimous man never loses his influence. He holds on through the ages. Think of Abraham Lincoln; what a hold he has upon our modern world. Why? Because his heart was too big to bear malice or enmity.

"You have more of that feeling of personal resentment," said he to one of his cabinet, "than I have. Perhaps I have too little of it, but I have never thought it paid. I shall do nothing in malice. What I deal with is too vast for malicious dealing." Can anyone forget those deathless words of his second inaugural address: "With malice towards none, with charity towards all, with firmness in the right as God gives us to see it, let us strive to finish the work we are in . . . to do all which may achieve and cherish a just and lasting peace among ourselves and with all nations." No wonder Stanton said of such a man when he had just breathed his last: "Now he belongs to the ages."

It was said of Henry Ward Beecher that no one ever felt the full force of his kindness until he did Beecher an injury. Well did Beecher confess: "My soul is too glad, too great, to be at heart the enemy of any man." Can we forget the words of Nurse Cavell? "I thank God for these three weeks of quiet before the end. This time of rest has been a great mercy. But this I would say, standing as I do in view of God and eternity, I realize that patriotism is not enough. I must have no hatred or bitterness towards any one." That is what God meant to lead all hearts to. The human soul cannot live unless it grows magnanimous.

                                                                            D. Ewart James

Magnificat

578   When Edward Gibbon, the historian, sat amidst the ruins of the Capitol in Rome, and fell to contemplating the vanished splendour of the ancient city, suddenly he heard from a neighbouring church the strains of the "Magnificat," and when the words reached his ears, "He hath put down the mighty from their seats, and hath exalted the humble and meek," Gibbon sprang to his feet, and in that moment received the inspiration for his monumental work, *The Decline*

and Fall of the Roman Empire. Gibbon, far removed from being a Christian, yet perceived the inner significance and permanent application of at least one part of the maiden's canticle.   Frederick C. Spurr

Man

579   As Pascal said, if the universe crushes man he is still greater than it, because he knows that he is crushed,—he can think and hope and pray. So that the victories of science, so far from belittling man, reveal his greatness, the while they show that "the soul of all improvement is the improvement of the soul."
Joseph Fort Newton

✳✳

580   Said Raphael: "I dream dreams and then paint my dreams." Shakespeare was greater than his plays, Wellington was greater than Waterloo, Luther was greater than his protest, Webster was greater than his greatest oration, Mozart was greater than his grandest oratorio. "I decline," says Dr. Dale, "to surrender my dignity in the presence of the material universe. I am greater than the sun, greater than the sea, greater than the planets, greater than the stars—greater than all. They are subject, but I am sovereign. They are bound, but I am free." Man is greater than any disaster which may overwhelm him or any honour which may be bestowed upon him.

James L. Gordon

Man, Worth of

581 ⋅ When an eminent French surgeon was sent for to perform an operation on a Cardinal Prime Minister of France, the Cardinal said to him as he entered, "You know you must not expect to treat me as you treat those miserable wretches of yours in the hospital." "Your Eminence," he gravely replied, "every one of those 'miserable wretches,' as you are pleased to call them, is a Prime Minister in my eyes."

F. W. Farrar

Mankind, Questions of

582   The German philosopher, Kant, tells us that there are three questions which mankind has always been asking: "What can I know?" "What shall I do?" and "For what may I hope?"

E. J. Hardy

Meditation

583   Mr. C. F. Andrews once confessed to a company of ministers that he was
in great danger of losing the spiritual quality of his life when he returned to the
incessant bustle and noise of the West from the quiet atmosphere of India. But
there was one habit which became his life-saver. In India it is the custom to rise
early, and by continuing that habit in New York and London he was able to use
the precious morning hours for prayer and for the spiritual adjustment of his
soul before the rush and roar of the day's traffic began.

George B. Dibden

Memory

584   If we could always forget what we wanted to forget, and remember only
what we desire to remember, we should find life very much simplified. There
would be no sense of guilt, no remorse, no passionate and vain crying to get rid
of the ghosts of the past. The murderer, the thief, the repentant prodigal would
in that case be haunted by no disquieting dreams. But God could not entrust us
with such a power over our own past. And so He has given conscience a memory
independent of our will. Macbeth and Lady Macbeth were the victims of this
inability to forget; he by day, in his waking moments, she at night in dreams and
nightmares, were pursued by the undying ghost of Banquo, which was but the
objectified image of their own conscience, as it drove its shadowy sword into
their inmost hearts till he cried: "Oh, full of scorpions is my mind, sweet wife";
and she wandered about in her sleep, striving in vain to wipe the blood spot
from her guilty hand. This involuntary ethical memory is one of the safeguards
of virtue, one of the restraints of vice. There are few of us, indeed, who have so
pure and unsullied a past, but that have some stinging recollections creep, at
times, with chill insistence into our happiest moments; we would give anything
to be able to forget, but we cannot, and it is well for us that we cannot do so of
our own accord. It is the Nemesis of memory that we are always liable to a
resurrection of a past which was thought to be buried beyond recall. Perhaps the
great Judgement means only—yet how much that is!—the revivifying of the
burnt-out embers, the unlocking of the barred and secret doors of our earthly
past, that its glory and shame may be seen in the burning light of the Divine
Countenance.

E. Griffith Jones

Men, Unchanging

585   During the war, a famous historian, Arthur Bryant, put out books dealing with Britain during the Napoleonic wars of 150 years ago. As one read these books, one had more than once to bring oneself up with a jolt to remind oneself that he was not reading the newspaper reports of the week, but the history of 150 years ago. There was the same war, with the same manoeuvres, the same strategy, the same patriotic speeches by politicians, the same sacrifice of truth, the same call for civilians to guard their shores against invasion. The names were different, the weapons were different. But the men were the same.

John A. McFadden

Middle Age

586   Miss Dorothy Sayers says, "I have never yet heard any middle-aged man or woman who worked with his or her brains express any regret for the passing of youth. That kind of talk is the escape mechanism of the lazy-minded, who want to shuffle off their responsibilities upon the shoulders of the young."

That hit me right between the eyes. But worse was to come, for it was Frank Hancock, writing in *The Christian Pacifist*, who ultimately dragged me face to face with reality. "Power," he says, "lies in the hands of the fifty plus. We old men and women hold at last the key positions in business, State and Church. The levers at long last are coming into our hands—those levers that we have so long waited for that we might use them to better purpose. For forty years we have striven and criticized and waited. And now, think of it, the premier positions and all the power for the next twenty years are in our hands—the hand of the fifty plus. It is God's opportunity—in us—at last."

Stanley Herbert

Minister

587   Dr. David Christie in *The Service of Christ* has a chapter on "The Temptations of the Ministry," in which he singles out three for special mention, the temptation to recline, to shine and to whine.   John Bishop

Minister, Personal Life

588   Woodrow Wilson was once asked whether a minister should wear clerical or ordinary dress. He replied, "It makes no difference what the minister wears.

But one thing matters supremely. He should never be in any company of men
for a single instant without making them realize that they are in the presence of
a minister of religion."   John Bishop

Ministry

589   The magazine *Time* reported that a Roper opinion poll showed that the
average citizen considers that the group doing the most good for the country
at the present time is the company of religious leaders. In five years this category
jumped from third to first place. Business leaders were placed next, with political
leaders, labour leaders following in that order. An editorial in the Boston *Herald*
appeared not long ago with this unexpected tribute: "This band of men, un-
recognized, underpaid, over-worked, unassuming, that never complain [I would
add, "Hardly ever!"], never strike, are accomplishing, under conditions that
make their performance little less than heroic, a work that is indispensable to the
stability and permanence of our religion." My young friend, this is a "majestic
fraternity" which you may be led to enter. As Dr. George Pidgeon said in the
closing words of his valedictory to this year's ministerial candidates, after a long
lifetime of consecrated service: "It is a marvellous opportunity and the richest
privilege on earth."   David A. MacLennan

✳✳

590   By a kind of perverse compliment, many people expect the minister to
have the sermonic skill of a Fosdick, the oratorical power of a Churchill, the
personal charm of a movie hero, the psychological insight of a Weatherhead, the
organizing and administrative ability of an Eisenhower, the wisdom of Socrates,
and the patience of Job! In addition he may be required to be the oiler of creak-
ing ecclesiastical machinery, the office boy for an official board, and the dispenser
of sweetness and harmony to members of rival groups of devoted church women!
It is a precarious calling, for even yet few ministers have any continuing city,
or home of their own. My dear cousin, the late Dr. William MacLennan, who
founded the Welcome Hall social settlement in Buffalo, used to say that the
hens owned by country ministers were so accustomed to the itinerant ministry
that after every annual Conference they would co-operatively lie down on
their backs and extend their feet into the air to be tied for shipment to the
next charge! In other professions maturity and age are considered assets, but
there are still benighted church committees who regard fifty and even fewer
birthdays as "too old" for the pastorate.   David A. MacLennan

✳✳

591   When "Dick" Sheppard, who served Christ with such singular power as the unconventional minister of St. Martin's-in-the-Fields, London, boarded a bus, wearing the uniform of his calling for the first time, he sat near two drunken working-men. One was in a belligerent mood, the other benevolent to the point of being maudlin. On catching sight of the young clergyman, who had just been ordained, the former remarked, "There's a ruddy parson!" But the other, full of genial intention, stopped him. "Now, George, don't blame 'im—it's not 'is fault. It's 'ard luck, that's what I says." That judgement of ignorance amuses us, but it is not far removed from the verdict some parents would be tempted to pass if they learned that a son or daughter felt inclined to "enter the Church."

David A. MacLennan

＊＊

592   Said Dr. Cuyler, in closing up a ministry during which he had preached 2,750 sermons, contributed 3,200 articles for various periodicals, and made 25,000 pastoral visits, "When I recall the joys of forty-four years of life spent in the gospel ministry, I shudder to think how near I came to losing them. Tempted to other pursuits, my decision lay trembling in the balance. But a single hour in a village prayer-meeting and the influence of my beloved mother tipped the scale, and in the right direction."

Howard W. Pope

＊＊

593   In that great day, how insignificant shall appear the offices or honours, the wealth and comforts of the earthly life, compared with the crown which shall be given to those who have conquered souls for Christ! Could I live a thousand years, I would proclaim the Divine message; but almost as soon as we learn how to live we must die. Had I a thousand lives, they should all be spent in the ministry of the Word.

Bishop M. Simpson

Ministry, Call to

594   One day in the last century a young lad sat in the gallery of the British House of Commons and listened to the majestic eloquence of John Bright. He went back home with the resolve in his heart that he was going to be a lawyer. The day before he was to sign the articles in a law office, he was walking through his native city when he came face to face with his Sunday-school teacher. He said: "I am signing the articles in a law office to-morrow." The Sunday-school teacher said: "That is a great profession," and then his face clouded and he continued, "but Henry, I have always hoped that you would be a minister of Christ."

In deep thought, the youth went to his home, and there in solitude he heard the call of the Eternal ringing in the chambers of his soul "as clearly as the morning bell rings in the valleys of Switzerland," and John Henry Jowett entered the Christian ministry. In Great Britain, and here in the pulpit of the Fifth Avenue Presbyterian Church, he exercised a ministry second to none in the twentieth century.   John Sutherland Bonnell

✳✳

595   Sydney Smith said he had only one illusion left—the Archbishop of Canterbury. I am not so entirely stripped of illusion as that; but if by illusion you mean a sort of mysterious interest attaching to a man or an institution, I can truly say, and in no irreverent spirit, that my strongest and most lasting illusion is the Christian ministry. A Congregational minister is an object of curious interest to me because he has been through an intensely interesting experience—the experience of the call to the ministry. For me it is the call—not the ordination, not even the induction by a Moderator—which invests the minister (I say it deliberately) with something of a priestlike apartness: for as I understand the call to the Congregational ministry it is a call, before everything else, to administer the sacrament of preaching.   Ernest H. Jeffs

Ministry, Common Sense in

596   A University student once asked his professor (a self-taught teacher of amazing knowledge, John Brown of Haddington): "What does a man most need to fit him to be a minister of religion?" The professor replied, "You need three things. First, a competent knowledge of the original tongues in which the Bible was written—that's a matter of mere plodding. Secondly, you need personal character and piety—that any man can get if he will ask for it. Thirdly, and above all, you need common sense, and if you don't bring that with you, I can't tell you where you can get it."

A hundred years ago Emerson was disturbed by the amount of nonsense written and talked about religion, and protested that the cure for such thinking was mother wit. "Nothing astonishes men so much as common sense and plain dealing."   Harold Bickley

Ministry, Dependent on Prayer

597   If your minister is to work effectively, you must pray for him during the week. His success is your concern. I have come to the conclusion, for a very long time, that if ever I preach a sermon that seems to have any special power

over the conscience and spiritual life of my own congregation, it is because people in the church have been especially praying for me and my work during the week. What success I have is theirs rather than mine. Never find fault with a sermon you may hear, if you have not been praying earnestly during the week that your minister may be filled with the Holy Ghost.

R. W. Dale

Ministry, Peril of Laziness in

598   The dead-line in the ministry, as in any other calling, is the line of laziness. The lawyer cannot use last year's briefs. The physician cannot depend on last week's diagnosis. The merchant cannot assume that a customer of ten years' standing will not be enticed elsewhere. And the preacher must be a live, wide-awake, growing man. Let him dye his brains, not his hair. Let his thought be fresh, and his speech be glowing. Sermons, it has been well said, are like bread, which is delicious when it is fresh, but which, when a month old, is hard to cut, harder to eat, and hardest of all to digest.

A. J. F. Behrends

Ministry, Qualifications for

599   Luther's ten qualifications for the minister: 1. He should be able to teach plainly and in order. 2. He should have a good head. 3. Good power of language. 4. A good voice. 5. A good memory. 6. He should know when to stop. 7. He should be sure of what he means to say. 8. And be ready to stake body and soul, goods and reputation on its truth. 9. He should study diligently. 10. And suffer himself to be vexed and criticized by everyone.

Ministry, Remembering Circumstances in

600   It is of the greatest importance to the preacher to remember the place and circumstances of his ministry. Henry Crabb Robinson relates that Chantrey, the sculptor, remarked: "The ancients worked with a knowledge of the place where the statue was to be placed, and anticipated the light to which it would be exposed." The preacher needs to keep in view the place and people. It is wonderful how we are apt almost entirely to ignore the environment. I knew a preacher who, in a down-town church, capable of seating 18,000, but attended by about fifty, commenced the service by giving out the hymn, "What means this eager, anxious throng!" The clergyman was equally oblivious who preached in the workhouse from the text, "Lay not up for yourselves treasures on earth." And

I fancy it was the same gentleman who opened his discourse in the country jail by remarking that he "was glad to see so many of them present," and who became immensely popular with the convicts by concluding the service with an earnest supplication that they "might all now be dismissed to their several habitations." Without being quite as absurd, we may seriously miscalculate the occasion and beat the air. A city congregation differs widely from a rustic one; a middle-class congregation from one of working-men. They alike need the great truths of the Gospel, but there are real, although subtle, distinctions, and happy is the preacher who understands what scientists call "concurrent adaptation."

W. L. Watkinson

Miracle

601   A century ago radio and aviation, radar and atomic energy, perhaps even the telegraph and the telephone, would probably to our bearded and crinolined progenitors have appeared miraculous. They would have seemed magical because the laws of which they are the practical application were still unknown. There is little doubt, further, that our own great-grandchildren will be familiar with and bored by speeds, rays, lunar week-ends, television marvels, which, suddenly exhibited to-day, would seem miraculous to us. If, then, we agree, and we can hardly do anything else, that the incidence of miracle varies with the level of knowledge, it should be possible both in the main to endorse the Biblical account of things and also remain loyal to our great conception of law. Supreme souls, personalities in tune with the infinite, may have discovered by intuition or learned through revelation a knowledge of other more majestic laws of Nature, and have acted in accordance with them to the amazement of the contemporary multitude and to the endless teasing of posterity.

D. W. Langridge

Mission Opportunity

602   We are living in a time of great opportunity to further missionary work.

Upon first consideration this does not appear to be the case. Everywhere there are difficulties and hindrances. These seem to make this anything but a propitious time for the winning of others to Christian allegiance. They may indeed seem so great as to make us feel, in Dr. Latourette's words, "The very existence of Christianity seems threatened. Seldom, if ever, has the menace to Christianity been so grave as in the present century. Were one simply to fix his gaze on the adverse forces, he might come to the conclusion that Christianity, like other religions, has reached the peak of its career and is irretrievably declining as a vital force in the life of mankind." There are, however, other circumstances to be considered besides those which constitute the difficulties and hindrances and the adverse forces. It is significant that Dr. Latourette follows the paragraph just quoted with these words: "Yet the world also presents Christianity with a challenge—a challenge not to survival but to advance and to fresh victories." He contrasts the threat of this time with, in fact, its opportunity.

H. Carter Lloyd

Missions

603 The conversion of the whole people to the worst (not to the best) form of Christianity ever known in the darkest ages would be a happy event. It is not necessary that a man should be a Christian in order to wish for the propagation of Christianity in India; it is sufficient that he should be a European, not much below the ordinary European level of good sense and humanity.

Lord Macaulay

❋❋

604 It is said that a young clergyman in the company of the Duke of Wellington was arguing against foreign missions. What was the good of taking Christianity to the heathens and unsettling their views? They were comfortable and contented without. The Duke rejoined: "Young man, what are your marching orders?"   J. Berry

❋❋

605 Adoniram Judson, the Apostle of Burma, was once flung into prison, a lonely, friendless man, at the mercy of his captors. It seemed a hopeless task to which he had set his hand; so at least his adversaries thought. He found frustration on every hand. As he lay in that foul Burmese prison his captors jeeringly said, "What about the prospects of Missions now, Judson?" The swift and unhesitating reply was, "They are just as bright as the promises of God."

F. C. Hoggarth

❋❋

606 You know what Dr. Duff said when he came back from India and stood in the midst of that great mass of people in Edinburgh. He talked to that great Presbyterian gathering and said: "Brethren, we are playing at missions, and that is all the Church of Christ has been doing—playing at missions."

J. J. Muir

❋❋

607   You remember the story of Morrison, the missionary to China. As he drew near to the scene of his work the American captain of his ship said to him: "And so, Mr. Morrison, you really expect to make an impression upon the Chinese Empire?" and Morrison replied: "No, sir, but I expect God will." You remember also that twenty-seven years later, when Morrison died, he left behind him not more than twelve Protestant Christians, and now they number some three million. This is an example of what the early missionaries sowed in blood and tears and of the fruits that have been reaped.   Geoffrey Fisher

※※

608   Robert Arlington was a munificent miser, spending nothing on himself that he might devote his fortune to spreading the gospel abroad. The austerity and simplicity of his daily life and his abounding generosity towards Christian missions are probably to be explained by reference to a letter from a missionary which was found after his death among his private papers. "Were I in England again, I would gladly live in one room, make the floor my bed, a box my chair, and another my table, rather than that the heathen should perish for lack of knowledge of Christ." Modern folk would perhaps class him as "a man with a one-track mind," but that track led to the establishment of the Church of Christ in Congo: an eccentric, yet thousands of redeemed Congolese rejoice at the results of his eccentricity.   S. G. Browne

※※

609   Marco Polo tells how in 1269 Kublai Khan sent a request from Peking for "a hundred wise men of the Christian religion. . . . And so I shall be baptized, and when I shall be baptized all my barons and great men will be baptized, and then their subjects baptized, and so there will be more Christians here than there are in your parts." "There is much to make us take this report seriously," Foster says. "Everything points to the fact that the Mongols were wavering in the choice of a religion. It might have been, as Kublai forecast, the greatest mass movement the world has ever seen. The history of all Asia would have been altered." But what actually happened? "Pope Gregory X answered by sending two Dominican friars" who got as far as Armenia and then could endure no longer but returned home. "So passed the greatest missionary opportunity in the history of the Church."   Roderic Dunkerley

※※

610   Fifty years ago a man went out from my adopted State of Texas as a missionary to Brazil. Later on, at one of the great conventions of our State, an eloquent preacher poured out his appeal for some young woman to go also to

Brazil and to teach the women and girls in that land. One little woman stood up in the vast hall and waved her hand, and said, "Papa, I will go." It was his own daughter. He staggered back and said, "Great God, child, I did not mean you." But she went, and she did a great work in Brazil, and she married that young man who had gone out earlier. And now, when Dr. Rushbrooke and I went to Brazil, we found five hundred Baptist Churches there, and many have been added since then. Indeed, the most triumphant march made by our Baptist people at the present time is in Brazil.

George W. Truett

**

611   It is almost impossible today to realize that Robert Morrison, after twenty-seven years of devoted labor, died with China still unopened and the gates still shut. It was on the little island of Macao, in a little stream which they say to-day has run dry, that Morrison baptized his first Chinese convert, and when he died there were but twelve. But he had put the Scriptures into Chinese, and he had left the record of an heroic life. He had suggested to every lad on the English countryside, and to every apprentice in the towns of this country, that he, too, might be a great hero, that he, too, might lead to the salvation of a continent; and his life, apparently barren, proved to be abundantly fruitful. And yet, when Giffith John went to China in the year that I was born, there were only five hundred Christians gathered into the Church by the half-century of Christian missions.

Robert F. Horton

**

612   On the mantelpiece of a certain home there stands the photograph of one of our young girl missionaries. It is the home of her mother's sister. An acquaintance who is untouched by the spirit of religion came in. "Who is this?" she said. "It is my niece," was the reply. "Where is she, and what is she doing?" asked the visitor. "She is in India as a missionary." "My word, couldn't she do any better for herself than that?" Her aunt fired up at this, and said: "Well, she has an honour degree in mathematics, and had a fine post in one of the best schools in England, but after three years she felt called to give up everything because Christ was calling her to serve Him wholly as a missionary." This was outside the comprehension of the visitor, who could only gasp: "My goodness, she must have a kink!"

Yes, she has a kink indeed. The same kind of kink as Francis Xavier and Father Damien. The same kind of kink as Livingstone and Carey, Comber and Grenfell, Mary Slessor and Albert Schweitzer (that multiple genius who, being first class in philosophy, in theology, in music, must needs qualify in medicine in order to bury himself in some dog-hole of a place on the west coast of Africa).

Gilbert Laws

✳✳

613   "Why did you become a missionary?" a friend asked Adoniram Judson. "I never thought of that," said Mr. Judson, and then said, "I became a missionary because I thought Jesus Christ would be glad to have me become one."

David A. MacLennan

✳✳

614   Two great names come to my mind. I think of Howard Somervell, the Mount Everest climber, becoming Howard Somervell, the Missionary Doctor of Neyyoor, South India. I recall how he descended from a great climbing expedition, conscious of his manly strength, to discover the diseased and weak bodies of the natives of Travancore, with little medical and less surgical aid at their disposal—one doctor for every ten thousand of India's millions even to-day—and I thank God as do countless people in India, that he, there and then, heard God's call to him—"I will send thee to the children of India"—and he dedicated his strength of body and mind, and all his professional knowledge and skill to the service of God in India.

The other name is that of Eric Liddell, Scottish Rugby Internationalist and Olympic champion. I think of him returning from the Olympic Games in Paris, where he had set up a world record, to receive the congratulations and praise of wildly enthusiastic crowds and assemblies of the great. I hear him in the midst of the great men of Scotland, after a complimentary dinner in Edinburgh, telling them that running was not to be his career, that he was training to be a missionary in China, and asking for help and sympathy and prayer. "What a hush suddenly fell," said a distinguished newspaper writer next day. "The Olympic Games were forgotten: the olive crowns and the thunder of cheers; and we saw this young men go forth on his mission." Yes, the Olympic hero heard God say, "I will send thee to the children of China," and he dedicated his strength to God's service in that land. In Howard Somervell, Eric Liddell and a host of lesser men and women we see Christianity in action as the religion of the strong in the service of the weak.

Ernest A. Buxton

Mistakes

615   I like the illustration of the Persian carpet: it taught me a wonderful lesson once when I was in Persia, and especially when I was able to confirm it

recently by a conversation with a Persian student in the train. When they are making a Persian carpet, or a Persian rug, they have planks across it at different levels on which little boys sit who are working away, and the artist is behind on the other side, and he shouts his instructions to them, and tells them what to do: and as he speaks to them so they move their colour or their pattern. In the carpet there are the colours blue, green, red: but in a real Persian carpet you may find a little yellow dot as big as a shilling. It ought not really to be there. Perhaps you will find that there is a black where there should be a red. I asked this Persian student in the train, "What happens when one of the boys makes a mistake?" "Well," he replied, "quite often the artist does not make the boy take out the wrong pattern or colour. He weaves the mistake into his pattern."

Is not that a parable of life? We are working on the wrong side of the carpet. In my ignorance I often put in the wrong colour. And my mistakes, and the mistakes of my fellows, spoil the pattern. But God is such a great Artist that He can take my mistakes and weave them into His own perfect purpose and plan. No mistakes can be made that He is not ready enough to weave into loveliness. Nothing can divert His purpose ultimately, or finally spoil His plan. I believe that if we go on co-operating with God in faith, putting our lives into His hands, He will one day bring us to the goal of our desires, and to the goal of His divine purpose.

Leslie D. Weatherhead

From *Why Do Men Suffer?* published by Abingdon-Cokesbury, p. 124.

Money

616   I was speaking to a man the other day who has travelled extensively. When he arrived at New York the customs officer, observing his Bible in his bag, said to him, "Say, brother, you'll have no time to read this in the States. We are all too busy making dollars. Guess the almighty dollar is our god."

Ronald K. Ross

Moral Resources, Need of

617   You may remember the wonderful parable of the Arab who sent his sons out to get learning wherever they could. They came back after four years, and he took them into the desert and showed them something. "What is that?" he asked the eldest son. "Why, the bones of a tiger," was the reply, as the son turned them this way and that. "His age when he died was seven years and three months, his length, from the tip of his tail to the tip of his nose, was seven feet nine inches." The father was surprised, and turned to the second son. "And what can you do?" This son quickly built up the complete skeleton of the tiger and set it on the desert sands. "What can you do?" the father asked the third son, still more astonished. The third son stuffed the tiger, covered it with skin, and put eyes in its head. "Now," said the father, "can I test the remaining son? There is nothing more to be done." "Wait a minute," said the fourth son. He stood in front of the tiger, uttered magic words, sent a blue spark from the tip of his finger into the tip of the tiger's nose. The tiger rolled its eyes, opened wide its mouth, made a mighty spring—and ate them all up!

Cannot you see how true that has become? We wonder that we have created a civilization which we are not strong enough to control. You come back there to the old personal problem. Here is the trouble. God gave us such a big nature, and we are not strong enough for it. If He had made us several sizes less, if He had given us the capacity to live a little less tumultuously, if He had made us a little less adventurous, a little less free, He might have us all safely tucked in bed every night at ten o'clock, with no anxiety to anybody—and precious little good either! If God had wanted tame rabbits, He could have had them. But He wanted sons and daughters. He created these extraordinary natures of ours that are too big for us to control, and we in turn have created an amazing civilization which we are not strong enough to control. Unless we can get a great access of moral resources we simply cannot get on.   W. Russell Maltby

Morality

618   Sir John Seeley reminded us that the whole difference between New Testament morality and the morality of the past was this, that the morality of the past was governing and measuring ourselves by acts done which were wrong, but that since Christ came all morality was to be measured not by what had been done but by what ought to have been done, and it is in proportion as you and I have fallen short of what we ought to have done that the measure of our guilt, the measure of our sin, is to be understood.   W. Boyd Carpenter

Morality, Christian

619   There is a great deal done today in the matter of social service, and I should be the last to decry it. But John Macmurray uttered a profound truth on the wireless the other day when he said that for many people social service is a substitute for Christian morality. Christian morality means loving—note that— loving the down-trodden and the degraded, the unlovely and the outcast, the un- attractive and the unclean. And that's infinitely harder than giving five or ten shillings to some philanthropic fund. The late Studdert Kennedy somewhere asks how many of us come up against a man completely knocked out on the Jericho road, with no hope in the world, everything gone, nothing but dark depression, and find to our horror we have no wine, no oil, nothing but ourselves to give. It is then we ask how much we ourselves are worth and fall on our knees asking God for help. Some of us have been there many times, says Kennedy, and find, God help us, that we are not worth much.

J. D. Jones

Mortality of Earthly Things

620   St. John says we should not love the world because the lust thereof passeth away. We sometimes sing:

> Fading is the worldling's pleasure,
>   All his boasted pomp and show:
> Solid joys and lasting treasure
>   None but Zion's children know.

The philosophy is better than the poetry. The worldling's pleasure is both fading and fleeting, swifter than a weaver's shuttle. Madame Récamier reigned by her loveliness in youth, but one day she was dethroned. "From the day when I saw that the little Savoyards no longer turned to look at me in the street, I understood that it was all over." Mrs. Carlyle said, "I married for ambition. Carlyle has exceeded all my wildest hopes and expectations, and I am miserable." That is how refined love of the world is rewarded. As for the coarse love of the world, it will not bear much thinking about. A day's delight, then only too often shame and remorse. Nothing can delight for long the man of the world. He may flit from flower to flower, but the sweetness will cloy, and the pleasure pall. If he then indulges himself, it is not because he is under any illusion about the pleasures of the world. He and the world understand. His attendance upon the world becomes a mockery. He knows that it has nothing for him. He has wasted his substance in riotous living, and there is no return. What does he say? That life is a weariness, and that he does not care how soon he shuffles off its mortal coil.

"The world passeth away." Some say, "Vanity of vanities." Others reply, "Let us eat, drink and be merry." What said Jesus? "My work is to do the will of Him that sent me." The Christian takes up the work, for he carries on the work; and he is happy in it, for he is sure of his reward. Let the end come when it will, he is ready for it. The man of God is neither foolish nor melancholy because the world passeth away; it leaves him untouched. "We know that if our earthly house of this tabernacle be dissolved, we have a building eternal in the heavens. Therefore we are always confident, knowing that, whilst we are at home in the body, we are absent from the Lord. Wherefore, we labour, that, whether present or absent, we may be accepted of Him." "He that doeth the will of God abideth for ever." Grave that word on the palms of your hands, write it on the tables of your hearts; you are here to serve your generation according to the will of God, and in His will is your peace and permanence. I call you to it in the name of Jesus Christ our Lord.   T. N. Tattersall

Mother

621   The late Dean Farrar, an eloquent preacher and writer, in old age wrote lovingly of his mother as "first among the influences which have formed my life. She passed her life," he says, "in the deep valley of poverty, obscurity, and trial, but she has left to her only son the recollections of a saint."

Alfred Thomas

✳✳

622   D. L. Moody, the great evangelist, had a wonderful mother. She was not very pious, but she had three principles which she instilled into her son: 1. Trust in God. 2. In our home fault-finding is not allowed. We are not to come home after a service and pick the sermon to pieces. (This is not a theological dictum. I am not sure that Christian people ought not to pay more attention to it. I have known the influence of a fine sermon to be entirely dissipated by thoughtless chatter round a table.) 3. Remember, a promise is sacred. Now, I think of that woman, and as far as I know she never wrote a line. She did write a gospel— her interpretation of Christ—and she passed it on.   F. Townley Lord

✳✳

623   During the Civil War of America a young man received a wound which proved fatal. In the hospital he called so constantly in his delirium for his mother that the surgeon dispatched a message for her; and she arrived as soon as trains could bring her. The surgeon informed her of her son's condition, hovering between life and death, and assured her that the excitement consequent upon his recognizing her presence would take away any hope of his recovery that might remain. So, according to strict orders, she sat for two hours outside the door of the ward, having the couch on which her son tossed to and fro in her direct line of vision. At length she said to the surgeon as he passed: "I shall die if I remain here any longer. May I not go and take the place of the nurse, only doing what she does in the way of smoothing his pillow and wetting his lips, and I promise you I shall do nothing to disclose to him who I am?" On those conditions she was allowed to take the nurse's place, and she faithfully

discharged her professional duties in a strictly professional manner until her boy, turning his face to the wall, uttered a deep groan, when she involuntarily placed her hand on his brow; whereupon the sufferer cried: "Nurse, how like my mother's hand!"   John Macmillan

✳✳

624   When fifty-eight years old Carlyle wrote the following beautiful epistle to his aged mother:

"Dear old mother, weak and sick and dear to me, what a day this has been in my solitary thoughts! For, except a few words to Jane, I have not spoken to anyone, nor, indeed, hardly seen anyone, it being dusk and dark before I went out— a dim, silent Sabbath day, the sky foggy, dark with damp, and a universal stillness the consequence, and it is this day gone fifty-eight years that I was born. And my poor mother! Well, we are all in God's hands—surely God is good. Surely we ought to trust Him, or what is there for the sons of men? O my dear mother, let it ever be a comfort to you, however weak you are, that you did your part honourably and well while in strength, and you were a noble mother to me and to us all. I am now myself grown old, and have various things to do and suffer for so many years, that there is nothing I ever had to be so much thankful for as the mother I had. That is a truth which I know well, and perhaps this day again it may be some comfort to you. Yes, surely, for if there has been any good in the things I have uttered in the world's hearing, it was your voice essentially that was speaking through me, essentially what you and my brave father meant and taught me to mean—this was the purport of all I spoke and wrote. And if in the few years that may remain to me I am to get any more written for the world, the essence of it, so far as it is worthy and good, will still be yours.

"May God reward you, dearest mother, for all you have done for me. I never can. Ah, no, but will think of it with gratitude and pious love so long as I have the power of thinking, and I will pray God's blessing on you now and always."

And when the mother of Thomas Carlyle was gone from earth for ever, how lonely was this strange and sad philosopher! How earnestly he could have breathed a prayer in the language of the following pathetic lines:

> Mother, come back from yon echoless shore,
> Take me again to your heart as of yore,
> Over my slumbers your loving watch keep,
> Rock me to sleep, mother, rock me to sleep.

James L. Gordon

✳✳

625   The greatest word is God. The deepest word is Soul. The longest word is Eternity. The swiftest word is Time. The nearest word is Now. The darkest word is Sin. The meanest word is Hypocrisy. The broadest word is Truth. The strongest word is Right. The tenderest word is Love. The sweetest word is Home. The dearest word is Mother.   James L. Gordon

✳✳

626   Do your children know that you pray? The great Frenchman, Lamartine, tells us of a secluded walk, in the garden of their country home, where his mother spent always a certain hour of the day. Husband and children all knew it, but they never intruded upon that sacred privacy. Little by little all knew how she paced that garden walk, her hands clasped, her eyes lifted, her lips moving. It was an hour of speech with God, an hour of earnest supplication that she might be strengthened, and that they might be blessed. It was an intercourse from which she returned refreshed and renewed. Do you wonder that she was the mother of a great man? One could quote hundreds of cases which only differ in detail. Do your children know that you pray? They most certainly know if you don't. A girl once went to a clergyman, and wanted to "join the Church." "Do you want to be like Jesus?" he asked. "I don't know, but I want to be like my mother," was the answer. And I'll warrant that was a praying mother.   W. R. Yates

✳✳

627   Now the remembrance that my mother so loved me, and that she dedicated me to mankind; the remembrance that it was her thought, and that it was the inspiration of her prayer that I was to be set apart not to be a great man for myself, but to be connected with the welfare of the human race—I have never lost the inspiration of it; nor have I ceased to be thankful to my mother, and to reverence her, that she had such a thought and wish with regard to me.

Henry Ward Beecher

✳✳

628   Consider this statement made at a women's conference held in America. A question was asked which was as follows: "What age is safest for a mother to present the claims of Christ to her children?" At the end of the meeting an elderly lady stood up to answer the question. She said: "I began with my first child twenty years before he was born by giving myself to Christ."

William Mudd

✳✳

629 The future of a child does not rest so much with itself as with its mother. The child's good or bad conduct, the child's happiness or misery, to a very great extent, hangs, I will not say on the wish, but certainly on the training and example of its mother. The mother is the greatest teacher for good or for evil that the child will ever have, and the scenes, experiences, and lessons of childhood will never be forgotten, and their influence will be felt through all the term of life. When Napoleon Bonaparte complained to a lady as to the flippant and frivolous nature of the education that the young were receiving, and put the question as to who was to blame, the lady's answer was, "Mothers!" And the lady was right.   P. Robertson

Mother, Influence of

630 One of the most important chapters of history will be entitled "A Mother's Influence." Who will write that wonderful story? The two brightest names of modern history are Lincoln and Cromwell. Lincoln affirmed, "All that I am or hope to be I owe to my angel mother." Concerning Cromwell, the historian says: "No other member of his family, neither his wife or father, influenced him as did his mother." He followed her advice when young, he established her in the royal palace of Whitehall when he came to greatness, and when she died he buried her in Westminster Abbey." A plain, robust, substantial character she must have been, for, the historian adds, "She cared nothing for her son's grandeur." Her only thought seemed to be for his welfare and comfort and the honour of his name and reputation.

From the mother of Augustine to the mother of John Wesley, and from the mother of John Wesley to Victoria, the mother of Edward VII, the story of Christian motherhood has been the brightest thing on the page of history. Henry Ward Beecher, whose mother died when he was three years old, said, "No devout Roman Catholic ever saw so much in the Virgin Mary as I beheld in the childhood vision and memory's dream of my sainted mother." That angel form was ever present in the life of the great preacher. She haunted his thoughts in youth. She hovered over the study hours of his maturity. She lingered near the sacred desk as her famous son entered the holy of holies in the house of prayer and petition. She stood by him in the moments of his fierce oratorical conflicts when he stood before angry mobs and opposing elements.   James L. Gordon

Mother of Jesus

631 Roman Catholics and Protestants are sharply divided in their ideas of, and attitude towards, Mary. Both of them have gone to unnecessary extremes.

The Roman Catholic who has deified her has in so doing spoiled the simple picture of her left upon the page of the New Testament. The Protestant who, on the other hand, ignores her has done himself and her a great injustice. But there is one point upon which both of them are agreed. It is this: that Mary stands forevermore as the first lady of the world. Above all princesses and above all queens, this simple village maiden stands resplendent. And for this reason, if for no other, that she was His Mother. That in itself is enough. But she remains also forevermore a pattern of great womanhood; the flower of her race; a lily amongst the thorns of Nazareth. Mary of Nazareth remains for ever in many respects a model for all women to the end of time.   Frederick C. Spurr

Mother, Opportunities of

632   Very beautiful is the testimony of John Ruskin. In *Fors Clavigera* he says: "It is strange that of all the pieces of the Bible that my mother taught me, that which cost me most and was to my child's mind most repulsive, the 119th psalm, has now become of all the most precious to me, in its glorious and over-flowing passion of love for the law of God." Only God knows how much the world owes to Godly motherhood, and to the faithful lessons of truth and good-ness which it teaches the little children in the holy, though often lowly, places of the home. The mother-love works often in obscurity; often also, as in Ruskin's case, against the inclination because above the judgment of the child. But what glorious fruitage it often brings forth in the after-years for the blessing of man-kind! Have patience, you Christian mothers—have patience, you Sabbath-school teachers. Sow on: You shall reap in due season if you faint not. Before Ruskin was thirteen years old his mother had taken him six times carefully through the Bible. Have you been through it once, even yet? It is worth reading once. It is worth reading carefully more than once. It is worth reading prayerfully many times. The indebtedness of the world's greatest and best to the Bible is a truism. Many great names might be mentioned, but there is no more remarkable case than Ruskin. He often refers to it. He says again in *Praeterita*: "Truly, though I have picked up the elements of a little further knowledge, and owe not a little to the teaching of many people, this maternal installation of my mind into that property of chapters I count, very confidently, the most precious, and, on the whole, the one essential part of my education."   W. B. MacLeod

Nations and God

633   I say that any nation which denies God becomes by an invariable law a degraded nation at last; and any age which denies God sinks in great measure

into an abominable age. History, alas, does not lack examples to emphasize the warning. We have seen what the last pagan century was. Let us think of the fifteenth Christian century. It seems to be characteristic of such ages that they should be at once glittering and corrupt, clothed, like the blaspheming Herod, in tissue of silver, but within eaten of worms. Christianity in the fifteenth century had largely ceased to be Christian. Priests turned Atheists made open scoff at the religion which they professed; the world was filled with pride and greed and pollution. There is not a single historian of the fifteenth century who does not admit that a fearful moral retrogression followed on the overthrow of it. Take another century in which unbelief was predominant, the eighteenth century. Then in the chambers of St. Louis, a king effeminate as Sardanapalus suffered infamous hands to toy with the crown of St. Louis. Then in Russia reigned Catherine II, an empress well-nigh as base as Messalina, whom the poet calls

> That foul woman of the North,
> The lustful murderess of her wedded lord.

In Saxony an Augustus the Strong filled with his shamelessness the trumpet of infamy. In Prussia a Frederick II was making his court the propaganda of infidelity. In England—alas! even in England—we had a grossly-tainted literature, a corrupt society, gambling, drinking, all but universal profligacy, and the election to Parliament of a man—John Wilkes—who had written an infamous book, and had taken part in the blasphemous orgies of Medenham Abbey. England was saved by the religious revival. But for Europe that epoch ended in the thunder-clap of the French Revolution; and amongst those frivolous and Atheistic kings the people, says Lacordaire, which had followed in the wake of their corruption, to feed upon its offal, flung the head of a king, shorn off by the ignoble axe of a machine. The boast of liberty ended in a Reign of Terror, with the boast of humanity in Paris drunk with blood; the boast of virtue in the desecration of churches by blasphemous obscenity, and the worship of a harlot on the polluted altars of Notre Dame.

Nor are our warnings a century old. The Scripture says that when God's judgements are in the world, nations will learn wisdom.

F. W. Farrar

Natural Rights

634 John Morley, writing to Joseph Chamberlain, rebuked his friend for basing some point of policy upon "natural rights." "Man has no 'natural rights,'" he said. Neither has he—except upon the Christian view that men are

the children of God and have the natural rights which a man may claim from the Author of his being. Even in this Christian view democracy is only secondarily a matter of rights. Primarily it is a matter of duties and responsibilities. The Christian must be a democrat because he must have freedom to discharge his duties and responsibilities as a son of God and a brother of men.

Ernest H. Jeffs

Need

635   Only one thing can save us now and that is a new moral sense, a spiritual conversion, a deliberate turning to God and Christ and goodness, with the resolve that first things will be put first and not last. If you reply that preachers have been saying that until you are weary of hearing it and put it down as pious and conventional verbiage, my concern is whether you can have noticed that columnists, educators, statesmen and scientists are now saying the same thing. A physicist in a State University recently put it in this way: "I have come to three conclusions. The first is that salvation is not to be found in science. Secondly, we must have a moral revival. Thirdly, we can have no moral revival without a living religion."

Robert James McCracken

✳✳

636   Superior as we moderns feel ourselves to be to savages and mediaevalists, we ourselves, after all, do not know very much. The unknown vastly exceeds the known. Brilliant though our recent progress in the advancement of learning has been, human knowledge is still but a beam in darkness. In the following directions, a handful chosen at random, the knowledge even of our experts is insufficient to guarantee control: cancer, the weather, how to tap the presumably inexhaustible supplies of heat and power in the center of the earth, the satisfactory treatment of social misfits, the determination of sex, the arrest of old age and death, the meaning of genius and the subleties of sin. This inventory of human nescience could be indefinitely extended. We cannot bribe the clouds, we can't reverse gravitation, we can't abolish disease, we can't control senescence, we can't redeem sin, we can't outlaw war, and we can't dodge death. In a word, despite all our pomp and circumstance, we are but creatures, and puny, primitive, frail and feeble creatures at that, creatures very precariously surviving amidst the wholly indifferent play of forces far too subtle to be known and far too massive to be grasped or controlled. We don't even know for certain whence we came, whither and when we go, or what we are. By comparison we humans are still like children crying in the night with no language but a cry. The courtesy and duty of worship, although widely disdained as beneath the dignity

of proud and confident moderns, and the privilege and comfort of prayer, recommended by religion, correspond well enough to the actual facts of man's position upon the earth.

D. W. Langridge

New Year

637   At the beginning of the year Paul's great testimony recorded in Romans 8:38–39, "For I am persuaded that neither death, nor life, nor angels, nor principalities, nor powers, nor things present, nor things to come, nor height, nor depth, nor any other creature, shall be able to separate us from the love of God, which is in Christ Jesus our Lord"—comes almost inevitably to mind. This is the kind of assurance we need as we face the unknown.

Dr. Parker once commented on these words quite characteristically but with a flash of true insight: "None of these great things can separate us from the love of Christ, but the smaller things might."   Leslie E. Cooke

✳✳

638   Picture to yourselves the Courtyard of the Gare de l'Est in Paris, where there was held the memorial service for the victims in a terrible railway disaster. M. Lebrun, President of the French Republic, and members of the French Cabinet were present, and M. Renaudin, chairman of the railway company, delivered the funeral oration. Now just listen to his words. "On Christmas Eve," he said, "many travellers left this station on a short journey, but all unknowingly they had embarked on the longest journey of all from which there is no return. Their friends on the platform cried 'bon voyage,' and in the firm belief of a future life, we can say, indeed, that they have made a bon voyage." Think of this in so-called agnostic France, and this from the president of a so-called soulless railway company; Christmas angels singing over railway stations in Paris. Those Christmas angels must be accustomed to finding God in queer places. "In the firm belief of a future life," he says, "we can say, indeed, that they have made a bon voyage." Men and women, no new and untried year can fail to be happy which we enter with the Lover of our souls. No journey, be it long, or be it short, can fail to be good which brings us to the Father's Home.

Hubert L. Simpson

✳✳

639   The uncertainty of human plans and schemes is best illustrated by the parable of the rich fool, boasting of his "much goods laid up for many years" on the very night on which his soul was required of him. It is such a spirit as

his that St. James denounces so sternly; not the careful forethought and providence which Holy Scripture never condemns but the forming of plans and designs without the slightest reference in word or thought to that overruling Will, on which all depends. Alexander is seized with mortal illness just at the moment when the world is at his feet; Arius "taken away" the very night before he was to be forced into communion with the Church; the statesman struck down by the knife of the assassin just when his country seems to need him most: these examples show the truth of the words which St. James had probably read, and which may well be compared with his own: "Our life shall pass away as a cloud, and shall be dispersed as a mist that is driven away with the beams of the sun and overcome with the heat thereof."

"Man proposes, but God disposes." The main subject is that of a prevalent manifestation of pride and worldliness; namely, the propensity to indulge in presumptuous self-reliance in relation to the future.

Alfred Thomas

New Year's Resolutions

640 "With good intentions," says William James, "hell is proverbially paved. When a resolve or a fine glow of feeling is allowed to evaporate without bearing practical fruit, it is worse than a chance lost: it works so as to positively hinder future resolutions and emotions from taking the normal path of discharge. There is no more contemptible type of human character than that of the nerveless sentimentalist and dreamer who spends his life in a weltering sea of sensibility, but never does a concrete, manly deed." So let us save ourselves from any mere emotionalism in our New Year resolutions.

A. Russell Tomlin

Obedience

641 John Ruskin tells of his first lesson in obedience. "First," he says, "I was taught to be obedient. That discipline began early. One evening, when I was yet in my nurse's arms, I wanted to touch the tea-urn, which was boiling merrily. It was an early taste for bronzes, I suppose; but I was resolute about it. My mother bid me keep my fingers back; I insisted on putting them forward. My nurse would have taken me away from the urn; but my mother said 'Let him touch it, nurse.' So I touched it; and that was my first lesson in the meaning of individual liberty. It was the first piece of liberty I got—and the last which for some time I asked for."

Henry J. Cowell

**

642   There was once a farmer who saw a party of horsemen out hunting over his farm. He had one field over which he was very anxious that they should not ride, as the young crop of wheat was just beginning to appear above the ground, and it would be injured by the tramping of the horses; so he sent a boy to shut the gate to the field, and told him on no account to allow anyone to pass through the gate. Presently a horseman came up, and ordered the boy to open the gate. This he refused to do, and he told the reason why. One after another of the horsemen spoke to the lad, and when they saw that speaking was not of any use they threatened him, and when threatening was of no use they offered him money, if he would let them through the gate. But all was in vain.

Presently one of the horsemen rode up and said, in stern, commanding tones, "My boy, you do not know me, I am the Duke of Wellington, and I am not accustomed to be disobeyed. I tell you to open that gate at once." The boy took off his cap and said, very respectfully, "I am sure the Duke of Wellington would be the last person in the world to wish me to disobey orders." The Duke was highly pleased with the reply of the boy, and said, "I honour the man or boy who can be neither bribed nor frightened nor threatened into doing what is wrong. With an army of such soldiers I could conquer the world." Handing the boy a sovereign the Duke put spurs to his horse and galloped away, while the boy, in high glee, returned to the farmer, shouting as he went along the road, "Hoorah, hoorah, I have done what Napoleon could not do, I have turned back the Duke of Wellington."   J. M. Mitchell

✳✳

643   Mary Slessor, the great missionary of Calabar, "she who lost herself in service," said, "Obedience brings health. We begin and end with God in our hearts." She went, after eight years' absence, back to the scene of some of her hardest work, at Akpap. Her arrival caused much excitement, and her stay was one long reception. All day the Mission House was like a market; from far and near the people came to greet their Mother. She could scarcely be got to come to meals. On the first day when she was called, she said, "These are my meat to-day," and then she told those about her what Christ had said to His disciples after His conversation with the woman of Samaria. She had won those people to Him. God give you such bread to eat! Work for God and "your bread shall be given, your water shall be sure."   G. C. Britton

Obscurity

644   In the Orchestra of Life most people are just second fiddlers. By the very nature of things the great majority of men and women must reconcile themselves to occupying positions of humble obscurity. Most of us can expect to be names and nothing more—producers and consumers, tenants and tax-payers, respectable, quiet, plodding folk.

That, however, is not all that can be said on our behalf. We must remember that the best part of human history is never written at all: family life, training children, patient service, quiet endurance—these things are never mentioned by the historian. Each of them, nevertheless, is highly significant and may be gilded with a glory peculiarly its own, and each can be discharged to perfection by men and women of the second place.

The man who leads an army in the organized slaughter that is modern war is immortalized in history, while the poor housewife, who makes a pound go as far as thirty shillings that her family may have as good a chance in the struggle for existence as possible, is not even known to have lived. It is not a difficult matter, however, to decide whose life is the more useful. Hitler and Mussolini are world notorious, while the honest father who has given his children a good training and striven to set them a noble example is probably not known to the majority of those who live in the next street. But again we have no difficulty in making a value assessment. Fame, glitter and brilliance are to be found on the upper rungs of the ladder of attainment; but life has other treasures, equally great, which all its children, irrespective of positions or gifts, may possess.

J. Cecil Armstrong

Old Age

645   A graceful and blessed old age must have three elements in it: a happy retrospect, a peaceful present, and an inspiring future. Old age cannot have either one of these three if the youth has been wasted and manhood has been mis-spent. "I am already being offered, and the time of my departure is at hand, for I have fought the good fight, I have finished my course, I have kept the faith; henceforth there is laid up for me a crown of righteousness"—a blessed retrospect, a peaceful present, an inspiring future.

Lyman Abbott

✳✳

646   Years ago, when but a child in school, I could never read Holmes's "Last Leaf" without a sense of sadness, as in sympathy I could anticipate a time when such would possibly be my own condition.

Fifty years after this poem was written Dr. Holmes, writing to his publishers, recognized himself then as the fulfilment of the prophecy of the last verse, in which he said:

> If I should live to be
> The last leaf upon the tree,
> Let them smile,
> As I do now,
> At the old forsaken bough,
> Where I cling.

"It was with a smile on my lips that I wrote it," said he. "I cannot read it now without a sigh of tender remembrance." And yet Dr. Holmes was one of the best illustrations in his age of a young old man that I can possibly think of. His intellect was never stranded. His interest in the progressive development of the world—in science, art, or religion—never failed to the very last. He continued to minister to its joy and gladness, even in his declining years, while he hung, like a last leaf quivering in the autumn breezes, upon that tree of poetic imagery that budded and grew with the nineteenth century.   Thomas Jay Horner

Outlook Brought by Jesus

647   H. G. Wells, in one of his novels, relates a curious kind of day-dream experience which he says visited him in his youth. "The visible world," he says, "would suddenly appear to be minute . . . the house and the furniture become dolls' houses and furniture, the trees, mere moss-fronds. I myself did not appear to shrink . . . it was only the universe about me that shrank." His experience illustrates in a way that new outlook on the world and material things which Jesus brings to me. Jesus cared not for things, but for men and women; things were of secondary importance; what was really great was man, a child of God.

                                                                        T. H. Roberts

Pain

648   Walt Whitman tells of a scene he saw in the awful American Civil War. A soldier had to pass through a terrible nerve-racking operation. An anaesthetic could not be administered. At the very last moment his courage failed. In the centre of the ward stood a beautiful cultured English girl, and the rough soldier, looking at her wistfully, said: "I think I could bear it if she would come and hold my hand." She came and held his hand and shared his pain, and the loneliness and fear of it passed away.

Christ does that for humanity. He longs to take the hand of every weak and suffering man and woman, and once having taken it, He will not let you go, but will lead you along life's highway into the painless land of Perfect Peace.

                                                                        H. H. Turner

Pain, Meaning of

649   Look at D. L. Moody, to whom the deacons went after he had spoken one day at one of the services in old Dr. Kirk's church in Boston, Massachusetts, and said, "Brother Moody, you mean well, but you haven't the talent. It is better for you not to speak in our services; please say no more in the prayer service." Savonarola—similar experience, until these men learned that difficulty is given to test the soul, to make the soul great and strong. People are always saying, "Why does God let the mountain difficulty be in my way? Does God know about it?" I think He does. "Why does He allow it to be in my way?" So that you can stand on the highest peak of it, so that you can see that you are bigger than the mountain. "Why does He let me suffer so?" So that you can conquer suffering in your self and help ten others or one hundred others to conquer. Never a pain without its meaning. As we look still further we see that the crown of thorns is the prophecy of the crown of glory—glory in this world possibly, if not certainly glory in the world to come.

Ernest W. Shurtleff

Palm Sunday

650   Savonarola was once preaching to a great congregation in the city of Florence. In the course of his sermon he said, "It is the Lord's will to give a new Head to the city of Florence. The new Head is Jesus Christ. Jesus Christ seeks to become your king." In response, the whole congregation, men, women and children, were on their feet, shouting, "Long live Jesus, King of Florence! Long live Jesus the King!"   J. Cecil Armstrong

※ ※

651   You know the story of Napoleon driving through the streets of Paris and greeted by the excited, cheering citizens. His aide-de-camp turned to him and said: "Sire, see how your subjects reverence their Emperor." "Bah," was the curt reply, "these same people would crucify me to-morrow!"

G. H. Clothier

Pardon

652   During the early part of the Civil War, one of the New York Volunteers was arrested upon the charge of desertion. As he was unable to prove at his trial that he was innocent, as he claimed to be, he was condemned and sentenced to a deserter's death. The case being brought to the notice of President Lincoln, he was convinced that an injustice had been done, and wrote a pardon for the man, on condition that he should return to the ranks and remain until his regiment was mustered out of service.

At the close of the last battle of the war, as the dead and wounded were being carried off the field, this man's body was found with that autograph pardon of the President close to his heart. Well might he love the man who had saved him from an ignominious death, and count as precious the sign-manual of his release.

Theodore L. Cuyler

Parenthood

653   Here is a letter which "Woodbine Willie" wrote to his wife when he was chaplain, telling her how he would like his little son to be brought up: "Make him a sportsman. Encourage him to play games and, above all, to play the game. Teach him to despise cowardice and never to be afraid of anyone or anything save God. Teach him what his body is for and show him the necessity for cleanliness in body and mind. Teach him that being a gentleman means using your life to help and serve your fellow-men. Teach him to love and reverence women and that the man who deceives a woman is a scoundrel. Last and most important, about his religion. Teach him to love Jesus Christ. Teach him that and leave him free. Don't force his religion in any way, especially if he has brains. Let him go his own way and don't be pained or shocked so long as he keeps his love for Jesus Christ. Guard him from vulgarity and snobbishness and never let him speak contemptuously of anyone or anything except a coward. I think that is all. Kiss him for me and give him my blessing and when he is old enough tell him my life story as you would tell it, knowing that I tried hard most of the time to do right, and when I sinned I was sorry in my heart, as I am now."

W. J. Lewis

Parents

654   C. F. Andrews writes concerning his parents: "They represented Christ to me. Through their eyes I saw Him and loved Him. Whenever I used to think of Christ, I would picture some one as gentle as my mother and with my father's genial good nature." They mediated Christ to the lad. They were Christians.

J. Penry Thomas

✳✳

655   In the *Life of Principal Rainy* there is a letter in which one of the daughters says that she could never think of her father without thinking of God. What a tribute! And Dr. W. R. Maltby has told of the spiritual impression his mother made upon him when he was a very young boy. He was in church with her, not very attentive, perhaps, but suddenly he caught sight of the look on his mother's face. Her eyes were looking into the kingdom of heaven. He knew then that God was real and that heaven was nigh.

W. Francis Gibbons

Parents, Example of

656   When Dr. F. W. Norwood was a minister in Australia he approached a certain man about joining the Church. The man refused quite brusquely. Says the preacher: "I did not get on my knees to the man to plead with him to join the Church. I wouldn't do that to any man. I just left him with his blank refusal." A few months later the man himself came forward for Church membership, and in response to the wondering question of Dr. Norwood he said: "You know I have a little boy. A week or so ago I was taking him for a walk in the country when we came to a rather rugged pathway where we had to walk in single file. I was going on ahead, and had forgotten that the lad was finding the way a little more difficult than myself. Suddenly I heard his small voice say: 'Be careful where you step, daddy, I'm coming on behind!' That settled it, sir. I want to join the Church."

John Pitts

Parents, Responsibility of

657   What do you think of a nurse letting a child drop, and the child being a cripple all the days of his life, because the nurse, by her carelessness, let it fall out of her hand? I have seen such cripples and I have always thought of the poor woman who, through her carelessness, let the child drop. Just look and see all that was the after life of the child through such a piece of carelessness. She could never forgive herself. Ah, but if they should become spiritual cripples. Ah, but if through a little carelessness of yours, the image of God upon the soul should be blurred; if they should be never able to move the limbs of the spirit rightly; if they should lose the birthright through it; if the door should shut upon them in the great day of all, because you let them drop in your careless spiritual nursing. Brother, sister, how would it be? Would not you hang your head down then as hardly worthy to enter because that one was shut out?

Henry Ward Beecher

Passions, Evil

658 A great Greek tragedy has a chorus about one who brought up a young lion in his house and petted it and played with it and delighted to see it film its glaring eye-balls and fawn at his feet and play with his little ones; but it was not long before the cub of the forest showed the wild tricks of its ancestors and ravaged his flock and bathed his house in blood. How many a youth has treated his own bad passions like that petted lion, and instead of making them come to heel by a strong will, the servant of a tender conscience, and keeping them bound in chains and controlled, has let them become his masters, and then he has at last felt himself driven to fight for very life, has been compelled to step into the arena like some wretched gladiator doomed for his crimes to fight the wild beasts on a second day, although he has been already wounded by their fierce bites and rending claws.

F. W. Farrar

Pastors, Successful

659 People are not at all interested to know what we don't believe; why should they be? They want to know what we do believe. "I know whom I have believed." "That which we have seen and heard declare we unto you." Dr. Buttrick says: "We know of a minister who for several years preached against Christian Science and against the saloon ad nauseam. He drove several of his congregation to Christian Science; how many he drove to drink is not told."

Let us be positive and constructive. Brethren, if we approximate to these ideals in preaching, worship, prayer, sympathy, tact, character, we shall inevitably become good Pastors.

Let me cite a quotation from Izaak Walton:

"I will tell you, scholar, I once heard one say, 'I envy not him that eats better meal than I do, nor him that is richer, or that wears better clothes than I do; I envy nobody but him, and him only, that catches more fish than I do.'"

F. I. Riches Lowe

Patience

660 Very early in my ministry I preached some sermons which created a great panic in the congregation. The people thought that I had forsaken truths they regarded as part of the substance of the Christian Gospel. But it was my felicity at that time—a felicity for which I can never cease to be grateful—to be colleague of one of the most venerable and saintly men in the ministry, a man who was regarded with honour and affection by all the Congregational churches in England and by his own church, of which at that time he had been the pastor for about fifty years, with unmeasured affection and devotion. After his death, I did not know it before, I learned that when the panic was at its height he went around privately to family after family in the congregation, and said to them: "Let him alone; the root of the matter is in him; the young man must have his fling."

R. W. Dale

Patriotism

661   Old Samuel Johnson was a great Englishman and a great patriot, but he scandalized his faithful satellite Boswell by defining patriotism as "the last refuge of a scoundrel." John Ruskin—another man of letters who was great both as an Englishman and a patriot—called it "an absurd prejudice founded on an extended selfishness." Other writers can be quoted in similar strain. For example, Havelock Ellis speaks of patriotism as a "virtue among barbarians," implying that it is far from being a virtue among civilized people; while Grant Allen describes it as "a vulgar vice, the collective form of the monopolist instinct." Why do these responsible writers speak so disparagingly of one of the greatest driving-forces in human life? Are they merely blind and prejudiced critics of this elemental passion in the human mind? Is it true patriotism, the genuine article, that they are castigating? Or is it only its debasement that calls forth their condemnation?

John Pitts

Peace

662   It is recorded of Dean Church that he once went (in mufti) to hear a certain missioner who was conducting an evangelistic campaign. After his address the missioner, according to his custom, went to different people in the audience, putting the rather pointed question, "Have you found peace?" Coming to Dean Church he addressed him with the same question, to which the Dean replied bluntly, "No, I have found war!" Which of these men was right? The answer is, they were both right.   W. C. Billington

✳✳

663   In one of Aristophanes' comedies an aged farmer dodders on to the stage. The old man is weeping. Both his ploughing oxen have been killed in the last invasion, and he and his family are pitifully hungry. And when they ask him what he wants, instead of asking for a brace of duck and a bottle of wine, he says that what he would like more than anything else would be a "drop of peace" poured into his eyes.

That is what all the simple decent people in the world want, but most leaders do not seem to know which is the right bottle on the medicine shelf. We like the short view and the quick method. It seems so obvious that, if some one is behaving badly, the simplest thing to do is to knock him down and sit on his chest. We seem to have believed that since time began. When Aristophanes was writing, the Assembly had decided that the only way to deal with the rebels in Mytilene was to kill off the whole male population as an example to the world. The Tiger Man seems so full of hard-bitten common sense. As a matter of fact, if people would only read that record of how not to do things which makes up so much of history, they would see that the Tiger Man is never in the long run successful, and, instead of his beetle eye-lashes covering profound wisdom, they cover something which is rather like profound nonsense.

McEwan Lawson

Peace, Christ and

664   For years the people of Argentine and Chile had been at enmity with the other. Much innocent blood had been shed. Many hearts and homes broken. Then some one saw the light. He fell down before it in rapturous wonder. He showed it to others. As a result, the cannons of destruction were melted down; a colossal statue of Christ made and reared up on the mountain boundary between the two countries. Underneath was placed the inscription: "Sooner shall these mountains crumble into dust than the peoples of Argentine and Chile break the peace which at the feet of Christ, the Redeemer, they have sworn to maintain." And so from that lonely peak in the Andes, for many years now, the light—the unarrested light—has been shining in the darkness.

Johnstone G. Patrick

Peace of God

665   The story is told of two friends who met one day in the street. "I've found peace," said the one. "Which peace?" asked the other. "The peace of God," came the reply. The other was silent a moment. Then he said, "God bless you. You have lived in the rough. Now you will live in the smooth."

G. Holland Williams

Peace of Mind

666   Recently, in New York, I called a taxi-cab. It was obvious that the driver was jittery. He stopped for a moment, in the traffic, and he seemed to think that the driver in the taxi next to us had come too close, so he leaned out the window and swore at him vehemently. As we came to intersections it seemed as though he was making a deliberate effort to run down pedestrians. We stopped at the door of a street-car as it opened, and my driver cursed the man at the controls.

After a few moments I said to the driver, "You certainly hate yourself, don't you?"

"What do you mean?"

I said: "I mean exactly what I say. I have never met a man who hates himself as much as you do."

"I don't hate myself."

"Of course you do. You despise yourself. No man could be so disagreeable with other people unless he hated himself. I don't know what your problem is, but something is burning you up inside."

He said nothing for a moment. That was a decided relief. He didn't ever tell me what his problem was, but just as I reached my destination he said: "You know, mister, you got something there. You put your finger on my trouble, I guess. I am going to think about it."   John Sutherland Bonnell

Peace, Search for

667   A story is told of how Dante, wandering one day over the mountains of Lunigiana, eventually drew nigh to a lone, secluded monastery. It was at a time when his mind was racked with internal conflict, and was seeking refuge from the strife. So he loudly knocked at the monastery gate. It was opened by a monk, who in a single glance at the wan, pale face, read its pathetic message of misery and woe. "What do you seek here?" said he. And with a gesture of despair, the poet replied, "Peace." Ah, it was the same old craving followed by the same old search. But neither the solitary places, nor the anchorite's cell, ever brought true peace to the afflicted heart. It comes not from without, but from within. We can have it in the winter of age or the spring of youth; in the lowly cottage or the stately castle; in distressing pain or in buoyant health. The secret of it is in comradeship with Christ. You can have peace in the midst of the storm, if you have Christ. He is the shelter from the tempest, the soul's haven of rest. If we have learned to value His friendship, we have mastered the secret of the "peace which passeth all understanding."   William Gilbert

Peaceful Spirit

668   Amongst the early settlers in America there were numbers murdered by the Indians. The Quakers refused to bear arms and protect themselves by any form of defence but right-doing and trust in God. What happened? The settlers were year by year exposed to the tomahawk and the scalping knife; the unarmed Quaker was never touched. Three Quakers only were killed; two of them, men who repudiated their faith, carried arms and were killed; the other a woman, who lost confidence, took refuge in the fort, and was killed. The State of Pennsylvania for seventy years had no military, no weapons of defence, and for seventy years was safe. Maryland, Virginia, New England had to meet the attacks of the Red Men; six Indian nations surrounded Pennsylvania, but that state, believing in God, had peace. Take it, then, as one of the great truths of God that if a man or a nation will say, and will abide in the saying, "Lord, Thou hast been our dwelling-place," that man or nation will also be enabled to say, taking up the word "dwelling-place" in another translation, "The eternal God is our Refuge, and underneath are the everlasting arms."

C. F. Aked

Penitence

669   There is a pathetic incident related of Dr. Johnson, the outstanding Englishman of his generation. Samuel Johnson was born in Lichfield. His father kept a second-hand book-shop and earned a somewhat scanty existence. One of his customers, impressed by the intelligence of the young Johnson, sent him to Oxford, and at Pembroke College he greatly distinguished himself. During a Christmas vacation the old man took ill, and asked Samuel to take his place at the stall in the market-place. The young Oxford undergraduate indignantly refused. The years passed, but Dr. Johnson never forgave himself for that refusal. Whenever he recalled it, a corroding remorse gripped him. Some fifty years later Dr. Johnson went down to Lichfield. It was market day, and snow covered the ground. For two hours the old man stood there hatless. No one recognized him, the crowd took him for some feeble-minded, eccentric old man, a few boys snowballed him, and at the end of two hours he slowly walked away.

It was a brave act of penitence; it makes one think more kindly of a somewhat quarrelsome and assertive old man; but even that brave act could not wipe out the tragedy of the day when he missed the opportunity of rendering a service of love to his sick father.   Herbert Dunnico

✻✻

670   I remember, when a boy, reading of a certain prince in a fairy tale. The prince was a favourite of the fairies, and one of them, when he was about to set out upon his travels, gave him a small ivory card, on which was written a magic sentence. Whenever he was in great straits and peril he was to take out the card and read aloud the sentence on it, and then deliverance was sure to come. But the strangest thing about it was this, that the writing was invisible until the reader's tears dropped upon the card, and then it was plain enough and quite easy to read, and when read, brought help and blessing; that is a fairy story, a child's fable, is it? It is a piece of glorious theology, of heaven-revealed wisdom.

Jackson Wray

✳✳

671   One incident of September, 1939, remains and will remain in my mind. A dear lady had just finished listening to the news and for a few minutes she realized fully all that the impending war meant to her family life. She began a tirade against what she termed "the people" who had neglected God, who had mocked the Sabbath Day by sea-side trips and card parties and dances, who had lived only for their own pleasures. My amazement knew no bounds, because she herself had shown no consciousness of any need of God and had never hesitated when opportunity afforded of joining the Blackpool Sunday rush, nor had the fact of Sunday ever been allowed to intrude upon her social side of life. "It's our sin," she railed, "which has brought this." But in a day or two she had recovered—the time of agonized uncertainty was passed and once again she had relegated God to the slumber room, and the idea would not be brought out again until the next crisis which touched her personally.

N. J. McLellan

✳✳

672   In one of his finest poems, "The Two Rabbis," Whittier tells of one, Rabbi Nathan, a good and wise man, who at last met with so severe a temptation that he fell into sin. He determined to visit his friend, Rabbi Ben Isaac, famed for righteous and forbearing love, to tell him all and to ask him to pray for him. Rabbi Isaac heard his tale with great patience and deep sympathy, and then confessed that he, too, had sinned, if not in act, at least in thought, and ended by asking Rabbi Nathan to pray for him. Then side by side they knelt and each prayed with his whole heart on behalf of the other.

L. Colin Edwards

Pentecost

673   Says E. Stanley Jones, "Why is it when you speak to the modern Church about Pentecost that cold shivers go up and down the spines of cultured people?" He goes on to tell how he announced the theme of Pentecost before a group of highly trained ministers. The head of an examining board for young ministers said that when he heard the subject announced he said to himself, "Good gracious, are we going to have some more rant?" When the head of an examining board looks upon Pentecost as rant there must be something seriously wrong. Where there is a theology that can dispense with the Holy Spirit, or a ministery that deems itself independent of Pentecost, there is a theology which becomes mere opinion and a ministry as withered as a sapless tree.

Gilbert Laws

People, Nature of

674   A man who had just moved into a small town in Pennsylvania fell into conversation with an old Quaker who was in the habit of sitting on a bench in the quiet square in the centre of the little township. "What kind of people live here?" asked the newcomer. The old Quaker replied, "What kind of people didst thee live amongst before?" "Oh, they were mean, narrow, suspicious, and very unfair," answered the man. "Then," said the Quaker, "I am sorry, but thee will find the same manner of people here."

Not long after another newcomer joined him on the bench and asked the same question and, like his predecessor, was asked, "What manner of people didst thee live amongst before?" A warm smile spread over the newcomer's face. "Friend," he answered, "they were the best folk in the world. They were always friendly, kind, and lovable, and I hated to leave them." The old Quaker beamed. "Welcome, neighbour," he said. "Be of good cheer, for thee will find the same people here."   David A. MacLennan

Peril of Mankind

675   In one of his books the Danish philosopher, Kierkegaard, tells a parable which has striking application to the world of to-day. The scene is a brilliantly lit theatre where a variety show is proceeding. Each turn is more fantastic than the last, and is applauded by a distinguished audience. Suddenly the manager comes forward. He apologizes for the interruption, but the theatre is on fire, and he begs his patrons to leave in an orderly fashion. The audience think this

is the most amusing turn of the evening, and cheer thunderously. The manager again implores them to leave the burning building, and he is again applauded to the echo. At last he can do no more. The fire seizes the whole building and the enthusiastic audience with it. "And so," concludes Kierkegaard, "will our age, I sometimes think, go down in fiery destruction to the applause of a crowded house of cheering spectators."   F. R. Schofield

Perseverance

676   Endeavour to excel in diligence and persistent application. Where a number of young people meet together for learning there is considerable mental diversity. Some may be richly endowed with genius, some of average intellect, others of feeble powers. Whatever your abilities, great or small, let nothing tempt you to neglect their cultivation. Plodding perseverance before uncertain spurts or the freaks of genius. Dr. Arnold always encouraged a plodding boy before all others. He says, "If there be one thing on earth which is truly admirable, it is to see God's wisdom blessing an inferiority of natural powers where they have been honestly, truly, and zealously cultivated." At Latcham he once spoke impatiently and sharply to a youth of this kind, when the youth looked up in his face and said, "Why do you speak angrily, sir? Indeed, I am doing the best I can." Years afterwards he used to tell the story to his children, and say, "I never felt so much ashamed in my life. That look and that speech I have never forgotten." Speaking of a pupil of this character, he once said, "I would stand to that man hat in hand." The plodder often succeeds where the genius fails. You remember the fable of the tortoise and the hare; and you know which won the race. It suits well to all the facts of life. Pursue the studies appointed for you, and in the prescribed way.   William Walters

Personality

677   There is a point, one single point in the immeasurable world of mind and matter, where science will always remain inapplicable. . . . That point is the individual ego. . . . Over this realm no outer power of fate can ever have sway. . . . Every advance in knowledge brings us face to face with the mystery of our own being.   Max Planck

Philosophy of Life

678   Mr. G. K. Chesterton writes: "There are some people—and I am one of them—who think that the most practical and important thing about a man

is still his view of the universe. We think that for a landlady considering a lodger it is important to know his income, but still more important to know his philosophy. We think that for a general who is about to fight an enemy it is important to know the enemy's numbers, but still more important to know the enemy's philosophy. We think the question is not whether the theory of the cosmos matters, but whether in the long run anything else affects it." Your view of the world shapes your action.   John Clifford

✻✻

679 W. L. Watkinson, who had a kind of genius for illustration, tells these two incidents which may be worth repeating. First of all, he recalls the story of a famous German physicist who kept two human skulls on his desk, suitably mounted on little pedestals. He had drilled a hole in each skull, into which he had fitted a candle: and every night as he worked, these candles were lit and shed their dim light on his papers or his experiments. He took great delight when his visitors were shocked at this exhibition, and assured them that he used these grisly emblems to keep himself humble, and to preach to all his friends the final vanity of all human dreams and aspirations. But there is little doubt that his grim choice of a candlestick was due to his own morose and bitter mind and to a melancholy sense of humour and good taste.

The second story is about the famous Italian artist, Leonardo da Vinci. Leonardo was an illegitimate child, and while he had a fair youth and good training, he had no rights he could call his own, especially no rights of inheritance and favour. At one time it was a question whether he would become a musician or an artist, for he seemed to be equally gifted in music and painting. In the end, to the world's eternal gratitude, he became one of the greatest painters of history. But even then—so the story goes—he combined the two great arts: for while he was working on some great canvas, he kept a small harp or lyre beside him. Whenever he came to a particularly difficult or delicate part of his picture, he would stop, pick up the little lyre in one hand, and begin to play softly on the strings. Sometimes—so his friends have said—he would have his brush in the one hand and the small instrument in the other: and as he filled in a line or a bit of colour here and there, he would strum gently on the strings of the instrument—and so he actually "painted in music."

Some people might say that the difference between these two great men was merely one of mood or temperament—the one was filled with the gloom of the old Teutonic forests, and the other lived under the charm of the Italian skies. But far more real than any difference of mood or temperament was the difference of an underlying "philosophy" about life and values, a difference which in the last resort is one of outlook and religion!   James Black

Piety

680   There is a revealing paragraph in the autobiography of Miss Petre, the Roman Catholic Modernist, the friend of Loisy and Von Hügel. She asks, "What has kept me to the Church of my childhood, and what has kept my religion alive and vital in spite of all the spiritual doubts through which I have passed?" And her answer is: "The spirit of piety." Piety she defines as that spirit of joy and delight above the mere sense of duty in which our religious obligations are fulfilled, the spirit of fellowship with God and her Church that exists apart from dogmatic beliefs.   J. G. McKenzie

Politics

681   I remember talking once with a very eminent statesman of the Commonwealth who told me that his father had wished him to be a Christian minister. "If I had been," he said, "I would have preached all my sermons from one text: 'Let that same mind be in you which was in Christ Jesus.'" What a perfect text for a statesman! It means simply this: that all our political decisions and acts will arise quite naturally—inevitably—from the Christianity that is within us. It means that though we may vote Conservative, Liberal or Labour, as the case may be, we shall not vote because we are Conservatives, Liberals or Labour people—by reason, say, of inheritance, taste or self-interest—but because, being Christians, we have to choose this or that political party as providing the nearest thing that we can see to a party which will express and "implement" our Christian ideals in politics. A Christian may often be puzzled as to which party he shall support at the polls. But at least he approaches the puzzle from a definite starting-point, the point at which he asks himself: "Am I thinking about this business with my mind or with the Mind of Christ?"

Ernest H. Jeffs

Power

682   Dr. J. H. Jowett once said that if he saw a tiny church alongside a mammoth armaments factory with its forests of chimneys belching smoke and its roar of machinery like a prelude to the din of battle, he would be quite sure in which of the two real power dwelt. Would we be sure? You and I must choose between the clamour and consecration, between the world's display and the soul's whisper.   George A. Buttrick

✶✶

683   There is a beautiful legend of St. Chrysostom. He had been educated carefully; was a man of culture, and devoted to his calling; and yet in his earlier ministry he was not remarkable for his success. At one time he had what seemed to be a vision. He thought he was in the pulpit, and in the chancel and round about him were holy angels. In the midst of them and directly before him was the Lord Jesus; and he was to preach to the congregation assembled beyond. The vision or the reverie deeply affected his spirit. The next day he ascended the pulpit he felt the impression of the scene. He thought of the holy angels as if gathered around him; of the blessed Saviour as directly before him— as listening to his words, and beholding His Spirit. He became intensely earnest; and from that day forward a wonderful power attended his ministrations. Multitudes gathered around him wherever he preached. Though he had the simple name of John while he lived, the ages have called him Chrysostom, the "golden mouthed."   Bishop M. Simpson

Power from God

684   They tell a story of Napoleon, that, on the eve of a great battle, he would summon his generals into his presence. One by one they would pass from an ante-room into the chamber where Napoleon waited for them; and each man as he came would find Napoleon standing to greet him, and Napoleon's hand outstretched towards him, and Napoleon's eyes looking into his own. And each man would go to his battle-station with the strength of ten within him, and the feeling that there was no exploit that lay beyond his powers that day.

And the people that do know their God and wait upon Him day after day, and see His face and feel His hand clasp their own—they shall go from His presence into the world where they are called to do battle for His Name, "strong in the Lord of hosts and in His mighty power." They shall say in their inmost hearts, "I can do all things through Him that strengthens me."

G. Holland Williams

Powers, Use of

685   Many will know the story of the fish in Mammoth Cave, Kentucky. These fish have lived for generations in the dark, so that at last the optic nerve has atrophied and they are quite blind. Similarly Darwin tells us that he lost completely his love of poetry and music, once very strong within him, simply because he ceased to develop it. This is true of all our powers, memory, concentration, capacity for hard work. We must use them or lose them.

Harold Nicholson

Praise

686 Oliver Wendell Holmes, after a great reception, before a Boston audience, where he had been applauded and cheered again and again, was approached by a friend and neighbour, who inquired: "You must get tired of all this?" His answer was simple, direct, and truthful: "I never get tired of the applause of an audience. I like it."

James L. Gordon

✳✳

687 On a certain rocky coast, where many a brave crew had perished for lack of guidance, the king ordered a lighthouse to be erected, and on its completion requested that the builder's name should be conspicuous on the base of the lighthouse, to be read by royal lips on the day of inauguration. The day came, and the name to be honoured, inscribed in letters of gold, was read by all admiring eyes and pronounced with high praises by the king. But that name soon afterwards disappeared under the action of stormy seas, and in its place came out clear in outline and deeply cut the name and titles of the king. The builder had been content with a layer of cement for his own name to shine in for a short season, and had cut the true owner's name in the granite beneath. "He that loseth his life" for the sake of Christ the King and true owner, "shall find it," amplified in capacity and sealed unto a share in His undying honour.

W. H. Jackson

Prayer

688 My old minister, F. B. Meyer, once said the secret of the great ministry of Samuel Martin (for whom Westminster Chapel was built) was that every Friday he locked himself in the building and went round, kneeling in seat after seat in prayer for those who sat there.

Ernest Fillingham

✳✳

689 In 1940 my father, a man of over eighty, got permission to see me for half an hour in the concentration camp at Sachsenhausen. On leaving he said: "My dear boy, there is one thing yet I want to tell you, because it will give you joy. The Eskimos in Northern Canada and the Rataks in Java send their greetings and are praying for you."

Martin Niemoller

✳✳

690   "Now I lay me down to sleep," was the evening prayer of Quincy Adams when he sat in the presidential chair.

＊＊

691   Everybody is still talking about "the miracle of Dunkirk," and it will be always so spoken of as long as the story of World War II is told and whatever the outcome may be. It ranks with some of the strange incidents of the last war, such as when the Germans ceased fire for forty-seven hours when they were within sight of Paris and the French had only eight hours' supply of ammunition at hand. Neither Von Kluck nor Hausen nor Bulow was ever able to explain why his men had given the French those forty hours' respite which saved the capital and turned the tide of the war. Or there was that remarkable and sudden veering of the wind at Ypres on April 22, 1915, which turned the first German gas attack back upon their own men. It was a local meteorological disturbance and Dr. Schmaus said that in forty years the wind had never been known to act so peculiarly. Or there was the sudden storm over the Piave River which changed it from a perfect calm to a raging torrent in an hour and cut off forty thousand Germans, saving Italy. *"Deus fecit,"* said General Diaz. And there was the blighting of the record potato crop in Germany in almost a day in 1917, so that Ludendorff said it was the failure of that crop which led to food shortage and mutiny and eventually defeat.

In much the same way the miracle of Dunkirk, following upon the National Day of Prayer, will take its place as one of the most remarkable events of history. The Prime Minister himself used the word "miracle" in speaking about it. There was the fog overhead, the calm of the Channel and the most amazing discipline and resourcefulness on both sides of the Channel. Most wonderful of all there was the saving of 335,000 men. And now, after a day of prayer for France in her extremity, we learn that she is bidding to lay down her arms. If that is God's answer to our prayer, and it may well be, then it is good. It is well also that the bulk of the British force, which had been in France, is now at home.

Never before have I so often been stopped in the street by people who have something to tell me about answered prayer—an incident in history, an event in their own family or an experience from their own life. People are telling one another these things quietly, with proper reserve, acknowledging that we must not take the name of Providence lightly on our lips. There is very little foolish talking, but people are thinking things over and their thoughts are turning to God.   H. A. Turner-Smith

＊＊

692   John Paton, that fine missionary to the New Hebrides, lived in childhood
with his parents in a small Lowland cottage having its "but and ben." Between
the two was a small room with a tiny window. To this room John often saw
his father retire, and heard from behind the closed door his father's voice lifted
in prayer—such pleading sincerity was in the prayers that John learned to slip
past the door on tiptoe. The light on his father's face was caught from his
practice of the presence of God, and his ear was quick to hear the voice of
wisdom, even the voice of the Saviour. They dwelt safely.

                                                                        Cyril T. Follett

** **

693   A few years ago a clergyman was invited to preach in a strange pulpit.
He was entertained over Sabbath at the home of one of the elders, an intelligent
consecrated man. Sunday the breakfast bell rang, calling the family together.
The minister was slow in responding to the call. One of the family was sent to
rap at the door, but returned, saying the minister was conversing with some one
in his room. "All right," said the father, "that's just as it should be; he will bring
his Friend with him to church." So he did, and they had a gracious visitation
of the Holy Spirit's power.   J. B. Campbell

** **

694   When some one during World War I asked Studdert Kennedy whether
prayer would make a man invulnerable to shot and shell, he said that fellowship with God in prayer made a man sure that though his body was shattered
his soul would be untouched.   John Bishop

** **

695   You will remember that impressive passage in *The Confessions* where
Augustine relates how his mother Monica prayed all night to God that he might
be prevented from going to Italy. Her heart's desire was that Augustine should
become a follower of Christ, but she thought that her wish would materialize
most surely under her own influence. She feared the evils that would beset him
in Italy, with its temptations and allurements. Even as she prayed passionately
that he might remain, he set sail. Her prayers seemed futile. But in Italy
Augustine met the great Ambrose who led him into the light, and he became
a Christian in the very place where his mother had pleaded that he might not
go. The prayer of her lips was unanswered, but to the prayer of her heart,
that Augustine should be converted, answer came "exceeding abundant above
all" that Monica could ask or think.   J. D. Jones

** **

696   Abraham Lincoln confessed once in a moment of self-revelation: "I am sometimes driven to my knees by the thought that I have nowhere else to go." At a perilous juncture in our national life in recent years a service of prayer for the nation was held in St. Paul's Cathedral. And there, kneeling devoutly among the worshippers, was a hard-bitten city man who had not been inside a church for years, and who had often sneered at religion, and religious folk. When the service was over a crony of his came upon him as he was leaving the building and twitted him on his presence in such a place: "Hello, old man, what in the world are you doing here?" "Oh, well," he replied, looking his friend straight in the eyes, "we need help from somewhere, don't we?" Yes, we do need help from somewhere, or rather from Some One, and we need it all the time. Deep down the soul of man knows its own need and its own Helper. Pity is it when, only in extremity, the soul turns to its own.

W. Ellick Kirby

✳✳

697   Archimedes said that he wanted a place to stand upon and a lever which was long enough and he would lift the world. He never found the place to stand upon nor the lever which was long enough. We have something to stand upon—the immutable word of God. We have a lever on earth—the power of prayer. With prayer planted on the Word of God we can lift the world heavenward, even up to the throne on high. Intercessors, girdle the world with your prayers! They have a power unequalled by any material agency. Storm the heavens with your prayers! They alone can pierce the blue vault and present your cause unto God.   D. A. Hayes

✳✳

698   "If He prayed, Who was without sin," said St. Cyprian, "how much more it becometh a sinner to pray!"   William M. Sinclair

✳✳

699   Mr. W. T. Stead was greatly interested in the 1904 Welsh revival. He went to Wales to see it, to study its methods and message and results. By and by, he wrote a pamphlet about it. The next March he gave an address about it in the Free Trade Hall, Manchester, in connection with the Free Church Council. He prepared his address with the hope that a similar work of grace might break out in Manchester and in England. Mr. Stead always had a praying friend with him, and that night the praying friend was in the gallery. All went well, and then the man in the gallery stopped praying. Mr. Stead declared that he felt the loss at once. He lost power, lost the grip of his subject and of his audience. When he came out he met his friend. "You were praying for me to-night? And you stopped in the middle of my speech? Oh, why did you? Why did you? All the power went out of me. I could feel it go. . . . Never do that again. To think we might have been in the thick of the revival this very night, if you had been faithful."   J. G. Bowran

✳✳

700   One night during the Civil War in America a stranger came to Henry Ward Beecher's house. It was night and Mrs. Beecher went to see who it could be. She found a stranger muffled to the eyes, who asked to see the great preacher. He refused to give his name and, because her husband's life was threatened at the time, Mrs. Beecher declined to receive him. She returned upstairs and told her husband of the stranger at the door.

Beecher never knew fear. He at once descended, and a few minutes later Mrs. Beecher heard her husband admit him, then she heard her husband's voice raised in earnest prayer. By and by, when Mr. Beecher rejoined her, he told her that the muffled stranger was none other than Abraham Lincoln. He, too, was in a crisis in the awful struggle. He felt his loneliness. He knew that the responsibility was his. He needed the man of prayer. It is always true. The man of action needs the man of prayer.   J. G. Bowran

✳✳

701   The ideal is, I think, that we should grow to be independent of our surroundings, but most of us have not reached that stage. St. Augustine, in a rather delicious confession, tells us how his prayers may be disturbed if he catches sight of a lizard snapping up flies on the wall of his room; certainly mine would be. I am sure it is best to say the bulk of what I would call our organized prayer in some place like the church, or in some corner that is arranged specially for the purpose.   H. R. L. Sheppard

✳✳

702   Some years ago Dr. John R. Mott made some inquiries into the sources from which vital and significant evangelistic work had come. In each case when he could penetrate far enough, he found that the source of successful work was always to be traced to prayer at the fountain-head. It is when man lays hold upon the source of successful work that he taps the ultimate power that can move the world.   E. Neville Martin

✳✳

703   Prayers need not be fine. I believe God abhors fine prayers. If a person asks charity of you in elegant sentences he is not likely to get it. Finery in dress

or language is out of place in beggars. I heard a man in the street one day begging aloud by means of an oration. He used grand language in a very pompous style, and I dare say he thought he was sure of getting piles of coppers by his borrowed speech; but I, for one, gave him nothing, but felt more inclined to laugh at his bombast. Many prayer-meeting prayers are a great deal too fine. Keep your figures and metaphors and parabolical expressions for your fellow-creatures. Use them to those who want to be instructed, but do not parade them before God. When we pray, the simpler our prayers are the better; the plainest, humblest language which expresses our meaning is the best.

C. H. Spurgeon

Prayer as Revolt

704   Consider our human situation in the light of some inspired words by the French writer, George Bernanos. He says, in his book, *A Diary of Our Times:* "Our rages, daughters of despair, creep and squirm like worms. Prayer is the only form of revolt which remains upright."

S. Myers

Prayer, Beginning of

705   One of the most dramatic sentences in the Bible—unconsciously dramatic: it was not written for effect, whoever wrote it—is the sentence which closes the last verse of the fourth chapter of Genesis: "And to Seth, to him also there was born a son; and he called his name Enos: then began men to call upon the name of the Lord."

Few people to-day would take that verse literally: in the sense, that is, of believing that at a definite and definitely known date or period—i.e., during the lifetime of Seth and Enos, no earlier and no later—the human race in general decided to pray to God. Yet the verse is both religiously and historically true in a broader sense; it is historically true that at some date or period in their pilgrimage men did begin to pray to God and to worship Him. It had to happen. The mystery and terror and pain of life—of life that ends with death, amid grief and tears—could not be endured by men in their own strength. In a desperate realization of their loneliness and weakness (not, as I think, in mere instinctive reference, still less in mere ecstatic contemplation of a field of daffodils) . . . "then began men to call upon the name of the Lord."

Ernest H. Jeffs

Prayer, Effect of

706   In Henry James's story, *Roderick Hudson*, the hero is an artist who has wandered to Rome and there sunk into a life of sloth and selfish indulgence. But through all his vicissitudes, his mother in the old home has ceaselessly interceded for him at the Throne of Grace. In those moments of prayer when, remembering her son, she poured out her heart's request, her face became illumined and purified, and gradually took on a calmness and refined spiritual beauty. At last she crossed the ocean in search of her son, and they met in the City of the Seven Hills. The artist son, looking at his mother in surprise, said, "What has happened to your face, mother; it has changed its expression?" "Your mother has prayed a good deal," she replied simply. "Well, it makes a good face," the artist replied. "It puts fine lines into it."

Horace E. Hewitt

Prayer, Intercessory

707   Here is a story of Professor Gossip's: "Once, at the Front, a man, outwardly of small religion, said to me, 'Why do you think it is that sometimes under heavy shelling, my nerves all a-twitter, suddenly and unaccountably I become calm and unafraid, ready to face anything?' And I replied, 'May it not be that somebody is praying for you?' Whereat he stood still, pondering a moment with a queer light dawning on his face, and then rapped out an oath, 'By God, Padre, you are right; it will be my mother.'"

Archibald Alexander

Prayer, Meaning of

708   It is said that once when Dr. Johnson was about to say grace, his wife stopped him by saying, "Don't go through the mockery of thanking God for what in a few minutes you will declare is not fit to be eaten." I am afraid many of our thanksgivings and prayers are often as superficial as Dr. Johnson's grace. But God is not one to accept words that have no meaning. He does not want the homage of our lips. He does not want petitions that sound well in the ears of men. What He wishes to hear is the frank expression of our feelings, the earnest desire of our hearts. When we ask Him to "Give us this day our daily bread," He expects us to believe that He can and does supply our wants. He expects us to act in such a way as to merit His countenance. He expects us to use His gifts as if they came from Him.

What, then, do you and I mean when we offer this prayer? What do we expect God to give us? How do we expect Him to act towards us? These are points for our consideration.

James Gilles

Prayer, Motives of

709   The chief librarian at Dagenham, England, recently investigated the history of an area on which there now stands an immense Ford factory. One of the first purchasers of the site was a certain John Ward, a member of Parliament, who bought it when it was flooded and therefore cheap, and then had a bill passed in the House of Commons to drain it at the public expense. After his death, there was found among his papers this extraordinary prayer: "Oh Lord, Thou knowest I have nine estates in the City of London, and likewise that I have recently purchased an estate in fee simple in the County of Essex. I beseech Thee to preserve the two counties of Middlesex and Essex from fire and earthquake, and as I have a mortgage in Hertfordshire, I beg Thee likewise to have an eye of compassion on that county; for the rest of the counties, Thou mayest deal with them as Thou art pleased." I hope I am not a malicious person, but you can't possibly know the mild and quiet satisfaction it affords me to tell you that John Ward died in a debtor's prison, and the fact that he died where he did does not shake in the least my confidence in the efficacy of prayer.

Robert James McCracken

Prayer, Silent

710   Dr. Joseph Parker of the City Temple often did and said the unexpected. Once, just before the opening prayer, he stretched out his hands and said, in thunderous tones: "Let us pray." Then followed a silence of several minutes at the close of which he said: "Amen." It was intended as an object lesson on the reality of silent prayer, a form of worship not so frequent in those days as now, though even now not so frequent as might well be. We glorify talk. We are for ever talking. But how moving and impressive the silent corporate lifting up of the heart of a congregation can be and how fraught with power and benediction the silent prayer of the lonely worshipper. God listens, it might be said, not to what we say, but to what we think. His ear is turned not to our lips but to our hearts. His ear is so quick that the lowest whisper reaches it, and the prayer that is not even a whisper.

W. Ellick Kirby

Preacher

711   When Jowett preached in the sermon class at Airedale College, Dr. Fairbairn said to the students: "Gentlemen, I will tell you what I have observed this
morning; behind that sermon there was a man."   John Bishop

✳✳

712   As Thomas Carlyle remarks, "the crowning hypocrisy is a false priest."
The best thing about a preacher is not the sermon he preaches, the visits he
makes, the prayers he offers, the truth he affirms, the instruction he affords,
the inspiration he generates, but the life he lives. The Earl of Shaftesbury said
concerning Charles H. Spurgeon: "Whatever he was in the pulpit he was in
private, and whatever he was in private he was in the pulpit." Magnificent
compliment!   James L. Gordon

Preacher, Judging the

713   I remember an office-bearer with more frankness than loyalty complain-
ing to me that his minister expected to be treated "like the Apostle Paul," but
was not willing, like Paul, "to spend and be spent." I met that minister later on,
and he certainly seemed a somewhat cold and ease-loving individual, whose
conception of his high office was not all that could be desired. But not so long
after I also met an old college friend of his, who told me that this particular
minister had started with a heroic devotion to the highest ideals, and was conspicuous among his fellows for an abandonment to the claims of his people
which bordered on the quixotic and at one time endangered his health. To know
the steps by which this deplorable change was brought about would be to get
an insight into unwritten Church history that might well make the most convinced critic walk softly all his days. One important lesson such a story teaches
us is that no preacher can be judged fairly until one knows his church, and
that even with such knowledge it is extremely difficult to gauge his capacity
and possibilities.   E. Hermann

Preachers and Hearers

714   A few years ago, after a minister had been preaching in a Wesleyan
chapel not far from my house, one of the older officials of the circuit began
to talk to him of the glories of the past generation, and said with some fervour,
"Ah, sir, there were some great preachers then." "Yes," was the reply of the

minister, who perhaps felt just a touch of human irritation on listening to the remark. "Yes, and there were great hearers then."   R. W. Dale

Preaching

715   The preacher is only at his best when he is most fervent in spirit. He must not only enter the ministry under the urge of genuine religious enthusiasm. He must "maintain the spiritual glow." We should face our many problems with a throbbing sense of the reality of the indwelling Spirit, and our people should be able to discern that we speak with spiritual authority. I think it is Gossip who tells of Alexander Whyte that some one said to him, "You spoke as if you came straight from the Presence." "Perhaps I did," he answered, shyly.

Alexander Hodge

✳✳

716   One day when Frederick Denison Maurice went to preach at Eversley, he asked his friend the Rector, Charles Kingsley, "What would your people like?" And Kingsley replied: "Never mind what they would like, tell them what they ought to know."   Frederick C. Spurr

✳✳

717   I remember years ago, when I came to London as a medical student, I became a member of a church in which was one of the most gifted ministers then living. When I heard him I went home thinking what a splendid preacher he was and what a grand sermon I had heard. But the next day, and all the days of the week, I found that I wanted something more than any sermon that was ever preached. I went elsewhere, to a very different man, and then went home not thinking either of the preacher or the sermon, but my heart glowed with love to my Saviour, my faith exulted in His power; and the next day I could go forth feeling that with such a Friend and Helper as Jesus Christ I could sing defiance to the gates of hell. Much, very much, depends upon the human minister of the Word.   Mark Guy Pearse

✳✳

718   "How is it," said one of Mr. Bradburn's hearers, "that he always has something so new and good to say?" "Because," was the answer, "he lives so near to God that God tells him things that He does not tell to other people."

J. Berry

✳✳

719   A familiar story of Coleridge tells us that he once said to Lamb, "Charles, did you ever hear me preach?" referring to a period when, as a young man, he used to speak in Unitarian chapels. Lamb, replying, startled his questioner by blurting out the confession with arresting strength, "Why, I never heard you do anything else!"   John Clifford

※ ※

720   A statesman never grows too old to be appreciated and sought for. Russell Broughman, Palmerston, Webster, and Clay were leaders as long as they lived. To-day Gladstone, Disraeli, Bismarck, and Gortschakoff are the men who control in great measure the destinies of Europe. Why should it not be so in the ministry? Why is it that men turn, in the most important interests of life affecting themselves and their families, from the counsels of age and experience to those of youth and less skill?

I may not be able to answer this question satisfactorily either to you or to myself. One reason is, I believe, the neglect of study on the part of many aged ministers. They lose that stimulus which belongs to other professions. To the physician every case is a new study. New remedies are discovered and recommended. He must keep abreast of the times, or some intruder will take away his practice. The attorney finds some new element in almost every case. New decisions are given by the Supreme Court, and he must study them. In statesmanship new complications are constantly arising. The connections of nations are so numerous, the questions involved are so various and sometimes so vast as to require the utmost comprehension to grasp them and the closest attention to the least minutiae and detail. The statesman has no old sermon that he can pick up and apply. He must think and study and write, and thus keep his mind ever active and fresh. There is no time for him to nod or sleep. But the old minister sits down under his vine or fig-tree, and there is no one to molest him or to make him afraid. He hurls thunderbolts at the heads of scientists who are a thousand miles away, and who will never hear his thunder; he descants upon the sins of the Egyptians, who have been mummies for thousands of years; or he discourses upon the pride of Babylon or Nineveh, which have been swept away for ages. He is pressed for time, and brings before his congregation of to-day a discourse which he had made twenty years ago, on an issue then living, but now almost forgotten. His thoughts are of the past; his sermons are of the past; and the generation of to-day feels that he is scarcely one of them.   Bishop M. Simpson

※ ※

721   There is a beautiful little picture in one of the Italian histories drawn by John of Bologna—I think it was of the year 1212—of how he heard Francis

was to speak at Bologna, and he says he went to hear him, expecting from so famous a man great oratory, and when he got there he found that Francis spoke quite quietly and colloquially. A great lesson for ministers there. But when Francis had done that colloquial address, which astonished John of Bologna by its simplicity and plainness, John says the crowd were all weeping, and men who would not scorn to shed eath other's blood, fell upon each other's necks and forgave past enmities. And as Francis passed out of that little place that afternoon, thousands of people knelt down to kiss the very hem of his frayed brown robe as he went out.   W. J. Dawson

✳✳

722   I am convinced that the world has not outgrown the preacher. If a man has a message he will always find people willing to listen to him. And despite the contention of many no subject is of such absorbing interest today to the mass of men as theology. This they confess by their attendance at the Church where great theological problems are dealt with at once frankly and reverently. In the existence of this interest a great opportunity presents itself to us. Listen to Carlyle's strong words—as true today as when the apostle of reality first gave them utterance: "This speaking man has indeed in these times wandered terribly from the point; has, alas, as it were, totally lost sight of the point: yet, at bottom, whom have we to compare with him? Of all public functionaries boarded and lodged on the industry of modern Europe, is there one worthier of the board he has? A man even professing, and ever so languidly making still some endeavour, to save the souls of men: contrast him with a man professing to do little, but shoot the partridges of men. I wish he could find the point again, this speaking one; and stick to it with a tenacity, with deadly energy: for there is need of him yet."   Hugh C. Wallace

✳✳

723   St. Jerome tells us that once when he asked Gregory of Nazianzus for the explanation of a difficult word in St. Luke that teacher humorously replied that he would prefer to explain it in the pulpit, because when there is an applauding crowd around you, you are compelled to know that of which in fact you are ignorant. It has been the temptation of the pulpit at all times to explain without understanding, and to substitute well-sounding phrases for real discussion. The presence of a sceptic or two in a congregation does a preacher good if it induces him on occasion to say, "I do not know."

                                    E. J. Hardy

✳✳

724   Somewhere in John Wesley's *Journal* it is recorded that he was asked to speak at a drawing-room meeting, and he confessed that seeing the amount of jewellery and gold ornaments displayed by the folk there he decided, so that they should not be out of their depth, to speak on the subject of the Rich Man and Lazarus! One cannot suppose Wesley was devoid of a very lively imagination.   Morley B. Simmons

✳ ✳

725   I remember Lloyd George, after attending one of my services, saying in the vestry, "I don't know how you ministers do it. I speak occasionally, here and there, to different audiences. I don't need to create my own atmosphere: it is there before me, electric and buoyant; my audience cheers the tritest remark or the most inane joke. But you are in the same place, speaking to the same people, twice a Sunday. The people don't come expecting fire-works or to be amused. And you have to speak, by and large, always on the same subject, and you have to stir or create your own atmosphere. I think that to be a minister in a settled church is one of the hardest arts of speaking known to me."

James Black

✳ ✳

726   David Hume, the sceptic, once went to hear John Brown, the saintly Scots preacher, and confessed when he returned, "That man preaches as though Jesus Christ were at his elbow."   Morley B. Simmons

✳ ✳

727   McLaren once was asked about his way of making sermons, and he replied: "I know of no method, except to think about a text until you have something to say about it, and then to go and say it, with as little thought of self as possible."   John Bishop

✳ ✳

728   Dr. W. L. Watkinson was about to begin his sermon on one occasion when the lights in the church were suddenly lowered. "Please put up the lights," he said, "I can't see my notes." When the lights were turned up again he pointed to the congregation and said, "You are my notes." It takes two to make an effective sermon—the preacher and the hearer.   John Bishop

✳ ✳

729   Sir Joshua Reynolds was requested, it is said, by a nobleman to paint for him a picture of his daughter. The picture was completed, and the bill

presented, amounting to fifty guineas. The nobleman objected to paying so large a price, saying that it cost the artist only the labour of a few days. Sir Joshua replied that he was mistaken. It had taken him forty years to paint that picture. So the sermon of to-day or the work of to-day, though just planned or executed, is really the work of years of thorough culture.

Bishop M. Simpson

** **

730 Perhaps you have prepared a sermon into which you have put all your best. When you had finished it, you said—humbly of course—"Now this will make somebody sit up and take notice: this ought to flutter the dovecots!" And after you had preached it, there was just a blessed silence of an unruffled pool. Then, a Sunday later, after a rushed and broken week, you preached a sermon for which you felt that you ought to apologize beforehand. Yet, somebody came round to see you, or wrote you, to say that this despised sermon had helped him beyond words. Not a ripple about the dandy sermon of which you were so proud, and a whole tide of feeling about the one for which you wanted to apologize! Isn't it queer? It is good to know that God can use the weak things of this world to confound the things which we thought mighty.

Let us be honest about our own work—and especially about our object in doing it. That fine sermon about which you were so proud was almost sure to drop like a dud: for you tried to be clever, and you tried to impress by the wrong kind of qualities. Whereas the sermon you considered slight and unimportant was at least written in a kind of clean humility, and didn't aim at dazzling folk or impressing them with your mastery of the subject. On the whole, I think it is the most comforting thing in the world to realize that God can use us apart from our own cleverness, and that the measure of our helpfulness is not merely the measure of our own brain-pan.

James Black

Preaching, Aim of

731 Paul tells how he preached this message of the Cross—it was not with rhetoric and eloquence, not with wisdom of words lest the Cross of Christ should be made of non-effect. Luther says, "He preaches best who aims at being understood rather than at being admired." "A good sermon," says some one, "is a sermon that does good."

Peter Fleming

Preaching and Study

732   You may have read Sir Roger de Coverley's instructions to his chaplain, who was required to have good sense rather than much learning, friendliness rather than studiousness; and who was expected to read from the pulpit on the Lord's Day one of a series of sermons selected from such masters as Tillotson, Barrow, and South. This chaplain was not a typical minister, for we prepare our own sermons to suit the needs of our own people. Still less is the true preacher like the roarer in Shakespeare's comedy: Snug was asked to play the part of the lion, and he requested a copy of his lines that he might study them, but the manager replied, "You may do it extempore, for it's nothing but roaring." Then Bottom, the weaver, desired the part of the lion. "Let me play the lion, too; I will roar that it will do any man's heart good to hear me; I will roar that I will make the duke say, 'Let him roar again.'" When told that he must roar so as not to frighten the ladies, Bottom gave this pleasing assurance: "I will aggravate my voice so as to roar you as gently as any suckling dove; I will roar you as 'twere any nightingale." The real preacher, however, depends neither upon the "fruits of other men's worthy labours," nor upon roaring, but day after day, five days of the week, he studies under the guidance of the Spirit of God.

Andrew W. Blackwood

✳✳

733   I have heard that Dr. Binney, when he was requested by his deacons to visit more, gave notice on a Sunday that he would visit all week. He selected the time for calling on people; he would call on gentlemen in the City about twelve or one, when they were in the very thick of business, and he would call on sisters at home, who had many children, just at the time when they were putting the children to bed. On the Sunday, after spending the whole week at it and after reading and praying and so on, he said, "I am very sorry, but as friends wished me to spend my time in visiting, I have done so, and have had no time to prepare a sermon, and I will, therefore, dismiss you with a benediction." I believe that during the afternoon he looked up an old sermon that he had given years before, and he told them he would give them that, but that as long as he was engaged in visitation, he could give them no new sermons at all. I believe they caved in, and thought that, on the whole, they had better have the preaching.

C. H. Spurgeon

Preaching by Life

734   Dr. A. T. Schofield, the Harley Street specialist, tells in one of his books that when his daughter was ill they engaged a nurse to look after her. At the end of two weeks the nurse came to him and said, "I thought you would like to know that I am now a Christian. When I came I was an unbeliever." The doctor said, "I suppose my daughter has been talking to you about religion." "No," was the reply, "she has not said a word about it, but I have never known anyone so cheerful and patient and I could not rest until I knew her secret." That girl on her sick-bed had been preaching the Gospel without words.

J. Ireland Hasler

Preaching, Delivery in

735   It is told of Dr. Fletcher, of London, a preacher of the early Victorian era, that he would sometimes preach for his father, a country minister in Scotland. When he did so there was always a crowd; when his father preached there was no crowd. The young man, to soothe his father's wounded feelings, declared that it was only because of his delivery that he was preferred. To prove this he preached one of his father's discourses, when he was heard with as much delight as when he preached his own. Certainly in many cases a poor sermon well delivered will equal, if not surpass, in effect a much superior production. We may say that in a very true sense manner is matter. The power of the human voice, when skilfully managed, is very great. An instance is mentioned by Dr. Fish: "M. Bridaine, a French missionary, and a peer of the most renowned orators of that eloquent nation, preached a sermon at Bagnole, at the end of which he lifted up his arms and thrice cried in a loud voice, 'O Eternity!' At the third repetition of this awful cry, the whole audience fell upon their knees. During three days consternation prevaded the town; and it is recorded that in the public places young and old were heard crying aloud, 'Mercy! O Lord, mercy!' " And it has been said that Whitefield, with his "Hark! Hark!" could conjure up Gethsemane before his audience. We do not plead for *vox, et praeterea nihil*, but we plead for much attention and training being given to the voice.   J. N. Russell

Preaching, Effect of

736   A poor woman returned one day from church, where she had heard a sermon upon dishonesty. When questioned as to the text she said she had for-

gotten, but she added: "I remember that when I came home I burnt the bushel measure." God give us more of such preaching!

J. Berry

Preaching in Writing

737   In a certain sense, it is only futile to say, "Tell us a story and don't bother about the moral." Surely if the author has thought about life at all, he must have come to some great personal judgements. And if he hasn't seen something which seems big and commanding to him, what is he writing about anyhow? He must have come to some views about life and the world, and some ideas of human motives and conduct. If so, say what he likes, he is subtly preaching them. It may be dirt he is preaching, or the meaninglessness of life, or that virtue doesn't pay, or indeed anything he believes—but he is preaching. If he is only preaching lust, he is preaching. It is comical that so many people say, "I don't want an author to preach," and all they mean is, "I don't want him to preach goodness and holiness." They don't seem to see that it is just cleanliness, or vulgarity or decency. But say what you care, every man who has the urge to write is preaching something he wants to say.

James Black

Preaching, Note of Crisis in

738   In modern preaching a note which is largely lacking is the note of crisis. Not long ago I heard a preacher say from the pulpit that if one were to question the first fifty men one met on the subject of personal religion, one would be forced to come to the conclusion that very few in these casual easy-going days took the matter seriously or made it an issue of life and death. One would like to state the conclusion somewhat differently. While it is undoubtedly true that an explicit sense of crisis is wanting in the average modern soul, it is a fallacy to deduce from this that men are more callous and obtuse to eternal issues to-day than they have been in the past. I believe that, on the contrary, men were never so persistently, if vaguely, haunted by the unseen, and that much of current surface flippancy covers a fluttering, frightened soul that hears eternity booming upon the horizon.

The juster conclusion to draw from their apparent carelessness is rather that in many cases the vague troubling of their soul has never been made explicit to them, that they have never heard the deep message that answers to their deep but inarticulate presentiment.

If so many church-goers lack a sense of the soul-crisis, it is largely because the pulpit has lost that iron note. The men of John Wesley's time were any-thing but spiritually alarmed, unless history be a liar; it was John Wesley's uttered sense of crisis that woke their own latent sense. And so it must ever be. Given preachers whose sense of the supreme and final issue is a passion, in every street there will be men asking, "What shall I do to be saved?" Given a pulpit which trails off into side-issues and irrelevancies, and carelessness will be written on the face of every passer-by. It is one of the initial functions of the pulpit to interpret the soul to itself, to help it to distinguish its many voices. There are instances in which this interpreting faculty of the preacher amounts to spiritual clairvoyance, and such a one will not be likely to complain of the callousness of the age. But even the less acutely endowed preacher who really believes that there is a great Either-or, and that it may take but a touch to awake the most apparently indifferent soul, will find deep calling unto deep.

E. Hermann

Preaching, Power in

739   There was a minister once, a minister of religion of all people, to whom with every passing day it became devastatingly apparent that his gospel was inadequate and ineffectual because it was not his own. One Monday he said to himself: "I have been preaching things that are not operative in me. I refuse to perjure my soul any longer. I am not going to preach again until I can preach reality. I'll give God until next Sunday to do something for me, and if He doesn't do something for me by then somebody else can preach: I won't." Desperate language, but if he was spiritually desperate it was because he was spiritually honest. Day by day of that week passed. Saturday came and he spent the greater part of it in retirement and prayer. The next morning he went into the pulpit and the people settled back in their pews to listen, as they thought, to the type of sermon they had been hearing from their minister for many a year. He hadn't been talking five minutes before they knew they had to reckon with another man. There were undertones in his words they had never heard before. When the service was over a worshipper was seeking what the minister had found.

Robert James McCracken

✳✳

740   Mr. Wesley, at the good old age of eighty-seven, in a letter to Alexander Mather, uttered these thrilling words: "Give me one hundred preachers who fear nothing but sin and desire nothing but God, and I care not a straw whether they be clergymen or laymen; such alone will shake the gates of hell, and set

up the Kingdom of Heaven upon earth." Grand words these from the old battle-scarred veteran whose sword, which so long flashed in the forefront of conflict, now hung feebly by his side.

Charles B. Galloway

Preaching, Purpose and Aim of

741   I should suggest that we, every one of us, do what we think best, and not say hard things about other people for doing what they think best. Anything on earth is better than letting those people go to hell. If you do not like the way I use, use your own way, brother. However, the question I am going into is how to get at them when you have got them, how really so to preach that you will get at their souls. We all mean business. We do not preach officially because we are called to perform that vocation, but we look upon it as something that has an end and purpose. We want these people's hearts and consciences to be touched, we want their souls to be saved. When I go into a house now-a-days frequently they do not offer me anything to eat—I do not find fault with that—but they hang the plates on the wall. Why don't they have them down and give us something? I have sometimes fancied that there are preachers who display their plates on the wall—very nice plates, fine sort of china—but the people starve. They don't want china, they want bread, they want meat, something that they can feed upon. You and I go in for the practical and useful. I do not believe we have a cracked plate amongst us that is not used; we have cracked plates, and chipped plates, and all sorts of plates, but they are all being used. I hope that is the condition of all of us, that everything is being put to practical account in the service of God.

C. H. Spurgeon

Preaching, Results of

742   Dr. Beecher once exchanged pulpits with a country minister. The day was cold and stormy; he urged his horse through the snow piled up. He reached the church, stalled his horse, and went into the church to find nobody there. He took his seat in the pulpit, and one individual arrived, looked around and sat down. One man. The doctor, a young man then, wondered whether or not he would preach. He decided he would. He took the whole service, and preached to the solitary hearer as he would a congregation. After the benediction he hastened from the pulpit to speak to the man, but before Beecher could reach him he had gone.

Twenty years afterwards Dr. Beecher alighted from the stage in a pleasant village. A gentleman came up and spoke to him, calling him by name. "I do not remember you," said the doctor. "I suppose not," replied the stranger, "but we spent two hours together in a house alone once in a storm." "I do not recall it, sir," added the old man; "pray, pray, when was it?" "Do you remember preaching twenty years ago in such a place, to a single person?" "Yes, yes," said the doctor, grasping his hand, "I do indeed; and if you are the man, I have been wishing to see you ever since." "I am the man, sir; and that sermon saved my soul, made a minister of me, and yonder is my church. The converts of that sermon, sir, are all over Ohio!"

Percy Hannah

Preaching, Zeal in

743   It is an old story that a minister once asked Garrick, the actor, why actors portraying fiction on the stage affected the people so much more profoundly than ministers in the pulpit discussing the most momentous realities. The great actor replied: "Because we represent fiction, as though it were fact, and ministers represent fact as though it were fiction." If actors displayed as little feeling on the stage as many ministers do in the pulpit, their career would be very short. Nothing but an earnest religion counts in this earnest age. What care busy men for a dull, lifeless presentation of any subject? Display a zeal for spiritual results as earnest as theirs for wealth, and they will listen. Speak to them as those whose eyes have been wearied in trying to compass the height and depth of life; speak as those who have stood on the verge of time and peered behind the veil where the mortal has put on the immortal and they will hear.

Charles E. Jefferson

Prejudice

744   We all travel through life with, as it were, a brief-case packed with ideas and maxims upon which we confidently rely and which we use from day to day, and yet probably very few of us could prove or have ever attempted to prove for ourselves the validity of a single one of them. They are, in fact, sheer prejudices; opinions formed in advance of any rational examination or scientific analysis. Naming a few of these prejudices at random, we might mention our belief that the earth is round, that it gyrates on its axis, and that it revolves around the sun; that man is besieged by myriads of microscopic organisms, and that but for the fact of our having a skin we should all succumb to this siege and be destroyed in a matter of weeks; that the supreme figure of Jesus once walked our earth, and that in the Bible we have the record of the promise of

His coming and a true report of His life, words, deeds and death; that our civil and religious liberties have been won for us at the price of bonds and martyrdom; and that if we carelessly allow a tea-cup to slip out of our hands it will not fly upwards and make a mess on the ceiling but will fall downwards and be smashed. These things we all believe, but none of us has proven, or perhaps could prove, the truth of any one of them. All of them, and scores of others too, quite as central and quite as practical, are then, in the strict sense of the word, prejudices.   D. W. Langridge

⁂

745   We have to take practically everything on trust. Prejudice or faith—call it which you like, it comes to the same thing—is the chart, compass, dynamo, daemon, star, steam, and whatever other and better metaphors you can think of, of human life. Liquidate the massive phalanx of his prejudices and, hapless and hopeless, civilized man would very soon collapse into primordial anarchy. We are saved by prejudice. Patriotism is prejudice. Religion is prejudice. Morals are prejudice.

The Ten Commandments themselves are so many ancient, venerable and impressive prejudices. We do not attempt to investigate from first principles the rightness of telling the truth and the wrongness of libel, the desirability of private property, of marital loyalty, or of the sanctity of human life. Without proof or analysis we take it for granted that it is evil to bear false witness, vicious to interfere with another man's property, and wicked to violate the sanctity of another man's wife or life. We honour the ten prejudices.

D. W. Langridge

Pride

746   Why do we hate so intensely to be put in the wrong? How is this well-nigh inveterate passion for self-justification, this passion which is native to us all and rooted deep in us all, to be explained? It can be explained in a single word, the word pride. It may be that more should be said in pulpits than is commonly done about pride. It is the parent sin, the root, indeed, of all that we call sin. It is the thing that rots human personality at the core. I noticed that Mr. C. S. Lewis calls it the essential vice, the utmost evil, the great sin, and at the same time contends that not a single person in the world is free from it. Everyone simply loathes it when he sees it in somebody else, yet with the exception of some Christians, hardly anybody supposes that he is guilty of it himself. People may admit, says Mr. Lewis, that they are bad-tempered, or that they can't keep their heads about girls or drink, or even that they are

cowards, but who ever heard of any, save Christians, accusing themselves of pride? And who ever heard of anybody showing the slightest mercy to pride in others? There is no fault which makes a man more unpopular. And the more we have it in ourselves, the more we dislike it in others. Without doubt it is the parent sin, the original sin. It leads to every other kind of sin. What is more, it is the complete anti-God state of mind.

Robert James McCracken

✳✳

747   Again, I think it is the mission of trouble that makes us feel our dependence on God. King Alphonso said that if he had been present when the world was made he could have suggested many improvements. What a pity he had not been present. I do not know what God will do when some men die.

T. DeWitt Talmage

Priesthood of Believers

748   M. Guizot, French Protestant scholar and statesman and at one time Ambassador to the Court of St. James, had a friend who tried to persuade him to join the Roman Catholic Church. In a private letter to this friend which has since been published, M. Guizot wrote: "My submission to the Divine Will has often been put to the test but God knows how deep is my conviction of His strength and of my own weakness apart from Him. Yet it is nevertheless true that I have never felt any need for priestly assistance in the relations between my frail soul and God. In joy and sorrow, in rendering thanks and in imploring protection, I always feel able to go spontaneously and directly to my God and speak to Him and He speaks to me. I live in trustful and immediate, though infinitely humble, communion with Him. Some persons may call this arrogance on my part. But this attitude of my soul has been and is being confirmed by all my experience of life."

W. Ellick Kirby

Principle

749   A non-Christian friend, reading in his newspaper of the moral stand taken by two bishops, turned to me and said: "That's the sort of thing that makes the Church unpopular." And so, no doubt, it is; but immediately the question arose in my mind: "Ought any action or word of Christian leaders to be condemned—condemned solely or mainly—on the ground that it is likely to make the Church unpopular?" Is popularity a safe guide in Church affairs? Are there not times

when the Church must risk the loss of popularity—both among her own people and among outsiders—in order to witness to, and to preserve, some essential principle?

Ernest H. Jeffs

Prodigal

750   It is recorded that a few years ago the body of a young man was found in the Mersey. On a paper in his pocket were written these words: "A wasted life. Do not ask anything about me. Drink was not the cause. Let me die, let me rot." Within a week the coroner received over two hundred letters from fathers and mothers all over England asking for a description of the young man.

P. Burnell

✳✳

751   A great preacher of my native land used to tell the story of a farmer he knew. His daughter ran away from home, once, twice, three times, and on going into the country town one day he was told that she was up before the magistrate for disorderly conduct. His landlord sat on the bench and said, "Mr. So-and-So, we all respect you, take your daughter home." But the old man said, "She is no daughter of mine any longer. I forgave her once, I took her back twice, but when she went away the third time I gathered my people together in family worship and took my knife and cut her name out of the family Bible." Men and women, we have run away from home not once, or twice, but some of us, a hundred times. We have grieved our God over and over again, but our name has never been erased from the Lamb's Book of Life. The dastardly shame of disobedience has been met by the overwhelming surprises of Divine forgiveness.

Thomas Phillips

Prodigal Son

752   Alexander Whyte says the Prodigal Son went away without kissing his father but, in spite of my idolatrous admiration for Alexander Whyte, I do not believe he did. I feel sure he kissed his father with tears in his eyes; a boy with glamour of the far country in his heart is seldom a nasty kind of boy.

There was no tragedy in his going away; only hope and immense possibility. He had not fallen out with his father. His father believed in him. The boy believed in himself. It is one of the loveliest pictures in the world, this of a boy taking leave of his father to set out for the country of his dreams.

Why, then, did the swine trough come into the picture? It came in because the boy lacked insight. He did not understand himself, nor did he know what spirit he was of. He thought that all he needed for perfect happiness, for complete life, was to get into the far country. But when he got to the far country he found what we all find—that the far country is not a bit more satisfying or secure than the little hollow we have left behind, and that what looked so glamorous in the distance is apt to lose its glamour when you live with it. The swine trough came in because the boy had learned next to nothing from his father, because he did not see in his father's life the things that made for peace and happiness. He did not realize that he was too big to be satisfied by a change of environment.   James MacKay

Progress

753   I think it was Bergson who said that the outstanding event of modern times has been the enlargement of man's body. "Telescopes and microscopes have increased the powers of our eyes; telephones have stretched our ears several thousands of miles; wireless has enabled the puniest voice to reverberate round the world; steam and electricity and petrol have enhanced the speed of our feet better than the seven-leagued boots of ancient fable. Gunpowder has given our fists a terrible range and power. Aeroplanes have enabled us to increase our high jump and our long jump from a matter of yards to thousands of miles." Never had man such a stupendous body, and never has the world we live in seemed so small, since the dawn of time.

H. G. Newsham

Promises, God's

754   John Ruskin, in his autobiography—and I should think that he had not a particularly happy childhood—tells us, "In my childhood I learned a lesson of faith, for nothing was promised to me that was not given; nothing was threatened that was not inflicted; and nothing was ever told me that was not true." Now, we may say of the words of Jesus that what He promises He gives; what He threatens He inflicts; and what He says is true. So you have a promise by a faithful, performing God.   Edwin Gorsuch Gange

Prophecy

755   As Sir George Adam Smith said, commenting on the life and work of Amos, so must we say:

To see the truth and tell it; to be accurate and brave about the moral facts of the day—to this extent the vision and voice are possible for every one of us. To see facts as they are and to tell the truth about them, this also is prophecy. We may inhabit a sphere which does not prompt the imagination, and seems as destitute as the deserts where Amos lived and worked. All the more may our unglamoured eyes be true to the facts about us.

S. Myers

Protestant Religion

756   The truth is that Protestant religion is only possible on the condition that it is profoundly religious. It is only possible on the condition that a man's private judgement is continuously, anxiously, sincerely and humbly submitted, in prayer and thought and study and self-abnegation, to the will of God, as he is given light to discern that will and grace to obey it.

Protestant religion, in short, is only possible on the basis of obedience—an obedience more complete and self-surrendering than that of the Catholic because it must be accompanied by the reasoned inward assent of the disciple. He knows he must obey God. He knows also that he must obey reason and conscience. Does this mean that he must necessarily experience a clash of loyalties? No. In the Protestant view of things nothing that clashes with reason and conscience can be thought of as having anything to do with God. If it is a Church tradition it must go. If it is a majority vote in a religious assembly it must go. Even if it is a text of scripture (or, rather, a text of scripture as traditionally or usually interpreted) it must go. It may be said without irreverence that the Protestant Christian has not only to choose daily whether he will obey God or not; he also has to choose daily what God he will obey.

Ernest H. Jeffs

Protestantism

757   France had the opportunity of embracing the Protestant faith, of a spiritual rebirth, of intellectual liberty. She spurned that offer, and on that dark and tragic St. Bartholomew's day massacred thousands of Protestants, and drove thousands into exile. But on a later day, when the monarchy fell, and the reign of terror swept over the country, when the guillotine was erected in her streets, and her barricades were piled with dead, she missed those men and women whose faith in God might have saved her such agony.

Years ago God gave Italy a prophet called Mazzini. She had at that time a clever politician named Cavour. Italy chose the politician, rejected the prophet, and ever since she has been the slave of militarism and military ambitions. According to John Milton, England flung away an opportunity more divine. The morning star of the Reformation first appeared in England's clouded skies, in the person of John Wycliffe. The ecclesiastical hierarchy of that day suppressed him as a heretic, an innovator of strange doctrines. Had the opportunity been accepted it is doubtful if the names of Luther and Calvin would have lived in history, and the glory of the Reformation would have been ours.

Herbert Dunnico

Protestantism, Busyness of

758   An American professor has said: "A generation ago the outstanding question was 'What have you been preaching recently?' " Later, another question forged to the front: "What are you doing with your young people now?" In these days a third question is asked with increasing frequency. "What changes are you making in worship?" What next? What will the next programme be? A bewildered and enfeebled Protestantism is unlikely to recover its spiritual vitality through concentration on church furnishings, even though the need to enrich our sanctuaries is obvious, and a very strong case can be made in favour of doing so. There always is a good case in favour of a strong programme. We should improve our worship, we should be concerned about our Sunday-school work, we must make provision for our young people, and—just as important—we must look after our old folk.

Yet the more activist Protestantism has become, the less spiritually compelling its witness appears. Our "busyness" has not even resulted in "successful" organization, since we not only suffer from depleted congregations—our finances are a constant anxiety. This prevents us paying our way, and this frequently means an excessive concentration of our limited energies on purely money-raising pursuits. In such circumstances we can hardly appear to the world as "more than conquerors." The work of the conscientious minister is made increasingly difficult. The more he realizes the need of spiritual renewal so that he can communicate spiritual power, the more he is called upon to devote himself to maintaining the material life of the church. The more he does so, the more his spiritual function is obscured or forgotten.

Arthur G. Reekie

Protestantism Different from Catholicism

759   The great error of Catholicism, as it seems to us, is in the emphasis it lays upon the Church as an ecclesiastical institution. Father D'Arcy finds the main difference between Catholicism and Protestantism to lie just here. The Protestant, he says, claims that Christ intended future generations to live by the record of His life and sayings in the Gospels, and in the letters of St. Paul, who never knew Him in the flesh. The Catholic, on the other hand, maintains that "Christ passed His authority on to the Apostles and bade them teach in His name till the end of time." "It is a hopeless business," says a Catholic writer, "to wish to distinguish in the Gospels the certain from the probable, the historical from the legendary, the foundations from the additions, the primitive from the dogmatic." Now the danger of that is illustrated in a well-known story told by Father George Tyrrell. A devout Catholic lady was speaking to her priest about the visions of St. Gertrude and Blessed Margaret Mary. "They tell us about our Lord," she said, "and without them one would know nothing of Him." "Do you ever read the Gospels?" asked the priest. "Oh, no, they are so dry." There is the danger. What are we to think of a Christianity that finds the Jesus of the Gospels an unattractive figure? At its worst it leads to the distorted vision that we see in the Mediaeval Church at its darkest period; the Body of Christ, when nothing was left in it of the Spirit of Jesus.

K. L. Parry

Providence

760   How does the Arctic tern fly twice a year from pole to pole? How does the swift fly from tropical Africa to the British Isles in seventeen hours? How can the tiny gold-crest cross the North Sea in the darkness of night? How is this wonderful flight accomplished? The law of gravitation is all the time against them. The theory that the body of the bird is lighter than air is now discarded. Instinct? Nature? These are but conventional evasions. Jesus Christ—unerring Naturalist—penetrates much further into this mystery when He declares: "Not a sparrow falls to the ground without your Father. . . ." There is a Divine Plan for the migration of birds—a higher law—and as they commit themselves to this higher control, they come safe to the haven where they would be.

H. Gresford Jones

* *

761   At the close of the American War of Independence the representatives of the people met to draw up a constitution for the newly-liberated country. For several weeks they talked but made little headway. Then Benjamin Franklin, the representative of Pennsylvania, who was in his eighty-second year, addressed the company. He called to mind that during the dark days of the war they had often met in that very room for prayer. Again and again had they been delivered.

Then he said that "if not a sparrow can fall to the ground without your heavenly Father, I am assured that no Empire worth rearing can ever be raised without Him." On his suggestion they went to prayer, and as a result the constitution of the United States of America speedily and satisfactorily came into being. And at about that same time George Washington was placing it on record that, though four times his coat had been pierced by bullets and twice his horse had been shot from beneath him, yet the God who marked the sparrow's fall had preserved him for the fulfilment of his providential purpose.

F. J. Miles

※ ※

762   Dr. Nehemiah Boynton had a delightful sea-side home, at which he loved to entertain visitors. On one occasion, at the end of a lovely summer day, a guest said gratefully: "You have provided a very wonderful day for us here, Doctor." With a quiet twinkle in his eye the Doctor replied: "To tell you the truth, I didn't provide it; but a very good friend of mine did."

Arthur Porritt

※ ※

763   Dr. Inge tells how in the Commonwealth period the Ambassador from this country to The Hague was spending a restless night. The news was so bad that he could not sleep. At length his servant ventured to ask him some questions. "Sir, will God govern the world well when you have left it?" "Undoubtedly." "Then can't you trust Him to govern it well while you are in it?" And the Ambassador went back to bed and slept quietly, and so was prepared for the labours of another day. It really makes all the difference if you believe that the Lord God reigneth.

Frank H. Ballard

Pulpit, Failure in

764   Rev. Richard Roberts, in *The Renascence of Faith,* is inclined to exonerate the man in the street at the expense of the preacher and the Church. The man in the street, he contends, has not essentially changed these two thousand years. Apostolic preaching captured him. If modern preaching fails to do so, the fault clearly does not rest with him. This view is shared by many of our younger men, but it may be gravely doubted if apostolic preaching did appeal to the individual who corresponded to our modern man in the street; it certainly failed with the Athenian who approximated most closely to the present-day type. Another and smaller school blames the man in the street. He is obtuse, apathetic,

unspiritual. The flesh is his only reality, and the mere mention of the Unseen evokes a broad and irritating grin. The pulpiteers of the coarsest and most sensational fibre may tickle his crude ear; to fail to attract him is a testimonial of the preacher's spirituality and faithfulness to high ideals. This view need not be taken very seriously; its thin fibre of truth is too grossly overlaid with caricature. Lastly, there is a wide section of critics who blame both the preacher and the crowd. Dr. Forsyth, for instance, distributes his mordant censure impartially between the purveyor of thin amateur heresies from the pulpit and the volatile and casual hearer who is fit on Sunday for nothing more strenuous than a tepid bath. These are all "inside" estimates of the situation. Criticism from the outside is undoubtedly valuable, and its salutary frankness and sharpness should not be shirked, but it is of necessity only a useful irritant; its one-sidedness and ignorance of the inward point of view deprive it of any positive therapeutic value.

These various efforts at locating the cause of the present ebb-tide recall a dictum of Thomas Carlyle's to the effect that the blame for any given abuse or wrong condition rests not with this one or that one, but with every man, woman and child who looked on and took no heed. The truth is that the present partial failure of the pulpit is due neither to the preacher, nor to the Church, nor to the masses, but to a certain set of social and spiritual conditions for which all alike are responsible in their measure, and for which the preacher of today has a more tender conscience and more sympathetic understanding than the majority of those critics who accuse him of apathy and detachment in terms of such feminine violence of emotion. And at any rate there has been enough of criticism, and many a preacher has failed ignominiously through trying to do what a host of ill-informed lookers on demand, when he might have achieved a valid success by quietly continuing as before.   E. Hermann

Pulpit, Hindrances to

765   When Alonzo Cano, the famous Spanish artist, was dying, he turned away from the crucifix held before his closed eyes, declaring that he could not bear the sight of such miserable workmanship. So the grandest truths of the pulpit may be rendered of no effect by the crude fashion in which they are presented.   W. L. Watkinson

Pulpit, Reality in

766   Dr. Boreham in one of his essays tells of a conversation he had in a train in Australia with an actor. "The thing one has to remember and the thing

an actor is most tempted to forget is that reality is on the other side of the foot-lights. If he forgets that, the tendency to artificiality will prove too strong for him. A subtle falsetto will creep into his voice and a suspicion of affectation will mark his behaviour. As soon as that happens, first-class work will be impossible. He can never rise above mediocrity. But as long as he remains conscious of the real people on the other side of the footlights he will talk as real men talk and act as real men act." "Only thus," concluded the actor, "can success be achieved in our profession or any other."

The pulpit is very much like the stage; it is easy to lose touch with real men and women and real life. It was said of an old Scottish minister that he was invisible all the week and incomprehensible on the Sunday. The one is the inevitable outcome of the other. The minister who gets out of touch with men will soon forget how to speak their language.   John Bishop

Purity

767   "Blessed are the pure in heart for they shall see God." Dr. R. F. Horton, one of the most scholarly preachers we have had, told how once he attended a village chapel when he was on holiday in the country. The preacher, a Methodist layman, was uneducated in the extreme. But he knew Christ, and Horton in his generous way says that he felt himself to be the merest beginner in the presence of that man.   H. W. Theobald

✳✳

768   The story is told of Percy Ainsworth, the famous Methodist preacher, who died young, that one night he was found with a bucket and scrubbing brush near his home, working hard at cleansing a brick wall in a mean street in Manchester. When asked the meaning of his strange behaviour by a surprised church official, Ainsworth told him that on his way home he had seen some obscene words there, and they had burned their way into his soul. He had tried to work in his study, but the picture those words had suggested persisted. He knew that children would read them and become corrupted in mind. He knew that grown men and women would be the worse for reading them. The preacher felt so unhappy that he said, "Before I can preach or do another thing I must wipe them out." So here he was, finding happiness in wiping everything out.   Arthur T. Rich

✳✳

769   General Grant, the great American General, was once visited by an officer who came into his tent brimming over with a good story which he was

eager to tell. He prefaced it by saying: "I hope there are no ladies here." And General Grant replied: "No, but there are gentlemen here," and the man, shamefaced, did not tell his story. There is also a story of the late Queen Victoria when she was quite young. At the table a gentleman was telling a doubtful story which caused a great deal of amusement. The young Queen asked him to tell it to her. He excused himself and said it was not worth telling; but she insisted, commanded him to tell it, and he was obliged to repeat it to the young Queen, and then she turned to him and said: "We are not at all amused." If every man and woman would even act in the spirit of General Grant and Queen Victoria we might work a great change in the tone and spirit of society, of business houses, of casual acquaintances. It is given to every one of us to be a purging influence wherever we go; not to yield to the corruption that is around us but to redeem it.

Robert F. Horton

Purpose

770   There was one king of legend who thought he could find satisfaction in an endless story. Have you not read how he offered great rewards to the story-tellers who could tell him one continuous story? Story-teller after story-teller tried, and in the end they all lost their heads except one man who told the story of the locusts and the grain of corn. "Another locust came and took another grain of corn; and another locust came and took another grain of corn . . ." until the king got so sick of the whole business that he gave the man his fabulous reward and sent him on his way. There is no satisfaction in something that is aimless, that has no definite aim, direction, purpose. Man desires an end in which he can rest. We are the children of time, and we must find something in which we can rest. That is a pulse that beats through the whole of human life. If we wish to become strong thinkers we must learn to clarify our thoughts, and if we want to possess a rich, radiant personality we must learn to define our desires after the highest ends. Tell me a man's desires, and I will give you a fairly true estimate of his character.   John Short

✳✳

771   A rude woman once blurted out to Thomas Carlyle's face the bluntly personal criticism: "Mr. Carlyle, you are so eccentric!" Swift as a flash came the cutting retort: "Not so eccentric, madam, if you only knew my centre!" Ay! That's it. "If you only knew my centre."   Ian MacPherson

✳✳

772   A story is told about Huxley, the scientist, who was on his way to a meeting of the British Association in Dublin. He arrived late at the station, threw himself into a jaunting car, calling to the coachman, "Drive fast." Away went the cab over the cobbled streets until at last Huxley called up to the driver, "Do you know where you are going?" "No!" was the reply, "but I'm driving fast."

E. G. Manby

Radiance

773   A certain Boston newspaper printed this item: "It was a dull, rainy day when things looked dark and lowering, but Phillips Brooks came down through Newspaper Row and all was bright." That is "Spiritual Glow." If we all possessed it, and we can if we will, we should be radiant Christians, help to fill our churches, and hasten the coming of Christ's Kingdom.

W. J. Redmore

Reading

774   I once used to know two ministers who were about the same age and near neighbours. One, whose training had been scanty, read comparatively little, but all he read seemed to become part of him: it lightened his conversation and it illustrated his sermons so that he seemed alive. The other had had greater opportunities in his youth, and he read more widely, but all he read seemed to make no difference; it gave no leaven to his private speech. It opened no windows in his preaching. Emerson, I suppose, is not read much now-a-days, certainly not in this country—and to our loss, I think: so stern a critic as John Morley wrote some shrewd words about him which are not irrelevant to the subject discussed in this paragraph: "He had the gift of bringing his reading to bear easily upon the tenor of his musings, and knew how to use books as an aid to thinking, instead of letting them take the edge off his thought." That comparison exactly describes the difference between the two men I mentioned above; and don't we all know men who read many books which seem merely to take the edge off their thought?

Albert Peel

Realism

775   There is a distinction between reality and realism. I hardly know how to define it. Murray's *Dictionary* gives it thus: realism is the semblance to or

suggestion of reality: reality is the quality of being real, the actual fact as distinguished from that which is apparent; the essential nature of a thing. G. K. Chesterton, in his brilliant way, put it thus: "Reality is frankness about our sins; realism is frankness about other people's sins."

Ebenezer Macmillan

Reconciliation

776   A married couple in Indiana became estranged by quarrelling, and great bitterness had grown up between them. After hard words one day, the husband said, hastily, "Well, we had better be separated. I will bring you a divorce." "Very well, I wish you would," was the wife's reply, not dreaming that she would be taken at her word. A few days after, her husband handed her a document, remarking, "There is the divorce you wanted; you are free to go." She calmly took the paper, and, after reading it, said, coldly, "I will pack my things at once; I wish you would see that I take nothing that does not belong to me." Her trunks were placed on the floor, and the work of packing commenced. Satan had possession of both of them, as, in pride, stubbornness and hatefulness of heart, the woman took her things from closets and bureau drawers, and the man sat in gloomy silence, watching as the trunks were rapidly filled.

Suddenly he was startled by his wife's dropping upon her knees by the lower drawer of the bureau and bursting into sobs and moans; he went to her side, and looked upon that which had caused her grief, and saw folded away in the drawer the clothing of the one little boy, who had once gladdened their hearts, but who had died years before. Unexpectedly, the mother had come upon the little jacket and trousers, the belt and boots, the cap and comforter, and all the precious treasures prized by the mother heart, and so long preserved. The man gazed for a moment, and the same emotions that had overcome the mother overcame him. He saw again the face of his darling boy, he bore again with the mother the bitter sorrow of the night beside the dying bed, and of the day of gloom when they laid the precious one away in the grave. He fell upon his knees beside his wife, and sobbed with her. In a few moments he took up the divorce and tore it in pieces, and said, "Wife, I have been wicked and wrong; will you forgive me?" "I have been more to blame than you, husband; I am the one to be forgiven." And in the presence of God, and of their angel child, they were reconciled. So "God was in Christ, reconciling the world unto Himself." Let us get men occupied with the crucified Redeemer and they cannot but repent.

D. W. Whittle

Redemption

777   Dr. Stanley Jones tells how one man was brought to realize his need of God's mercy in Christ: how the words sin, suffering and salvation, became flesh to his heart. The man was happy in the love of his devoted wife. Their home was in India. Being absent from that land, he broke his covenant to cleave to her alone and sinned against God, man and woman. His innocent wife's trust in him tortured him and he was miserable. He resolved to confess his sin to her and did so. He expected her to say one word, "Go!" When he revealed his secret unfaithfulness to her, he could see that his sin was torturing her as she clutched at the pain in her heart.

The expected storm did not break. Instead, she said to him, "I love you still, and I will not leave you." This man confessed: "Then I saw in the anguished love of my wife the meaning of the Cross. From her love I stepped up in thought to the Cross. I was a redeemed man from that hour."

Adam A. Reid

✳✳

778   The world may have grown indifferent to pious phrases; it is not unmoved by shining personal goodness, integrity of character, a Christ-like compassion. C. J. Jung in his most recent writings states that Christianity has its counterpart in the unconscious life of man. He believes that the study of man's deepest mental life reveals the profound need of redemption. He suggests that the psychologist's task is to make his patients aware of this need within.

Many people are becoming set in materialistic habits of thought and life, and increasing numbers are becoming imprisoned in words and slogans that have lost validity. It is our primary task to discover the words that quicken men and women to their true need; to proclaim the mystic word, the liberating word, the word through which God works His salvation.

Arthur G. Reekie

✳✳

779   We have two stories in the Bible: one in the Old Testament of a woman taken in adultery, and a javelin was struck through her and she died instantly; and one in the New Testament of a woman taken in adultery, and she was brought before my Master and your Master, and He stooped and looked upon the ground, that He might not look upon her flushing face and add to her shame, until all her accusers had gone out one by one, and then He lifted Himself up, and said, "Go, and sin no more; neither do I condemn thee." Which of

these two stories has had the greater effect in the redemption and purification of humanity? I doubt not; do you?

Lyman Abbott

Reform

780   I hold intensely with Horace Bushnell, that the soul of all improvement is the improvement of the soul. I hold with George Sand—who certainly is an unprejudiced witness—that all real reform begins within. I heartily agree with the working-man who spoke some years ago at a railway-men's meeting at Exeter Hall, when I was also a speaker, who said: "A great many persons say at the present day, 'Educate, educate, educate!' So say we," exclaimed the railway driver. "We desire to promote education to the utmost extent. And there are others who say: 'Legislate, legislate, legislate!' So say we; but in addition to that," added this Christian artisan, "we also say: 'Regenerate, regenerate, regenerate!'" And there was nothing that brought down the house that day so much as that remark.

C. H. Spurgeon

Reformation

781   Principal T. M. Lindsay used to labour to impress upon his students; for he held that the Reformation was not a sort of unnatural miracle that contradicted all the mediaeval past, but was the natural growth and fruit that evolved from great roots that were already there. Trevelyan shows with great power that the foundation of the ancient grammar schools up and down the land almost made the Reformation a logical necessity. For they brought knowledge and education for the first time into popular custom: and in the end they enabled people to read the Bible for themselves.

James Black

Reformation, Darkness Before

782   It is no exaggeration to say that for three centuries before the Reformation Christianity in England seems to have been buried under a mass of ignorance, superstition, priestcraft, and immorality. The likeness between the religion of this country and that of the apostolic age was so small, that if St. Paul had risen from the dead he would hardly have called it Christianity. As to ignorance, there were no English Bibles in the land. The facts which were brought to light on Bishop Hooper's visitation to the diocese of Gloucester, even so late as in the

time of Edward VI, are sufficient proof of what I say. Out of 311 clergy of his diocese, he found 168 unable to repeat the Ten Commandments. The worship, so-called, consisted of services in Latin (which hardly anybody understood), masses, and prayers to the Virgin and saints. The practical religion of most lay people was made up of occasional alms-giving, mass-attending, penance, absolution, and extreme unction at the last. Preaching there was hardly any, and what there was, was unscriptural rubbish not worth hearing. In short, it was a period of darkness that might be felt.

Herbert E. Ryle

Regeneration

783   Regeneration is not turning over a new leaf. It does not mean that. People have doubtless been turning over new leaves all their lives. It is not making good resolutions, either. Before I was converted I wrote some resolutions once and signed them with my own blood. I was anxious to keep them, and I thought that that would help me do it. Well, it didn't. The power to serve God must come before we can serve Him. We must get the power first, and not afterwards. That is the trouble with most people. They want to accomplish things before they are prepared for them. The preparation is a hard part. To get the power we must receive Christ. The power is outside of ourselves. Now, many people say, "Well, how can I receive Christ? I cannot receive Him tangibly. How am I to do it?" Well, the Bible says you can receive Christ by receiving His Word. That is the way. Do it. Lay hold of God's Word by faith; that is for you to do.   D. L. Moody

Relativism

784   It is notorious that our age cannot sound out the positive note. We are not cock-sure today about anything. We tend to deal in negations: it is of our uncertainties that we are certain. It is not our fault but it is our misfortune that we cannot answer questions, we can only ask them and leave them open. "Our age has taken the note of interrogation as its emblem," as a famous cartoon of Max Beerbohm reminds us. "Everything being now relative"—(I take the sentence from our leading novelist)—"there is no longer absolute dependence to be placed on God, Free Trade, Marriage, Coal or Caste," i.e., a boundless relativism everywhere throws the old landmarks down: the more men feel their deep need for a palpable, self-authenticating authority which they can make their own, live by and rejoice in—the more wistfully do they confess their obvious lack of it.   John S. Whale

Relaxation

785   The Apostle John used to amuse himself—according to tradition—by playing with a tame partridge. One day a noble youth, chancing to come upon him when engaged in this pastime, expressed unbounded astonishment that a man of his saintliness and reputation should be so engaged. "What is that in your hand?" said the saint. "It is my cross-bow," replied the youth, "with which I have been ranging the mountains." "And do you keep it always strung?" "No, certainly not." "Why not?" "Because, if always bent, it would lose its elasticity." "Well," replied the Apostle, "it is for the same reason that I occasionally unbend my mind with what may seem to you a trivial occupation. It is a relief from overstrain, and then when the mind is refreshed it returns with renewed force to the contemplation of heavenly mysteries."

James Stalker

Religion

786   A sceptic age is never a great or golden age; an infidel people can never be a noble or creative people. For deed, for achievement in politics or letters, for the highest creations in art, in poetry or sculpture, in architecture or painting, religion is a necessity.

A. M. Fairbairn

⁕⁕

787   A religion that does not purify the home cannot regenerate the race; one that depraves the home is certain to deprave humanity. Motherhood must be sacred if manhood is to be honourable. Spoil the wife of sanctity, and for the man the sanctities of life have perished. And so has it been with Islam. It has not reformed and lifted savage tribes; it has depraved and barbarized civilized nations. At the root of its fairest culture a worm has ever lived that has caused its blossoms soon to wither and die. Were Mohammed the hope of man, then his state were hopeless; before him could only lie retrogression, tyranny, and despair.

A. M. Fairbairn

⁕⁕

788   We know how bad the world has been with its religions; could we imagine what it had been without them?

A. M. Fairbairn

Religion an Opiate?

789   Mersault, in the brilliant French novel, *The Outsider*, has no sense of sin and no scale of values. He ends his days on a scaffold condemned for the murder of an Arab. It is climax of fierce unyielding despair. "Gazing at the dark sky, laying his heart open to the benign indifference of the Universe, exulting in the howls of execration by the spectators, he passes out." How different is the story of Allen Gardiner, the missionary to Picton Island at the extreme south of South America, as he faces the worst. His unburied body was found on the shore by the belated relief ship. The last entry in his diary is typical of all he wrote. The date is September 5, 1851, and he writes, "Great and marvellous are the loving kindnesses of my gracious God to me. He has preserved me all my days."

Is all this dope, as the Communists would have us believe? How much anaesthesia is there in the Kingdom of Christ that harnessed all the powers and all the days of Grenfell in an evangelistic campaign and sent him to the icy coast of Labrador?

How much escapism is there in the love of Christ that cares for all sorts of despised peoples and that commissions the brilliant Dr. Schweitzer to serve in the primeval forests of Africa?

How much illusion is there in the transforming grace which changed the sufferings of Bishop Berggrav, the Primate of the Church of Norway, under a ruthless enemy which surrounded him with a guard armed with pistols and truncheons. His tragedy was transformed into a glorious testimony to Christ's all-sufficiency.

Christ-controlled men and women are proof against evil in its most diabolical form. The promise of God has been tested to the hilt and it never fails. "In all these things we are more than conquerors through Him that loved us."

J. Leonard Clough

Religion Condescends to the Average Man

790   "The practice of high religion," as Walter Lippmann points out, "had to mean separation from human society and violence to human nature." Men expected, if they lived the lives of monks or hermits, to overcome all the fever of human passions—greed, love of money, love of power and every evil desire. Their expectation failed. High religion did not come that way. Their separated lives did not assure them self-control; their isolation did not serve, in any useful way, the needy world; their withdrawal did not procure them the mind of

Christ. For He did not live the hermit's life. He was a social being, mixing, eating and drinking with men, fraternizing with publicans and sinners and children and women. He suffered and defied all our temptations in open, daily contact with men. "High" religion there is, without doubt; and there is a religion of a lower or popular type. It partakes very largely of the spirit of the age; it condescends to the average man.

G. G. Britton

Religion, Cure for

791   When Jesus was crucified there was at Delphi in Greece a shrine to which seekers had come for ages, to get the oracles of the gods. Older than the Roman Empire, it appeared likely to outlast the Empire—a religion so seemingly permanent that when it began to dwindle men could not believe their eyes. Two generations after Christ, Plutarch wrote that men had been "in anguish and fear lest Delphi should lose its glory of three thousand years." Well, Delphi did peter out, but it was not irreligion that ended it; it was another religion that ended it, although to pit the Christ on Calvary against the authority and splendour of Delphi would at first have seemed insane. There we face a universal truth of history: the only cure for religion is religion—never irreligion.

Harry Emerson Fosdick

Religion, Destroying

792   Who destroys religion? Goethe was once asked, "What drives poetry out of the world?" He answered laconically, "Poets," and added, "Poetry will flourish when there are inspired poets." So in religion, the only people who can harm and slow down and destroy religion are religious people. People who call Christ Lord and do not the things which He says. People who make religion distasteful in the eyes of ordinary folk. Jesus bluntly charged the religious leaders of His day: "You are destroying religion, your out-look is not God's but man's. Your religion is outward form lacking inward spirit. You are at great pains to get minor details exact, but you obscure the central spiritual realities like justice and love. You shut the door of eternal life to ordinary folk. You block up the way to God the Father. You deny the dispossessed, the outcast, any share in God's mercy. You make religion a dull and dead thing, when it ought to be the loveliest and happiest thing in the world. No wonder ordinary folk turn from religion. You, who ought to be commending religion, are killing it in the lives of people."

Harold Bickley

Religion, Enjoying

793   There used to be a sharp story told of a stingy millionaire in New York who was solicited to contribute towards rearing a statue to Washington. The miser refused with the excuse, "I keep Washington always in my heart." "Well," replied the indignant solicitor, "I don't believe the Father of his Country ever got into such a tight place as that." This story occurs to me when I hear certain professors of religion complain that they "do not enjoy their religion"; they have not enough of it to enjoy.

Heber Newton

Religion, Ineradicable

794   The fierce old half-gods of blood and soil have taken the place of the God and Father of Jesus. Some form of religion seems inevitable, and the abiding choice is between God and idolatry. Whitehead, a modern scientist, sums up the process in a sentence. "The movement of thought," he declares, "is never from religion to irreligion, but invariably is from one form of religion to another." And Miss Sheila Kaye Smith, the novelist, says, "Religion may be suppressed, inhibited, or misdirected, but it is still there, colouring and directing human life, for good or evil, according to whether it is or is not given healthy expression." And there is no lack of proof before our eyes that the ancient word of the Psalmist is tremendously true, "Their sorrows shall be multiplied that exchange the Lord for another God."

Harry B. Miner

Religion, Loss of

795   Some years ago a remarkable book was written which was called *The Eclipse of Faith,* and in it the author imagined that the world awoke one morning to discover that the Bible had entirely disappeared. From every library the Bible had gone. From every house the Bible had gone. And not only so; but from every book the quotations from the Bible had gone. And as English literature at its height is made very largely of quotations from the Bible, there were blanks in all the greatest books. English literature was as good as ruined because the Bible had gone. And in that book Henry Rogers followed with great ingenuity and skill the consternation and the disastrous results which followed from the sudden loss of the great religious book of the world.

I am asking you to imagine an eclipse of faith more than that. According to

M. Guyot's notion, I am asking you to imagine not only that the Bible has gone, not only that Christianity has gone, but that religion has gone; and you have surrendered everything which now passes under the general idea of religion in human life. I am asking you, therefore, to suppose that men have now agreed that the word "God" can be neglected; have agreed that Christianity, like every other positive religion, has got away into the past. They are agreed that now we need not have churches or chapels; they can be turned into music-halls and public houses. We do not want ministers or preachers, they can be music-hall artists or publicans. The security for the public against ever hearing the name of God is that no one would be tolerated in decent society who mentioned it. You may be sure that no one in public speech will ever remind you that you have a soul; that no one will ever plead with you to come to God; that no one will mention Christ; that no one will speak of the Cross. You may assume that our little children will no longer be marked with the sign upon their forehead at the font: That when we are grown up and are married we shall be married at the registry office without any mention of God or of Heaven; and that when we die we shall be shovelled into the earth or burned in the crematorium without any impertinent references to immortality. You shall imagine, if you will, and consistently imagine, that we have got into that non-religion of the future which M. Guyot imagines; and that we have at last become a people without religion, a people without God, a people without worship, and a people therefore without hope.

R. F. Horton

Religion, Practical

796   When I myself was a little over twenty I walked into a meeting in the East End of London. I had never been at a similar meeting before; it was presided over by Mr. Moody. I had always thought that religious meetings were tedious and unpractical. I shall never forget that meeting, because I nearly went out. Some gentleman on the platform was praying at great length and worried me, so I got up to go, when Mr. Moody suddenly stood and said, "Let us sing while our brother finishes his prayer!" I thought I would stay and hear him, as he was going to speak; I thought he sounded practical. Of course, the old gentleman stopped instantly! Mr. Moody got up to speak, and the one feeling he left on my mind was this—Is the religion that I have (which was very little, I am afraid) really of any value? Before he went out he asked us to make up our minds whether we wished to serve Christ and whether we were serving Christ.

Wilfred T. Grenfell

Religion, Scorn of

797   Montesquieu, on his visit to England, observed that, in the higher circles of society, "every one laughs if one talks of religion." In Yale College, in the early part of this century, there was only one undergraduate present at a celebration of the Lord's Supper.

James M. Whiton

Religion, Second-Hand

798   Said a student at Edinburgh University, "I believe in God because Marcus Dods believed in Him." One can understand and appreciate that. And one bears in mind how, to begin with, all belief is mediated; our first approaches to it are made through the impact on us of godly men and saintly women, through the home and the Church, the Bible, and the hymn-book. It comes down to us out of the past as a rich inheritance and a priceless treasure. Only a fool would carelessly repudiate such a legacy or regard it lightly. But no one should ever be permanently satisfied with a borrowed belief, however rich and priceless. To begin with, belief is mediated; our responsibility is to make it immediate. Otherwise it may become an echo of an echo, the lifeless mechanical repetition of what others have triumphantly affirmed.

Robert James McCracken

Religion, Substitutes for

799   1. Art. There are those who would have us believe that art will supply all our nature demands. If we see good pictures and listen to delightful music, we shall be satisfied. But religion consists of something more than emotion.

2. Reason. Tom Paine argued strenuously for reason as a substitute for religion and professed his belief that the time would come when reason would destroy religion. But man has something in addition to mind.

> Dim as the borrowed beams of moon and stars
> To lonely, wandering, weary travellers
> Is reason to the soul.

Reason renders support to religion, but can never take its place.

3. Science has some remarkable achievements to its credit, and there are those who assert that it alone will prove the saviour of mankind. Yet there are many leading scientists of our time who are recognizing its limitations. I heard

Sir Oliver Lodge himself say that "science knows nothing of origins." There is nothing in science to contradict the Christian belief expressed in the sublime words: "In the beginning God created the heaven and the earth." Science has no gospel for the sinner. It cannot wash away sin, nor can it purify the heart.

4. Social Service. Here again we find that many declare they find an outlet for good desires and that nothing more is needed. But religion is more than the performance of acts of charity.

None of these succeed in satisfying both the desires of the heart and the perplexities of the mind.

W. B. Hoult

Religion, Supremacy of Christ in

800   I wonder if you heard about that World Congress of Religions that we had in Chicago many years ago? I believe there were there representatives of thirty-six religions of the world, and they compared notes; they looked for the various things of note and strength in their religion; and they stated their case. By and by it came to the turn of Joseph Cook, who has spoken from this platform, to state the case for Christianity, and he stood up there in that great hall and in a few words he stated the case for Christianity.

He dramatically pictured Lady Macbeth vainly seeking to wash away the awful blood-stain on her hand, and turning abruptly to one and another—to the representative of Buddhism, to the representative of Confucianism, to the representative of Mohammedanism, and to others, he said, "Is there anything in your religion that can wash out that sin-stain from the world?" and they each in turn shook their heads. And this great champion said, "By this token I proclaim the supremacy of the gospel of Christ. Christ alone can wash away that stain from the world." You are not surprised at the effect. The great Hallelujah Chorus began, and as they sang some who were present have told us that the great building seemed to rock under the sound of that Hallelujah Chorus. "And He shall reign for ever and ever." And as they sang the representatives of these various religions left one by one, and ere that great chorus had reached its final notes, not one of them was left. Just a picture of what it is going to be. "His name shall endure for ever."

George W. Truett

Religion, Survival of

801   If religion is to survive, it seems to me that it can only survive by becoming more religious, not less; by having more of God in it, not less. It can only

survive as it proves itself necessary to the individual man or woman who is not satisfied to think that life has no meaning at all except that one eats and drinks for seventy or eighty years and then makes way at the table for somebody else. Religion says: "For God's sake make a better world in all material matters. Be ready to toil and fight, and even to die, rather than let one little child grow up to be bitterly disappointed in this world which it believes to be so lovely and wonderful. But for God's sake, too, don't let that same child grow up to believe that it is just an animal, without a soul to cherish and a God to pray to, to give the people life—life to the full, enriched by all that good government and sound culture can provide—but give them something greater than life as well: give them a vision of the end and purpose of their life as children of a God who is their Father, and who must therefore need their lives for all eternity." If religion does not say that, what has it to say that any high-minded politician cannot say?

Ernest H. Jeffs

Religious Experience

802   The story goes that Huxley, engaged once upon some scientific work with a friend, was compelled to spend the week-end in a small town. "I suppose you are going to church," said Huxley to his friend. "What about staying indoors and talking to me about religion?" "Oh! I couldn't do that," was the reply. "I'm not clever enough to argue with you." "But what," said Huxley, "if you just tell me your own experience—what religion has done for you?" He stayed, and spoke of what Christ meant to him; and presently there were tears in the eyes of the great agnostic as he said: "I would give my right hand if I could believe that." Nothing convinces like experience!   G. R. C. Fuller

＊＊

803   Says Dean Inge, "The saints do not contradict each other. It is the theologians who do that—a very different matter." It will be found that these men of acknowledged and pre-eminent saintliness agree very closely in what they tell us about God. They tell us that they have arrived gradually at an unshakable conviction, based not on inference but upon immediate experience, that God is a Spirit with whom the human spirit can hold intercourse; that in Him meet all that they can imagine of truth, beauty and goodness; that they can see His footprints everywhere in nature, and feel His presence within them as the very life of their life, so that in proportion as they come to themselves they come to Him. They tell us that what separates us from Him and from happiness is firstly self-seeking in all its forms and secondly, sensuality in all its forms; that these are the ways of darkness and death which hide from us the face of God; while the

path of the just is as a shining light which shineth more and more unto the perfect day. As they have toiled up the narrow way the Spirit has spoken to them of Christ, and has enlightened the eyes of their understanding, till they have at last begun to know the love of Christ which passeth knowledge, and to be filled with all the fullness of God. If you dismiss the verdict of religious men as mere illusion, you have to dismiss, in that way, Amos, Isaiah, Paul, Augustine, Aquinas, Francis of Assisi, Luther, William Law; and if these men were not truly great men, I do not know whom to call great.

A. Herbert Gray

Religious Faculties

804   When G. F. Watts wished to illustrate the religious faculties he held out his hand. The thumb, he said, stood for Reason, the forefinger for Reverence, and the other fingers for Devotion, Faith, Hope.

Henry J. Cowell

Renunciation

805   Some years ago it was my privilege to meet that Indian Christian Sadhu Sundar Singh. He was a member of a high caste family. He went to a Christian school in India, and his father said to him one day: "You will turn a Christian." "No," he said, and to prove it, he burned his Bible. But he did become a Christian. He told his father and mother and they said: "You have broken caste. You cannot live here any longer; your life is not worth anything; you will have to go." And he did go. I heard him say that it was during the wet season, and the rain was coming down as he left the house clad in his flimsy Indian robes; and he sat all night under a tree, soaked to the skin; but he was so radiantly happy that he forgot his physical discomfort. He came to be spoken of as the apostle of India. He moved up and down the country telling the Gospel story. He went into Tibet; he was arrested; he was put into a pit; he was branded with hot irons and bore the scars all his life. When he was here in England he said: "I am going back to do what I have done. I am quite aware of the cost." A few years ago he disappeared; and he has never been heard of since. Undoubtedly he suffered a martyr's death.   W. Graham Scroggie

Repentance

806   During the first world war the Churches organized a Mission of Repentance and Hope. Horatio Bottomley, in *John Bull*, was incensed by this. His theme was: "What right has the Church to talk to our splendid men about repentance? They don't need repentance; they are saints, every one of them. To preach repentance to them is an insult." G. A. Studdert Kennedy, as a padre, saw this outburst. Armed with a copy of *John Bull* he went amongst the men. "When Mr. Bottomley says you are splendid fellows," he said, "I'm with him all the way. But when he says you're all saints! . . . well, take a look at one another," and on the crest of the roar of laughter he swept in to preach—repentance. We might do well to follow his words, and take a look at ourselves, our personal life of devotion and service, at the corporate life of our churches.

S. Myers

✳✳

807   Dwellers in a certain Scottish border county are familiar with a well-known landmark. It is a square tower built on an eminence commanding an extensive view of both sides of the Solway. It bears the name of "Repentance Tower," and was built hundreds of years ago by a border-reaver. Abandoning his wicked life, he spent his remaining years in doing good. The building overlooks the scenes of his former escapades. It still stands, the monument of a man's repentance.

Dora Donaldson

Reputation

808   We are told that a man once wrote the late Mr. Spurgeon saying that, unless he received from him within two days a specified sum of money, he would publish certain things that would go far to destroy the great preacher's hold upon public estimation. And Mr. Spurgeon wrote back upon a postcard, "You, and your like, are requested to publish all you know about me across the heavens."

Ambrose Shepherd

Resolutions

809   Jonathan Edwards, early in life, adopted a fivefold resolution—namely:
1. To live with all my might while I do live.
2. Never to lose a moment of time.
3. Never to do anything which I would despise in another.
4. Never to do anything out of revenge.
5. Never to do anything which I would be afraid to do if it were the last hour of my life.

✳✳

810   New Year resolutions are so notoriously breakable that they have become quite a jest amongst us. By the end of January most of us are laughingly confessing that our will-power has proven once again too weak for our good intentions. Indeed, as the years roll on, we more and more tend to take the weakness of our wills for granted, and cease even to "go through the motions" of making good resolutions; though perhaps we still mark the New Year by giving ourselves a sort of general promise of personal improvement.

Yet the brittleness of good resolutions is rather a poor subject for jesting: rather a dangerous subject indeed. When a man takes the weakness of his will for granted—when he no longer thinks it an important matter that he should try to be a better man in the new year than he was in the old—he is in serious danger of making both his life and his religion meaningless to himself, as well as unserviceable to his fellow-men. It means that he is ceasing to think himself important to God and man—and that is, in effect, something like practical atheism. A far healthier mood is that which is expressed in such a passage as this which Boswell quotes from the *Meditations* of Dr. Johnson: "I have now spent fifty-five years in resolving; having, from the earliest time almost that I can remember, been forming schemes of a better life. I have done nothing. The need of doing, therefore, is pressing, since the time of doing is short. O God, grant me to resolve aright, and to keep my resolutions, for Jesus Christ's sake."

Ernest H. Jeffs

Resurrection

811   Christianity celebrates Good Friday but once a year; the Resurrection is celebrated fifty-two times; every Sunday is the Day of the Lord. Dr. Dale, after his personal experience of the presence of the living Christ, used to have an Easter hymn every Sunday morning at Carr's Lane Chapel. A visitor one November morning heard the hymn given out, "Christ is risen: Hallelujah," and on his expressing his surprise to Dr. Dale was told this: "I want my people to know the glorious fact that Christ is alive and to rejoice over it, and Sunday is the day on which He rose."

John Bishop

✳ ✳

812   Hall Caine tells us that Rossetti was not an atheist, but simply one with a suspended judgement; in face of death his attitude was one of waiting; he did not know. Now the great work of Jesus Christ touching the doctrine of immortality was to convert it from a speculation into a certainty. The evidence for His resurrection, which carries with it the doctrine of our incorruptibility and immortality, is overwhelming. As one has said, it is the best authenticated fact in history.

W. L. Watkinson

Resurrection, Meaning of

813   Christ's resurrection is a pledge of personal immortality. Richter, desiring to invest atheism with its own horrid darkness, represents Jesus as returning to a group of shadows gathered in a church, and as saying: "I have traversed the worlds, I have risen to the suns, with the milky ways I have passed athwart the great waste places of the sky; there is no God. And I descended to where the very shadow cast by Being dies out and ends, and I gazed out into the gulf beyond, and cried, 'Father, where art Thou?' But answer came there none, save the eternal storm which rages on, controlled by none; and toward the West, above the chasm, a gleaming rainbow hung, but there was no sun to give it birth, and so it sank and fell by drops into the gulf. . . . Shriek on, then, discords; shatter the shadows with your shrieking din, for He is not!" If this were true, well might we say of man, "That petty life of thine is but the sigh of nature, or the echo of that sigh. Your wavering, cloudy forms are but reflections of rays cast by a concave mirror upon the clouds of dust which shroud your world—dust which is dead men's ashes. A mist of worlds rises up from the ocean of death; the future is a gathering cloud, the present a falling vapour." This is a poet's dreary dream. Christ's resurrection is reality! He did return, and returning, His very presence did proclaim that there is a Father's heart in the universe, and that it beats in sympathy with the suffering and oppressed. As He emerged from the charnel-house He said, in substance, "Though the Father permitted the cross and the scourge, He was not unmindful of His son; and though He may permit you to be tried and afflicted sore, He has not abandoned you, and in evidence of which witness My resurrection." Yes, the resurrection is proof of a Providence which overrules the sins of men, which cares for the oppressed, and which will vindicate the right, if not in this life, then in the life to come. Of the certainty of that immortal life the resurrection is the assuring pledge. Such a pledge we sadly need. The utterances of Mr. Mill, of George Eliot, of Mr. Conway, and of Mr. Emerson plainly show how insufficient is reason to solve satisfactorily the problem of existence. Left to the vague reasonings of our philosophers, our faith in immortality could never have been more than an inspiration; but resting in Him who has said, "Because I live ye shall live also," we look with confidence beyond this vale of death to those unseen hills on which the light of life falls forevermore.

George C. Lorimer

Resurrection of Christ

814 An Irishman once took this line. He was accused of theft. "At least four people have seen you take the article," the judge told him. "Sure, your honour," he replied. "They may swear to that, but I can bring you forty people who will swear that they did not see me take it." Negative testimony has no weight against the evidence of those who actually saw Christ after His Resurrection.

J. Calvert Cariss

Resurrection, Proof of

815 In *The Jesus of History*, the late Dr. T. R. Glover said, "Something happened, so tremendous and vital, that it changed not only the character of the movement and the men—but with them the whole history of the world. The evidence for the Resurrection is not so much what we read in the Gospels as what we find in the rest of the New Testament—the new life of the disciples. They are a new group. When it came to the Cross, His Cross, they ran away. A few weeks later we find them rejoicing to be beaten, imprisoned, and put to death."

Johnstone G. Patrick

Revelation, Christ and

816 An old thoughtful Hindu doctor, at one of Dr. Stanley Jones's "table talks" in India, gave this testimony: "I have been an agnostic, but I have worked my way from agnosticism to faith in a personal God. And Christ has been the path along which I have travelled to this faith. He is the supreme revelation of God."

Horace E. Hewitt

Revenge

817 Recently a Greek mother said to a Swiss Red Cross worker: "Last month I had three children, but there wasn't enough food to go round, so I had to let my daughters die." "How did you decide which of the children to keep?" asked the worker. "Oh!" she replied, "I had to keep my son so that he could revenge his sisters."

Leslie D. Weatherhead
From *Christian World Pulpit*, Vol. 146

Reverence

818   Goethe, discussing once the subject of education, said that however much a man might have learned, there was one more thing which he must have, and without which he would be something less than man. That was reverence. A young artist once came to William Blake for tuition; Blake merely looked at him and asked: "Do you work with fear and trembling?" "Yes, indeed I do," replied the other. "All right then," said Blake, "you'll do!" He meant that if anything great is to be achieved, there is need at the outset for reverence, for the sense that what one is about to do is a high and holy calling.

E. L. Allen

※ ※

819   B. M. Bower has a western story. It is the night before July 4th, and the ranch hands are faced with the task of branding hundreds of calves before a threatening storm breaks, if they wish to finish their work and get to the town in time for celebrations. They are all very cross and irritable, sweating and fuming at their heavy toil. At last, by great industry, the last calf has scampered "blatting" to his mother in the herd and the men set off at a gallop towards town. Presently they come to a river-ford, but find it impassable by reason of the heavy floods. They turn to a point higher upstream. Then they come suddenly upon the huddled wreck of a man lying in the fringe of tall grasses by the bank.

The lad turns out to be a hunted cattle-thief, quite unknown to them all, who has struggled off his drowning horse despite a fatal gun-wound in his breast. Between his gasping breaths he tells his story, begging them to see him decently buried so that his parents may never know his shame. The spirit of the range is touched. Every man is on his honour. And when the burial is over, without a word of suggestion or a thought of religion, regardless of Independence Day, the village girls, the dancing and the wine, every man turns his pony's head back to the round-up camp. They stood together, they risked arrest, they put their realities first.

Edward Beal

※ ※

820   Principal Sir George Adam Smith tells us that he was once climbing the Weisshorn above the Zermatt. valley with two guides on a stormy day. They had made the ascent on the sheltered side, and, when they had reached the top, exhilarated by the thought of the view before him, and the triumph of having attained the summit, but forgetting all about the gale, he sprang to the top of the peak and was almost blown over the edge by the wind. The guide caught hold of him and pulled him down, saying: "On your knees, sir. You are safe here only on your knees."

J. W. Roberts

Revival

821 When one of our Arctic companies of explorers went to search years ago for your noble Englishman, Sir John Franklin, among snows and icebergs—alcohol froze in a bottle by their side, and the thermometer went to 70 degrees below freezing point—the poor fellows, overcome with cold, lay down to sleep. Warm homes and delightful firesides mingled with their visions. But the leader knew that half an hour more of that lucid sleep would leave every one of them corpses on the ice. He roused them up. They said, "We are not cold; we only want a little rest." Half an hour more would have left them stiff. So their leader struck them, boxed them, bruised them—anything to drive off the slumber. Poor fellows! They staggered down into the cabin, but they were saved. The arm that roused them was the arm that saved them. Oh, immortal hearers, the arm that rouses is the arm that saves.

But, my dear brethren, is there not something like this in the history of the Church sometimes? When a church lies down and is frozen into such a spiritual torpor that the whole church becomes an orthodox ice-house, and the pulpit a refrigerator; when they ask to be let alone; when they say they are doing very well, they are satisfied with the pew rents, satisfied with the music, and, above all, satisfied with themselves—satisfied to see souls stumbling into hell over their own bodies because they want a certain sort of conservative dignity in their worship and in their Christian living—I tell you God sometimes sends to such an ice-bound Church as that a strong arm to stir them up, or a terrible calamity to bring them to their senses. When the Spirit of God comes down and arouses them, and brings them to reflect, the stiffening limb is aroused and works again, and those who have not prayed for so long that they have become tongue-tied begin again. The life has been kindled not by a human voice or influence, but kindled through the power of Christ's Spirit to save.

Theodore L. Cuyler

Revival, Resisting

822 When Dr. Norwood and Lionel Fletcher were given a send-off at the City Temple on their evangelistic campaign, Leslie Weatherhead charged the Church of Christ with resisting revival by three things: First, the selfishness of church-going people, who are concerned only with their own salvation and make no effort to touch or reach the Godless multitudes around them. Second, the idea that religion is merely an interest or a hobby, like music, or football. And, third, the fear of emotion. "When you talk sometimes to the University student type," he said, "you find that as soon as there is the slightest sensationalism, or anything verging on emotionalism, they develop a sort of protective armour."

W. Stuart Scott

Revolution

823   Dr. T. R. Glover tells a story of two children, brother and sister, who were debating the question: Which is the last book in the Bible? The little girl argued that it was Timothy, but her brother would not have that at all. "No, Barbara," he said. "The Bible does not end with Timothy. It ends with Revolutions." As Dr. Glover remarks, "A child's blunder will sometimes hit the truth," and that particular blunder reminds us that the Bible is essentially a revolutionary Book.

G. Holland Williams

Rewards

824   A lady once dreamed that she was in heaven. An angel met her and showed her around. They came to a palatial mansion and the angel said, "This mansion is for your coachman." "What! for my coachman?" asked the lady in surprise. I am afraid heaven will be a place of surprises. "Yes," replied the angel, "for your coachman." Shortly afterwards they came to a little cottage, and the lady wondered for whom was that. "This cottage," said the angel, "is your home for ever." "What, my home, impossible!" She felt extremely indignant. But the angel quietly answered, "Your coachman, madam, sent us on enough materials to build a mansion; you have only sent on sufficient to build a cottage. This cottage will be your home for ever." I am told that the lady was delighted— when she awoke.

W. Rowland Jones

Rewards of Faithfulness

825   There is a story of an old mediaeval monk who, on his death-bed, said, "It is true; it is all true," and they said to him, "Brother Ambrose, why do you keep saying that? What is all true?" And he said, "Well, although I have given up all my possessions to the poor, and although I have come into a monastery,

yet I never could really believe those words, 'Whosoever giveth up father, or mother, or houses, or lands, for My name's sake shall even in this life receive his full reward, and shall enter into life eternal,' but now I am dying I have found it is true, it is all true."   Frederick W. Farrar

Sacraments

826 It is said that once a clergyman was conducting a communion service. He noticed a poor woman, weeping, who, when the bread and wine were offered to her, declined them. He stepped down from the platform and coming to her, urgently said: "Take it, woman! It's for sinners!"   J. G. Bowran

⁑

827 Emil Brunner speaks of the gifted minister who lives by his own wisdom rather than from the Scriptures. He says that an audacious minister can so interpret the words of Scripture that the words speak the opposite of the intent. And if it were not for the sacraments his church would stand on no Biblical footing whatever. In such a case, says Brunner, the sacraments are the flying buttresses which save the Church from collapse. For the most audacious minister has not yet dared to lay his hands on the sacraments. The sacraments have a language of their own, and will speak no other even though the pulpit go astray.
                                                                        Gilbert Laws

Sacrifice

828 Anatole France tells of a juggler who, now too old to ply his craft at country fairs, had retired into a monastery. He saw there that all the brothers gave the service of their work freely for the love of the Virgin Lady, and his heart was sad, for he had nothing that he could give to her. One day he disappeared from the common-room, and the Abbot, visiting the Lady Chapel, saw there a strange sight. The old juggler stood before the figure of the Virgin, and he was throwing up the juggler's balls before her, and catching them in his hands, as he was wont to do in past days at the fair. The Abbot watched him, and the eager face that looked up in earnest supplication to the smiling Virgin, and stealing out of the Chapel, he said, "His service is richer than mine, for it springs from a loving and dedicated heart."   Angus Watson

⁑

829 Sir Harry Lauder's only son had just laid down his life in France, and one evening Lauder was sitting in the window of the house in which he was staying, looking sadly down the darkening street. He was brooding over his loss, when he noticed a tiny point of light spring up on the pavement opposite. By and by there was another, lower down, and this was followed at intervals by light after light. The lamplighter was going his rounds and behind him he left the light by which men might see the footwalk and reach their homes in safety. But it was as though a lamp had been lighted in the singer's soul. He saw then what his son had done, yea, what every gallant youth who had given his life for his country had been doing. They had kindled a light by which the path of peace and of deliverance might be seen. And though they might not share in the blessings they had made possible, their sacrifice was effectual.

J. W. G. Ward

* *

830   When a friend once wrote to Dr. Livingstone about the sacrifices he was making in spending his days amongst the savages of Central Africa, he made the spirited reply: "Is that a sacrifice which brings its own best reward in healthful activity, in the consciousness of doing good, peace of mind and the hope of a glorious destiny hereafter? Away with such a thought. I never made a sacrifice."

W. MacIntosh Mackay

* *

831   In Buffalo, a few years ago, a working-man was driving to his factory on a spring morning. He left at home a wife and five children. His station in life was humble. By the shores of a little lake he heard the cry of a lad for help. The lad was drowning. He rushed in and saved him, a twelve-year-old boy. In the act he lost his own life. When the news spread through the city, it was as though a miracle had been wrought. Life grew more beautiful. Buffalo was a better place in which to live since Walter Little went to his death. So valid did his conduct seem that, within two days, funds sufficient had been provided, voluntarily, to deliver the family from possible want the rest of their days and to provide an adequate education for each of the children. It seemed valid because it is just right that one man should take upon himself the welfare of a helpless boy. The validity of that sacrifice can be expanded to world proportions. The heart of humanity is susceptible to its appeal.

Miles H. Krumbine

Saint

832   Rita Snowden writes in one of her charming books: "I cling with real affection to the idea of a saint given me by a little Quaker girl. She sat in a beautiful church. She had never been inside a beautiful church before, and when she sat as quiet as a mouse in her tall pew and asked what the lovely stained-glass window was, she was told it was a saint. She thought she had never seen anything so beautiful. She was silent. Now she knew what a saint was. A few days after, she was crossing the park with a friend when they saw an aged woman with flowers and a full basket going her way towards the poorer part of the village. "There was a saint if ever there was one," said the friend. And the little girl was puzzled. On Sunday a saint was a beautiful stained-glass window, and now it was an old woman. How could that be? She puckered up her brow in doubt. Then it came to her; in the next moment she added, "Oh, I know, a saint is some one who lets the light shine through."

Horace E. Hewitt

✳✳

833   Dean Inge has told the world of his little girl Paula. She died when she was eleven years old. Her father wrote: "It has been my strange privilege to be the father of one of God's saints." She was ill for eighteen months. She bore her illness with astonishing serenity and patience. During the last weeks she asked to discontinue her child-like practice of saying her prayers aloud to her mother or her nurse. "If you do not mind," she said to them, "I should like best to be quite alone with God."

J. C. Bowran

Salvation

834   There's a delightful story of a poor woman who wanted to buy some of the flowers which grew in the king's garden, for her sick daughter. The gardener angrily repelled her. "The king's flowers are not for sale," he said rudely. But the king happened to overhear, gathered a bouquet and gave it to the woman. "It is true," he said, "the king does not sell his flowers; he gives them away." So, too, the King of Kings does not sell salvation; He gives.

G. H. Clothier

✳✳

835   There is a beautiful story told of Dr. Charles Berry, the famous English Nonconformist preacher, how one night, in the early days of his ministry, a Lancashire mill girl, wearing clogs, and with a shawl over her head, was shown into his study. "Are you the minister?" she asked. "Yes," answered the minister. "Would you come then and get my mother in?" But thinking it was a case of drunken parent, the minister suggested, "Wouldn't it perhaps be better to get a

policeman?" "Oh, no," said the girl, "my mother's dying, and I want you to get her into Salvation!" So the minister, without further demur, accompanied the girl to the slum where her mother lay dying. And as the Doctor himself told the story, "I sat down and began to talk to her about the beautiful example of our Lord." But the woman interrupted him. "That's no good, mister, no good for the likes of me. I'm a poor sinner, and I'm dying." "And," confessed Dr. Berry, "there was I face to face with a poor dying soul, and I had no gospel for her." A master of Israel, and yet he knew nothing of these things! Then he bethought him of the simple truths his own mother had once taught him, and he began to tell the poor dying woman the old story of the love of God in Christ Jesus. And at once the poor woman sat up excitedly, and she said, "Yes, now you're getting at it. That's the story for me." And as Dr. Berry loved to conclude the telling of that incident, "I got her in, and I got myself in too."

Donald Davidson

Sanctification

836   Dr. J. H. Jowett used to tell of a man who had lived a vicious life and whose face bore the terrible marks of dissipation. One day he was confronted by the Living Christ who became his companion on life's way, and gradually the old marks were erased. Jowett said "his face became like a cathedral window lighted up at eventide."

Cyril T. Follett

Sanctification, Need of in God's Work

837   Two or three weeks after Mr. Moody began his evangelical work he felt certain something was wrong, a screw loose somewhere (souls were not being saved), and he determined to find out where it was. He heard the leader of the choir impatient at their mistakes utter language not usually to be found in classical text-books. "I see where it is," said Mr. Moody; "I am trying to do God's work with unsanctified material." That choir-leader's appointment was immediately cancelled, and from that day onwards unmistakable blessing rested on the work of the great American evangelist.

George H. Knight

Saviour

838   William Jay saw John Newton just at the end of his life. The mind and the tongue of the old preacher were past their work. "My memory is nearly gone," he murmured, "but I remember two things—that I am a great sinner, and that Christ is a great Saviour." Those two things burned into the heart of John Newton and made him one of the great powers of the eighteenth century. Those two things, experienced and known by any man living, will make him a power among men. Strictly speaking, there is no man we want to know more than the man who knows that he is a great sinner, and knows also that Christ is a great Saviour.   Robert F. Horton

※※

839   "The life of Christianity," says Luther, "consists in possessive pronouns." It is one thing to say, "Christ is a Saviour"; it is quite another thing to say, "He is my Saviour and my Lord." The devil can say the first; the true Christian alone can say the second.   J. C. Ryle

Saviour, Christ the

840   When Napoleon was going with the troops across the Alps and making their way to the Plains of Italy, a little drummer-boy slipped down many hundreds of feet with an avalanche of snow, and it was utterly impossible for him to get from there without help. The soldiers who witnessed the accident looked back, but they dared not stop and go to his rescue without orders. The little boy commenced to play on his drum the relief call, and the soldiers heard him; and Napoleon himself was told of the accident, but the life of a little drummer-boy was of no value to him; so on they went and still he played the relief call. He watched the army fast disappearing and no help or relief coming, and when he saw there was to be no rescue, he began to beat his own funeral march, and many of the soldiers wept as they heard it, and after they reached home they told the story to their wives and children, and they also wept. That is not the way that God treated us in our fallen and lost condition. He heard our relief call and came to our rescue. He did not leave us behind to perish and to beat our own funeral march and die, but He came in Jesus Christ to our rescue and deliverance. His love was so wonderful that He came Himself to deliver and redeem us. "He loved me and gave Himself for me."

William Jones

Saviour, Need of

841   In the mighty play of *Prometheus Unbound*, Prometheus, the representative of humanity, is chained to the rock, torn by the vulture, and is told to expect "no limit to this thine agony till one of the gods appear as a successor to thy toils, and be willing to descend for thy sake into the sunless Hades and gloomy abysses of Tartarus." Socrates could see no hope for the deliverance of mankind until one of the gods should come down to take man's nature, and to suffer for him and to enlighten him. From Seneca was wrung the confession that man cannot save himself. Accordingly, from the earliest days when the Fall had introduced sin into the world, the self-slain, miserable exiles from Paradise received the prophetic hope of the seed of the woman who should bruise the serpent's head. In very truth the belief in the gift of a Saviour is involved as a necessary consequence in the belief of the love of God.

F. W. Farrar

Scepticism

842   When scepticism has found a place on this planet ten miles square, where a decent man can live in decency, comfort and security, a place where age is reverenced, infancy respected, womanhood honoured and human life held in due regard—when sceptics can find such a place ten miles square on this globe, where the gospel of Christ has not gone first and cleared the way, and laid foundations, and made decency and security possible, it will then be in order for the sceptical literati to move thither and ventilate their views.

James Russell Lowell

**

843   A medical man, who through pressure of a great sorrow had lost for a time all faith in religion, said to his clergyman, "If you ever meet with cases like mine, advise them to go and hear sceptics lecture. I went, and it was they who drove me back to Christianity." On the same principle we preachers should often ask God to save us from driving our hearers into infidelity. If the ignorance, unfairness, irreverence, and want of imagination of the lectures and publications of secularism should strengthen Christian faith, not less should the unwarrantable demands upon belief made by some occupants of the pulpit, the caricatures of Christianity they unconsciously draw, and their evident inability even to see the difficulties of thoughtful men tend to weaken it.

E. J. Hardy

Scepticism, Cause of

844   Dr. Marcus Dods once read a paper before the Pan-Presbyterian Council in London, on the question "How far is the Church responsible for present scepticism?" In that remarkable paper—which called forth much criticism—

occurred the following fearless utterance: "The unbelief within the Church is mainly responsible for the unbelief outside. Were the members of the Church leading a supernatural life, unbelief in the supernatural would be impossible. Were the supreme, living, present power of Christ manifested in the actual superiority of his people to earthly ways and motives, it would be as impossible to deny that power as it is to deny the power of the tides or of the sun. Offences come, and sceptics are made chiefly by the worldliness and poor, unreformed lives of professed believers." After uttering this sharp and solemn indictment, Dr. Dods adds: "These are grievous things to have to say, but we must look the facts in the face, and recognize our responsibility. If any conduct of ours, or if the tenor of our life, or any infirmity, be gradually impressing on the mind of some child, or youth, or wavering person, that there is little reality in religion, no duty can more urgently press upon us than an inquiry into our conduct and a strenuous endeavour to make our religion more real than ever."

Theodore L. Cuyler

Science, Effect of, on Belief

845   Science, so far from destroying belief in the importance of the present, should strengthen it. It teaches us that nothing can happen without producing some effect. Sir James Jeans has written: "Each time the child throws its toy out of its baby carriage, it disturbs the motion of every star in the universe." It is hard for the lay mind at least to believe that this is anything but a ridiculous exaggeration. It is equally hard to believe that every deed and every thought of every moment has incalculable consequences, which continue down the centuries. But scientifically it is so. There is no effect without its consequent result; no action which does not produce, like the stone cast into a still pond, its ever-widening circle of reactions. What happens in the present, therefore, is literally of immeasurable importance.

R. E. Thomas

Science and God

846   One of the ablest of contemporary scientists, Professor Max Planck, delivered a lecture on "Religion and Science." One of the points which he makes is that the greatest impulse to scientific advance in modern times has come from men who were actuated by a specifically religious motive. He instances Kepler, Newton and Leibnitz, all men who conceived their task as scientists to be that of "thinking God's thoughts after Him." The discovery of the laws of planetary motion was for Kepler a revelation from God, and the prayer with which he dedicated his work is that of a man awed by the greatness of the privilege

granted to him. "I thank thee, my Creator and Lord, that thou hast given me these joys in Thy creation, this ecstasy over the works of Thy hands. I have made known the glory of Thy works to men as far as any finite spirit was able to comprehend Thy infinity. If I have said anything wholly unworthy of Thee, or have aspired after my own glory, graciously forgive me."

Another point which he makes is that for him, as a working scientist, the law behind all laws is that Nature acts throughout as if it were governed by a rational and purposive Will. He takes an illustration from the passage of light from the stars to the earth. It is a well-known fact that when light travels in a slanting direction from a rarer to a denser medium, as from air to water, it is bent aside from its course. That is what happens when light travels from a star to our earth, passing as it does through many layers of atmosphere of varying density. But the significant fact is that, while the light-ray is thus forced to describe a zigzag path, it takes at any moment the shortest of all possible paths, just as if it were seeking the maximum result for the minimum expenditure of energy. As Professor Planck rightly urges, that is in no sense a proof of God, but it does mean that the scientist can work with the assumption that all things in heaven and on earth do act if they were ruled by Mind.   E. L. Allen

✳ ✳

847   Half a century ago unbelief was very aggressive under the influence of materialistic science. Not all the front-rank representatives of science then any more than now were definitely irreligious, but the prevailing assumption among them was that the universe could be explained in terms of physics and chemistry and of the operation of mechanical laws. But what is happening today? As Sir James Jeans put it, science has taken a hairpin bend in the past century, and ordered thought is following suit. I bid you take note that along with this change of attitude towards the mystery and majesty of the universe and our relation thereto there has come a new emphasis upon the value of religion and our need of God. It has little direct connection with the churches as yet, which makes it all the more significant. We are hearing on every hand from the leaders of thought that religion must be restored to its former central place in the interests of mankind, because without religion idealism cannot sustain itself.

R. J. Campbell

Science and Moral Values

848   There is an interesting paragraph in Max Planck's new book in the chapter on "The Answer of Science." "Science brings us to the threshold of the ego and there leaves us to ourselves. Here it resigns us to the care of other hands.

In the conduct of our own lives the causal principle is of little use; for by the iron law of logical consistency we are excluded from laying the causal foundations of our own future or foreseeing that future as definitely resulting from the present." In another paragraph the writer reinforces this position: "Science enhances the moral values of life, because it furthers a love of truth and reverence—love of truth displaying itself in the constant endeavour to arrive at a more exact knowledge of the world of mind and matter around us, and reverence, because every advance in knowledge brings us face to face with the mystery of our own being."

It is this freedom to "face the mystery of our own being" that science claims to have secured for us, and it is the allotted task of the present generation of religious thinkers to grasp this freedom boldly and explore with daring vision the realm of this "ego" over whose threshold science cannot pass.

Percival Gough

Science and Religion

849   Some years ago Lord Kelvin, the great scientist, gave an address to an audience in which he pointed out the proportion of scientific men who were Christians, and it was seen that the proportion of men of science who are earnest believers is equal to the proportion of lawyers and doctors and bankers and business men.   John Storrs

Science Needs Moral Control

850   Carel Kapek, in one of his plays, describes men caught on an island and mastered, and eventually massacred, by the machines they had made. It is not an untrue account of much in modern civilization. Science has given us power over nature, but not power to control ourselves. We are children playing with bombs and finding that they burst. We have created a machine which tears us. Nor is there at present much hope in the world. Even youth seems often burnt out. In the economic confusion each nation tends only to stand in its own threatened fortress telling of its hunger and need. Few speak of helping another nation. Our crying need is for some new vision of God, His Kingdom, and the trustworthiness of the human race.   McEwan Lawson

Scientists, Faith of

851   In our neighbourhood there once stood a little chapel built by an obscure Scotch sect who were named after their founder, the Sandomanians, and a mem-

ber of that sect was the most brilliant scientific genius of his day, Michael Faraday. On one occasion he was lecturing before a crowded audience of London scientists on the nature and properties of the magnet and giving some of his great discoveries. He concluded with a certain triumphant experiment which woke the enthusiasm of the house as I suppose it had never been awakened before. And during the applause the Prince of Wales rose to propose a motion congratulating Faraday. The motion was seconded and when they turned to look for the hero of the evening he was not to be found. Only a little handful of people knew where he was. He was at the prayer-meeting in that little meeting-house. He had slipped out as soon as the lecture was over to get away from the applause--to renew his fellowship with God.   C. Silvester Horne

※※

852   It is not true that science leads to unbelief. Whose name stands first in the modern era of science? The name of Sir Isaac Newton. Was he an unbeliever? He was one of the whitest, purest, simplest, most believing souls that ever lived. Whose name stands first in science in our own generation? The name of Michael Faraday. Was he an atheist? His friend found him one day bathed in tears, and asked if he was ill. "No," he said, "it is not that"; but pointing to his Bible, he said, "While men have this blessed Book to teach them, why will they go astray?" It has been sometimes assumed that Charles Darwin was an unbeliever; yet he wrote in his book on the descent of man: "The question whether there is a Creator and Ruler of the Universe has been answered in the affirmative by the highest intellects that ever lived."

F. W. Farrar

Scripture

853   After the death of Signor Gavazzi, a well-known orator who in his earlier years had been a priest in the Church of Rome, there was found a locket hanging around his neck, containing a leaf of the New Testament, readable at the 8th Chapter of the Epistle to the Romans. Italian mothers put a charm around a boy's neck in infancy which they believe will help to keep away all evil from him. On leaving the Romish Church, Gavazzi had kept the case for his mother's sake, but had put this chapter of the Bible in room of the charm. Light had come to him through that chapter. He believed that the true charm, the true deliverance from evil, was to be found there, and full of the Divine love and hope it revealed to him he lived and died.   J. S. Maver

※※

854   To use St. Augustine's words, "Scripture is a long letter sent to us from our eternal country, and we who hope in time to reach its shores should learn what we can about it, and about the conditions of reaching it while we may."

H. C. Ryle

Scriptures, Appreciation of

855   Daniel Webster tells an amusing story of a French infidel. In a drawer of his library he found one day a stray leaf of, to him, an unknown book. The book was the Bible, and the leaf contained the third chapter of Habakkuk. He was a man of fine literary culture, and he was captivated with the poetic beauty of the piece. He read it at his club in the evening. "Who is the author?" he was asked eagerly on all hands. "A man by name Hab-ba-kook, a Frenchman, I believe," was his reply. But the truth of the authorship was soon discovered; let us hope that it led to an inner appreciation of the Holy Oracles.

Andrew F. Forrest

Self

856   Edward Gibbon, the historian, begins his famous *Memoirs* with these two sentences, "In the fifty-second year of my age, I now propose to employ some moments of my leisure in reviewing the simple transactions of a private and literary life. Truth, naked unblushing truth, must be the sole recommendation of this personal narrative"; I wonder if this is not the greatest of all our self-deceits—that we imagine we can be entirely honest about ourselves!

James Black

※ ※

857   Arnold Bennett in one of his essays suggests we look at ourselves objectively. Suppose we were one of a small party sitting in a drawing-room when our own name was announced. Presently the door opens and we enter. Whom shall we see, and should we like what we saw? Should we like or detest our mannerisms, our dumb or voluble expression?

R. Morton Stanley

※ ※

858   Once, at a meeting presided over by William Temple, Sir Walford Davies was trying to teach some four hundred people to sing. He began with some well-known hymns, which, because the people knew them, they sang badly.

Then he tried some new things—a quartette from the Temple choir sang them first, and then the audience—and Sir Walford Davies said: "Don't try to sing: forget about yourself. Let the music sing itself." Again and again he pulled them up and said: "Stop trying. Just enjoy the music." At the end he said to the Archbishop: "That's good theology, isn't it?" Of course it is. Look away from self to God.

John Bishop

Self, Confidence in

859   I was talking with Secretary Stanton once. He was speaking of a prominent individual who was an able man; and he said to me, "That man, if all the offices of the whole world were offered to him to-morrow, would accept them, and he would think he could conduct them all."

Henry Ward Beecher

Self, Crucifixion of

860   We remember the heroic landing at Gallipoli on April 25th, 1915. Here is a story brought from the trenches of Gallipoli by one who served there as chaplain. It will be recalled that one of the worst problems of that cruel campaign was the water shortage. Shiploads of water had to be brought even from Egypt, and all through the scorching summer rations were desperately small. During a battle a senior officer met this chaplain in the rear trenches, and said: "Padre, have you any water in your water bottle? If so, you will find forty fellows further along that trench badly wounded and crying for water. For God's sake go and give them some." The padre found the pathetic little bunch of casualties, and, fortunately, his bottle was full. But some here may remember how little a military water bottle holds on a hot day. He went to the first man and gave him the bottle, saying, "Here you are, lad; drink. But, remember, there are thirty-nine others who want it as badly as you." So he went from the first to the next, and right along the line, and, "Do you know," he said, when he told us, "it was the last man who got the most water."

E. A. Burroughs

Self-Denial

861   Let me very briefly tell you a story, a memorable one, which may be new to a few of you, but which never leaves one's memory when once it has gained a lodgement there. The story comes from the strange period of the

Crusades, in which there was so strange a mixture of good and evil. You know how the Crusaders, after manifold difficulties and delays, at last succeeded in capturing the Holy City, and then proceeded to set up there in Jerusalem the Christian kingdom. They elected a king, and chose the chivalrous, the stainless, the peerless Godfrey of Bouillon. They offered him the crown; but he set it aside, saying he could not wear the crown of gold in the city where his Master had worn the crown of thorns.

Brethren, let those of us who would be real Christians look around in the world. It is still the world of that great city where our Lord was crucified. If we are disposed to hug ourselves in selfish ease away from the struggle and the troubles of mankind, then look steadily at that figure of Christ, and swear, in the inmost recesses of your moral being, where you swear those great oaths which through all weakness and failure really determine the courses of men's lives, that you will not wear a crown of gold in the city where your Master wore the crown of thorns.

Charles Gore

Self-Discipline

862 Not self-indulgence but self-discipline is the Christian rule. Did I say the Christian rule? If one wants to be or become something in any field of life it is the universal rule. The artist, the author, the musician, the scientist, the tight-rope walker, can only achieve success by innumerable renunciations, by an immense concentration, by killing out the smaller centres of interest. There can be no frittering of energy, no mixture of motives. "Every poem," Francis Thompson said, "is a human sacrifice." One of Ruskin's pupils told him, "The instant I entered the gallery at Florence I knew what you meant by the supremacy of Botticelli." "In an instant, did you?" said Ruskin. "It took me twenty years to find out." Ask any master of his craft for his secret—Einstein, Kreisler, Fosdick. You always get the same answer: Genius is an infinite capacity for taking pains. And you never have that without self-discipline.

Robert James McCracken

Self, Facing

863 Dostoievsky says that there are some things we tell the world about ourselves, some things we tell to a small number of friends, other things we tell to our personal confidant; there are certain things we only tell to ourselves, but there are things which we are afraid to face about ourselves and never look at. This Russian is right; he has diagnosed the weakness in most of us.

A man who has not faced himself has not learned to live. If there is anything we are afraid to face, that thing may hinder us from exercising the influence we should. I was passing a jeweller's shop, and noticed a little instrument revolving, and was intrigued, so I stopped to look at it. To my amazement, when I stood in front of it, it stopped, when I moved away it started again. It was a radiometer. When I stood between the rays of the sun and it, it stopped. How delicate. It is tragically possible for us to get between people and God.

A. Jeans Courtney

Self, Honesty About

864   Who has not shivered when seeing Sir John Martin Harvey as Sydney Carton in *The Tale of Two Cities,* regarding his drink-sodden features in the mirror and saying thickly, before he shatters his wine-glass to fragments, "Sydney, my boy, you're a fool!" Yet one feels there is hope for Carton from that hour. A man is issuing into the sunshine when he has the courage to see himself as he is. We recall the words of Phillips Brooks to the effect that when men pray they should not be content with calling themselves miserable sinners and leaving it at that. "Call yourself a coward, a liar, a cad, a thief, if you like, but never by such a general term as sinner."   Arthur T. Rich

Self, Inescapable

865   We must not only live—we must live with ourselves. That is a companionship we can never escape. When we are bored by people we can find comfort in the knowledge that we are not compelled to remain for ever with them. But when we are tired of our own company where shall we flee? I believe it was Emerson who once said: "I went to Naples, and lo! Emerson was there." This self is our Siamese twin inseparably bound up with us. We may not always be conscious of our own country, but it is always there. It is one of the compulsions of life that we must always live with ourselves.

The kind of self that we live with, however, is of our own choosing. We select the self that goes with us all our days. If, therefore, we find ourselves difficult to live with, it is our own fault. We have chosen badly.

Foster Sunderland

Self, Opinion of

866   "I do not care," said President Garfield, "what others may think or say concerning me, but there is one man's opinion which matters supremely, that

of James Garfield; others I need not think about. I can get away from them, but I have to be with him all the time. . . . It makes a great difference whether he thinks well of me or not."

John Waddell

Self-Reliance

867   The story is told that at Yale University the grey squirrels which hibernated among the trees near the college grounds were fed by the students during term time. Because they obtained their food so easily they ceased to lay in a store for the winter, with the result that during the long vacations many of them died of starvation. One student who loved animals left a legacy to the University to provide a constant supply of food for the squirrels. The colony is still there, but it has lost all of its old frugal self-protection; it must now either be hand-fed or it dies.

Herein is a parable for any nation which forgets the ultimate laws that govern life. "If thou hast run with the footmen, and they have wearied thee, then how canst thou contend with horses? and if in the land of peace, wherein thou trustedst, they wearied thee, then how wilt thou do in the swelling of Jordan?"

The great and urgent question for our young citizens of to-day—and upon them must rest the future well-being of our Empire—is "Have we the moral reserves to face a great crisis if, in the future, this is in store for us?" Personally, I have no doubt that this challenge must be faced by us all sooner or later.

Angus Watson

Self-Sacrifice

868   "The history of self-sacrifice during the last 1,800 years," says Lecky— and no one would think that he is prejudiced in favour of Christianity, "has been mainly the history of the action of the teachings of Jesus Christ upon the world. The Name which is above every name has evoked a passionate love during the course of these centuries which no other name given under heaven has ever called forth."

Caleb Scott

Sentry Duty

869   On a dark night in December, 1602, when the inhabitants of Geneva, lulled by peaceful professions, slept, but never dreamed of danger, a daring

attempt known in history as the "Escalade" was made by their foes. The Savoyards scaled the walls, and would have admitted their comrades, but for the discharge of the musket of one of the sentries. He fell a martyr, but the crack of his piece brought the citizens from their beds, and the city was saved, while Beza, then eighty years of age, returned to God public thanksgivings, announcing the 124th Psalm for singing. There is work for our sentinels to-day.

John T. Briscoe

Sermon, Making

870   As compared with to-day, it is interesting to note that not only did Gibbon write his millions of words with his own scribbling pen, but also he sent his great book to the press in "my first rough manuscript." I wonder if any publisher would accept such a manuscript to-day, with its natural erasures and insertions? The secret with Gibbon is that he didn't attempt to put anything on paper until he had it crystal-clear in his own mind. I am reminded of Stacy Aumonier, a master of the short story, who said, "A short story must be finished before it is begun. You must think it all out clearly and in detail before you begin to write." If we do that (say in our sermons), without needing to chew the end of our pen, we may hope to rival Gibbon in our own way. No one should start a sermon till he has his conclusion!

James Black

Sermon on the Mount

871   The Bishop of Lichfield tells the story of a Chinese Christian farmer who had been recently confirmed. This farmer went one day to see the English missionary who was a great friend of his. Directly as he got into the house he sat down and repeated by heart the whole of the Sermon on the Mount, about 110 verses of the Bible. At the end of the recital the missionary said he thought it was very good but added that he supposed the point really was not just to know the Sermon by heart but to practise it. "Oh," said the Chinaman, "but that is exactly how I learnt it. You see, I'm only a simple farmer and when I tried to learn the words by heart they wouldn't stick. So I hit on this plan. I learnt two verses at a time and then went out and practised them on my neighbours until I got them right. Then I went on doing it like this right through to the end of the Sermon. That's how I learnt it." That was just a simple Chinese Christian's way of taking Jesus seriously.

L. A. M. Parsons

Sermons

872   A sermon should be persuasive, Bishop Hensley Henson once said. "A good sermon must satisfy four requirements. It must be interesting or it will not be listened to. It must be intelligible or it will not be understood. It must be relevant or it will have no effect. It must be edifying or it will do no good."

John Bishop

※※

873   The *Congregationalist* says that it was Professor Park who first made the bright remark, "A sermon, to be preached a second time, must be born again." If so, how many lives some sermons ought to have!

Servants, Faithful

874   On the walls of a little church in the West of England there is a tablet erected to the memory of a humble woman, by a grateful master. It is recorded of her that "for 40 years she was a faithful servant," and I feel there is something fitting in this. If the instinct is right to place memorials in God's House to great statesmen and brilliant soldiers, why not to faithful servants?

H. G. Doel

Service

873   The *Congregationalist* says that it was Professor Park who first made keep the fertility of your soils you must use them, or others will." That is what we must do. If we would reap a bountiful harvest we must cultivate all our resources. We must minister to the people's need, and this must not be just on the physical level. We must meet the deepest need of the whole man, physical, mental, moral and spiritual. The challenge of Christ is that the harvest should be a bountiful one.   J. W. Price

※※

876   Through the lips of D. L. Moody, I first listened to the Master's call to me to leave the shallows, the beach, of human life on which so many pass their days, playing with sand, or, fearful and distrustful, fail to see that which alone makes the span of human life worth while, so losing its glorious opportunities to serve.   W. T. Grenfell

※※

877   A young artist was once called by his instructor to complete a picture which the master had commenced, but, through growing infirmities, could not finish. "I commission thee, my son," said the aged artist, "to do thy best upon this work. Do thy best." The youth shrank from so great a task, but the old man's calm, firm answer was, "Do thy best." Then the young painter threw himself upon his knees before the canvas, and, looking up to heaven, prayed: "It is for the sake of my beloved master that I implore skill and power to do this deed." Rising with deep emotion, he took the brush and began the work. His hand grew steadier as he progressed. His mind became engrossed with his inspiring task. Love for and enthusiasm in his work possessed his breast, till he had steadily and successfully completed it. The infirm but beloved master was conveyed into the studio to inspect the picture and offer his criticisms. After a steady gaze the venerable artist burst into tears, and, tenderly embracing his pupil, exclaimed, "My son, I paint no more." That youthful painter— Leonardo da Vinci—subsequently produced "The Last Supper," a picture which is still an attraction to worshippers of art. Let it be thus with us who are engaged in painting the features of Christ's character upon those about us.

J. Hiles Hitchens

✳ ✳

878   Dr. Leslie Weatherhead told his City Temple congregation on Sunday night that, twelve years ago, one of the most distinguished specialists in London gave him two years to live. He remembered seeing at about that time his portrait in a newspaper and being startled by his haggard appearance. It was a dark time and he would never forget it. He, frankly, did not expect to recover or ever to preach again. After months of depression and disappointment and sadness, he was able to resume that part of his work which consisted in interviewing people who were in trouble. The first person he saw gripped his hand at the end of the interview and said, "Thank you. You have helped me very much." From that moment, with the consciousness of being able to help somebody else, the tide of his own recovery set in.   Ernest H. Jeffs

Serving Christ

879   A famous preacher used to say that he would have been pleased to have blown the bellows for Handel, to have picked up the fallen brush for Michelangelo, to have held the spy-glass for Christopher Columbus, or to have carried Shakespeare's bag. If men count it an honour to do some humble service for the world's great heroes, what distinction lay in the opportunity of serving the Saviour of men?   Thomas Cameron

Sharing

880   Daly was a victim of the depression and was reduced to ordinary mercenary begging on the streets. He was standing one evening at the door of a down-town restaurant when a well-dressed couple came along and started into the restaurant. Daly stretched out his hand and asked for something to get a bite to eat. The man passed him by, saying he had no change, but the woman turned back and gave him a dollar. "Remember," she said, "when you are spending this you are eating Christ's bread." Daly wasn't sure what the woman meant, but he took the money and disappeared down the street. He had not gone far when he came upon another man who in turn asked Daly for something to get a bite to eat. Touched by his appeal Daly took the man with him into an eating-place and while they ate told him about what the woman had said. "What do you think she meant, when she said, 'You are eating Christ's bread'?" The man was no shakes at interpreting such profound matters, and hardly knew what to say. As they finished their meal, however, Daly noticed the man wrapping up a portion of his meal in a napkin, and he asked him why he was doing so. The man confided that he had a friend, a news-boy, who was sick and impoverished, and that he wanted to share his meal with him. So Daly, interested in this loving thoughtfulness, went with the man to see the boy. On their way a stray dog came up to them and wagged its tail friendly-like. Daly stopped to rub his glossy fur and noted that the dog wore a collar with name-plate attached. Realizing the dog was lost and the owner doubtless greatly concerned, he decided to take the dog to its home. The owner greeted him with both surprise and pleasure, and immediately offered him a ten dollar bill.

"Oh, no," Daly replied, "I can't accept any money." And then he told the man about the remarkable chain of events which began with the woman's remark: "When you spend this, remember you are eating Christ's bread."

"Well," the man answered, "I want to say two things. The first is, I want you to take the ten dollars with my gratitude. And the second is this: I have a place of business where I need an honest man: I have a job waiting for a man like you." Will anyone say there was a false ring to Daly's discovery of the law of sharing?   John W. McKelvey

※ ※

881   In the end, only by sharing himself can man save himself from hardness or heart-ache. Only by healing others can he heal his own deep hurt. Here, too, is the precious secret of self-escape by which alone man can ever win happiness, if he ever wins it at all.

It makes me angry for a man to preach at me. If he must preach at all, let him preach to me, not at me, or about something that does not interest me. That is to say, he could share himself with me, tell me his secret, if he has one, and what meaning or music he has found in the strange adventure of life. One day Emerson went to church, but he could not tell from the sermon whether the preacher had ever loved, sinned or suffered—had ever heard the laugh of a child or looked into an open grave. Such a sermon was a dud, because the man in the pulpit did not share himself. If he had ever lived, he did not let anybody know it.

Share your life, and find the finest joy man can know. Do not be stingy with your heart. Get out of yourself into the lives of others, and new life will flow into you—share and share alike.

Joseph Fort Newton

Silence

882   John Kelman has said that every preacher has to face the "two great silences"; and he describes them as the silence of God and the silence of the soul. It is in dealing with the first that the preacher becomes a prophet, interpreting the message of God to man. It is in dealing with the second that he becomes a priest, interpreting the message of man to God.

Morley B. Simmons

Sin

883   The modern world, we are told, is not troubled about its sins; it regards them as adventures in experience; and even if the consequences of these adventures are often disappointing or disquieting, there is no guilt attaching to them. Mr. Gladstone was once asked: "What is the chief want in the modern world?" and he answered: "The sense of sin."   Cosmo Gordon Lang

✳ ✳

884   It is significant that many modern novelists whom the multitude follow deride the realistic view of human nature upon which Christianity, the Bible and the Church insist. That view is very well expressed in the General Confession:

"Almighty and most merciful Father; We have erred and strayed from Thy ways like lost sheep. We have followed too much the devices and desires of our own hearts. We have offended against Thy holy laws. We have left undone those things which we ought to have done; and we have done those things we ought not to have done; And there is no health in us. But Thou, O Lord, have mercy upon us, miserable offenders. Spare Thou them, O God, which confess their faults. Restore Thou them that are penitent; According to Thy promises declared unto mankind in Christ Jesus our Lord."

Christianity asserts these as facts which must be faced. Clever, but irresponsible, writers have asserted that this is nothing but the essence of morbidity and have made it a subject of mirth and ridicule. And those who are only too glad to deny the fact of sin and to stifle their sense of guilt have hailed them as emancipators, and so have rejected one of the first axioms of Christianity. The late Mr. H. G. Wells attempted to by-pass these facts upon which Christianity insists. He tried to laugh them out of existence. He endeavoured to assure the world that the mind of man could rise superior to all such morbid thoughts. Before his death Mr. Wells found out that there were facts he had not taken into account. The title of his last book, *Mind at the End of Its Tether,* sounds like a wail of despair. Spurn the facts of human guilt and sin, and the corresponding facts of God's redemption, and the utmost effort of the cleverest brain comes to the end of its tether in a cul-de-sac. It is indeed true that "We must recover something of the old sense of sin which our forefathers felt and knew." Christ took the sinfulness of man for granted.

Charles E. Garritt

✳✳

885   For years it has been unfashionable to discuss the problem of "personal sin." It was not a respectable subject. That all was not perfect in a bewildering world might have to be admitted, but our failures were but the birth-pangs of an advancing civilization. Life's evils would gradually disappear when financiers had found the solution of our economic problems, when we had a finer education, and higher wages, and decent housing. Lord Passfield has assured us of the "inevitability of gradualness" and in time all would be well. The preacher hesitated to speak from the text, "The heart is altogether evil and desperately wicked" (Jer. 17:9). He was on safer ground in a discussion on Freud's psychology and the "inferiority complex." To-day we know where we are. There is no evil of which the undisciplined heart is not capable; no barbarism that has been perpetrated by man since time began is greater than the horrors that have been unleashed by so-called civilized man during the last few years.

Angus Watson

✳✳

886   I have heard of a poor woman who one winter's day was busy with her washing and was rather priding herself on the whiteness of her linen. She took

it out and hung it upon the line. The landscape was covered with snow. When she looked at the linen against the background of the snow she was disappointed and exclaimed sadly, "Ah, that is just it, nothing can stand against God Almighty's whiteness." Yes, dear friends; nothing can stand against "God Almighty's whiteness," as it shone in the perfect life of Jesus of Nazareth.

J. Tolefree Parr

※※

887   An Alexander who, in the name of culture, ruthlessly sweeps away whole populations. A Napoleon who can write to Josephine rejoicing in a victory which leaves behind a million murdered men. A Mussolini who bares his head at the singing of a Te Deum to celebrate the studied murder of thousands of hapless Abyssinians. There is not a civilization in the world which is free from the stain of Cain.

Frederick C. Spurr

※※

888   A Danish poet relates a dream of death. On his passing into the world beyond an angel met him and showed him a great golden book. "What is that?" he inquired. "It is the book of your life," was the reply. Looking closer he saw that there was some writing on the first page. "What is there?" he asked. "These are your evil acts," said the angel, "and you see that they are many." The angel turned the page, and the dreamer saw that the next sheet was more closely written. "These," said the angel, "are your evil words, and you see that there are more of them than there are acts, for a man speaks more than he acts." The poet trembled. The next page was still more closely written. "What are these?" asked the dreamer. "These are your evil thoughts, and you see that there are very many, for a man thinks more than he speaks and acts." With trembling voice the dreamer asked what the fourth page contained. The angel turned it over, and lo! it was black as midnight. "This represents your evil heart," said the angel. "For it is out of the blackness of the heart that all thoughts and words and acts come." Such a vision enforces the lesson of our need of pardon, that all sin may be washed away in the blood of the Lamb.

R. P. Anderson

※※

889   Adolf Hitler has left his mark on the theology of the age. The most influential Christian teacher of our day is Dr. Reinhold Niebuhr, who in a series of brilliant books has emphasized our human frailty in such stark fashion as to create in many minds a feeling of blank hopelessness. Man, he insists, is a

sinner, must always be a sinner to the end of time. Sin distorts his vision, corrupts his thinking, and confuses his motives even when the ends he seeks are relatively pure. "Politics are a contest of power, and in such a contest forces are never engaged for the defence of ideal ends if immediate ends are not also served." Individuals, Dr. Niebuhr allows, may perhaps be delivered from their natural immoralism, but mankind is irredeemable. A disinterested person is a possibility, but not a disinterested state.

H. Ingli James

❋❋

890   Says W. R. Maltby: "The world is what it is, not because of the superlative wickedness of a few bad men, but because of the ordinary selfishness, prejudice, ignorance, and laziness of mankind—that is of you and of me—which has worked up to this sum of wickedness and cruelty. If we see around us a world which cannot unify itself, cannot exercise its baseness, cannot even keep its wounds from festering, some of us remember a story very like all this much nearer home." If a man cannot unify his own life, need he wonder that the world at large cannot do the greater things?

J. D. Jones

❋❋

891   The greatest sin of the heart is hate. The greatest sin of the intellect is insincerity. The greatest sin of the will is indecision. The greatest sin of the spirit is fear.

James L. Gordon

❋❋

892   I remember, now over five-and-twenty years ago, staying in Yorkshire with a clergyman conducting some meetings in his parish. One night we were talking. In our conversation he said: "I will show you something interesting. Forty years ago I was going to preach one Sunday morning, and I could not understand why the words 'crimson' and 'scarlet' were used as describing sin. Near to my home there was a man just going into the dyeing business, when dyeing was first being introduced into this country. I wrote him asking what colours were most difficult to deal with in the process of dyeing." My friend went on to explain to me that he gave the man no reason for asking the question. I saw the letter he received in reply, in which the writer said: "The colours most impossible to deal with are crimson or scarlet. Black is easy."

Crimson and scarlet! These are the colours which cannot be dyed out. You can make them look like other colours for a little while, but presently the red

will work through. God says if men will argue with Him they will come to a
sense of sin as being crimson, scarlet. The sense of sin will become acute.

G. Campbell Morgan

* *

893   Coventry Patmore tells us of his little motherless boy who every evening
climbed upon his knees and romped and played. One evening the boy was
disobedient and his father sternly rebuked him and sent him to bed. A few hours
later Coventry Patmore rose to retire, and found his pockets full of the boy's
toys. A tender mood came over him; he went quietly upstairs to the boy's bed-
room, and there he lay fast asleep, his cheeks still moist with tears. The father
stooped and gently kissed the boy. We have all sinned against God, but I like
to feel that some day, when we sleep, God will stoop, and, in spite of ourselves
give to each, if we truly repent, the kiss of pardon.

Herbert Dunnico

* *

894   John Wesley made this entry in his diary on his seventy-second birthday,
"God be merciful to me a sinner."

John McNeill

* *

895   Mother, to little girl who had been sent to her room for naughtiness:
"Did you tell God about being so naughty and ask to be forgiven?"
    Little girl, firmly: "No, I didn't think you'd want the scandal known outside
the family."   Author Unknown

* *

896   Dr. J. D. Jones told how travelling in the train one day from Bourne-
mouth to London he was handed a newspaper cutting by a fellow-passenger. It
turned out to be an article by Mr. David Kirkwood, the Clydeside M.P., and
it related the life stories of some of the acquaintances of his youth. He divided
them into two groups of twelve. The first group consisted of the sons of well-to-
do people. The other twelve were sons of the workers and had been brought up
in a sort of puritanic simplicity. The twelve sons of the richer parents formed
themselves into a Club. "The Jolly Boys" they called themselves. Their notion
of being jolly was to travel up to Glasgow and drink and gamble and generally
go the pace. Mr. Kirkwood gave the life history of eleven out of the twelve
Jolly Boys (the twelfth he had not been able to trace). Every one of the eleven
went down in drunkenness and shame. Eight committed suicide before they

were forty. All of them were dead. Of the other twelve every one had made good.
I am not concerned, as Dr. Jones went on to do, to point the moral or adorn the
tale. I am concerned simply to point out that the way of life represented by the
Prodigal and the way of life represented by all who take the same road, is a
denial and an all too common denial of God. When we give ourselves to follow
the allurements of sin and the enticements of evil, when our steps are turned
out of the way and our heart walketh after our eyes, then have we denied God.

A. Stanley Hill

✳✳

897   Sin is transgression of the law, and a broken law holds me in its bondage.
There is an appalling sequence proclaimed in the word of God, and it is confirmed in human experience. And the sequence is this: sin brings forth death.
This death is not some penalty of remote judgement to be inflicted when this
life is ended; it is a death which begins at the moment of sin. When a man lies,
he begins to die to truth. John Ruskin said a day's communion with daubs
would impair a man's vision of artistic truth. That is to say, the artistic transgression makes the artist begin to die to the artistic ideal. And so it is with the
moral transgression; sin works benumbment, and the higher powers die downwards with every new iniquity. "Sin and death"; that is a sequence of "gluttony
and indigestion." It is a law of the Lord, and it cannot be escaped.

J. H. Jowett

✳✳

Sin, Conviction of

898   A young village artist, conceited, of course, has painted a picture that
would make a man crawl, and yet he thinks it is beautiful. His mother thinks
it is thrice beautiful, his aunts think it is four times beautiful, and they all
pamper him. Suppose, now, a professor should come in and undertake to say
to him: "This colour is hard, and these forms are almost grotesque"? He would
not believe it. What would you do? Take another picture, and put it alongside
of his. He has a true eye, and a true sense of colour; and though at first he says,
"Well, I don't see anything," he comes in every morning, and looks at that
one and then at this, and begins to say to himself, "By George, that is rather
harsh, isn't it? Oh, that I could get that graceful curve." Keep that picture,
which is beautiful in all its elements, by him, and he will burn up his own in
a short time.

There is nothing that is so convicting of sin as putting over against sinfulness
right conduct, the element of the beautiful, the holy, the true. It is not fear

which has been the principal instrument of striking conviction into men's hearts. That is not the most powerful and fruitful in producing a sense of sinfulness. The beauty of holiness, the wonder and glory of love, are more convicting of sin, a thousand times, to a generous soul, than the thunders of hell itself. Sinai may smoke; but let Calvary sigh, and say, "Father," and Calvary is the mightier of the two.   Henry Ward Beecher

Sin, Definition of

899   No better definition of sin can be found than that of Susannah Wesley. She said to her famous son, John: "If you would judge of the lawfulness or the unlawfulness of pleasure, then take this simple rule: Whatever weakens your reason, impairs the tenderness of your conscience, obscures your sense of God, and takes off the relish of spiritual things—that to you is sin."

John Pitts

Sin, Its Effects

900   A certain father had a wayward son. His patience was sorely tried, for all attempts to make the lad good seemed to have failed. What could be done? Pondering this problem one day, a new idea occurred to him; accordingly, he called his boy, and took him to a post in the garden. After once more remonstrating with him, he said, "Now, in future, whenever you disobey me, I shall knock a nail in this post, that you may see how often you do wrong." In course of time the wood got pretty well studded; there was hardly room enough for another nail. The father summoned the culprit, showed it to him, and asked, "Are you not sorry? Are you not ashamed? Oh, won't you try to do better? See! if you will really do your best to be a good lad, I will help you all that I can. Listen, for every right act which you do, I will pull out a nail." The effect was magical; ere long the post was cleared and the glad parent triumphantly exclaimed, "Not a nail left! Not a nail left! Thank God." To his surprise the boy looked grave; he turned pale, his lips quivered and tears came. "Why do you cry, my boy?" said the father. "The nails are all gone." "Yes," he replied, "but the marks are left." Ah, who of us cannot understand that? There is something responsive in the experience of each. Wrongs which we did years ago have been pardoned, but the marks are left in our memories; sins which we committed long ago have also long ago been absolved, but the marks are left in our reputation; follies very remote from today have been generously forgiven, but the marks are left in diminished social influence.

T. R. Stevenson

Sin, Original

901   Professor Niebuhr says that the rejection of the doctrine of original sin (or rather the fact) "has robbed our democratic social reforms of real wisdom." They treat man as a "harmless creature" for whom a little educational or economic adjustment will put everything right. That is a "sentimental" view.

E. Aldom French

Sin, Punishment of

902   I knew an Army officer during the Great European War. One night he left his mess to consort with a woman of the streets in a foreign town. Many men would excuse his conduct, although he was a married man. Only on the one occasion he so forgot himself, and when he finally returned home when the war was over the temporary lapse was only a memory to him. A year after, his first and only daughter was born, but she was born blind. He had contracted syphilis without knowing it, and the seeds of his ill-doing had blighted the life of the precious little soul that had been given into his charge. Every day as he watched the small groping figure as she felt her way about the house, he was reminded again of the action that had brought blindness to her. For him the teaching of the punishment of hell was the dominant one in his life. For his sin he knew he was forgiven and pardoned, but the nemesis of retribution had dwelt with him right through his life.

Angus Watson

Sin, Reminders of

903   The old Puritan preacher, Thomas Goodwin, in a bit of rare autobiography, which recalls hints given to his son, who, also, was aspiring to preach, says: "I do not think I ever went up the pulpit stair that I did not stop for a moment at the foot of it and take a turn up and down among the sins of my past youth. I do not think that I ever planned a sermon without doing the same thing, and many a Sabbath morning when my heart has been cold and dry, a turn up and down in my past life before I went into the pulpit always broke my hard heart again, and made me close with the Gospel for my own soul before I began to preach."

W. Jones Davies

Sin, Suffering Over

904   For a long time it was a subject of wonder and surprise to me why Burns should have taken such a grip of the popular mind of Scotland. I know he made the ballads of the nation, I know he wrote the "Cotter's Saturday Night," and the other poems which will never be excelled in your day or mine, and I know he sometimes dipped his pen in smut, and he wrote verses that are a shame to his name and memory. Byron put it truly when he said that "his genius was a mixture of dirt and deity." But I think I understand it better after having once more read his life. I think it was because Burns could not sin without suffering, that at his worst he never hardened his heart, but felt his own transgressions and mourned over them.

Samuel Horton

Social Justice

905   Sir Robert Peel once ordered a birthday gift for his daughter. It was a riding habit. A few days after it had first been worn the girl sickened of a malignant typhus fever and died. It was then discovered that the habit had been made in an attic in East London. The seamstress had used it to cover her husband as he lay dying of the same disease. Thus the daughter of a statesman paid the price for a social sore, sweated labour, which was permitted to fester beneath the nation's life.

Alan Walker

Socialism

906   Mr. Bruce Glasier says, "Socialism in truth consists when fully resolved, not in getting at all, but in giving; not in being served, but in serving; not in selfishness, but in unselfishness; not in the desire to gain a place of bliss in this world for oneself and one's family—that is the individualist and capitalist aim—but in the desire to create an earthly paradise for all. Its ultimate moral and its original biological justification lies in the principle, human and divine, that as we give so we live, and only insofar as we are willing to lose life do we gain life." But this is Christianity. This is the Kingdom of God. This is what Christ taught, and this, as we understand it, is what Christ alone can effect.

Robert F. Horton

Society, Changing

907   For society to be radically altered, we need a radically new conception of its form perhaps, and certainly we need the radical changing of individual men and women. To quote Professor Angus: "We all want a new order of things, but this can only come about by the work of new men and women. It

cannot come through mass conversions from the skies, or by an Act of Parliament. It will come by the conversion of the individual. Christ began His work as an individual, and we must begin with the conversion of our own disagreeable selves."   J. A. Hunter

Sorrow

908   When Prometheus was assaulted by an enemy, an arrow struck a swelling which had threatened his life. The swelling was opened, and so the life of Prometheus was saved. So I think it is the mission of the arrow of sorrow to open great swellings of pride and to cure the diseases of the soul. You never feel your dependence on God, and you never feel your own weakness until you have trouble.   T. DeWitt Talmage

Soul, Neglected

909   As Alexander Whyte was preaching in Free St. George's he mentioned the crown of thorns that was forced so cruelly on the Saviour's brow. He paused, and then, with an emphasis which those who heard it never forgot, he said, "I wonder in what sluggard's garden they grew." That is the most dreadful thing about a neglected soul. It is often in our neglected gardens that men find the thorns with which they crown our Saviour in derision. Let us see to it that they are neglected no longer.   James MacKay

Speaking

910   It is interesting to ask what makes a man a great talker. In the first place, he must have a fairly encyclopedic mind with a wide range of knowledge and an interest in men and things. In the second place, he must be quick, receptive and ready, catching points immediately and being able to give a quick summary or reply. Thirdly, he must have an "urge to express himself," almost a touch of exhibitionism. And finally—for the really great talker—he must have that indefinable and elusive quality we call "wit," to give point to his wisdom and judgements.   James Black

Speech, Extemporary

911   When Cato rose in the Roman Senate and held up a ripe fig, saying, "This fruit was gathered at Carthage three days ago," to illustrate the nearness of their enemies, and all Rome exclaimed that Carthage must be destroyed, we

should find it hard to imagine that Cato, before he did it, climbed into a box four feet square, and which came up almost to his armpits, and that he drew out of his pocket a very illegible manuscript, and glasses, then adjusted his specs, and then bent down his head, looked twice at his paper to see if he was right, then muttered, "Brethren, this fig, no, this fruit,—Brethren, this fruit was gathered—I say was gathered,—at Carthage three days ago," and then fumbled in his pocket till he found the fig, and then laid it out upon the board on top of the box where he rested his manuscript. It would be hard for us to imagine that this was eloquence; and we should feel very certain that, if this course had been taken, all Rome would have shouted, "Cato must be destroyed! Cato must be destroyed!"   Author Unknown

Standards

912   It is said then when Michelangelo corrected the drawings of his students he would take the brush and sketch the scene that his pupil was trying to reproduce. Side by side the great master's work stood with that of the learner. Has not that been the Father's method of correcting the faulty attempts of His human children? The perfect picture has been painted on the canvas of our human nature. In all points He was made like His brethren. A life has been lived, not in cloistered quietness, but in labour of body and soul, in hunger and thirst, in homelessness and loneliness, in sorrow and struggle, amidst the opposition of foes and the misunderstanding of friends; a life that passed for a time into the dread darkness through the gateway of a shameful death, but which is felt to be the one truly ideal life. What is unregenerate and degenerate in human life stands out in dark contrast against the stainless beauty of the life of Jesus. What many a student felt in Michelangelo's studio, that, and far more than that, have many of us felt as we have read the story of the ministry of Jesus.

T. H. Champion

State, Duties to

913   After the fall of France, a Frenchman writing in a New York paper and saddened at the fate which had overtaken his country, attributed the French lack of morale and endurance to the same sort of thing. "My people looked upon the State as a milch cow which would never run dry. They concentrated upon their dues and not upon their duties," and he pleaded with Americans to take heed while there was still time.

W. Edwin Bywater

Statesmanship

914   Dr. Frank Gunsaulus has written that true statesmanship consists in discovering the way in which God is going, and then moving things out of the way for Him.

A. E. Willmott

Stewardship

915   When John Wesley preached his great sermon on stewardship, his first division was "Make all you can," and a deacon farmer down in front said, "That is right." The second division was "Keep all you can, save all you can," and the farmer said more emphatically, "That is better." And the third division of the sermon was, "Give all you can," and the farmer's face dropped and he said, "That has spoiled the sermon." Now that farmer had a vision of steward-ship in making and in saving, and that is Scriptural; but he lost the vision, if he ever had it, of giving.

A. C. Dixon

✷ ✷

916   A London journalist, in one of his books, quotes a text which he says has been heard often in Parliament as an argument to take over the property of others. This is the text: "The earth is the Lord's." And he suggests that those who make use of the text have given no promise that the Lord would get much of the earth if they got possession of it.

D. W. Montgomery

Stillness and God

917   There is a connection between God and stillness. Will you allow me to make one personal reference? There is a sense in which God never seems so near to me as when everything about me is hushed and I myself am quiet and still. I do not say He is any nearer then than when I am pressed by many duties, but it is in these moments I myself am most conscious of His presence. Now and again, when I can get away from all the stir and bustle of life and there comes perfect calm, I seem to know that God is real. If that were only my own isolated experience it would be hardly worth while to mention it. I discover, however, that it is the experience of many men, and of men quite different from myself in temperament and outlook. It was in lonely fellowship with nature that Wordsworth felt the presence, the sense sublime, of a being

deeper than nature. It is so with men of a scientific mind. A brilliant young scientist who often questioned God's existence told me once there was an experience in his life when his doubt was shaken, and he felt that, after all, God was real. They were moments in which he was alone under a starry sky. This is true again and again of men of action. Captain Peary, who discovered the North Pole, once said it was impossible for a man to spend his life amid the mysterious loneliness of miles of unbroken ice without feeling that there is a God. A famous Alpine climber in one of his books tells of a mountaineer who, resting on a height half-way up a mountain, scribbled idly on the rocks, "There is no God"; but when he reached the top and saw beneath him range after range of snow-clad peaks, there crept into his soul such a mysterious sense of awe that as he descended he changed what he had previously written into: "The fool hath said in his heart there is no God." In the absolute stillness of that mountain summit, far away from the rush of human life that man's soul had discovered God. We find, then, this interesting and most suggestive fact, that men of quite different types, the preacher, the poet, the strong man of action, when they get away from the turmoil of human strife and activity into the great solitudes, find that the reality of God grips them with convincing force. There is a connection of some sort between knowledge and stillness.

Harry Bisseker

Success

918   In their unredeemed days, it is said, the South Sea Islanders launched their canoes by using the dead bodies of their enemies as rollers. There are lots of people like that: they have launched out to what they called success over the sufferings of others.   Leslie E. Cooke

* *

919   We have a phrase that nothing succeeds like success. But a hard-headed business man who knows history has amended it. "Nothing recedes like success," he says. The judges who condemned Socrates, Jesus, St. Joan and Hugh Latimer, the conquerors who ruled by violence, the men of slick methods and easy consciences—they have had their little day of cheap victory. They thought they had closed the case, but nothing recedes like success. So the psalmist found. "I went into the sanctuary of God: then I understood. Surely thou didst set them in slippery places," and from a later age we hear words with the authentic Christian note, "The things which are seen are temporal; but the things which are not seen are eternal."

R. G. Martin

Success in Pulpit

920   You remember those oft-quoted words of C. H. Spurgeon: "People have often asked me, 'What is the secret of your success?' I always reply that I have no other secret but this, that I have preached the gospel—not about the gospel—but the gospel; the full, free, glorious gospel of the Living Christ, who is the Incarnation of the Good News. Preach Christ, brethren, always and everywhere."

J. H. Vincent

Suffering

921   Bacon thought of God sitting serenely remote from suffering. "In this world God only and the angels may be spectators." Bacon had forgotten his Bible. "When thou passest through the waters I will be with thee and through the rivers, they shall not overflow thee. . . . Fear not, for I am with thee." No one who has grasped the meaning of the Cross and of Christ's deathless words, "He that hath seen Me hath seen the Father," thinks of a remote God. He is in your tragedy with you, sharing with you His spiritual power and leading you on to victory.   J. Leonard Clough

❋❋

922   A musician ordered of a violin maker the best instrument he could make. At length the musician was sent for to come and try his instrument. As he drew the bow across the strings his face clouded and he became angry. Lifting the instrument he dashed it to pieces on the table, paid the price he had contracted to pay, and left the shop. But the violin maker gathered up the broken pieces and set to work to remake the instrument. Again the musician was sent for, and drew the bow across the strings as before. The violin was perfect. He asked the price. "Nothing," the violin maker replied. "This is the same instrument you broke to pieces. I put it together, and out of the shattered fragments this perfect instrument has been made." This is the way God does ofttimes with men's lives. They are not what they ought to be. Outwardly they may seem very beautiful, but no sweet music comes from them. They are lacking in spirituality, and the likeness of Christ does not appear in them. Then God permits them to be broken in sorrow or suffering, and with the fragments makes a new life which yields praise, honour and blessing.

J. R. Miller

❋❋

923   Those who heard Jenny Lind, the sweet singer of Stockholm, have written of the wonderful quality of her voice and the charm of the songs she sang. Yet few realize that she owed as much to the school of suffering and of sorrow as to the Academy where her powers were developed. Her childhood was full of sadness. The woman with whom she lived locked her in the room each day while she went out to work, and the only means of whiling away the long hours was for the child to sit by the window and sing to herself. One day a passer-by heard the voice of the unseen singer. He detected in it possibilities, for he was a music-master in the city. He called a friend to his side, and together they listened to this wonderful voice within. They got in touch with the child's guardian and made arrangements for the almost friendless girl to be given her chance. There were many difficulties to be overcome, but step by step she mounted the ladder of fame. She astounded London and Paris, Vienna, Berlin, and New York. Some say there never was such a voice, trilling like the thrush, pure as the note of the lark. But those who knew her best realized how the sorrows of her childhood gave a richness and depth to her song that otherwise were unattainable. She herself once wrote:

> In vain I seek for rest
>   In all created good:
> It leaves me still unblest,
>   And makes me cry for God.
> And safe at rest I cannot be
>   Until my heart finds rest in Thee.

J. W. G. Ward

✳✳

924   Sundar Singh once was put in prison in Nepal for preaching Christ; so he preached to the other prisoners, as did Paul on a similar occasion. The governor then had him thrust into solitary confinement, in a foul-smelling cowhouse tied by hands and feet, with clothing taken away, and leeches thrown on his body. He lifted up his heart to God, and sang His praises, "Though I am a very poor singer," he adds. His accuser said to the jailer, "What do you think of this man? He is so happy though he is suffering." "He must be mad," the jailer replied. The jailer went to the governor. "Our purpose is not being fulfilled," he said. "We hoped with this punishment to make this man sorry and leave off preaching, but we are only adding to his happiness." Then the governor said, "He is only a madman: let him go."

P. N. Bushill

✳✳

925   You remember Charles Dickens' beautiful story of the poor little father whose one joy in his life was the love of his blind child. He lived in poverty and served a brutal employer who often came near to breaking his heart, but he managed to keep these things from the growing girl. Whatever he might have to endure he was always cheerful and buoyant to her, and never allowed her to think he had a care in the world. Then came a day when the child, who had now attained to maturity, was to receive her sight by the performance of an operation which, at an earlier time, would have been impossible. The brave, simple-minded man consented to it, and then lived in dread as to what those eyes would discover. His child had pictured him a handsome man; he was small and ugly. She had thought of the home as a house beautiful; it was poor and mean. She had believed that everything was well with him in his daily toil; she would now know that he had stinted and starved himself to provide her with comforts and pleasures. The fateful day came, and with it the revelation; the eyes of the girl were opened, but they were opened to something the father himself had never seen—the glory that had crowned his life of self-devotion.

Probably there are some to whom this parable is no parable but the simple truth. God has opened your eyes to see something which but for the darkness and struggle of earth you would never have seen, and that is the glory that rests upon the brows of those near and dear to you who have taught you most that you know about the sacred meaning of life.   R. J. Campbell

✳✳

926   Dr. George Matheson experienced the sense of a great loss and the pang of a great sorrow. In the darkness of that moment he wrote the hymn, "O Love that wilt not let me go," a composition which takes its place among the permanent possessions of the Christian Church. "My heart was composed," he related afterwards, "in the Manse of Innellan, on the evening of June 6, 1882. I was at that time alone . . . the rest of the family were staying overnight in Glasgow. Something had happened to me which was known only to myself and which caused me the most severe mental suffering. The hymn was the fruit of that suffering."

> O joy that seekest me through pain,
> I cannot close my heart to Thee;
> I trace the rainbow through the rain
>   And feel the promise is not vain
>   That morn shall tearless be.

Horace E. Hewitt

✳✳

927   "I cannot see," Huxley once wrote to Kingsley, "one shadow or tittle of evidence that the great Unknown underlying the phenomena of the Universe stands to us in the relation of a Father—loves us, and cares for us as Christianity asserts." "And," comments George Jackson, lifting the discussion to the highest level of all, "perhaps if I looked for evidence only where Huxley looked, I should say the same; but I have seen Jesus, and that has made all the difference. It is He who has made me sure of God. He felt, as I have never felt, the horrid jangle and discord of this world's life; sin and suffering tore His soul as no soul of man was ever torn; He both saw suffering innocence and Himself suffered being innocent, and yet to the end He knew that love was through all and over all, and died with the name 'Father' upon His lips. . . . And, therefore, though the griefs and graves of men must often make one dumb, I will still dare to believe with Jesus that God is good and 'Love creation's final law.' "

Robert James McCracken

✳✳

928   It is told of Robert Hall, the great preacher, that, suffering much from disease, he was forced often to fling himself down and writhe in paroxysms of agony on the ground. From these he would rise with a smile, saying, "I suffered much, but I did not cry out, did I? Did I cry out?"

John Waddell

Suffering, Fellowship in

929   Mr. Philip Inman in *The Human Touch* tells of a Bermondsey stoker who had to undergo an operation. In the hospital he shared a room with a German and at first rejected rudely all the approaches of the other to friendliness—his reason being that in the last war his son had been killed in battle. "Was he your only son?" asked the other. "No, I've two left, but they weren't old enough to fight." In a broken voice the German replied, "You've got two boys left. Both my boys were killed and I've no son left." "I'd like to take back all I've said," muttered the stoker, "you've got my sympathy." Later, when the stoker's life was in danger through loss of blood, it was the German who gave a pint of his own for transfusion. May we not hope that the sufferings now being undergone by the peoples of many lands, both friends and foes, may eventually help to a larger understanding?   J. Ireland Hasler

Suffering, Overcoming

930   Katherine Mansfield, the wife of Middleton Murry, and a creative literary artist in her own right, was a great sufferer, and in her journal has left

a noble passage, "in which," as the Chaplain of Marlborough College has written in his helpful little book on the Beatitudes, "she seems to have sounded the deeps of the doctrine of Jesus."

"I do not want to die without leaving a record of my belief that suffering can be overcome. For I do believe it. What must one do? There is no question of what is called 'passing beyond it.' One must submit. Do not resist. Take it. Be overwhelmed. Accept it fully. Make it part of life. Everything in life that we really accept undergoes a change. So suffering must become love. That is the mystery. This is what I must do. I must give to the whole of life what I gave to one. . . . The fearful pain will fade. I must turn to work: must put my agony into something, change it. 'Sorrow shall be turned into joy.' It is to lose oneself more utterly, to love more deeply, to feel oneself part of life—not separate."

David A. MacLennan

Suffering, Sensitiveness to

931   William Lloyd Garrison saw an insufferably bitter situation and he helped to sweeten it with his whole might. But it cost terrifically. Mobbed, hunted, half-starved during one period of his career, he would not retreat a single inch, and he would be heard. Life is sensitiveness, and the more deeply we live in the company of Jesus the more sensitive we become, not for self, but for others. Hutton said of F. D. Maurice, that valiant colleague of Charles Kingsley, that he felt "a sort of self-reproachful complicity in every sinful tendency of his age." The hope of the world lies in men and women whose consciences have been made so sensitive that they experience that sense of "self-reproachful complicity" in the evil tendencies of our age. The blessed are always those who find it perfectly intolerable to pretend to be religious without caring for those who suffer.

David A. MacLennan

Sunday

932   Lord Macaulay said in one of his Parliamentary speeches, "That day is not lost while industry is suspended, while the plough lies in the furrow, while the Exchange is silent, while no smoke ascends from the factory; a process is going on quite as important to the wealth of nations as any process which is performed on more busy days. Man, the machine of machines, the machine compared with which all the contrivances of the Watts and the Arkwrights are worthless, is repairing and winding up, so that he returns to

his labours on the Monday with clearer intellect, with livelier spirits, with renewed corporeal vigour. Therefore it is that we are not poorer, but richer, because we have through many ages rested from our labour one day in seven."

John Macmillan

Sunday School

933   Think of the Gloucester printer, Robert Raikes, in 1781—a man of ordinary endowments, of ordinary position, ordinary in everything, except the priceless gift of a loving Christian heart. He saw the ragged children rioting about on Sunday in the streets of Gloucester. Hundreds of others must have noticed the same thing, but it had never even occurred to them to remedy the mischief. Convinced that crime is the daughter of ignorance, he hired four poor women to teach those children the Bible and the catechism on Sundays. I never pass his statue on the Thames Embankment without a sense of pleasure. "As I asked, Can nothing be done?" he tells us a voice answered "Try." "I did try," he says, "and see what God hath wrought." There are now Sunday-school teachers by tens of thousands all over the world; but, humanly speaking, they all owe their origin to that one word "Try," so softly whispered by some voice Divine to the loving and tender conscience of Robert Raikes a hundred years ago.

F. W. Farrar

Sunday School, Teaching

934   Just as the twig is bent the tree inclines; poison the fountain and the river will be impure. The Sunday-school teacher has been compared to the pointsman at the railway switches, who by a slight touch can send one train rushing to Aberdeen, and another to Hull. The late President Garfield used to say that there was a certain court-house in his native town of which the roof was a natural watershed, so that a single breath of air or the flutter of a bird's wing was enough to decide whether a water drop should find its way to the torrid Gulf of Mexico or the frozen Gulf of St. Lawrence. Even such is the work of a Sunday-school teacher. "Like as the arrows in the hand of a giant, even so are the young children."   F. W. Farrar

✲✲

935   Mr. Moody tells us how, when once he was an ignorant, ragged, shoeless boy in the streets of Chicago, he found his way to a Sunday school by one of those unseen providences which men nickname chance. He was shy and sensitive, and very nervous lest the other boys should laugh at him because he could not find his places in the Bible. The teacher observed his embarrassment, and with gentle and silent tact saved him from his trouble by finding the places for him. But for that little kindness he might never again have entered the Sunday school; but for that little nameless act of love and sympathy a career of memorable beneficence might have been lost to the world.

F. W. Farrar

Sunshine

936 We may not agree with the writer of Ecclesiastes in all that he says, for he has been too well off and gives one the impression that he is weary and sated with life's many gifts. But when he says: "Truly the light is sweet and a pleasant thing it is for the eyes to behold the sun," his words strike a note of agreement in almost every heart. Poets and plain people are at one with him here, the children playing in the fields, the aged sitting at the window or the cottage door, young men and women—all rejoice with Wordsworth to declare: "The sunshine is a glorious birth."

We can all sympathize, therefore, with Diogenes in his famous reply to Alexander the Great. That youthful world-conqueror, you remember, came to visit the cynic philosopher in his tub, and asked what gift he would like to have as a token of interest and respect. What did the man reply? Nothing but this: "Will you stand a little out of my sunshine?"

D. W. Langridge

Surrender

937 There is a quaint story which Dr. D. L. Moody tells in one of his books. A lawyer came to him at the close of a mission and held out a document, saying: "I want you to take this." Dr. Moody looked at the sealing wax and red tape, and said: "Take it away. It has nothing to do with me, for I don't understand those things." "But it has to do with you," said the lawyer. "It arises out of your mission." Moody tried to look intelligent, and failed. He said: "I give it up. What is it?" The lawyer said: "It is a deed of gift, sir. I have been attending your mission night by night. You kept on saying, Give yourself to God. I felt like it, and I wanted to be right with God, but I did not clearly understand it, and nothing happened. Then last night, sir, you were more insistent than ever that we should give ourselves to God. I went home thinking, thinking, thinking about it. All of a sudden it flashed upon me: Why, again and again in your professional work, you have executed a deed of gift for a client. A certain sum has been transferred to a child, or a friend. So I said, Do it for God. And, Mr. Moody, this morning when I went down to the office I got a deed of gift drawn up. I gave my life to my Saviour. Then, sir, I called my office staff in and got them to witness to my signature. So here is my deed. My life for God." Curious? Quaint? I do not know why it should be. I do not know why we should not treat our Lord as sensibly (may I say it reverently) as we treat one another in such matters.

George Allen

Sympathy

938 How difficult it is to keep our sympathies fresh. I remember the first funeral I conducted. It was that of a little child, and the parents were heart-broken. I stumbled over that service; I am sure I left something out, and I nearly broke down. I am not afraid now I shall break down, I am rather afraid that I shan't; that familiarity with sorrow will mean that I shall be no earthly good to people in trouble. To stand between God and men as inter-cessor is at once a privilege and a terrific responsibility. Standing between I may stand in the way.   F. I. Riches Lowe

※ ※

939 Some years ago, just after Mr. Gladstone had been staying at Dollis Hill, I was visiting a poor sufferer who kept a little shop of knick-knacks on the Finchley Road. She lay bed-ridden in the shop, where she earned her living by selling to any chance customer. Beside her bed there was a box which contained her personal treasures, and as she talked to me she pulled out of the box a book and passed it to me, saying, "Mr. Gladstone gave me that." I was aston-ished; but I opened to the title page, and there, sure enough, was the inscription in the well-known half-illegible hand, the woman's name, and "from her friend W. E. Gladstone." I asked her how it came to pass. She did not seem to see that there was anything very wonderful about it; but he had passed along the Finchley Road, he had discovered by a fine instinct that there was a sufferer there, and he had gone in again and again to read and to pray with her, and he had given her the little book, a book, so far as I remember, of private devotion, as a memorial of their friendship.   Robert F. Horton

※ ※

940 If we had ever stood, as George Gissing puts it, utterly alone, just clothed and nothing more than that, with the problem before us of wresting our next meal from a world that cares not whether we live or die, with what different eyes we should look upon those whose lot is hard and bitter. He found a child in a lonely spot in a woodland, sobbing his heart away. He had been sent with sixpence to pay a debt, and he had lost the money. "Sixpence dropped by the wayside and a whole family made wretched. I put my hand in my pocket and wrought sixpennyworth of miracle." He knew what it was from his own experience to be in need. He was able to sympathize with the boy who had lost his sixpence because of his own knowledge of human struggle. He was not only sorry for the boy, he suffered with him, and that is true sympathy.   John Bishop

✳✳

941   I wonder how many Christians ever really take the burden of man's sin upon their prayers, and thus at least watch and brood, even if they can do no more. I wonder how often we read the newspaper reports of police and cases with morbid interest, but with hardly a stir of atoning desire, hardly a thought of the divine heart of suffering within the shadows.

H. H. Farmer

Tempo of American Living

942   A citizen from the Argentine recently visited in New York. A friend of his, who has lived in this city for some time, and who believes that he understands our habits of life, gave the visitor a list of suggestions to help him to adjust himself to New York modes of living. One of the suggestions was this: "When you are on the street always walk fast, even if there is no place in particular to which you want to go."

John Sutherland Bonnell

Temptation

943   Napoleon used to mass his forces on the weak point of the enemy's army; and the devil is a master strategist who follows the same tactics in assaulting the soul. A good deal of building tumbles to the ground in an evil mood or in the sudden onslaught of a fierce temptation, which could have been saved if more attention had been paid to the place and power of the minor moralities.

D. Sutherland

✳✳

944   You remember that incident related of Frederick W. Robertson of Brighton. Some one went to a little shop in that town and asked the trader

inside if he remembered anything of the great preacher. His reply was to take the visitor to a little room at the back of the shop and show a picture of Robertson. "There," said the shopkeeper, "is the man of whom you ask, and do you know, whenever I am tempted to do a mean thing in my business, I come in and look at the picture, and I cannot do it, I cannot do it." That is what the friendship of Jesus should mean for you and me: He would exercise a restraining, uplifting, and ennobling influence in your life and mine, so that we would go forth with fresh courage and hope in our hearts and a Te Deum on our lips.

T. H. Roberts

**

945   It is said that once there came to a wise king a youth who asked to be told the secret of happiness and of victory over sin. The king filled a cup of wine and handed it to him, bidding him carry it through the streets of the city and bring it back to the palace without spilling a single drop. "And if thou spillest any," he declared, "the soldier who followeth thee with drawn sword shall remove thy head." The youth, followed by the soldier, went forth bearing the cup most carefully. He carried it safely through the streets and brought it back at last unspilled.

"Well," said the king, "what didst thou see and hear by the way?" "Naught, O king," the youth replied. "What!" exclaimed the king. "Sawest thou not the beggars by the wayside, nor the sellers in the market, nor the players and dancers in the booths, nor the roisterers in the taverns?" "Nay, sire," said the youth. "I neither saw nor heard any of these." "So," answered the king, "learn thy lesson. Set thy heart on God and give all thy mind to obey Him, as thou didst fix thy thought on the bearing of the cup, and thou shalt not hear the voices of temptation, nor be enticed by the vanities of this world."

Harold Derbyshire

**

946   There is an old story which I suppose we all of us were told in Sunday school to illustrate the meaning of the text, "Thou God seest me." A father went out to rob an orchard, and took his boy with him. At a point where two paths crossed, he looked this way and that way and listened, and then held out his bag for the boy to hold while he put in the fruit. The boy was a Sunday-school scholar, and he said: "There was one place you didn't look, father." Startled, he said, "Where?" "You didn't look up, father." That orchard was not robbed that night.

Norman Webster

**

947   No amount of resolving to do right will save you if you remain under the influences that lead you to go wrong. As Henry Ward Beecher once bluntly said, "If a man wears garments in which powder is wrought into the texture, he cannot safely go and hire out in a blacksmith's shop."

Theodore L. Cuyler

** **

948   The Indians have a superstition that the strength of every enemy a warrior slays in battle enters into his own limbs. This is an actual truth in regard to a Christian. He becomes stronger for every temptation whose "scalp" he wins, and every besetting sin that he slays. Next to the joy of saving a soul is the joy of victory in a hard fight with a spiritual foe. Three things make a happy Christian Endeavourer: they are, prayer, labours of love for Christ, and triumphs over strong temptations.

Theodore L. Cuyler

** **

949   Give the lie to that saying of Horace Walpole, and believed by many in these days, "Every man has his price." Satan thought so in the days of Job; he thought that Job was bought by the mercies of his God; but God said, "Try him." And he took away all, stripped him of all the good things that God had given him; but he came back. "Have you succeeded?" "No." "Have you yielded?" "No; I offered too low a price." "Try him again." "Touch now his bones and his flesh, and he will curse thee to thy face." "Try him again." And he struck him with a loathsome disease, but when he heard him cry, "The Lord gave, and the Lord hath taken away; blessed be the name of the Lord! Though he slay me, yet will I trust in Him," Satan never tried Job again.

Herber Evans

Thanksgiving

950   Dr. Hazen Werner tells of a conversation with a member of one of our service clubs following an address on the Christian home. This man stopped him in the lobby and said:

"Would you be interested in knowing what happened in our home in respect to what you have been talking about? My wife and I were not religious people. A little boy was born into our home. When he was old enough to go to school he came home one day and said, 'I have learned a thanks to say at the table. May I say it?' So from that time on we were quiet while our boy thanked God for the food. My wife and I began to be disturbed. We didn't know quite what to do about it. It ended with our having prayer in the home. We have prayed as a family from that time on. Eventually we said: 'If we are Christian people like this, we ought to find a church and join up with other Christian folks.' We found a church a few blocks away. We've been members of it for some time, in fact, I am a member of the board at the present time. It made a great deal of difference in our family when our little boy came home that day years ago and said: 'I have learned a thanks to say at the table. May I say it?'"

We have a duty of thanksgiving. Your children can start us on "the shortest, surest way to happiness." Blessed are the child-like who give thanks in everything, and for everything! For theirs is the kingdom of deep and abiding joy.

David A. MacLennan

✳✳

951   I read recently of a school in Nuremberg, Germany, where ten-year-old schoolgirls were asked by their teacher to write an essay on "The Most Beautiful Day in My Life." One of these grey-faced little girls wrote: "The most beautiful day of my life was February 17, 1947, when my brother died, and I received his shoes and his woolen underwear."

Gerald Watkins

✳✳

952   It is told of Dr. White, the great minister of St. George's, Edinburgh, how in the course of his visiting one afternoon, he went in to see a woman, old and poor. Throughout the twenty minutes of his stay she complained, complained about everybody and everything, while he sat silent. Then he rose to go, and, as he shook hands with her to bid her good-bye, with one of his rare smiles, he said: "And mind you, forget not all your benefits." And don't you think that is the best way to take life's set-backs? "Forget not all your benefits." When we do, even the dark days can help us see the happier days in brighter relief.

J. G. Grant Flemming

Thanksgiving, for Sanity

953   In one of his letters Frederick Denison Maurice tells us of a poor creature in a lunatic asylum who, in a lucid moment, snatched by the arm a lady visiting the institution, and exclaimed, "Have you thanked God for your reason to-day?" and then relapsed into fury. For the common blessings and comforts of life— health of body and strength of mind, food and clothing, warmth and light and air, the peace of home and the sacred ties of love—we are far from being as grateful as we ought.

Henry Varley

Theology

954   A skimmed theology will not produce a more intimate philanthropy. We are not going to become more ardent lovers of men by the cooling of our love for God. You cannot drop the big themes and create great saints.

                                                          J. H. Jowett

Theology, Test of

955   The main question in any theological movement is whether it has raised or lowered men's ideas of God. The Reformation definitely and distinctly raised man's conception of God. It swept away a mass of superstitions, and of dogmas by which the character of God had been obscured, and Calvin's theology was a sign of advancing thought about the Divine dealings with men. Methodism was another advance. It forced the Church to look at the masses, and to feel that it had a message of love and mercy to fallen men everywhere.

                                                          Samuel Pearson

Time

956   Sir James Jeans tells us to image a penny reposing on the top of Cleopatra's needle and placed on that a postage stamp. The height of the needle, he goes on, represents the age of the world before the appearance of human life; the thickness of the penny the time that man has existed; and the thickness of the stamp the time that man has been civilized. That is the parable of the patience of God, who waited countless aeons before He had prepared the earth for man.   Horton Davies

⁂

957   One of the illusions is that the present hour is not the critical, decisive hour. Write it on your heart that every day is the best day in the year. No man has learned anything rightly, until he knows that every day is Doomsday.

                                                          Ralph W. Emerson

Time, Passing of

958   In some of our moods we feel, like Charles Lamb, that we want to "stand still at the age to which we are arrived . . . to be no younger, no richer, no handsomer"; but, we should not accept the present moment as a permanent

possession if it were really offered to us, because our interest is always in the future. The old fairy story gives us the truth. "A genie gave a child a ball of string, and said to him, 'This is the thread of your life; take it. When you want time to pass quickly for you, unwind the thread; your days will pass fast or slowly as you have unwound the ball quickly or not. So long as you do not touch the thread, you will remain at the same hour of your existence.' The child took the thread; first he unwound it to become a man, then to marry the betrothed he loved, then to see his children growing up, to get offices, to gain honours, to overcome troubles, to avoid the griefs and diseases that come with age, and finally alas, to put an end to burdensome old age. He had lived just four months and six days after the visit of the genie." You and I would undoubtedly do the same with the ball of string. "Without a stop, we pelt into the future, until at last we stumble over our own grave."   James MacKay

Time, Value of

959   I was reading the other day about the value of the gold dust or filings that fall from the work in jewellers' shops; and I remember that the writer said a workman's old waistcoat would be worth more than a new one; that, in fact, the story of Aladdin and the magician who offered to exchange new lamps for old is paralleled in modern times by second-hand clothesmen, who give new vests for old ones, because of the fine gold dust which accumulates in the cloth, and which is collected again and sold. Spare moments are the gold dust of time. Of all the portions of our life, spare moments are the most fruitful in good or evil. They are the gaps through which temptations find the easiest access to the garden of the soul. And they also afford the most precious opportunities for doing good. Yet how many of our young friends lost much of this gold dust; scattering it, not in single grains, but casting it away by the handful.

F. Wagstaff

Tolerance

960   On a Continental holiday Harry Jeffs met a charming Roman Catholic priest who became his travelling companion.

On parting Jeffs asked the priest whether he thought—not as a priest of the Roman Church, but as an individual—that he (Jeffs), being a heretic, had any hope of happiness in the life to come. The reply of the understanding priest was: "Well, Mr. Jeffs, speaking quite unofficially, mind, I think you stand as good a chance as some of our fifteenth century Popes."   Arthur Porritt

⁂

961   As G. K. Chesterton once said, "Merely having an open mind is nothing. The object of opening the mind, as of opening the mouth, is to shut it again on something solid." This is a day for decision.   Cyril T. Follett

⁂

962   There is a legend that one day Abraham was standing by his tent door when he saw coming along the way a very old man, weary with his journey, and with bleeding feet. With true hospitality he invited the old man to share his meal and be lodged with him for the night. But he noticed that the old man asked no blessing on the meal, and inquired why he did not pray to the God of Heaven. The old man said, "I am a fire-worshipper and acknowledge no other God." At this Abraham grew angry that a man should be such an infidel and thrust him out of his tent into the night. Then God called to Abraham and said to him, "Where is the old man that came to thee?" And Abraham answered, "I thrust him out, because he did not worship Thee." Then said God, "I have suffered him these hundred years, though he dishonoured Me—and couldst thou not endure him one night?"

Frederick H. Wiseman

Traditions

963   Professor Drummond used to tell the story of an eagle that was seen one spring morning hovering over Niagara. Its quick eye detected amid the blocks of ice the carcass of a sheep. It was but the work of a moment for the hungry bird to swoop down upon the tempting meal and press its talons into the fleece of the dead sheep. On swept the river to the thundering falls, but the bird fed on, oblivious of the danger, till just above the awful brink it spread its wings to rise. Alas, however, it was not to be. Its talon had become frozen to the fleece. It no longer held the carcass; the carcass held him and with a wild despairing shriek the bird passed over the falls into the doom. We also can be so shackled to our traditions, so self-satisfied with past achievements, so gripped by soul-destroying customs, that we can no longer rise to the opportunities and the challenge of the new world.

W. J. Lewis

Treasures

964   You remember the story that Browning tells in one of his poems concerning a young girl who was reputed to be a person of beautiful character. She had long golden hair of which she was very proud. As she lay dying she

expressed the wish that no one should cut her hair, and that it should be dressed after her death in the way she herself indicated. She arranged her hair about her shoulders with great care, and extracted the promise from those around her that she should be laid in the tomb with her hair untouched; and she was. And everybody mourned the death of this sweet and beautiful girl, and people talked in succeeding centuries of canonizing her. And then one day the body was taken away from the sepulchre in which it had been buried, and they found in her hair a number of gold coins. And the interpretation that Browning gives to the incident is that the girl, with all her seeming beauty of character, was greedy at heart; she wanted to take her money with her; she could not bear the thought that anyone else should profit by her death. So she hid the gold coins beneath her golden tresses, and cherished them to the end.

J. E. Rattenbury

Treasures in Heaven

965   R. L. Stevenson, in a letter dated 1873, describes a day's walk in Fife, during which he came upon a labourer cleaning a cowshed. They fell into conversation. As they talked together of this and that, one simple memorable remark betrayed the real man. The labourer said in his quaint dialect, "He that has something beyond need never be weary." "And that," comments Stevenson, "from a man cleaning a cowshed."   Wilfred Salmon

Trinity

966   So great was the importance which Maurice attached to the doctrine of the Triune Name that in his book on *The Religions of the World* he applied it as the test by which they were to be measured and judged. Confucianism and Mohammedanism could not rise to the truth of the fatherhood of God because they lacked the knowledge of the Son, through whom alone fatherhood could be fully revealed. Brahminism abounded in incarnations of the divine, but they ended in themselves because the knowledge was wanting of the Eternal Father. Buddhism dreamed of an infinite Spirit in which all men shared, but because it did not know the Father and the Son its doctrine of the Spirit was void, as its highest goal was also reduced to Nirvana.   A. V. G. Allen

✳✳

967   Dr. Martineau, of the Unitarians, wrote a wonderful paper many years ago. It is called "A Way Out of the Trinitarian Controversy." He reminds Unitarians that all their conceptions of God are taken from the character of the

Son, and that their real object of worship is the God revealed in Christ. Only in Christ do we know God. Without the Son God is to us a dark blank of infinite possibility; a mere mute immensity. He states the doctrine in a way which few Trinitarians will object to accept. The Father is God in Himself; the Son is God manifested in the universe and in history, and brought to focus in the drama of Redemption; while the Holy Ghost is God in communion with our inner spirit.

It is from a letter written to him by a clergyman in the North of England: "I have just returned from a united prayer meeting at which ministers of all denominations were present, and have been struck by the way in which the prayers of all the earnest and able men present point to the fact that Trinitarianism does supply a real need. The prayers were prayed almost entirely to Jesus as God, Jesus as the Way, the Truth, and the Life. The Heavenly Father was for the most part a great far-off Original, of whose love they could only say that but for Jesus Christ they could never have believed in it, and but for a belief in Jesus Christ's power as co-equal with the Father they would still despair of its continued and steady presence by means of the Holy Ghost, the Comforter."   J. Day Thompson

※ ※

968 It was F. C. Bauer, the celebrated head of the Tübingen School, who said that Christianity would have lost its claim as the universal religion of mankind, if at the Council of Nicea, A.D. 325, Arius, who denied the Godhead of Christ, had gained the victory over Athanasius. With the Godhead of our Saviour would have fallen our faith in the Triune God, and with it Christianity would have been hurled down from its lofty position as the only true religion. Truly the doctrine of the Trinity is the rock-foundation of our blessed religion. In our denominational life we may cherish special principles, which we find in the Holy Scriptures, but with all the Christians, dwelling in all the lands of the earth, we put our trust in the Father, the Son, and the Holy Spirit.

Nicholas M. Steffens

Trouble

969 Dr. Fosdick tells a story of a soldier in the war of 1914–1918 who was ordered to attend a lecture on the stars. It had been arranged by the War Office, so that men lost at night might be able to find their way home again. This soldier, an officer, was profoundly bored. Astronomy seemed to him an abstract affair, which had no bearing on the mud and death of the front. But one night he and his men were sent out to reconnoitre in No Man's Land. They were discovered by the enemy, were fired upon, became confused, ran at random, lay down, and then tried to creep home. But where was home? Then he remembered the stars. They were no longer remote, but relevant, the supremely relevant things in the universe. They had a message for him that made all the difference between life and death, and, reading that message and acting upon it, he got his men safely to his own lines.

That story is a parable of many a life. To many people God is only an abstraction. He seems to have no bearing on life as they know it. He has nothing to say to their peculiar problems and their pressing needs, and therefore they pass Him by. But then comes the Valley of Trouble, awakening a dire sense of need. And that sense of need makes God necessary. He becomes real, and they discover Him as One who does not disappoint them or let them down, but who has the very word that they cry for. And out of that valley they journey on, having tested and seen that the Lord is good. And what they learn then remains with them, so that life thereafter is a new creation.

G. Holland Williams

Trouble, Effect of

970   Some time ago I was in the company of a foreman at one of the Clyde shipyards, who told me the story of one of his apprentices—an undisciplined lad who belonged to a razor-slashing gang. There was a day when the foreman called him into the office, to give him a reprimand which he richly deserved. The boy stood there sullen and resentful, finally taking a knife out of his pocket and opening and shutting it viciously, and evidently lusting to use it. In due course, however, he joined the Navy, and the shipyard was glad to see him go. But some months later, while home on "leave," he paid the foreman a visit, and it was obvious that he was greatly changed. "If I were back here now," he said, "I wouldn't give you the trouble I gave you before." "I'm glad to hear it," said the foreman. "What has happened to you?" "Oh," replied the lad, "I thought I was tough—that was the trouble with me. But I discovered what I was when I found myself crying like a child on the beaches of Sicily."

G. Holland Williams

Trust

971   One of the most able churchmen ever produced in America was Bishop William A. Quayle, who was often referred to as "the Skylark of Methodism." The Bishop was eloquent, imaginative, poetic, and of good humour. Once in a sermon he described how he had faced a problem one night

that seemed too difficult to solve. He prayed, but his prayers seemed to get nowhere. He lay on his bed and tossed, unable to sleep. Then, he said, about midnight God spoke to him and said: "Now, William, you go to sleep and let Me sit up for the rest of the night."

David John Donnan

** **

972   My father was an invalid part of the time, and despotic. My mother—the second—was naturally fearing and doubtful. Father was living on a salary of eight hundred dollars a year, at Litchfield, with a family of eleven growing children. How ministers ever lived in those times I cannot conceive. I remember that at the table, one time (I was not supposed to be in existence; for children do not amount to anything, ordinarily), he was drinking his tea in his way—having it poured into a saucer to cool, and resting his two elbows on the table. Mother sat opposite, murmuring, in her sweet, refined, gentle, sad way, that the bills were due; that she had no money; that indeed she did not see how they could get along; that for her own part she expected to die in the poorhouse. At that my father dropped his hand to the table. His eyes sparkled. Something was coming. "My dear," he said, "I have trusted God now for forty years, and He never has forsaken me, and I am not going to begin to distrust Him now." That woke me up. It was better than the catechism; it sank into me, and during my earlier life I went through perils of sickness and poverty, and all forms of limitation and trouble; but I never lost sight of that one single scene. This sentence never was out of my ears! "I have trusted God now forty years, and I am not going to begin to distrust Him now."

Henry Ward Beecher

** **

973   A soldier of the world war wrote thus of his experiences at the front: "We realize at the front that the issues of life and death are not in our hands. But just because we do the only right thing and realize that everything else is out of our power, there comes to us a peace of mind and content. We take the one step and trust the rest. It is the beginning of the peace of God. We do the only right thing and realize that everything else is out of our power."

Alfred Bond

** **

974   I remember a story of Martin Luther. Great-souled Martin Luther could believe and doubt against any man of his time; in believing he could excel the angels, and in horrible thoughts of doubting he could almost match the devils.

Great-hearted men are subject to horrible fits of faintness and despair, unknown to minds of smaller calibre. One day he fell so low in spirit that his friends were frightened at what he might say or do. Things were going ill with the great cause, and the Reformer might in his dreadful condition have upset everything. So his friends got him out of the way, saying to themselves, "The man must be alone, his brain is overworked, he must be quiet." He rested a bit, and came back, looking as sour and gloomy as ever. Rest and seclusion had not stilled the winds nor lulled the waves. Luther was still in a storm, and judged that the good cause was shipwrecked.

I will now give you my own version of the method adopted for the great man's cure. He went home, but when he came to the door nobody welcomed him. He entered their best room, and there sat Catherine his wife, all dressed in black, weeping as from a death in the house. By her side lay a mourning cloak, such as ladies wear at funerals. "Ah," says he, "Kate, what matters now? Is the child dead?" She shook her head and said the little ones were alive, but something much worse than that had happened. Luther cried, "Oh, what has befallen us? Tell me quick! I am sad enough as it is. Tell me quick!"

"Good man," said she, "have you not heard? Is it possible that the terrible news has not reached you?" This made the Reformer the more inquisitive and ardent, and he pressed to be immediately told of the cause of sorrow. "Why," said Kate, "have you not been told that our Heavenly Father is dead, and His cause in the world is therefore overturned?" Martin stood and looked at her, and at last burst into such a laugh that he could not possibly contain himself, but cried, "Kate, I read thy riddle—what a fool I am! God is not dead, He ever lives; but I have acted as if He were. Thou hast taught me a good lesson."

C. H. Spurgeon

Truth

975   "I do not know," confessed the great Sir Isaac Newton a short while before his death, "what I may appear to the world; but to myself I seem to have been only like a boy playing on the sea-shore of knowledge; and diverting myself in now and then finding a smoother pebble or a prettier shell than ordinary, whilst the great ocean of truth lay all undiscovered before me."

J. D. Roberts

※ ※

976   Cicero tells of a prisoner who, having spent his entire life in a dark dungeon, and knowing the light of day only from a single beam which filtered through a crack in the prison wall, was full of distress when he was told that

the wall was to be pulled down, "because," he said, "it will rob me of my gleam of light." He did not know that the destruction of the wall would bathe him in noontide splendour and gladden him with the infinite glory of the outer world.

So, the Jews of old feared the pulling down of the middle wall of partition; so, philosophers to-day resent any criticism of those systems of thought which let in the light through the chinks; but the faith of Christ swallows up the dim and partial light in the splendour of the spiritual knowledge with which it floods the soul.

In Christ is the fullness of truth, and in Christ is the perfection of beauty.

G. H. Clothier

Truth, Power of

977   Gibbon, in his *Decline,* tells the dramatic story of Julian's election by the army to the throne of the Caesars. No sooner is he elected and in control of the treasury than the army demands he shall pay for the honour they have conferred on him—so much to every man. It is a dramatic scene. Confronted by the legions, 10,000 angry men, he refuses. "I will not pay," he says, "because I cannot. The Roman Republic is bankrupt." Because it was the truth those angry men had to bow in its presence, for it had a power more terrible than death. We can burn, hang, or murder one another but no man can burn, hang, or murder truth.

Cyril T. Follett

Truth, Search for

978   "Where are you going, holy man?" a peasant man of India said to an old traveller as they stood together under the shade of a tree. The old man answered: "To a city far away." "In India?" he asked. The answer was: "Further." "In Asia?" "Further, further, friend, further; for that city I seek is Truth and it is hidden in the heart of God."

William Morrison Kelly

Unbelief

979   A blind man by the roadside whispered to Christ that he had been waiting for Him for a long time, and Christ, praying, touched his eyes. But, instead of light breaking through, he sat unchanged in his black prison. Grey, negative minds do incalculable harm. Flaubert tells of a stupid French village doctor who with his incompetent fingers fumbled over a tendon operation on

a club-footed ostler. Gangrene set in, the leg had to be amputated, and afterwards the doctor had to meet daily a man maimed for life. Our dreary agnostic
minds have only to look around a home or a world and see souls we have
helped to blind or murder. Christ calls His disciples, in a living belief in the
present power of God, to make lame men walk, the blind to see, and to set
the world free. And, instead, our unbelief often clamps heavier bolts on the
dungeon doors.   McEwan Lawson

Unction

980   There is an old Romish tale of a monk who had converted great numbers
of persons, that on a certain day he was detained on his journey, and did not
reach his congregation in time. The devil thought this a fine opportunity, so,
putting on the cowl of the monk, he went into the pulpit to preach. He preached
of hell (a subject with which he was well acquainted), and they listened; but
just as he was getting well into his discourse, the holy man appeared, and made
the devil disclose himself in his proper form. "Get thee gone, Satan," said he.
"But how ever could you have preached the truth as you have done, for all and
everything that you have said has been true? How could you do it?" "Oh,"
said he, "I knew it could not do any hurt to anybody, nor any good either." So
where there is no unction it does not matter what or how we preach.

                                                                 C. H. Spurgeon

Union

981   There is a story of a young man who wished to impress his young lady
with the extraordinary keenness of his eyesight. He put a drawing pin into a
tree at the end of a field across which he proposed later on to walk with her.
When he did so, he pointed to the tree away in the distance and said: "Look,
someone's left a drawing pin in that tree!" She could scarcely even make out
the tree. "I will go and get it," he said, and as he ran across the field he tripped
over a cow. We shall make a like error if we fix our eyes only upon the distant
goal of reunion.

We shall trip over the great solid Christian convictions which are incorporated
in the denominational structures. The serious Anglican is not an Anglican
merely because he believes from the bottom of his heart that the unity and continuity of the Christian faith is preserved by the apostolic succession of bishops;
but because he believes that the Lord's Supper can only be rightly celebrated by
one who stands within the field of that unity and continuity. Similarly the
serious Congregationalist is so because he believes, and from the bottom of his

heart, that the individual church is responsible to no earthly king, to no parliament, to no bishop or archbishop or pope, but directly and immediately to the King of Kings Himself. He believes in the Crown Rights of the Redeemer. He believes in the priesthood of believers that Henry Barrow and John Penry and John Greenwood died martyr deaths 350 years ago not fighting windmills, but fighting for something which was vital to the understanding of the gospel itself.

Philip Lee Woolf

Unity in Civilization

982   Raymond B. Fosdick, in his report to the Rockefeller Foundation for 1941, says: "For although wars and economic rivalries may for longer or shorter periods isolate nations and split them up into separate units, the process is never complete because the intellectual life of the world, as far as science and learning are concerned, is definitely internationalized, and whether we wish it or not, an indelible pattern of unity has been woven into the society of mankind. There is not an area of activity in which this cannot be illustrated. An American soldier wounded on a battle-field in the Far East owes his life to the Japanese scientist, Kitasato, who isolated the bacillus of tetanus. A Russian soldier saved by a blood transfusion is indebted to Landsteiner, an Austrian. A German soldier is shielded from typhoid fever with the help of a Russian, Metchnikoff. A Dutch marine in the East Indies is protected from malaria because of the experiments of an Italian, Grassi; while a British aviator in North Africa escapes death from surgical infection because a Frenchman, Pasteur, and a German, Koch, elaborated a new technique. In peace as in war we are all of us beneficiaries of contributions to the knowledge made by every nation in the world. Our children are guarded from diphtheria by what a Japanese and a German did; they are protected from smallpox by an Englishman's work; they are saved from rabies because of a Frenchman; they are cured of pellagra through the research of an Austrian. From birth to death they are surrounded by an invisible host—spirits of men who never thought in terms of flags or boundary lines and who never served a lesser loyalty than the welfare of mankind. The best that every individual or group has produced anywhere in the world has always been available to serve the race of men, regardless of nation or colour. What is true of the medical sciences is true of the other sciences. Whether it is mathematics or chemistry, whether it is bridges or automobiles or a new device for making cotton cloth or a cyclotron for studying atomic structure, ideas cannot be hedged in behind geographical barriers. Thought cannot be nationalized. The fundamental unity of civilization is the unity of its intellectual life."

Samuel Trexler

Vanity

983   Now-a-days we can laugh at the strutting dictators we sometimes see on old newsreels, with their masses of armed, saluting men, manning innumerable tanks and guns. But we did not smile when first we saw those films in the days before the storm broke. We were apprehensive of that show of power just as we are apprehensive of another display of similar power further east to-day. This too, will fade away like every one of its predecessors . . . or else history teaches us nothing.

John E. Barker

Victory

984   The Duke of Wellington knew what war was, and after the battle of Waterloo he wrote that his heart was broken for the loss of his beloved comrades, and that, except a battle lost, there is nothing in the world so melancholy as a battle won.

F. W. Farrar

Victory, Pyrrhic

985   About three hundred years before the birth of Christ there lived in Epirus, a province of Greece, a king whose name was Pyrrhus. He was the first to test the power of Greece against the power of Rome. He led his armies against the Roman army, and met with it at a place called Heracleia, near the gulf of Tarentum, and there, being a brilliant soldier, he won a brilliant victory. He was so crippled, however, and impoverished, that he was unable to follow up the result of his victory, and although time after time he led it to the subjugation of Rome, he was each time so severely crippled he was unable to follow up his advantage, till at last he was forced to abandon the attempt. His victories are known in history as Pyrrhic victories; he was less than conqueror.

P. D. Thomson

Virtue

986   Dean Inge says: "It was the so-called bourgeois virtues that made England a going concern; if it becomes a gone concern, it will be because these virtues are no longer held in honour." It could not be put better.

Author Unknown

Vocabulary, Christian

987   For many reasons we have tried to content ourselves and other people with a merely human Jesus, and with a merely human programme of reform. In Christian circles the old language lasted on. As Mr. Whale has written, men "continued, hesitatingly and a little rebelliously, to use the old theocentric language about sin and man's need of redemption; but they relied in fact on their own resources, substituted a little sanctified psychology and a diluted socialism for the Faith, and talked with sentimental enthusiasm about the brotherhood of man as though Utopia were just around the corner." And so a generation has grown up in which men and women, if they use the Christian vocabulary at all, use it with little understanding and conviction. We have given a great deal of lip-service to the Christian gospel. But often we have never truly faced its tremendous claims nor begun to think in its terms about our life. For it speaks to us in terms not of problems, but of sins; not of progress, but of reconciliation and redemption; not of reform, but of a new birth, a new life in Christ Jesus.

Frederic Greeves

Vocation, Christian

988   Peter, James, John, Paul and the other apostles—our Lord Himself—each was a layman. So, as Dr. John Oliver Nelson of the Federal Council of Churches said, "God calls everyone to be a minister, whatever form that ministry may take in his or her life work. . . . Church vocations are just one sort of vocation to which God calls young people. He has a call, a summons, a plan, for every young person that's born." Said Martin Luther, "A shoemaker, a smith, a peasant, anyone, has the office and work of his trade and yet, at the same time, are all consecrated bishops and priests." "Seeing that we [all] have this ministry" let us look to our calling, magnify it, and discharge it with fidelity and zeal.

David A. MacLennan

Vocation, Commonplace

989   The lowliest, the most commonplace earthly calling may still be a sacred vocation, rich in service, full of blessing both to you and your fellow-men. We read D'Aubigné's history of the Reformation with glistening eyes and bated breath as we follow the dramatic episodes and hairbreadth escapes of Martin Luther in his struggles against Rome; but it is an open question whether that little man fiddling about with a few wooden blocks in that little German work-

shop and inventing the art of printing did not do more to establish the Reformation than even the great Luther himself. We read with throbbing breasts the story of the wars of the Roses, and delight to visit the places where those epoch-making battles took place; but the effect of those dread conflicts on the history of Yorkshire and Lancashire and England was as nothing compared to the changes wrought by that simple working-man who invented the spinning-mill. We are proud of the prison philanthropist John Howard and Wilberforce and Florence Nightingale, but the services rendered to mankind by those were not greater, were not anything like so great, as the services rendered by that patient, unknown chemist who taught humanity the use of anaesthetics. The man who cut the Suez Canal, or tunnelled the Alps, or gave us the telegraph, did quite as much for human brotherhood and the unity of the race as some of the social champions we delight to honour. To maintain an honest business is noble; to do the humdrum mercenary business of life in a proper spirit is to serve your God and your generation.   F. R. Smith

Vocations

990   Some years ago one of our greatest oil companies said, "We want to open up a great oil office in China." The man to be in charge of that office was to have four qualifications: He must be under thirty, be well educated, must know the Chinese language, and he must have the quality of leadership. They could not find such a man until at length some one said, "I know a man who has all those qualifications, but I do not think you could get him." "Well," said the officials of the company, "what is he receiving now?" The reply was, "He is one of our Baptist missionaries and he is getting a salary of 600 dollars a year." The oil company said, "If he will go we will make his salary 10,000 dollars, or 12,000, or, if it is necessary, 15,000 dollars." The offer was transmitted to the young missionary, and his reply was, "I am not interested." "But," they said, "the salary is magnificent." "Yes," he agreed, "the salary is magnificent, but, sir, your job is too small. I would rather have my 600 dollar salary and point China to Christ, than your 15,000 dollar salary and sell oil to the people."

George W. Truett

Voice Within

991   Kant, the great philosopher, said that as a result of his ten years' search for the way of salvation he came back at the end to where the simplest peasant stands, viz., reliance upon the voice within which he took to be the voice of God.

Samuel Jones

War

992   Recall what General Eisenhower said at Ottawa in January of 1946: "War is always negative. The best we can do is to get rid of it. . . . I hate war as only a soldier who has lived in it can, as one who has seen its brutality, its futility, its stupidity." Scientists who know the scope of atomic and other modern weapons plead with us to join the ranks of the peacemakers with an urgency unsurpassed by the religious idealists of the days before the atomic bomb became a reality. Some one asked Dr. Albert Einstein if he knew what would be the weapons used in World War Three. He replied, "I do not know. But I can tell you what the weapons of World War Four will be—stone clubs!" He is sure that another global war will reduce civilization to a most primitive barbarism. You may have read Arnold Toynbee's prophecy that "if mankind is going to run amok with atom bombs, I personally should look to the Negrito Pygmies of Central Africa to salvage some fraction of the present heritage of mankind."

David A. MacLennan

War, Abstraction in

993   In the German war-novel, *All Quiet on the Western Front*, the author tells us that he was once left behind in a shell-hole. A heavy body stumbled and fell in beside him. He struck out. Then he looked at his victim, and spoke: "Comrade, I did not want to kill you. But you were only an idea to me before, an abstraction that lived in my mind. It was that abstraction I stabbed. But now for the first time I see you are a man like me. Now I see your wife and your face and our fellowship. Forgive me, comrade. We always see it too late. Why do they never tell us that you are just poor devils like us, that your mothers are just as anxious as ours, and that we have the same fear of death and the same dying and the same agony? Forgive me, comrade. How could you be my enemy? If we threw away these rifles and this uniform you could be my brother. If I come out of it I shall fight against this that has struck us both down." The German novelist is right. Dealing with men as abstractions, and forgetting that they are persons and human beings, and "just poor devils like us," is something that brings loss and hurt not only to them, but also to us.

G. Holland Williams

War, Christianity and

994   Adolf Harnack was a great scholar—perhaps the greatest New Testament scholar of his day—and he was not a pacifist. After considering the position with

the utmost care Harnack says bluntly: "The truth is that war can never be reconciled with the Gospel, nor can we believe that Christ would ever countenance it."

For a century and a half after the Crucifixion, the Christian Church recognized this truth and acted upon it. Its members refused to enter the army or to take any part in war. Justin Martyr, a Christian writer of the second century, declares that Christians preferred death to participation in war. Origen, who lived a century later, remarks that "the Christian Church cannot engage in war against any nation. They have learned from their Leader that they are children of peace." In that period many Christians were martyred for refusing military service. On March 12, 295, Maximilian, the son of a famous Roman veteran, was called upon to serve in the Roman army and he refused, saying simply: "I am a Christian." The Pro-Consul ordered the attendants to hand Maximilian the badge of service, and the lad—he was only twenty—refused to take it. "No," he said, "I shall wear no such sign. I have a sign already, the sign of my Lord Jesus Christ." Maximilian was put to death, and his father offered thanks to God that he was permitted to bring Him so great a gift.   H. Ingli James

Weakness

995   Good Father Staempfle, a priest of great learning, editor of a paper at Miessbach, spent months rewriting and editing *Mein Kampf*. He eliminated the more flagrant inaccuracies and the excessively childish platitudes. Hitler never forgave Father Staempfle for getting to know his weaknesses so well. He had him murdered by a "special death-squad" on the night of June 30, 1934.

Charles Kellett

* *

996   The Greeks told how Achilles was dipped in the Styx by his goddess-mother to make him invulnerable; but she held him by the heel as he went under the water, and by the heel it was that the arrow entered which took his life. And the Germans had their story of Siegfried, whose mother bathed him, for the same purpose, in dragon's blood; but as she bathed him, a leaf fluttered down from the branch of a tree, and touched his back, and there death found him at the last.   E. L. Allen

Wealth

997   When the richest American of his day was in his last fatal illness, a Christian friend proposed to sing for him; and the hymn he named was, "Come,

ye sinners, poor and needy." "Yes, yes," replied the dying millionaire, "sing that for me; I feel poor and needy." Yet at that moment the stock-markets of the globe were watching and waiting for the demise of the man who could shake them with a nod of his head. "Poor and needy!" How the sand sweeps from under a man's soul in such an hour as that!   Theodore L. Cuyler

⁂

998   Mr. T. P. O'Connor reports an interview with Mr. Andrew Carnegie: "As we drove to the station I was remarking how I envied him his wealth. He said, 'I am not to be envied. How can my wealth help me? I am sixty years old, and cannot digest my food. I would give all my millions if I could have youth and health.' Then I shall never forget his next remark. We had driven some yards in silence, when Mr. Carnegie suddenly turned, and in hushed voice, and with bitterness and depth of feeling quite indescribable, said: 'If I could make Faust's bargain, I would. I would glady sell anything to have my life over again.' And I saw his hand clench as he spoke."

J. G. Henderson

Welfare

999   James Smetham has an entry in his diary: "I have been to class to-night. Old Father Barnes was there. He had a terrible cough and looked like Fagin. Yet I question whether Father Barnes would not be better off than any of us if the soul were taken into account." Indeed the soul must be taken into account if you would properly assess a man's prosperity.

Cyril T. Follett

Will of God

1000   At a student conference at Lake Geneva, one summer, great emphasis was put upon the thought that one ought to seek to know and follow the Will of God in the choice of his life-work. One evening a young man of twenty-two, who had just graduated from college, asked one of his old teachers to walk off in the woods with him. "I want to do this thing they are talking about," he said; "I want to find out God's Will for me, and do it, unless He wants me to be a doctor, or a preacher, or a missionary. Do you think that is all right?" The teacher felt fairly sure that God did not want him to be any one of the three. He knew that the boy was planning to go into business with his father, and it seemed to be just the thing that he was cut out for; and, so far as the teacher could tell, what God wanted him to do. But the teacher felt that that was not for him to decide, so answered quietly: "One might as well not pray at all about his life-work as to pray with reservations like that." They talked the thing through; and the boy surrendered his will to God in prayer: "O God, show me what you mean for me and want me to do; and I'll do it."

It was late when they went back to their tents to sleep, for they talked over many things. Early the next morning the boy was back for one more word. "I wanted to tell you, sir, what happened last night. I couldn't go to sleep, for I kept worrying about what I had done, and wondering what God has cut me out for and wants me to do; when all at once I thought of something. I said to myself: Here, Bob, you've been planning to go into business next month, not because you know that you will succeed, for you don't know a thing about it, but because your father is a good business man, and you're just following his judgement. And then it occurred to me that that is just what I am doing now with God. I'm only trusting my heavenly Father's judgement. Then I turned over and went to sleep." The boy had caught the secret of real religion through his appreciation of earthly fatherhood.   Luther Allan Weigle

Wisdom

1001   Dr. Fosdick tells of a letter he received with a pathetic story of a muddled and disordered life which ended: "It just beats me. A doctor of philosophy and unable to solve my own troubles!" Wisdom lies far deeper than the intellect or any mere accumulation of knowledge.   Graham W. Hardy

Witness

1002   Years ago, we read, there was an outbreak of Asiatic cholera in Oxford, and Charles Marriot, the saintly vicar of St. Mary's, was visiting one of the dying victims. He had with him Sister Marian, of the Incarnation. The dying woman was blaspheming, and crying aloud: "I don't believe in Christ." As the Sister bent over her the Vicar said: "You believe in Sister Marian?" There was a silence, and then the poor creature pulled the Sister's head down to her and kissed her cheek, sobbing out: "Yes, I believe in Sister Marian." Another silence, and at length, with her last breath, she said, "I believe in God! Lord Jesus, have mercy!" What are you and I here for, but that one thing, so truly and effectively to believe in God, body, soul and spirit—all we are, and all we have—that His children, all these our hapless brothers, may also believe in Him: may come home with "the ransomed of the Lord unto Zion, with songs and everlasting joy upon their heads"?   Adam W. Burnet

✳✳

1003   Quite recently I heard the story of a man who had travelled with his friend to play golf. By odd chance one of them had seen the other entering a place of worship, and so met him with the challenge, "I didn't know you were a church-goer." "Oh, yes; I have been for years," came the reply. "Oh, funny thing," said the friend. "You've always been keen to talk about golf, but you've never said a word about God."   William Mudd

✳✳

1004   Every way of preaching which ends in a man's being brought face to face with Christ is evangelical preaching, which should be as varied and interesting as human life itself. There is nothing in the ministry more worth doing than helping a man's life to turn to goodness and his soul to find God, and there is nothing that brings greater joy. When John Broadus was sixteen he accepted Christ as his Saviour, and at once began to introduce others to his new-found Friend. His first convert was a school friend. These two lived most of their lives in the same city, Broadus a professor in the university, the other a truck-driver; and Broadus said that he never met that man during all those years but he touched his cap as they passed and said, "Thank you, John, thank you." "I know just what he will say when I meet him coming down the golden street of heaven," said Broadus. "It will be just what he said this morning, 'Thank you, John, thank you.'"

> 'Tis worth living for this
> To administer bliss
> And salvation in Jesus' name.

John Bishop

✳✳

1005   I read somewhere of a French lieutenant in the days of Napoleon who in the heat of battle was separated from his regiment and was lost. "Step in anywhere," said a superior officer. "There's fighting all along the line." So, too, with the Christian host. There is work in the Church for all who are ready to serve. Never a day goes by but a Christian may make some witness in word or deed that he belongs to Christ. He can show by unmistakable signs that he is not ashamed of the gospel.   Ralph H. Turner

✳✳

1006   The only religion in the world which I have ever heard of that men were ashamed of is the religion of Jesus Christ. I preached in Salt Lake City, and I did not find a Mormon that was not proud of his religion. I never met an unconverted Chinaman who wasn't proud of being a disciple of Confucius; and

I never met a Mohammedan who wasn't proud of the fact that he was a follower of Mohammed. But how many, many times I have found men ashamed of the religion of Jesus Christ, the only religion that gives men the power over their affections and lusts and sins.   D. L. Moody

※※

1007   It was but a brief and simple question proposed by Robert Haldane to Merle d'Aubigné, when a young student at Geneva, that led to his becoming a faithful servant of Christ. D'Aubigné was in Haldane's Greek class, and the Epistle to the Romans was the subject of study. D'Aubigné remarked that he saw the doctrine of the depravity of human nature taught in the epistle, when Haldane quietly inquired, "Do you see it in your heart?" That was an arrow sent quivering into his spirit by the Holy Ghost. It may be but a single word that you speak to the young man; but God can make that word like the command upon the field of war that secures the victory—or, like the word of the marriage ceremony that links two lives for ever.   J. Hiles Hitchens

※※

1008   A distinguished Chinese leader said, "What we need is not lawyers who are Christians, doctors who are Christians, teachers who are Christians; we need Christian lawyers, Christian doctors, Christian teachers—expressing through their actual daily work their calling under God."

David A. MacLennan

※※

1009   It is related by his biographer Sir David Brewster, that Sir Isaac Newton was very often subject to the sarcastic and sneering comments of his atheistic friend, Dr. Halley. But it is recorded that Newton on no occasion permitted his friend's immorality and impiety to pass unreproved. And when Dr. Halley ventured to say something disrespectful and derogatory of religion, Newton invariably checked him and said: "I have studied these things, Halley, you have not."   J. D. Roberts

Word, Power of

1010   Here is one poor monk, Savonarola, his sole coign of vantage, his pulpit in St. Mark's, Florence, the solitary prophet of righteousness, in a city whose corruption was appalling; yet because this one man was faithful in speaking the truth as he saw it, behold, an incredible change! This is the account of the effect of Savonarola's preaching, given by a sober historian, not a romancer:

"The aspect of the city was completely changed. The women threw aside their jewels and finery, dressed plainly, bore themselves demurely; licentious young Florentines were transformed as by magic into sober, religious men; pious hymns took the place of Lorenzo's carnival songs. Most wonderful of all, bankers and tradesmen were impelled by scruples of conscience to restore ill-gotten gains amounting to many thousand florins." Voluntarily the people gave up their evil books and pictures, and on the last day of carnival these were all piled up in the great square, and burned as a bonfire, to the glory of God. Verily, the Word was with power, as it ever is on the lips of faithful men."

                                                                                J. Warschauer

Words, Meaning of

1011   One man can say a word and it is as superficial as a saucer, another man can use the same word and it is as profound as possible. I heard a scavenger say the other day, when he had swept a street, "Now, I think it is clean," and the very next day I heard a surgeon say the same thing, "You must have your instruments clean." But I don't think the scavenger and the surgeon used the word with precisely the same meaning. When a surgeon uses the word "clean" he uses it with almost incredible intensity. When a surgeon uses that word he means something quite different from the scavenger. They are both employing the same term, but one with almost incredible depth of power, and the other with a considerable amount of shallowness. Well, anyone can use the word "virtue," but the meanings are divided by an infinite gulf.   J. H. Jowett

Work

1012   A lady standing in front of the noble cathedral of Cologne heard some one behind her say, "Didn't we do a fine piece of work here?" Turning she saw a man in the plainest working clothes and said to him, "Pray, what did you do about it?" "I mixed the mortar across the street for two years," was the cheerful reply. God's work to-day needs cheerful, patient, and diligent mortar-mixers. Mixing mortar is one of the hardest and most disagreeable things to do in rearing a building. But what sort of a building could be made without mortar? Then thank God and take courage if your lot is cast among the mortar-mixers. "Whatsoever ye do, do it heartily, as unto the Lord, and not unto men."

                                                                                Ida Q. Moulton

                                        ✳✳

1013   Here is a blacksmith working at his forge. With his big, brawny arm he is striking vigorous blows on the hot bars of iron before him. He is welding together links of a great chain. This chain is to hold the anchor of some ship of the line. The blacksmith does his work faithfully and well. Every link was made of good iron, and all are firmly and truly welded together. The man put conscience into his work. His work was a part of his religion.

Months and years go by. The old blacksmith is dead and forgotten. A ship is on the sea and a wild storm is raging. They are compelled to cast anchor and wait. The anchor is dropped. The winds are fierce, and the waves terrific. The safety of the whole ship's crew and passengers depends on the chain that holds the anchor down in the sea. All through the dark night and the wild storm the ship is held fast and sure. At last, when the storm is ended and "The sunrise splendid comes blushing o'er the sea," all gather on deck and with glad and reverent heart join in hymns of thanksgiving to God for deliverance. Yes, praise God for safety, and praise God because that old God-fearing blacksmith put his conscience and his religion in the chain he made for the cable. Heaven will disclose heroes and heroines of whom this world never dreamed. Multitudes of them will come from humble homes and obscure corners.   J. B. Silcox

✳✳

1014   Some time ago, a well-known surgeon in Britain, discussing the whole problem of work and wages, had this to say: "What is happening to-day is that nobody works for the sake of getting the thing done. The result of the work is a by-product; the aim of the work is to make money to do something else. Doctors practise medicine not primarily to relieve suffering, but to make a living—the cure of the patient is something that happens on the way. Lawyers accept briefs, not because they have a passion for justice, but because the law is the profession which enables them to live." "The reason," he added, "why men often find themselves happy and satisfied in the Army is that for the first time in their lives they find themselves doing something, not for the sake of the pay, which is miserable, but for the sake of getting the thing done."

Robert James McCracken

Work, Lasting

1015   Are not the words of the great American orator, Daniel Webster, most true? "If we work upon marble, it will perish; if we work upon bronze, time will efface it; if we build temples, they will crumble into dust; but if we work upon immortal souls, if we imbue them with just principles of action, with fear of wrong and love of right, we engrave on those tables something which no time can obliterate, and which will brighten and brighten through all eternity."

F. W. Farrar

World

1016   Dr. Mott has said, "We are meeting, in my judgement, at the most fateful moment in the life of the world. . . . Never has there been such unparalleled intensive need." Dr. Mott challenged any of his listeners to disprove his statement. His knowledge had been gained from unceasing travel, a lifelong study of history, and meetings with all sorts and conditions of men. Having put forward disturbing facts concerning starvation, disease and dislocation throughout the world, Dr. Mott delivered himself thus: "Notwithstanding all that I have said about our living at the most momentous moment in the life of the world, I want to put on record that John R. Mott said that in his judgement we have come to the most hopeful moment in the life of the world." Briefly these are the reasons for his unwavering hope: (1) The power of suffering to bring people to an appreciation of Christ's teaching; (2) that always "man's extremity is God's opportunity"; (3) never before has there been so much knowledge and experience in the world; (4) the world had never before had so many genuine Christians; (5) the large amount of money being set free in the world; (6) the powers of organization, which were "the means of distributing force most advantageously." "We have to-day," added Dr. Mott, "a larger Christ, larger in the sense that there are now so many more individual Christians that know Him." In Dr. Mott's opinion there is no door in any part of the world that will not open to the friendly and constructive messenger of Jesus Christ—and he did not hesitate to mention the name of the country to which he was referring.

Worship

1017   The danger of worshipping outward beauty of form is a grave danger; it is the digging of the grave of real beauty. It has so often led to perversion and degradation. Pompeii is not the only city that has worshipped external beauty to the exclusion of the soul and of character. When Pompeii was uncovered pictures were revealed which had to be covered up again; they set forth such a perverted development of the cult of the physical. As Dean Church has said, "The idolatry of beauty in Italy ended at last in the degradation of both art and character." Worship is a window through which we look to something other than ourselves; and if that on which we look, and to which we ascribe worth, is not worthy of all that we ascribe to it, the result is disastrous. Hence the urgent question: "What shall we worship?"

Leonard Plested

✳✳

1018 I like the story of the eminent doctor who, seated one day in his study, very busy, noticed his small son come sidling into the room; he came and stood, silently, at his father's side. The doctor, preoccupied with his work, put his hand into his pocket, took out a coin and offered it to the boy, only to be met with a decided refusal; "I don't want any money, Daddy." Surprised, but still engrossed in his work, he went on with his writing; the child still standing at his side. After a few minutes he opened a drawer in his desk, took out some sweets and passed them over; but again the child shook his head, "I don't want any sweets, Daddy." At which the father laid down his pen. "You don't want money, you don't want sweets. Whatever do you want then?" "I don't want anything, I only wanted to be with you." That is worship, surely.   H. V. Larcombe

✳✳

1019 In his famous Cambridge address, Mr. Emerson said that the hold which public worship had on men was gone or was going. It was not the first time nor the last time that a passing mood has been mistaken for a permanent tendency. Social worship is one of the everlasting necessities of humanity. A Church where the idea of worship is most exalted was never as attractive as it is to-day. Men cannot live by knowledge alone.   J. A. Hunter

✳✳

1020 The explorer Edward Wilson, who was a colleague of both Shackleton and Scott on their polar expeditions, tells how he found the ship's crow's nest to be the place where God's presence was most real. Writing to his wife while with Scott's expedition he said in one of his letters: "I simply love the crow's nest— it's my private chapel. I spend the happiest times imaginable there—alone with God and with you."   H. Vernon Thomas

✳✳

1021 We should regularly attend God's temple:

1. From a sense of duty, gratitude and love to God, the Giver of all good things.

2. Man needs worship. A God is a necessity of man's being.

3. The soul needs exercise and cultivation as do the mind and body. A neglected soul will fall into feebleness and decay.

4. Man needs social worship. We are formed for fellowship and mutual help.

5. Because Christ was a regular attender. "And He came to Nazareth, where He had been brought up, as His custom was, He went into the synagogue on the Sabbath Day and stood up to read."

6. Because of the educational benefits to be derived.

7. A church-goer nails his colours to the mast. He clearly distinguishes himself from the unbeliever.

8. Church-going is a public protest against atheism. Heb. 10:25, "Not forsaking the assembling of ourselves together, as the manner of some is."

9. It stimulates love and zeal.

10. It emphasizes the fact that we have souls as well as bodies.

11. Spiritual isolation breeds fanaticism and spells eccentricity, cowardice and selfishness.

12. The times need a public expression of faith in God's presence and providence.

13. Second-hand religion is a poor substitute.

14. Unity is strength. Guerilla warfare, even spiritually speaking, lacks effectiveness. "A merely unorganized Religion might dechristianize England in a hundred years."

15. Empty pews in the temple of God means empty hearts, homes emptied of true religion, Sunday desecration and eventually spiritual ruin.

Let Dr. Hutton add some other reasons. "I go to church because my father and mother went before me, and I worship the God of my fathers. Moreover, because I would like my children to go after me, and by reason of the fact that more and more I want to go, otherwise certain things would become blunt and dubious within me under my neglect."   Alfred Thomas

※ ※

1022   I came across a short French story which tells how a wolfish outcast of the street stole the picture of a dainty girl from a public gallery and hung it on the wall of his squalid garret. For the first time in his neglected life, eyes of interest and of beauty seemed to rest upon and follow him, and they so worked on his hidden nature as to wean him from his brutish habits. Great is the mystery of godlikeness and the influence of worship. We are here to put ourselves under the spell of a Real Presence that can draw us into His own likeness and magnetize us with His own Spirit, according to the workings whereby He is able to subdue all things unto Himself. Come then to this Living Stone, this Headstone, this Lovestone, and under His magnetism be caught into His fellowship and service.   A. Norman Rowland

※ ※

1023   John Wesley said that worship always consisted of four things: Thanksgiving, praise, deprecation and intercession!

※ ※

1024   Dr. Fosdick tells us that in a Danish Protestant Church, well on into the nineteenth century, folk maintained the custom of bowing when they passed a certain spot on the wall. The reason, which no one knew, was discovered when removal of whitewash revealed a Roman Catholic Madonna. For three centuries the worshippers had been bowing before the place where the Madonna used to be. So today some people worship God, not as a present reality, but as a tradition.   John Bishop

※※

1025   I was once wicked enough to get two young friends of mine to take shorthand notes of the conversations carried on in a certain church while people were waiting for the service to begin. The church in which I contrived this wickedness was a very popular place of worship crowded with well-to-do people. They were good people too, generous, kindly, sincere; but I shall not disclose what they talked about as they waited for worship to begin. It would surprise you. The point about it was that it showed no kind of desire to begin the enjoyment of God. And even if we grant that the failure to enjoy God in public worship is to be traced to the lamentable and apparently incurable dullness of the preacher, can we feel that people enjoy God very much more in private worship? I wish the answer could be "Yes."   James MacKay

※※

1026   Do you remember in A. J. Cronin's *The Citadel*, how on that Christmas Eve the doctor came home from his rounds and found the presents his patients had sent? None of them had great intrinsic value. But as he looked at them and saw how an old widow had, out of her penury, struggled to offer something to show her gratitude, Andrew Manson's heart was full to overflowing and those gifts meant more to him than fat cheques or costly presents. It is only so that worship can find its true expression. When the Master commended the widow who had dropped two mites into the treasury, He made it clear that the reason why the gift was acceptable to God was not because it was a similar proportion of her income to that which other wealthier folk gave out of their income. It was because the woman could only give her gift as a result of costly sacrifice.
                                                    Barnard R. H. Spaull

※※

1027   In the days when the great Augustine was feeling his way to the Christian faith there was one, Victorinus, who went to a Christian named Simplicianus, saying that he was a Christian. "Never," said Simplicianus, "will I believe this until I have seen thee in Christ's Church." "Do walls make the

Christian, then?" inquired Victorinus. "No" was the reply, "the Church is much more than walls; but a Christian acknowledges his brotherhood with all who have been redeemed by Christ. Thus he makes public profession of an inward conviction."

We say the same to-day, not only to young people pondering what they are going to do with their lives, but to many who for years have hesitated and wavered and hid their light under a bushel.   Frank H. Ballard

✳✳

1028   What is worship? A glance at the Lerolle painting of "The Arrival of the Shepherds" on the morning of the Nativity, may give us a hint. The scene is drawn with realistic verity, devoid of halos, but with a penetrating insight into the deepest intimacies and attitudes of the soul. The herdsmen stand huddled against the rough tree trunks which support the roof of the cave-like stable, and over all is the hush of a mingled awe and joy. One shepherd has dropped upon his knees in adoration, lost in wonder, his feeling of unworthiness speaking from his whole body. The second lifts himself on tiptoe, gazing timidly over the shoulder of the kneeling figure in front of him, watching with wistful, inquiring eyes, seeking the answer to the riddle of life in the lighted face of Mary, and the Child at her breast. The third shepherd, the oldest and most thoughtful of the three, has lifted his hand, as if swearing allegiance to a vision he has vowed to serve and obey.

These are the three elements which enter into worship as the ultimate art, Adoration, Inquiry, and Allegiance; and we may think of them in order. When the late Baron von Hügel, one of the noblest spiritual teachers of our generation, was asked to define the essence of religion, he replied in one word—Adoration. The deepest need of man, he said, deeper than duty, honour, or happiness, deeper than petition, contrition, or even thanksgiving, is the mood of adoring prayer, in which the soul is lost in the Otherness of God, finding rest, release and renewal in One who is like yet profoundly unlike itself. Other forms of prayer do not, indeed, disappear from our lives; they are caught up, fused and united in a detached, disinterested giving of our being to a Being other than ourselves to be cleansed, taught, mastered, possessed. Such prayer yields all, asking nothing; it seeks God for Himself alone, as both the source of prayer and its answer, and the end of all desire. St. Francis used to spend whole nights in an intense stillness, uttering no words but "God! God! God!" loving God, rejoicing in God, surrendering all to God.

As Eckhart said long ago, when we seek God for our own good and profit we are not seeking God. It is religion as an end in itself, like art for the sake of art, which must be our aim and ideal if we would be free; religion God-centred and ineffable. To attain it man may well invoke the aid of every art, striking on all the outward senses of the soul that from dull insensibility it may be awakened to know God and live in Him.

Joseph Fort Newton

✳✳

1029   What is the idea of public worship? What are we in point of fact doing when we meet together with this end in view? What lies behind this time-honoured custom, and why is its necessity so insistently stressed? To answer this question we must grasp intelligently the various factors which make it the unique thing it is.

Let it be noted firstly that its sphere of reference is always God. As the origin of the impulse is in God, so its direction is always towards Him. That is to say its necessity lies not in us, our need and inability, but in the nature and revela-tion of God. It is a response from us to something God has done for us. In other words, it is not a subjective but an objective act.

Secondly, worship is sacrifice. It is not something we receive, but something we give. "Bring an offering and come into His courts." In worship we make an offering of ourselves, of our hearts in gratitude to God for His mercies, of our minds to the understanding of His truth, of our witness to His claims on our allegiance, of our wills to the realization of His purposes. Thirdly, worship is a communal sacrifice. It is an oblation offered in association with others like-minded. It is a social exercise, a response made by the whole believing com-munity to the full revelation of God in Christ. Fourthly, it is a vicarious obla-tion. It is offered not only for our own sake, but on behalf of the sinning world. Even the world of physical Nature is included in this act. Nature herself is voiceless and expressionless until its adoration is made articulate by the self-conscious offering of the Church.

Robert Menzies

✳✳

1030   On Sunday morning when the bells ring to call the congregation and minister to church, there is in the air an expectancy that something great, crucial and even momentous is to happen. How strong this expectancy is in the people who are interested, or even whether there are any people whatever who consciously cherish it, is not our question now. Expectancy is inherent in the whole situation. . . . We need to-day ministers who take their work seriously. We need ministers who are efficient but not necessarily efficient in business.

Karl Barth

✳✳

1031   A beautiful story is told of a minister's wife, bringing her first-born son to church one Sunday morning while he was yet but a few months old. The little fellow, only accustomed to the confines of the room at home, wonderingly opened his eyes in this strange place. He stared in utter mystery, and then, the minister opened the vestry door and mounted the steps of the pulpit. The babe caught sight of this movement, and evidently saw something familiar about the form and face. Presently with a joyful sense of discovery it chortled out, "Daddy!" The mother was discomfited and the minister embarrassed. At the close of the service the minister was apologetic to his church officers for the interruption. A dear old saint tremulously said, "Don't apologize, sir. Many of us forget what we come for when we assemble in the sanctuary. Your little son saw nothing but his daddy. Would to God we all but discerned here the face of our Father." True! And then the Church would reveal the Father to all and sundry.   Ernest R. Squire

Worship, Effect of

1032   F. A. Atkins, in one of his choice little books, tells us of a walk which he took in Central Park, New York, one Sunday morning after he had attended a short service in one of the churches. He describes the people whom he met who had been to no place of worship. Their faces, he said, looked hard, arrogant, and fretful, and many gave the impression of being care-worn and crushed. And then he met a stream of people altogether different. They seemed to have escaped the prison house of care. They looked serious, yet they were sunny. In their eyes there was the glow of victory. Who were they? They were those who had been at the service in Fifth Avenue Presbyterian Church, where Dr. J. H. Jowett was then engaged in a glorious ministry. Under that ministry the church was one of "spiritual glow."

Every church cannot have a Jowett as its minister, but "spiritual glow" is not for outstanding men, not for particular churches. It can be the possession of every minister, every church, and every individual. And any church, wherever it may be situated, that can send people out into the world possessing the triumphant spirit will never be played out.   W. J. Redmore

Youth

1033   To the young we should say, don't wait until middle life before you offer yourselves for Christian service. Put on your armour now. Remember, Martin Luther was only twenty-seven when he climbed the Santa Scala at Rome. George Whitefield at twenty-one was moving England. Dwight L.

Moody in his twenties was doing marvellous work as an evangelist. C. H. Spurgeon at twenty was preaching in the great London Tabernacle. David Livingstone at twenty-three was spending himself for Christ in darkest Africa. They were all adventurers, and both young and old can emulate their glowing witness as they throw off the shackles of officialdom and abandon fetishes for the fuller life of a free, unhindered faith in God.   William Mudd

✳✳

1034   I heard of two thousand Christian workers meeting in Boston. A speaker asked all to rise who were "converted" after they were fifty years of age; only two rose. Then he asked those to stand who began the Christian life before they were twenty years old, and nearly the whole two thousand were instantly on their feet. It is affirmed that not one out of ten of the Moravians can give an account of his "conversion"; so early are they initiated, in the home and the Church, into the experiences of the Gospel of Christ.   John Clifford

✳✳

1035   Our writer tells us that history is full of stories of a youth of high moral promise dashed by the later years. He says that had Henry VIII died young he would have been acclaimed as a hero rather than as a monster. Even Nero, it appears, as a youngster, had excellent aspirations.   Stanley Herbert

✳✳

1036   Plutarch in his *Lives* gives a graphic description of the Spartan youths. He tells us that it was customary at the festivals to have three choirs corresponding to the three ages of man. The old men with their grey locks and tremulous limbs began by shouting, "Once in the battle bold we shone," then the men of middle age answered, "Try us: our vigour is not gone," and the youths, full of energy, concluded by singing, "The palm remains for us alone." As it was then, so it is still, the palm of victory over self and sin; the palm of honour in art, science, literature, or social life; the palm of success in the contest with physical, mental, or moral difficulties remains within the reach of our young men. Hence it is not surprising that, as Disraeli wrote, "The history of heroes is the history of youth." To whatever calling in life we turn we shall find it honourably filled by young men.   J. Hiles Hitchens

Youth, Achievement of

1037   The names of men who have immortalized themselves whilst yet young crowd upon us from all quarters. Amongst Warriors we see Alexander the Great sighing for another world to conquer before he was thirty, and dying at thirty-three; Napoleon, only twenty-seven when he led his army for the grand campaign in Italy; Washington, about the same age when he covered the retreat of the British troops at Braddock's defeat, and was appointed to the command of all the Virginia forces. Amongst Philosophers we see Francis Bacon discovering the futility of Aristotelian philosophy when a mere lad, and publishing a learned work when only nineteen; David Hume, planning his *Treatise of Human Nature* before he was twenty-one, and publishing it at twenty-seven; Blaise Pascal, issuing a treatise on Conic Sections when only sixteen years of age. Amongst Orators we see Demosthenes pleading his own cause at seventeen, and taking a conspicuous public position at twenty-seven; Cicero appearing at the bar, and pleading the case of Quinctius at the age of twenty-six. Amongst Musicians we see Mozart playing before the Emperor of Germany when six years of age; Handel composing a set of sonatas at the age of ten; and Mendelssohn distinguished as an able composer at the age of sixteen. Amongst Poets we see Dante publishing his *Vita Nova* when only twenty-seven; Pollock publishing his *Course of Time* before he was twenty-six; Keats his "Endymion" in his twenty-second year; Campbell his "Pleasures of Hope" when twenty-one; Shelley his "Queen Mab" at eighteen; Thomas Moore writing for the *Dublin Magazine* when fourteen; Pope writing poetry at the age of twelve, Chatterton at the age of eleven, and Samuel Rogers at nine. Amongst Theologians and Divines we see Innocent III, the greatest of popes and the despot of Christendom when thirty-seven; John de Medici, a far-famed Cardinal when fifteen; Ignatius Loyola, only thirty years of age when he penned his *Spiritual Exercises*; Calvin publishing his *Institutes* when twenty-six; John Wesley, fellow and tutor of Lincoln College, Oxford, when twenty-three; and John Kitto contributing essays to the *Plymouth Journal* when nineteen years of age. Were it necessary to complete this list by names of men within the memory of most of us, we should point, amongst others, to Earl Beaconsfield, William Ewart Gladstone, Lord Wolseley, Henry M. Stanley, and Charles Haddon Spurgeon, all of whom had engraven their names "upon time as on a pedestal," whilst they were yet young men. It is worthy of remembrance what Philip James Bailey, when only twenty, wrote in his "Festus":

> We live in deeds, not years; in thoughts, not breaths;
> In feeling, not in figures on a dial.
> We should count time by heart throbs. He most lives
> Who thinks most, feels the noblest, acts the best.

J. Hiles Hitchens

Youth, Dreams of

1038   A young man once called on the eminent Rowland Hill, and desired admission as member of his church. The youth began by giving an account of his experience and relating a dream, which had greatly impressed him. Having listened very intently, Rowland Hill said, "I will tell you what I think of your dream after I have seen how you go on when you are awake." Yes, young man, it is your thoughts when you are awake, your actions when you daily mingle with your fellow-men, your prevailing passions and principles, of which you are conscious, which make or mar your present and your future.

J. Hiles Hitchens

Youth, Influence of

1039   In the biography of Dr. Cairns we read of the two most potent influences in his young life. They were the hearing of his father at prayer, and, in the early morning, the observance of his mother at work. Doubtless, there was instruction and to spare in that home; but it was the example that bit in to the boy's mind. Edmund Burke affirmed that "example is everything. It is the school of mankind, and they will learn at no other." It has not entered into the heart of man to conceive what kind of noble men and women there might be in this land in the next generation if the thought of God only dominated home life. "As for me and my house, we will serve the Lord," would be youth's chief preservative from "wandering fires and quagmires."

D. D. Smith

Youth, Teaching of

1040   We are told by the late Mr. C. F. Andrews that in India there is "a very profound religious ceremony which takes place at the time of adult age, when anyone is initiated into the deeper meaning of the spiritual life." At that propitious moment the teacher whispers in silence some text from the sacred books of their religion into the ear of the young initiate "in the good hope that it will remain in his mind for the rest of his life." And he has sometimes remarkable success in doing it. "A wise spiritual teacher," it is said, "will be able to choose a single great text which will make a marked impression upon the whole subsequent career of his disciple."

Frank Y. Leggatt

Zeal

1041 When one of the early Methodist preachers, William Lockwood, was speaking in the open air at Newark, and could not be silenced in any other way, the mob fetched the town fire-engine and turned the hose on him. At last, half-drowned, he had to cease, but cried as he escaped, "You can't quench the fire within."

John Bishop

SUBJECT INDEX

(Listing is made according to item numbers)

387

AUTHOR INDEX

(Listing is made according to item numbers)